The End of Commitment

Books by Paul Hollander

From the Gulag to the Killing Fields (editor)
Understanding Anti-Americanism (editor)
Discontents: Postmodern and Post-Communist
Political Will and Personal Belief: The Decline and Fall of Soviet Communism
Anti-Americanism
Decline and Discontent: Communism and the West Today
The Survival of the Adversary Culture
The Many Faces of Socialism
Political Pilgrims
Soviet and American Society: A Comparison
American and Soviet Society (editor)

The End of Commitment

Intellectuals, Revolutionaries, and Political Morality

Paul Hollander

Ivan R. Dee
CHICAGO 2006

 For information, address: Ivan R. Dee, Publisher, 1332 North Halsted Street, Chicago 60622. Manufactured in the United States of America and printed on acid-free paper.

www.ivanrdee.com

Library of Congress Cataloging-in-Publication Data:
Hollander, Paul, 1932–
The end of commitment : intellectuals, revolutionaries, and political morality / Paul Hollander.
p. cm.
Includes bibliographical references and index.
ISBN-13: 978-1-56663-688-9 (cloth : alk. paper)
ISBN-10: 1-56663-688-4 (cloth : alk. paper)
1. Communism—Moral and ethical aspects. 2. Political ethics. 3. Fanaticism. I. Title.
HX73.H64 2006
172'.1091717—dc22

2006000933

Acknowledgments

Roger Kimball deserves thanks for putting me in touch with Ivan R. Dee and recommending this study to him while it was still in a planning stage.

The research help required for this book was performed by Rebecca Jost, a conscientious and dependable assistant. These expenses were borne (as on other occasions) by the Earhart Foundation, a longtime generous supporter of my work.

A number of people read portions of the manuscript (in part according to their interests and expertise), as I did not wish to inflict the entire manuscript on anyone. Each of them made helpful comments of varying length or provided specific information or advice. I thank them all: Anne Applebaum, Anthony Daniels, Jorge Dominguez, Christopher Hurn, Peter Kenez, Don S. Kirschner, Harvey Klehr, Hilton Kramer, Michael Walzer, and Martin Whyte.

This is also the place to thank those among the subjects of this book who agreed to meet with me and respond to questions about the evolution of their political beliefs: the late Herbert Aptheker, Eugene Genovese, the late Andras Hegedus, Doris Lessing, and Christopher Hitchens. David Horowitz responded to questions in writing. I also met with Jozsef Hegedus, who helped with information concerning the politics of his father, and I received useful information from Andrew Kravchenko about his father Victor. Oleg Kalugin advised me about some Soviet sources.

Finally I wish to express my appreciation for the exceptionally thorough editing and many thoughtful critical comments provided by Ivan Dee.

P. H.

Northampton, Massachusetts
February 2006

Contents

The End of Commitment

ONE

Political Belief and Personal Morality

> Political engagement, even more than the pursuit of private pleasure, is incapable of meeting high expectations of personal fulfillment.—Peter Berger[1]

> The curtains of Communism are drawing to a close, yet a mystery remains: what were the attractions of revolutionary Marxism that drew so many passionate intellectuals to its flag? What was the faith that . . . summoned many to die for a cause? In one respect the answer is simple: what once had appealed in the name of God crossed over to the banner of History. . . . Marxism was a secular religion.—Daniel Bell[2]

I

In the course of the twentieth century, political beliefs increasingly replaced religious ones as sources and determinants of personal morality. Personal morality as well as immorality—the latter expressed in, among other things, mass murders and persecutions—acquired and continue to display political roots. Much new evidence (if more is needed) supports the notion that beliefs do influence behavior and that these beliefs need not be anchored in or reflect any discernible material or "class" interests.

The commitment to ideas that generated or influenced socially and politically consequential behavior often led to unanticipated and horrific results. It is also among the lessons of the past century (as well as that of earlier ones) that questionable or totally wrongheaded political beliefs and judgments are compatible with intellectual excellence and accomplishment.[3] This book is one more inquiry into the relationship between ideas and political behavior as well as between personal and political morality in a particular historical context.

Deeply rooted ideological convictions and the discarding of them—the subject of this study—both shed light on the connections between ideas and behavior. Both invite questions, especially in connection with prevailing or residual (a matter of dispute) left-of-center, adversarial beliefs at the end of the twentieth century and the beginning of the twenty-first. It is far from clear why and how these beliefs survived in the wake of the momentous and increasingly well-documented historical events of the twentieth century and especially why these events and experiences have failed to discredit decisively these beliefs, already compromised much earlier in the course of their attempted realization.

It is worth asking once more, Can it ever be anticipated that the pursuit of attractive ideals or ends will lead to mass murder and widespread suffering? This is a particularly relevant question in relation to Marxism and the practices of Communist movements and states that adopted it, since Marxism is an impressively idealistic body of ideas ostensibly developed in the service of human liberation or emancipation. If the consequences of the attempted realization of these ideals were both unintended and unanticipated, it is important to understand if this was due to the nature of the ideals, the character of the human beings seeking to realize them, or the historical conditions in which their realization was attempted.

While it is not easy to comprehend why some intellectuals cling to dubious or discredited beliefs, it is equally if not more difficult to understand when and why political disillusionment or a conversion experience may occur. Ingenuous and stubborn attempts of the believers to salvage their commitments are more frequent than the renunciations of deeply held beliefs. Those seeking to protect their commitment to dubious causes or discredited ideas most often fall back on the claim that their validity has never been properly tested and remains unimpaired, notwithstanding the practices of the fallible human beings seeking to realize them.[4]

Little is known about the conditions that create insoluble and intolerable conflicts between personal morality and political conviction, and about the types of personalities likely to undertake the painful, wrenching reassessment of deeply held beliefs. Sometimes individuals cling to outmoded or discredited beliefs and commitments by ascribing their attitude to a commendable consistency, and take pride in their "stubbornness."[5] Claud Cockburn, a British journalist and ex-Communist, characterized those who broke with the Communist movement (and divulged it in public) as "the people who spend twenty years or so in the Communist Party and presently dash out, tearing their hair and beating their breasts, to tell the waiting world what a murderous brothel they have been living and working in all that time."[6] It was not the kind of behavior he approved of.

When youth and the acquisition of political beliefs coincide, pleasant recollections of the former tend to validate and ennoble the latter. Youthful idealism is especially cherished in retrospect, in middle and old age, as for example by Eric Hobsbawm, who is discussed below. Saul Bellow wrote:

> I have observed that most people are incapable of altering their early beliefs. Most, I've noticed, think of their first education as a sort of investment made during their best, most vital years. Many of the Marxists I've known are unwilling to give up the labor they put into mastering difficult texts. They tend to hang on to the very end.[7]

It was probably Isaac Deutscher, a leftist author and biographer of Trotsky, who formulated most explicitly and unhesitatingly the critique of disenchantment with communism, or at any rate of its vocal and emotional expression. In his essay on *The God That Failed* (the book of essays by famous former supporters of the Soviet Union*), what he found most objectionable was that these "heretics" or "renegades" rejected not only Stalinism (or the Stalinist Soviet system) but communism itself, and even stooped to defending capitalism. He blamed their "irrational emotionalism"; they were carried away by their disillusionment and forgot the point of departure of their original commitment:

> Having broken with a party bureaucracy in the name of communism, the heretic goes on to break with communism itself. He claims to have made the discovery that the root of the evil goes far deeper than he at first imagined. . . . He no longer throws out the dirty water of the Russian revolution to protect the baby; he discovers that the baby is a monster which must be strangled. The heretic becomes a renegade.

**The God That Failed*, edited by Richard Crossman and published in 1950, included the following contributors: Louis Fischer (1896–1970), American writer and journalist; André Gide (1869–1951), French writer and 1947 Nobel Prize winner; Arthur Koestler (1905–1983), Hungarian-born British writer of fiction and nonfiction; Ignazio Silone (1900–1978), Italian writer; Stephen Spender (1909–1995), English poet and writer; and Richard Wright (1908–1960), black American writer.

Deutscher correctly described the typical progression of disillusionment as it expands from a critique of means to one of ends, but he took it for granted that the ends were immune to criticism; digging for deeper causes was mistaken and pointless. He believed, as Arthur Koestler put it, that "the foundations" of the undertaking remained "unshaken" and need not be questioned. Deutscher's attitude was no less emotional and irrational than what he ascribed to the "renegades," as indicated by his observation that the ex-Communist's "former illusion at least implied a positive ideal. His disillusionment is utterly negative." That is to say, illusions were preferable to the barrenness of their abandonment.

Deutscher was committed to the notion that strongly felt disillusionment had to be irrational and conducive to "anti-communist frenzy" (ascribed to Koestler); that it was "incoherent" and led to a "blind alley." He connected such disillusionment with a "characteristic incapacity for detachment." Deutscher saw the ex-Communist as a person of weak character and poor judgment, beholden to mood swings, who jumped to conclusions. Even worse, "the ex-communist's utter confusion of intellect and emotion makes him ill-suited for any political activity. He is haunted by a vague sense that he has betrayed either his former ideals or the ideals of bourgeois society. . . . He then tries to suppress his sense of guilt and uncertainty . . . by a show of extraordinary certitude and frantic aggressiveness." Deutscher was especially angry with those who went over to the other side and became "leaven to contemporary conservativism."

While Deutscher was capable of recognizing the motives that originally drew ex-Communists to the cause as idealistic and pure ("experience of social injustice . . . the craving for a great ideal or purpose . . . the miseries of the old capitalist order . . . the glowing light of the Russian revolution . . . ," etc.), he could not admit that a praiseworthy idealism (untainted by "irrational emotionalism") could also motivate disenchantment. He suggested that such people had unrealistically high expectations: "socialism, classless society, the withering away of the state—all seemed around the corner. Few of the newcomers [to the party, or the cause] had any premonition of the blood and sweat and tears to come. . . . Our ex-communist now bitterly denounces the betrayal of his hopes." Deutscher implied that such bitterness was out of place; he failed to realize that people were just as much attracted to communism for emotional reasons as they were repelled by them, and that such attraction was also quite capable of adding a less than fully rational quality to their thinking and judgment.

The attribution of unbalanced judgment culminated in the proposition that the ex-Communist became "an inverted Stalinist": "he continues to see the world in white and black but now the colors are differently distributed." This did happen sometimes but, as will be shown below, most of the disillusioned remained quite capable of nuanced judgments while understandably preoccupied with the political evil they were most closely involved with.

In the end, Deutscher questioned even the unconditional rejection of Stalinism:

> Worse still is the ex-communist's characteristic incapacity for detachment. His emotional reaction against his former environment keeps him in a deadly grip and prevents him from understanding the drama in which he was involved. . . . The picture of communism and Stalinism he draws is that of a gigantic chamber of intellectual and moral horrors. Viewing it, the uninitiated are transferred from politics to pure demonology. . . . Of course the story of Stalinism abounds in horror. But it is only one of its elements; and even this, the demonic, has to be translated into terms of human motives and interests. The ex-communist does not even attempt the translation.[8]

Deutscher meant to convey that even the Stalinist horrors had to be properly understood (rather than overemotionally rejected and demonized), so that they would cease to be unadulterated horrors and so their other, presumably less horrific, "elements" would be appreciated.

Deutscher's critique of disillusionment with communism had its obvious roots in his determination to fend off his own disillusionment, to limit it to the "excesses" of Stalinism. He seemed to believe that even if noble ends led to morally problematic means (party bureaucracy and worse), this had no bearing on the morality and desirability of the ends. Deutscher, of course, was a supporter of Trotsky, whose ideas seemed to promise finding a narrow path between anti-communism and Stalinism.[9]

It is not difficult to explain why a discussion of these matters invariably points to intellectuals rather than to any other group. They are the kind of people whose sense of identity is most closely and self-consciously anchored in the ideas they hold, many of which are political. They also gravitate to the role of the critic of society and the status quo, and are disturbed by the inability of their society to live up to its highest ideals. The task of the social critic, according to Michael

Walzer, is to expose false appearances in his own society, express "his people's deepest sense of how they ought to live. . . ."[10]

Richard Posner has noted attributes of this group that further explain their involvement with the ideas and political positions here discussed:

> A proclivity for taking extreme positions, a taste for universals and abstraction, a desire for moral purity, a lack of worldliness, and intellectual arrogance work together to induce in many academic public intellectuals selective empathy, a selective sense of justice, an insensitivity to context . . . an impatience with prudence and sobriety, a lack of realism and excessive self-confidence.

In the same empirical-quantitative study, Posner found a "two-thirds preponderance" of left-leaning individuals in the sample of prominent contemporary intellectuals.[11]

In the modern world it is the intellectuals who tend to articulate moral convictions and values and often seek to infuse political activities with moral concerns and considerations. Intellectuals also often aspire to the role of spokesmen of the less articulate, the downtrodden masses, and see themselves as the conscience of society. While socially conscious intellectuals seek to identify with the oppressed, often such identification is highly selective. The concern with the oppressed, the underdogs, the victimized tends to be ideologically defined; it does not extend, in equal measure, to *all* victims of injustice. Rather it is the victims of particular political systems, institutions, or socio-economic forces who are the focus of their compassion and attempted identification.

Definitions of and attitudes toward the incarnations of the victim are also influenced by the romantic notions of the "outsider." As one author put it, this is "an age still enamored of a Romantic paradigm according to which it is the outsider and the outcast who represents the most exciting possibilities. . . ."[12] This "romantic anti-rationalism" among adversarial intellectuals has led to the glorification of selected victim groups, especially since the 1960s.[13]

In modern Western societies, where the possession of a well-defined sense of identity is often problematic and something consciously achieved rather than taken for granted, the social critic's role is all the more cherished and identity-giving.

II

Despite my sociological training I have always believed, with Isaiah Berlin, that a focus on "the wishes and purposes of identifiable individuals," their aspirations and motives, offers the best hope for understanding human behavior as well as historical events—as distinct from scrutinizing history's impersonal forces, economic interest, or the grip of short-lived situations in which individuals find themselves. This is not to say that the latter are irrelevant, nor that behavior driven by unconscious motives should be ignored, nor to dismiss genetic factors.

I have been especially interested in political beliefs that inspire and sustain the certainties of radical-extremist movements and totalitarian systems, that is to say, in the connections between idealism and fanaticism which contributed so much to the great historical outrages of the twentieth century and continue to do so today. It is one of the most remarkable of all human beliefs—displayed by both present-day Islamic terrorists and the Nazi and Communist officials and architects of mass murders—that large doses of violence can be an appropriate and even indispensable means to the creation of a better world, or a better society; that the willingness to inflict such violence itself can be proof of the moral rectitude and superiority of those dispensing it; and, finally, that the means used to attain such lofty goals have no bearing on the ends sought.

The Islamic terrorists of our time exemplify a watertight, overdetermined connection between belief and behavior, or idealism and fanaticism, reflected in their serene and joyful embrace of indiscriminate, premeditated mass murder, often combined with self-destruction. The pages and profiles that follow, while unrelated to this type of fanaticism, may indirectly contribute to a better understanding of various types of political fanaticism and of those who personify the authentic true believers of our times.

In the course of reading the sources that are the foundation of this book, it became clear to me that political disillusionment and its associated moral conflicts cannot be understood without some consideration of the antecedent "illusions" that were abandoned. Some familiar questions must be raised at least briefly: Why did these ideas and ideals, and the political systems that seemed to implement them, appeal to many intellectuals? Why did so many among them surrender their well-honed critical impulses for extended periods of time, in some instances for their entire life?

Even in the aftermath of the collapse of Soviet communism (which removed an apparent alternative to the social systems many Western intellectuals hold in contempt), the discontents of intellectuals have persisted. These discontents may be especially bitter because they are experienced in a period bereft of radical revolutionary hopes. Edward

Shils's observation made a quarter-century ago remains applicable to this day:

> . . . the discontent seems to be no less great than it used to be; the tone of rancor has not abated. The ideal seems as far off as it ever was. There have been modifications of accent on the ideal and its earthly location but basically the views of a very large bloc of the intellectual stratum have remained as they were, despite the numerous changes made in accordance with their demands on the societies which they criticize.[14]

As I wrote some time ago, it remains "one of the mysteries of our times why so many well-meaning, idealistic people bent on liberating themselves and others become supporters of highly intolerant political movements or systems, why such movements or systems were so doggedly misidentified as liberating and worthy of dedication, and why the phenomenon keeps recurring."[15] After 9/11 such sympathies remain rooted in the same impulses and are manifest in the advocacy of "nonjudgmental" attitudes toward Islamic terrorists and the demand for a proper "understanding of them."[16]

My interest in the darker connections between ideas and behavior (or ideology and political practice) has concentrated on the Communist or radical leftist variety because when I began (and throughout) my professional career, communism was still a going concern, a phenomenon to be reckoned with (unlike Nazism), and because the ideas and ideals associated with Communist systems had an enduring appeal for intellectuals.[17] Nazism, needless to say, never inspired comparable devotion among reputable intellectuals, or only briefly. It was not merely crushed militarily and politically but also thoroughly discredited by its well-documented mass murders and the racist doctrines that inspired them. By contrast, Communist systems and their supporting ideas remained far more respectable and capable of inspiring sustained devotion and commitment.

As Mark Lilla wrote, "What made Communism different . . . [was] that it demanded and received a psychological investment rendering it virtually impermeable to rational or empirical refutation."[18] Hence it was axiomatic for George Lukacs, the famous Marxist philosopher, who knew well from personal experience the darkest sides of Communist systems, that "even the worst socialism is better than the best capitalism."[19] Likewise Eric Hobsbawm, the acclaimed historian, at the end of the past century could reaffirm his loyalty not merely to the ideals that played a part (to say the least) in the massive slaughters under Stalin, but to the "Soviet experiment" itself.[20] In turn, Jacques Derrida, similarly disposed, defended Marxism in the wake of the demise of the Soviet Union:

> . . . all men and women, all over the earth, are today to a certain extent heirs of Marx and Marxism . . . heirs of the absolute singularity of the project—or of a promise. . . . The form of this promise or of this project remains absolutely unique. . . .
>
> Whatever one may think of this event, of the sometimes terrifying failure of that which was thus begun, of the techno-economic disasters, and the totalitarian perversions to which it gave rise . . . whatever one may think of the trauma in human memory that may follow, this unique attempt took place. A messianic promise, even if it was not fulfilled . . . will have imprinted an inaugural and unique mark in history.[21]

Derrida's defense of Marxism and the Soviet Communist experiment exemplifies a stubborn, undiluted utopianism, an irresistible attraction of the "messianic promise" that the mundane politics of Western societies failed to deliver. As in the case of Hobsbawm, the "messianic promise" mattered far more than the enormous costs of its attempted fulfillment.

Equally remarkable for Lilla is that many Western intellectuals sought to "justify the actions of modern tyrants, or as was more common, to deny any essential difference between tyranny and the free societies of the West. . . ."[22] This denial, which persists to this day, used to be incorporated into assertions of moral equivalence between the United States and the former Soviet Union (sometimes the United States and Nazi Germany); in the wake of 9/11 it came to be used to equate the alleged wrongdoings of the United States in the Arab world (and elsewhere) with the atrocities of Islamic terrorists.

As Lilla further remarks, "Distinguished professors, gifted poets and influential journalists summoned their talents to convince all who would listen that modern tyrants were liberators and their . . . crimes noble, when seen in the proper perspective. . . . What is it about the human mind that made the intellectual defense of tyranny possible in the 20th century?"[23]

These are precisely the questions that preoccupied me a quarter-century ago and led to the writing of *Political Pilgrims*. Lilla's raising them anew testifies to their continuing importance and the scarcity of satisfactory answers to them.

III

The present book is in some ways both a continuation and a counterpart of *Political Pilgrims*. That study focused on political illusions, indeed on a political infatuation which deprived many intellectuals of their powers of discernment and of the capacity to exercise their critical faculties; the present undertaking seeks to understand the complementary process: the abandonment of illusory political beliefs as well as the conditions and circumstances associated with this process.

There is no way to know how many intellectuals in the Western world have become disenchanted with Communist systems and their supporting ideologies over time, or since the collapse of Soviet communism. We only learn of such disenchantment when it finds public and especially written expression by individuals who decide to write about these matters and are sufficiently well known to come to our attention. But only a very small number of the disenchanted have written about their changed convictions. It is impossible to locate and analyze more "representative samples" of them or the remaining hardened believers. (An attempt to do so may be found in Chapter 7.)

The disenchantment examined on these pages has not been confined to Communist systems, few of which remain, and even fewer of which can still inspire enthusiasm. More generally I have been interested in disillusionment with the residual radical leftist (or adversarial) outlook which finds expression in the rejection and denunciation of Western pluralistic societies, especially the United States and capitalism, or its more recent incarnation, "globalism."

I have used several criteria in selecting the individuals I have written about. The essential requirement was the availability of autobiographical or biographical writings, without which little if anything could be learned about the change or persistence of political attitudes and beliefs. Such writings are the primary source of this study, supplemented by other studies and in a few instances interviews.

It is an old and much debated question to what extent autobiographical writings may be treated as reliable sources of information. Most autobiographies seek to vindicate or validate the life and accomplishments of their author; few reveal genuine flaws of character, and serious self-reflection is often in short supply.

It is possible to detect and minimize subjective and questionable information in such writings by relying on other, less subjective sources (against which highly subjective assertions may be checked) and by applying more elusive standards of psychological plausibility and congruence. Whatever we know about human nature from scholarly research or personal experience may be used to evaluate the credibility of autobiographical revelations and assertions. There may not be substantially less reason to believe what people say about themselves in their autobiography than what they say about their political and social beliefs, sex life, or income to an interviewer in a survey or opinion poll.

The second criterion for selecting these authors was their importance, reputation, and intellectual merit. It is of greater interest to comprehend the political attitudes of well-known figures than obscure ones, of people of demonstrated accomplishment. This is especially the case when inherent limitations of space make it impossible to discuss a large number of cases. I also felt that it was worthwhile to include some lesser-known yet remarkable individuals who deserve recognition or renewed attention, such as Bui Tin of Vietnam, Zdenek Mlynar of Czechoslovakia, Miklos Gimes and Julius Hay of Hungary, Davit Wolde Giorgis of Ethiopia, Gioconda Belli of Nicaragua, and Rafael Del Pino of Cuba as well as Maurice Halperin and Sidney Rittenberg of the United States, among others.

Third, I have attempted to locate figures from different periods, generations, and societies, being interested in disillusionment not only with old-line Soviet-type political systems but also with the more recent Third World varieties such as Cuba, China, and Vietnam.

Arguably three separate studies could have been written about these matters: one about disillusionment with Communist states among those who had lived in them and subsequently escaped; a second about similar rejection by former supporters in the West; and a third about those who resisted such disenchantment. Combining these three inquiries may, I hope, illuminate the broader questions about the change and persistence of political attitudes outlined earlier.

Given the variety of its sources and the diverse national origins of their authors, this book will also help increase our understanding of the discontents generated by different Communist systems, and not only among those who have written about such matters. Most remarkable is discovering how many flaws these systems—in different parts of the world and in different periods—had in common.

IV

Questions of political morality come into sharp focus when believers conclude that their beliefs and commitments no longer deserve their support and dedication, that the ends pursued are unrealizable and the means used in their pursuit unacceptable and morally defective.

What precipitates such change of belief? What does it take for different individuals, and especially those with a long-standing commitment, to reach such conclusions, to become incapable of silencing their doubts and even to express them in public, and finally cease to support the cause?

An answer to these questions must consider what may be called the moral thresholds of individuals, their varied ability to tolerate or refuse to tolerate certain actions, policies, or moral transgressions. This threshold determines or at least shapes the relationship, or the balance, between political beliefs and objectives on the one hand, and deeply felt, individual moral standards or sensibilities on the other.

Surprisingly little has been written about the sources and nature of disillusionment with Communist systems in recent times, especially as compared to the volume of such writings about earlier disillusionment with the Soviet system and the Communist movements supporting it. This is all the more surprising since, in all probability, the number of Western intellectuals who admired Mao's China, Castro's Cuba, Communist Vietnam, and Sandinista Nicaragua during the 1960s, '70s, and '80s was similar to if not larger than those who were enamored with Soviet socialism in the 1930s and '40s.

The contrast in the amount of available information about these sets of attitudes may be explained in two ways: either the more recent, Third World communist systems are still held in a high esteem that precludes public soul searching, or if they have also stimulated disenchantment, its expression has been muted for reasons discussed below.

We do not know what proportion of Western admirers gave up on China, Vietnam, or Cuba, or for what reasons. Attitudes toward these systems vary: Cuba still enjoys considerable sympathy among those on the left (apparently due to its unbending hostility to capitalism and the United States and the longevity of its still somewhat charismatic leader). China, no longer revolutionary and anti-capitalist, has lost most of such support. Interest in Vietnam too waned following the war and perhaps also, in a small measure, due to the "boat people," the hundreds of thousands of refugees who had no desire to enjoy the blessings of Vietnamese socialism. Sandinista Nicaragua was unexpectedly voted out of existence in 1990, to the total amazement of its Western supporters, and thus ceased to be the land of the last hope for a humane and slightly exotic socialism. Of late some Western intellectuals have come to admire and idealize Palestinians, but not because they have built a new, purer variety of socialist society (that has not even been attempted) but because they are now seen as an authentic Third World victim, which provides new grounds for reaffirming hostility to the United States and its apparent surrogate, Israel.

The differences in the public expressions of disenchantment with various Communist systems (mainly Soviet versus non-Soviet) have some plausible explanations. One is, I believe, that the more recent, 1960s generation of sympathizers belonged to a much larger subculture, or counterculture, than did their pro-Soviet predecessors. The size and influence of this subculture made it easier to resist the reexamination and repudiation of beliefs (including the admiration of repressive Third World Communist states) that were widely and comfortably shared. In any event, for the sixties generation the critiques and rejections of American (or Western) society mattered more than finding plausible alternatives elsewhere, though sometimes these processes were joined.

There were also differences in the organizational support enjoyed by Communist systems in the West. For the sixties generation there was nothing comparable to "the Party," which at earlier times sought and channeled support for the Soviet cause. As Ignazio Silone recalled: "To join the Party of the Proletarian Revolution was not just a matter of signing up with a political organization: it meant a conversion, a complete dedication."[24] Demands on party members sometimes led to conflicts between the rigid, centralized, authoritarian hierarchy of the Communist party and those idealistic supporters possessed of a strong individualistic disposition. There were no comparably durable and disciplined organizations during and after the 1960s to sustain similar political devotions, but by the same token their absence also made it easier to drift away from the cause or the movement *without* a dramatic break with its underlying beliefs, and without compelling political self-examination.

Between the 1960s and 1990s leftist sympathies and impulses coalesced, for the most part, in loose and undemanding subcultures, not rigid organizations like the Communist party. The "counterculture" or "adversary culture" was a far more amorphous, flexible, and accommodating entity than the Communist party and provided a spiritual-emotional home for a wide range of grievances, resentments, estrangements, and types of social criticism. The very size and pervasiveness of this subculture (less and less "sub" as the years have gone by) has provided a comfortable supporting environment, dispensing nostalgic solidarities and greatly reducing the need to reassess one's past political activities and beliefs.

One point of departure and basis of comparison of this study of political disillusionment is *The God That Failed*, the classic collection of testimonials by former Communists, regarded at least by one prominent neo-conservative as the book that legitimated anti-communism among American intellectuals.[25] If so, this legitimation did not last long. The present book differs from *The God That Failed* in several respects. While that book consisted of autobiographical essays, I use such personal accounts as source material. Second, I wish to expand the discussion from the Soviet Union to various other Communist states that inspired disaffection; when *The God That Failed* was written, the Soviet Union was the only such state. Third, it is now also possible to note the impact of the collapse of Soviet communism on the attitudes examined in this volume. Fourth, and perhaps most important, I am writing about the disillusionment of both individuals who were born and lived in Communist systems for a large part of their lives and those in the West who contemplated these societies from a distance. Finally, in this book I also briefly examine resistance to disillusionment and some of its prominent representatives.

V

Notwithstanding the collapse of Soviet communism and subsequent revelations about Communist systems, numerous Western intellectuals and those under their influence managed to retain their core commitments and resisted disillusionment, especially with the ideals these systems allegedly sought to realize. Those among them who conceded the failure of these systems rarely considered the possibility, indeed the likelihood, that the ideals were resistant to realization, that theory and practice diverged in part because of the defects of theory.

The preservation of old and seemingly discredited beliefs leads to the broader question, Why are some individuals more successful in resisting political disillusionment than others? Is it a matter of being spared certain transforming experiences or information, or of belonging (or not belonging) to certain groups or communities that bolster belief even in the face of potentially disillusioning experience? Is it a matter of personality?

The proposition that political beliefs have deep emotional roots is hardly original. Arthur Koestler, a most perceptive witness of these phenomena, wrote: "Reason may defend an act of faith—but only after the act has been committed. . . . Persuasion may play a part in a man's conversion; but only the part of bringing to its full and conscious climax a process which has been maturing in *regions where no persuasion can penetrate*"[26] [my emphasis]. Although such emotional allegiances often distort political judgment, this observation need not become an all-purpose polemical device to discredit wholesale political convictions and positions when their emotional roots have been uncovered.

It is impossible to specify at what point or under what conditions feelings overwhelm reason and undermine political judgment, although they clearly and frequently do. Often this process finds expression in "selective perception," whereby certain aspects of reality, certain facts, go virtually unnoticed while others loom large and acquire great significance. Such selectivity mirrors emotional dispositions, originating in "the regions where no persuasion can penetrate" as Koestler put it. It is these deeper predispositions which underlie and compel the selectivity, the implicit and often subconscious ranking of phenomena and their moral significance and salience. I refer here to a selective moral-emotional concern with or attention to particular events, situations, or experiences, some of which are deemed to be truly important and overshadow others which can be ignored or dismissed. Such moral-emotional selectivity is at the bottom of most political judgments and preferences.

Louis Fischer, one of the contributors to *The God That Failed*, called this attitude "one's general alignment." He wrote:

> One's general alignment with a cause is more compelling than all but the most shocking facts about it. Just as religious conviction is impervious to logical argument and indeed does not result from logical processes, just as nationalist devotion or personal affection defies a mountain of evidence, so my pro-Soviet attitude attained complete independence from day-to-day events. Developments which seemed detrimental to Russia were regarded as ephemeral, dishonestly interpreted or canceled out by more significant and countervailing developments. . . . How could you complain about the scarcity of potatoes when you were building Socialism?[27]

Closer to the present, Noam Chomsky (among many others) personifies the same attitude. He would not dismiss outright the horrors of September 11 or those of the Gulag, but they fail to mobilize his deeper feelings of moral outrage and indignation, which are reserved for the far more important and salient outrages he associates with and blames exclusively on the United States. Thus one may admit (as he does) that something morally repugnant took place somewhere, but atrocity X will not elicit the same response or emotional resonance as atrocity Y, which truly matters. Chomsky's predisposition ("general alignment") energizes and prompts him to fierce denunciations of American policies—and great compassion for those he sees as their victims around the globe, from Nicaragua to East Timor—but he has little attention or emotional energy left for, say, the victims of the Cambodian genocide, the horrors of the Chinese "Cultural Revolution," or the brutal, unwavering repression in North Korea. Chomsky went to great and (in retrospect) embarrassing length to deny, dismiss, or belittle the dimensions of the Cambodian mass murders under Pol Pot[28] before it became a legitimate concern in left-liberal circles, in the wake of the Vietnamese overthrow of his regime.

Chomsky is by no means exceptional in his partiality except for the degree of rationalistic posturing he engages in, claiming or suggesting that his judgments and opinions are always factual, verifiable, and untainted by partisan bias and emotion. (His attitudes and polemical tactics are further discussed later.)

At the time of this writing I was struck by the remarks of an American advocate of peace with Iraq (she had visited it sixteen times), which also illustrated the attitude here examined: "Asked repeatedly about Mr Hussein's rights abuses, Ms Kelly acknowledged that there had been excesses in Iraq. But each answer was cast in a way that shifted the topic quickly back to what she sees as America's transgressions."[29] More vehemently, Ramsey Clark charged the United States with "a deliberate, systematic genocide of a defenseless population" but refrained from any criticism of Saddam Hussein; he actually accused his critics of "appealing to prejudice" (by which he meant that they noted Saddam's extravagant spending on luxuries) and of offering "false excuses to continue the sanctions."[30]

As the foregoing suggest, the key to political judgments is more likely to be found in the identity of the putative wrongdoer than in the nature of the wrongs inflicted. Orwell was well aware of this tendency: "Actions are held to be good or bad, not on their own merits but according to who does them, and there is almost no kind of outrage . . . which does not change its moral color when it is committed by 'our side.'"[31] If so, political judgments are determined by an implicit, sometimes subconscious scenario in which the identity and ranking of the forces of good and evil are already clearly and durably established. Intellectuals are no less immune to entertaining such scenarios than others. As the social psychologist Stanley Milgram put it, "Context dominates meaning. . . . The meaning of any act can be altered by placing it in the appropriate context."[32]

How this selective moral-emotional responsiveness or predisposition evolves is difficult to establish and trace; presumably it is a matter of personal experiences which culminate in the patterned, predictable if often implicit readiness to arrive at moral-political judgments and conclusions based more on this predisposition than on the facts or dimensions of particular moral outrages. Especially difficult is to discern and establish how indignation over some large-scale social-political injustice merges with, or originates in, some hidden personal injury.

Political disillusionment (like attachment) is located at this intersection of the political and the personal-emotional realm. Such disenchantment, at least initially, is solitary, even secretive, as it might result in ostracism, in personal-social isolation in the West and far worse than that in Communist states. The process is also emotionally exhausting and painful.

The intersecting realms of "the personal and the political" became popular subjects of discussion in the 1960s when radicals (and especially the feminists among them) proposed and fervently insisted that these realms could not and should not be separated, that the political (i.e., considerations of power) penetrate and infiltrate even the most intimate personal relationships and situations. This was not merely an observation but a recommendation: these radicals believed that the personal deserved to be subordinated to the political—provided, of course, that the political values and intentions in question were "correct." It was a conviction which, among others, found expression in the Weathermen's slogan to "smash monogamy," that is, to subordinate exclusive personal attachments to a dedication to the cause, to political agendas and objectives. The same conviction prompted the feminist insistence on the political significance of who, in a male-female household, should take out the garbage or do the dishes. It was a peculiarity of many radicals of this generation that they managed to combine such beliefs (in the priority of matters public and political) with a highly individualistic sense of entitlement and self-righteousness, exemplified (among others) by Bill Ayers, who is examined later in these pages.

The politicization of personality and personal relationships was not invented by the radicals of the 1960s, however. Various earlier generations of revolutionaries extolled the same idea as an expression of dedication to the good of society or mankind; they too were enamored by notions of "wholeness" or "organic unity," by the triumphant eradication of the divide between the personal and the social/political.[33] It is not widely realized that the radicals of the 1960s and those of the

1930s shared a preoccupation with "wholeness," though the term was not widely used in the subculture of the American Communist movement of the 1930s and '40s.

Vivian Gornick, among others, who belongs to the generation of the sixties, was profoundly impressed by American Communists who displayed "the sensation of 'wholeness,'" which entailed selfless idealism, passionate commitment, abundant moral energy, strong feelings, sincerity, caring, and a willingness to subordinate personal life to the demands of the party. Her admiration for this older generation of "activists," their good intentions and pursuit of "wholeness," prompted Irving Howe to observe that Gornick "suffer[ed] from unacknowledged religious appetites"[34]—another often overlooked attribute linking the two generations of American radicals. Gornick ended her book about American Communists with a ringing affirmation of the wonders of the politicized personality:

> For better or worse, radical politics—full of sorrow and glory—embodies the stirring spectacle of human beings engaged, alive to the beauty and rawness of self-creation. American Communists were caught up in a magnificent sorrow. They gave themselves to it passionately, with a wholeness of being. For this I honor them. . . .[35]

Christopher Hitchens (one of those disillusioned in more recent times) has taken critical note of the conflation of the personal and the political and some of its manifestations:

> I remember very well the first time I heard the saying "The Personal is Political." It began as a sort of reaction to the defeats and downturns that followed 1968: a consolation prize . . . for people who had missed that year. I knew in my bones that a truly Bad Idea had entered the discourse. . . . People began to stand up at meetings and orate about how they *felt*, not about what, or how they thought, and about who they were rather than what (if anything) they had done or stood for.[36]

What the radicals advocating the unity of the personal and the political had little knowledge of and failed to grasp was what actually happens when the dividing line between the two spheres is weakened or obliterated, as it was under the totalitarian systems of the twentieth century. These systems too denied the autonomy of the private-personal realm, advocated the unity of the personal and the political, and upon this denial erected the institutions that performed the most sweeping invasion of privacy and deprivations of personal freedom in recent history.

VI

The most obvious and general conclusion one may draw from *The God That Failed* is that political disillusionment originates in the recognition of discrepancies between "theory and practice," between what was expected and experienced, between hope and reality. It was rarely a particular event or experience by itself that made the difference but rather the conflict it created with expectations and ideals.

Most accounts of disillusionment, including *The God That Failed*, further suggest that *unawareness* of the defects or failings of the systems (or movements or ideologies) in question did not play a major part in blocking or postponing disenchantment. Rather it was the capacity to relegate the negative or problematic phenomena to insignificance, the neutralization of their moral-emotional importance, that made possible the preservation of the original commitment. Thus Arthur Koestler learned while in the party that

> . . . facts had to be appreciated not on their face value, not in a static but in a dynamic way. Living standards were low [in the Soviet Union] but under the Czarist regime they had been even lower. The working classes in the capitalist countries were better off . . . but that was a static comparison: for here the level was steadily rising. . . . At the end of the second Five Year Plan the two levels would be equalized; until that time all comparisons were misleading and bad for the Soviet people's morale. . . .[37]

This was the attitude Koestler later called the doctrine of "unshaken foundations," the bedrock, nonrational belief in the transcendent goodness of the cause to which commitment had been made. This doctrine enabled the believer to resist and overcome doubt when confronted with morally problematic attributes or specific defects of the system, the *foundations* of which remained "unshaken" in his wishful judgment. This capacity to perceive the foundations as "unshaken" required (under the circumstances) an irrational commitment quite similar to the beliefs of deeply religious individuals who can maintain their faith even when confronted with seemingly meaningless and inexplicable tragedies.

More recently, Tony Judt has noted the irrelevance of factual information to political attitude change: "The question is when you decide to acknowledge what you know—when you become accessible to truths that you already possess, and to their implications for your behavior and your allegiances."[38]

A well-defined line separates the public disillusionment of Western intellectuals (such as those confessing in *The God That Failed*) from those living in Communist states and especially the occupants of high positions in their hierarchies. There are crucial differences between disillusionment with communism among those who live in a Western society as opposed to experiencing the same process inside a Communist system. In the West such disillusionment may have little noticeable impact on a person's way of life; it may be an entirely internal process. In a Communist society the same process has far more momentous and devastating consequences unless it remains carefully concealed. As we shall see, many people managed to hide their feelings of disenchantment, but it was a difficult and psychologically costly endeavor.

It is not surprising that those living in Communist states found it more difficult to nurture political illusions than those in the West; idealization is not sustainable for long when daily experience contradicts (and compels the questioning) of the ideals and their alleged fulfillment. This is not to say that the close experience of moral decline is incompatible with committed support, but such sentiments differ from the enthusiasm of foreign supporters safely separated from the realities of life in a Communist state. Living inside these systems that routinely made extravagant claims of their virtues and accomplishments, and being in a position to compare and contrast these claims with reality, was a far more potent source of disaffection than the occasional glimpses of such realities available to Westerners.

The true believer living in a Communist state experienced conflicting pressures: on the one hand he was in a far better position to experience disillusioning realities; on the other hand he was embedded in a demanding and unforgiving political environment in which the public questioning of his own political beliefs (and of the official verities) was a dangerous luxury he could not afford. Political disaffection in Communist societies had to be carefully concealed until the dissenter could remove himself from them, or until the state became more permissive and tolerant of public expressions of disbelief or criticism.

For those living in Communist states there was additional tension between the quality and duration of political commitment. Just as long-lasting personal relationships lose their romantic intensity and fervor over time, long-term political involvements too become routinized and come to settle for more modest expectations and a greater willingness to compromise with reality. For the insider and outsider alike, political disenchantment followed the discovery—provided it was confronted, not repressed—that the means used to promote the cause were tainted or outright repellent, and discredited their goals. At a further and final stage in political disenchantment (not always reached), the ultimate goals themselves become critically scrutinized and finally rejected as deeply flawed, unrealistic, or unreasonable from the outset.

Fidelity to the original commitment and the long-term goals could be retained by redefining and diluting them, by making them less specific, and by concentrating on their general desirability. For instance, Ignazio Silone wrote: "I do not conceive Socialist policy as tied to any particular theory, but to faith. . . . Socialist values are permanent. . . ."[39]

Much of the inner conflict that accompanies disillusionment revolves around the matter of ends and means, and for many, even among the disillusioned, the ends retained their sanctity as long as the faithful could focus on long-term goals while overlooking the means, here and now. Stephen Spender wrote: "It is 'humanitarian' weakness to think too much about the victims. The point is to fix one's eyes on the great goal, and then one is freed from the horror and anxiety. . . ."[40] This remark helps us understand the importance of good intentions for the believers.

Good intentions, sincerity, strong and apparently pure feelings—these mitigate the corruption of the means used in the political struggle and the behavior of particular human beings. In the 1960s and early 1970s on American college campuses, while professors lamented the destructive student protests, they almost invariably complimented their perpetrators for their goals and their sincerity. Apologists for Communist systems and movements were always impressed by the good intentions they radiated (as in Vivian Gornick's *The Romance of American Communism*). The future orientation of these systems and their supporting ideology helped avoid the questionable means used here and now.

The preoccupation with pure beliefs and good intentions may originate in a romantic outlook that dates from the early nineteenth century. Isaiah Berlin wrote:

> . . . the idea of sincerity as a value, is something new. . . . Muslims who died for Islam were poor, foolish, misled creatures who died for nonsense; so for Catholics, were Protestants and Jews and pagans; and the fact that they held their beliefs sincerely made them no better. . . . No marks were given for sincerity until the notion that there is more than one answer to a question . . . became more widespread. That is what led to value to be set on motive rather than on consequence, on sincerity rather than on success.

In our times these attitudes culminated in a willingness to give some credit even to mass murderers provided that sincerity could be detected in their motivation. As Berlin further noted:

> To cause pain, to kill, to torture are in general condemned; but if these are done not for my personal benefit but for an ism—socialism, nationalism, fascism, communism, fanatically held religious belief, or progress, or the fulfillment of the laws of history—then they are in order.[41]

Berlin's observations are particularly relevant to the recent Islamic suicide bombers and pilots who are sometimes given credit for their self-sacrifice, courage, and determination to call attention to various real or alleged social-political injustices.[42] In the Arab world they have been treated as heroes and role models.

The cult of sincerity, strong feelings, and the willingness to act on them—that is, of authenticity—became especially pronounced in the 1960s. The prevailing rejections of American society were grounded in perceived gaps between appearance and reality, in sensing and deploring hypocrisy, pretense, and duplicity—in short, inauthenticity. Lack of feeling and impersonality were also high on the list of repugnant traits. By welcome contrast, Communist revolutionary systems such as Castro's Cuba, Mao's China, and various guerrilla movements appeared authentic, action-oriented, passionate, and capable of bridging the gap between theory and practice, word and deed. It was precisely this action-orientation that captivated the radicals of the sixties and became their hallmark.

Radicals in Europe in the same period and later shared these sentiments. Antonio Negri, the intellectual voice and inspiration of the Red Brigades in Italy, wrote: "Every action of destruction and sabotage seems to me a manifestation of class solidarity. Nor does the eventual risk bother me: rather it fills me with the feverish excitement as one waiting for his lover."[43] Even apolitical criminals, if sufficiently violent and ruthless, earned the admiration of some intellectuals (such as Norman Mailer) when criminal violence became seen as a hallmark of authenticity since it involved risk-taking and a defiance of the social order.[44]

VII

Some of the specific experiences that stimulated the disillusionment of the contributors to *The God That Failed* should be noted here.

For Louis Fischer, André Gide, Arthur Koestler, and Ignazio Silone, visits to the Soviet Union revealed troubling discrepancies between ideals and realities. They encountered authoritarianism, high-handedness, and mendaciousness among party officials. Silone touchingly complained about the "utter incapacity [of these Communists, including Lenin and Trotsky] to be fair in discussing opinions that conflicted with their own. The adversary, simply by daring to contradict, at once became a traitor, an opportunist, a hireling. An adversary in good faith is inconceivable to the Russian Communists. . . ."[45] Silone was also upset by the demand of the Soviet leaders that foreign Communist parties endorse a resolution denouncing Trotsky without being given an opportunity to see the documents that made the case against him.

Richard Wright's disillusioning experiences were confined to his dealings with functionaries of the Communist Party of the United States (CPUSA), who treated him with contempt and suspicion upon discovering that he was unwilling to subordinate himself unconditionally to the party's changing demands. He reached the conclusion that "The Communist Party felt that it had to assassinate me morally because I did not want to be bound by its decisions."[46] These attempts at "moral assassination," for even minor acts of insubordination, mirrored the similarity between the internal structure and policies of Communist parties around the world and the totalitarian character of the Soviet Union which nourished and controlled these parties at the time.

André Gide, unlike most well-known Western visitors to the Soviet Union, was repulsed by the hospitality lavished upon him. He also noticed with sadness and indignation the inequalities that prevailed in Soviet society. This was a classical case of hopes and ideals foundering on the discovery of specific realities:

> . . . all these favors [his treatment while visiting] reminded me constantly of the privileges and differences where I had hoped to find equality. When I escaped from officials and went amongst the workers, I discovered that most of them lived in the direst poverty, while I was offered a ceremonial banquet every evening . . . what distressed me most was . . . to find there [in the USSR] everything from which I had always fled at home—the privileges which I had hoped abolished forever.[47]

Gide's visit to Bolshevo, a model penal colony, also led to moral outrage, though not immediately:

> When I visited it, it seemed to me one of the noblest and most successful experiments in the Soviet Union. . . . It was only later that I

discovered, what I did not know at first, that only informers—those who had betrayed their fellow-convicts to the authorities—were granted the privilege of living in this model settlement. Could moral cynicism sink lower than this?

Gide also noted the connection between the subservience of writers and the privileges bestowed on them—that is, upon "the right-thinking" among them: ". . . in the Soviet Union it is the writer who is most favored and indulged. The immense privileges I was offered amazed and terrified me. . . ."[48] By contrast, many Western writers and intellectuals who visited the Soviet Union in the same period and were treated in similar ways reacted differently: they saw the privileges of Soviet writers as a laudable expression of the moral seriousness of the system. It was a matter of giving proper attention to artists and intellectuals, the attention they deserved.[49]

Louis Fischer reported the case of a Soviet writer who was rebuked by officials for mentioning in a manuscript that workers traveled great distances to work in old buses over bad roads. He was asked how long it would take him to finish the book. Upon saying it would take another six months, he was told: "Then the censoring will require a few months and printing a few more. Your book won't appear until a year from now and in a year we will have good roads, new buses and new apartment houses near the plant. So why not describe these roads, buses and homes as already existing?"[50] The suggestion revealed the basic principle of socialist realism (the official theory of literary-artistic creativity): the abolition of the divide between the present and the future, or between "is" and "ought." Socialist realism sought to legitimate the system and excuse its failings by emphasizing its promises and future accomplishments.

Fischer made other disturbing discoveries. He recalled the "Shakti Trial" he attended in 1928, in which a key prosecution witness "repeated his story like a tutored automaton . . . had merely enacted a part invented for him in the cellar of the GPU." Fischer was further shocked by the exile of and implausible accusations against Leon Trotsky, whose "crime consisted of doctrinal and political differences with Stalin. . . ." He also found "the fawning adulation and saccharine glorification of Stalin" hard to take. Fischer's belief and loyalty were further eroded by the rapidly changing official definitions of good and evil, right and wrong: "If Trotsky was a Fascist and Ivan the Terrible a Soviet hero, all fixed standards of judgments vanished and nobody knew what to believe." The final blow to his faith was delivered by the Nazi-Soviet nonaggression pact of 1939. He concluded that it was a profound error to believe, as he himself did, "that a system founded on the principle of 'the end justifies the means' could ever create a better world or a better human being."[51]

Stephen Spender, during his short membership in the British Communist party, was also disturbed by the attitudes of party officials. The party leader, Harry Pollitt, criticized Spender for expressing doubts about the guilt of defendants in the Moscow purge trials and faulted him for not displaying sufficient hatred of capitalism. During the Spanish Civil War, Spender disapproved of the Communists' control of the International Brigade. He became increasingly troubled by the "crude propaganda" of the Communists in Spain, especially the "slanderous attack against groups within the Republic who were unfriendly to Communism." He found no excuse for the liquidation of the anarchists (the POUM). He had negative reactions to the 1937 International Congress of Writers at which the Communists vilified Gide for his report of his visit to the Soviet Union. The Russian delegates in particular "were impressive only for their arrogance and mental torpidity . . . they snarled at Trotsky and Gide, praised Stalin. . . ." Spender "gradually acquired a certain horror of the way in which . . . [his] own mind worked," being capable of applying double standards which made it possible for him to cling to political commitments and objectives furthered by unsavory means. He wrote:

> During the Spanish Civil War it dismayed me to notice that. . . . When I saw photographs of children murdered by the Fascists, I felt furious pity. When the supporters of Franco talked of Red atrocities I merely felt indignant that people should tell such lies. In the first case I saw corpses, in the second only words. . . .
>
> It was clear to me that unless I cared about every murdered child impartially, I don't really care about children being murdered at all.[52]

For long periods of time such apolitical moral indignation could be stifled. As Koestler and others noted, the clash between expectations and experiences could be averted, and the committed could stave off doubt by continuing to believe that some important goal or ideal was still in place and being realized, or was on the way to realization notwithstanding some morally problematic discrepancies between ends and means.

VIII

In the course of reading the accounts and recollections that form the basis of this book, it became clear to me that they are of interest not solely because of the light they shed on political attitude change and the pathways to disillusionment, but because of the insights they offer into Communist systems. Probing the matter of disillusionment proved to be impossible without exploring the real and imagined attributes of these systems, their original and essential promise. It also became apparent that what these individuals came to reject about these systems were in fact their major, defining characteristics.

It may be asked whether we need more information about the workings and appeal of Communist states, especially since most of them are gone and some of those remaining are substantially transformed. I believe these systems remain of historical, political, and social-psychological interest for a number of reasons: the huge utopian, social-engineering projects they attempted; the immense suffering these attempts produced; and the strikingly similar megalomaniacal traits of their leaders. These systems, especially in their revolutionary stages, manifested a doomed idealism leading to a profound divergence between political promise and social reality. To this day these political entities remain poorly known and increasingly forgotten.

Attempting to raise the levels of such historical knowledge is particularly compelling in American society not known for its commitment to instruct new generations about the facts and lessons of history, especially outside the United States. American society has long been distinguished by an indifference toward, even a distaste for, and "an innate cultural bias against 'dwelling on the past.'"[53] We may scour in vain the catalogues of colleges and universities for courses about Communist states, let alone the high school curricula; nor will references to such topics be found in the mass media. Surveys of public opinion, if ever undertaken in such matters, would unearth staggering levels of ignorance and incomprehension regarding the history, policies, institutions, and leaders (including their names) of Communist states, the duration of these systems, and the circumstances of their rise and fall. Nor has much scholarly attention been paid to the connections between the official ideals and theories that guided these systems and the dismal social-economic realities they produced; few social scientists or "public intellectuals" have raised the larger questions of what their rise and fall may tell us about human nature and the human condition.

A belated attempt to better understand these systems finds justification in what Christopher Hitchens called "an unmet need, an unanswered yearning, for an intelligible past."[54] Dwelling on the past can be enlightening. Few would dispute, for example, that lessons have been learned from exploring the moral outrages committed by Nazi Germany or during the history of slavery. It may be similarly instructive to probe the conduct and misconduct of Communist systems even when refracted through the disappointments of their former supporters.

And finally there is the chilling and thought-provoking connection recently demonstrated anew between high levels of idealism inspired by a combination of religious and political convictions and the serene murderousness displayed by Islamic fanatics. Although Communist systems rarely inspired such suicidal fanaticism, their true believers and ideologically committed elites had little hesitation to bring about the death of millions for the imagined benefits of a distant future, and to undertake the repressive regimentation of their societies in order to create the new socialist citizen. These systems, not unlike the suicide bombers, strove (at least during certain stages of their existence) to unite theory and practice, ideals and actions. Thus there may be substantial benefits from learning more about Communist systems from the disillusionment they inspired in some of their devoted followers.

TWO

Behind the Iron Curtain: The Soviet Union and Eastern Europe

Nothing better illuminates discontent with a social-political system than the determination of its citizens to physically remove themselves from it. The willingness to leave behind families, friends, language, culture, and homeland is a good measure of the intensity of discontent. Since Communist states rarely permitted legal emigration, the dangers and difficulties of illegal escapes were further indications of the depth of alienation these systems created.[1]

From the substantial literature produced by defectors (as they used to be called), I chose those who had earlier been supporters of these systems, often officials of some kind, and who left primarily for political rather than economic or personal reasons (as for example the desire to escape a bad marriage). Given our attention to political attitude change, I excluded those who had never supported or sympathized with these systems.

Although it is often difficult to separate the mixture of motives leading to such a life-changing decision, most educated, highly skilled, and often high-ranking defectors were not motivated by expectations of economic gain in the West.[2] In fact they often experienced a loss of status abroad since their old skills were not necessarily useful and a new language had to be learned.

There are compelling reasons for writing about the political disillusionment of this group, largely overlooked as a source of information by Western authors, including social scientists and social historians.[3] J. Arch Getty for one (better known for seeking to lower estimates of

Soviet purge victims) argued against the use of defectors' accounts for a better understanding of the Soviet system, referring to them as "second-hand personal memoirs, gossip . . . and lurid accounts by defecting spies eager to earn a living in the West."[4] While a handful of exceptionally well-known authors such as Alexander Solzhenitsyn were given respectful attention, the group as a whole has been ignored as a source of information both about these systems and about political attitude formation and change. Sometimes their message was trivialized and caricatured, as for example by Mary McCarthy:

> Every age has a keyhole to which its eye is pasted. . . . In our own day, this type of sensational fact-fiction is being produced largely by ex-Communists. Public curiosity shows an almost prurient avidity for the details of political defloration, and the memoirs of ex-Communists have an odd resemblance to the confessions of a white slave. Two shuddering climaxes, two rendezvous with destiny . . . the first describes when the subject was seduced by Communism; the second shows him wrestling himself from the demon embrace. . . .[5]

Sometimes even high-ranking, knowledgeable defectors were ignored by officials in the United States.[6] When not ignored, defectors were often treated with outright scorn and hostility. Victor Kravchenko in particular was subjected to an orchestrated campaign of denigration and denunciation by Soviet authorities, with some help from leftist Western intellectuals. Frederick Schuman, an American historian, called him a "socially myopic and politically unworthy careerist" and ridiculed his revelations about Soviet terror.[7] Theodore Von Laue, a professor of Russian history, proposed that American support of defectors "accentuate[s] the insecurity of the Soviet state" and thus increased the danger of "nuclear confrontation"; by "rejoicing over defectors, the American people . . . wage a ruthless political offensive against the Soviet system."[8]

Such attitudes toward defectors are in spectacular contrast to the recognition lavished on some of the most unreliable observers of the Soviet system. Walter Duranty, the *New York Times* Moscow correspondent, was awarded the Pulitzer Prize in 1932 as the "best foreign correspondent for an American newspaper." The committee selecting him had this to say of his work:

> Mr. Duranty's dispatches show profundity and intimate comprehension of conditions in Russia. . . . They are marked by scholarship, profundity, impartiality, sound judgment and exceptional clarity and are excellent examples of the best type of foreign correspondence.[9]

This was the correspondent who wrote about the Soviet labor camps that conditions in them were far from difficult since "the Kremlin has a spark of softness in its heart for politicals." These camps, organized in "communes," were "comparatively free." "Politicals" were paid union wages for work that was "for the good of the community." Duranty was further distinguished by a determined and prolonged denial of the famine of the early 1930s. It was "sheer absurdity," he wrote, to call it a famine when he could see "mile after mile of reaped grain in the fields" and "gigantic piles of wheat." Village markets were "flowing with eggs, fruit, poultry, vegetables, milk and butter. . . . A child can see that this is not famine but abundance."[10]

Susan Sontag was one of the few Western intellectuals who publicly recognized the value of what the defectors had to say and also noted the resistance to their message on the part of her fellow intellectuals. In her famous speech in 1982 that affirmed the legitimacy of Western intellectuals' opposition to communism, she said:

> The emigrés from Communist countries we didn't listen to, who found it far easier to get published in the *Reader's Digest* than in *The Nation*, or the *New Statesman*, were telling the truth. . . . Why didn't we hear them before, when they were telling us exactly what they tell us now? . . . We didn't love truth enough. . . . We tried to distinguish *among* Communisms—for example treating Stalinism, which we disavowed, as if it were an aberration and praising other regimes outside Europe, which had and have essentially the same character.[11]

The huge numbers of anonymous refugees from Communist states who did not write about or otherwise publicize their experiences were also widely ignored as sources of information. Only a handful of studies utilize their experiences for a better understanding of the societies they left behind.[12] More often, they too were considered unreliable sources, especially in regard to the hardships and repression of such systems.[13]

In the following pages I examine the disillusionment of some important figures, first in the Soviet Union and then from Eastern Europe.

ALEXANDER ORLOV (1898–1970) was a high-ranking official in the NKVD (the Soviet political police) who defected in 1938, taking advantage of his assignment as adviser to the Republican government of Spain (in matters concerning counterintelligence and guerrilla warfare) during the Spanish Civil War. Among his responsibilities in Spain was the transfer of the entire gold reserves of the Spanish government to

Moscow. His earlier positions included a role in the drafting of the first Soviet criminal code, commander of the Transcaucasian frontier troops, and chief of the Economic Division of the Foreign Department of the NKVD.[14] It was written of him that his loyalty to the system was "total and unquestioning. . . . If he had any doubts about the increasingly repellent system he was serving, he suppressed them at the time and only gave vent to them later in the qualified form of personal onslaught against . . . Stalin. When eventually, Orlov ran, it was mortal fear not moral repugnance that drove him."[15]

His book, *The Secret History of Stalin's Crimes*, is less a memoir than a selection of the highlights of what he considers Stalin's crimes, based on personal recollections, firsthand experience, and familiarity with many of the protagonists and victims. While there is no attempt to chronicle his political disaffection or outline its major stages, the sources of his rejection of the system can be readily discerned. Throughout the narrative he implies that the Soviet system, from its inspiring beginnings under Lenin, hopelessly degenerated under Stalin. Unlike Trotsky, Orlov offers no theory or explanation as to the causes of the process, except the suggestion that Stalin and his henchmen were responsible. As he sums it all up: "the painful truth . . . [was] . . . that the revolution, with all its alluring promises, had come to an end and that Stalin's regime had squatted on the Soviet land . . . with the same overwhelming weight with which the czarist dynasty of the Romanovs sat for three hundred years."[16]

Apparently Orlov's dedication to the system, spanning two decades, was undermined over a long period. No abrupt turning points are discernible; the defection itself was motivated by fear for his life. Much of his book details Stalin's misdeeds, his exceptional deviousness and ruthlessness culminating in the Moscow Trials and the killing of his potential rivals, all stalwart revolutionaries. In other words, the repressiveness, brutality, and mendaciousness of the system, intimately linked to Stalin's policies and personality, accounted for Orlov's disaffection. It is not clear if, absent Stalin, he would have found the system more acceptable—and of course we cannot know how different the system would have been without Stalin. To be sure, Lenin initiated the terror, if on a smaller scale, and Trotsky too was ruthless when he considered the system under attack. In any event, contempt for Stalin is Orlov's major theme throughout. He points out that Stalin "had never visited a single factory during working hours, being afraid to come face to face with the workers." He also refers to Stalin's notorious "theory of sweet revenge," which he shared with Kamenev and Dzerzhinsky in

1923: "To choose one's enemy, to prepare every detail of the blow, to slake an implacable vengeance and then go to bed. . . . There is nothing sweeter in the world." Orlov attributes "such a barbaric philosophy" to Stalin's growing up in the Caucasus, land of blood feuds; he was a man "indifferent to human suffering." Orlov recalls that even the NKVD chiefs who "knew Stalin's insidious character, his predatory ways and restlessness . . . were amazed by the purely beastly hatred which he displayed toward the arrested Bolsheviks, especially toward Kamenev, Zinoviev, and Smirnov."

Orlov was also repelled by new laws that extended the criminal culpability of children: in 1935 "the Soviet Government published a law unheard of in the civilized world, which decreed that children from the age of 12 and older who were found guilty of thefts and various other crimes would be subject to punishment on the same basis as adults, up to the death penalty." Orlov also learned "that as far back as 1932, when hundreds of thousands of stray children, driven by hunger, had jammed the railway stations and big cities, Stalin issued orders to shoot secretly those children who were . . . stealing food from railway cars. . . ." The same law also made it easier to threaten political prisoners with harm to their children unless they made self-incriminating confessions. "The relations among children," Orlov writes, "reflected, as in a mirror, the beastly relations that existed among adults," including a propensity to suspiciousness and a "passion for denunciation."

Orlov's other major target of criticism was the new inequality, including the reintroduction of both symbolic and tangible status distinctions, such as the new titles, uniforms, and privileges bestowed on the military in 1935 as well as the substantial material privileges of the party elite and their families. The latter included "the newest products from abroad" and "the latest automobiles, pedigreed dogs, wines and radio sets; for their wives . . . Paris dresses, silks, perfumes . . . for the children expensive toys." A gap between privilege and poverty steadily grew: "from 1929 to 1935, Russian citizens could see butter only through the display windows of the special Torgsin stores where goods were sold only for gold and foreign currency. . . . In 1935, when rationing was abolished, butter appeared in the so-called commercial stores at 25 rubles per pound. That equaled the earnings of a worker for five days."

By 1938 all of Orlov's former friends and colleagues in the NKVD were liquidated. He wrote, "I could not but realize that my turn was near."

Grigory Tokaev (1909–2003). The case of Grigory Tokaev is an excellent illustration of the influence of personality and temperament on political attitude formation and especially disenchantment. His strong sense of ethnic identity and pride in his ethnic heritage also played an important part in the uncompromising positions he had repeatedly taken: "He was not a Russian but a North Caucasian of the Ossetian national minority, born to the full tradition of a proud independent patriarchal peasant culture."[17] While a student at the Soviet air force academy, his commanding officer (well disposed toward him) advised him: ". . . You are too straight, too frank, and this will make life very hard for you. You must grasp one simple truth: the Party is not to be argued with. . . . [it] requires absolute loyalty."[18]

Tokaev came from a peasant background. He became a laborer at age thirteen and later a tractor driver in his village. A voracious reader from an early age, he was sent to a workers' university in Leningrad and subsequently to the Military Air Engineering Academy. He belonged to all the appropriate political organizations: two years in the Pioneers, six years in the Komsomol (both official youth organizations), and sixteen years in the party—from which he was repeatedly expelled and readmitted.

Tokaev's clashes with the authorities were innumerable; he was fired from various jobs; his certainty of eventual fair treatment led him repeatedly to higher authorities in pursuit of satisfaction. As a tractor driver at the age of eighteen, he went on a one-person strike to protest poor working conditions. He lost the job as well as membership in the Komsomol. On one of the numerous occasions when he was admonished at a party gathering (prior to expulsion) he refused to take part in the ritual of self-criticism, thereby further weakening his own position. He did not respond to such setbacks by losing faith in the regime or ceasing to worship "the very principle of the dictatorship of the proletariat. For me, it was not the system that was wrong, but only certain individuals." As a young man he was "convinced that it would be wrong to generalize from these few petty and perhaps inevitable local phenomena." This was the time-honored fallback position of many idealists until deeper and darker realizations eroded their faith and compelled them to conclude that indeed it was justified to generalize from the phenomena they dismissed earlier as insignificant.

As a youth, Tokaev was also naive enough to seek admittance to the Kremlin to thank Stalin personally, as "a fellow Caucasian," "for sending us our first tractor." The rudeness of the policeman who turned him away left him "flabbergasted."

While in Leningrad he was vocally critical of the cancellation of stipends to students (including himself) who, as a result, had to find jobs as dockworkers to support themselves. He debated the matter with the party secretary who warned him to stop his "anti-Soviet agitation." He recalled: "My naively taken stand shows to what extent I still believed in the earlier ideas of the Revolution; in their light it was impossible for there to be a party boss, still less for that boss to threaten a worker."

Despite his clashes with the authorities, Tokaev rose to a high position as professor of aviation at the Moscow Engineering Institute and reader in aerodynamics in the faculty of special aircraft equipment; later he became a member of the scientific council governing higher policy in all scientific matters in the Academy of the Soviet Air Force. Subsequently he was "Stalin's direct emissary on jet aerial propulsion" in East Germany.[19]

Tokaev's numerous critiques of the system include the human costs of industrialization:

> [the] clumsy general management of the State, terrorization, forced collectivization of the peasantry, and a general ideological recession towards dogmatism. The net result was increasing famine. Even in the fruitful Caucasus people had begun to feed on wild roots, and cats and dogs disappeared into the pot. Provincial towns scarcely obtained a twentieth part of what they needed. . . .[20]

He had opportunity to observe the impact of collectivization:

> On my . . . visit home I had a glimpse of the impoverishment which collectivization brought to the countryside. . . . These areas once had a flourishing patriarchal agricultural life. The inhabitants were industrious and capable, lived in well-built houses set amidst gardens and orchards, wore good clothes. . . . Now the countryside looked as if a ravaging army had swept over it . . . gates, and garden and field fencing had gone for fuel . . . streets were overgrown with weeds . . . houses had not been repaired. . . . Through these ruined shells of homesteads moved . . . gaunt figures only given human shape by the loose rags which half covered them . . . hunger had destroyed and aged them all.[21]

In his second book he compared rural and urban poverty:

> I had seen poverty in Moscow but not this grim kind. . . . I shared a meal: scraps of sour black bread, half-empty bowls of watery soup. To this low level of life . . . had Stalin's forced collectivization

brought some of the most competent, diligent, hard-working farmers in the world.[22]

Another source of deep disappointment for Tokaev was the public capitulation to Stalin and humiliation of major political figures at the 17th Party Congress in 1934, signaling the end of any opposition to Stalin (which he witnessed while attending the Congress as a visitor). The men included Bukharin, Rykov, Tomsky, Kamenev, and Zinoviev,[23] who were later tried and executed. Tokaev personally knew and admired Bukharin and other major figures destroyed in the purges.

He was also well aware and critical of the new inequalities, including those that benefited him as a cadet at the Air Force Academy. He contrasted the status of military and nonmilitary students:

> We had all been trained . . . to believe that the starved-beggar level on which we existed was the utmost that the country could afford while it strained . . . to accomplish the first steps of industrialization, and it was hard to believe that the same sacrifices were not exacted everywhere. This sharp differentiation of two types of student—the civilian and the military—was far more impressive than any treatise on the development of a new stratification of the community would have been.[24]

The stratification of health care was another manifestation of inequality:

> We of the upper stratum [in the Air Force Academy] had our own Polyclinic. This was next door to the Polyclinic of the workers. . . . Ours was a fine building, the other a flimsy hut. The principal activity of the workers' medical staff was to prevent the men from going off work—ours, on the other hand, cared for us like prize stock. . . . Our medical examinations were strictly private. . . . But the masses were seen by their doctors in public, several doctors using the same room at once. . . .[25]

The other major source of his rejection of the system was its ethnic policies. He wrote: "What a nonsense all the talk about the fraternity and moral-political unity of the peoples of the USSR proved to be! We were to be trusted only when the motherland was in mortal danger." These policies turned more repressive after World War II, when the Politburo decided "to wipe off the map the Chechen, Ingush, Balkarian . . . Crimean tartar and Don Kalmuk countries." The resettlement of the vacated lands included "turn[ing] mosques into barns; museums

. . . gutted. . . . A visitor from another planet . . . would get the impression that these lands had always been the home of Russians!"

Tokaev was also disturbed by his observations of the treatment of civilians by Soviet troops in East Germany: "My reactions were all the more painful since . . . the mass humiliation of the Germans was mainly the work of Soviet soldiery." On one occasion he personally intervened to prevent the rape of young German girls by Soviet soldiers and arrested them at gunpoint. But the officer to whom he delivered his captives warned him not to meddle.

In his writings Tokaev offers no theory as to the reasons of the degeneration of the Soviet system. He clearly believed that the October Revolution was a noble undertaking and held Stalin responsible for the moral and political decline that followed. "We were never against genuine socialism. We were only against Stalin's sinister caricature of the idea."

Despite his misgivings and defiance, Tokaev reached high positions and mingled with leaders who were anxious to use his expertise in aerodynamics. After the end of the war he was assigned to East Germany to assist in the recruitment of German scientists who had worked under the Nazi regime. While stationed in East Germany he also came to object strongly to the new push for rearmament and the pursuit of new weapons: "What faced us was the wholesale squandering of industry on weapons of war, to the detriment of the long-suffering peoples of the USSR." More specifically, he objected to the attempt to create, with the help of German scientists, a new rocket-powered plane capable of reaching the United States. He was also charged with persuading important German scientists to come over to the Soviet side (from the Western zones). Great pressure was put on him by General Serov (head of the political police at the time) to cooperate in the kidnapping of one of them. This he refused, and his relationship with Serov became increasingly envenomed. While he detested Serov for "annihilating" the Caucasian nations, Serov in turn "could not forgive me for being a Caucasian." Increasingly Tokaev was placed under surveillance; his phone was tapped, his "every step was shadowed." For a long time he resisted the idea of defection, feeling that "flight abroad meant a life of isolation from my country, my comrades, my relatives, my people. The thought of the sudden descent from membership of the Scientific Council of so great a country to nothingness chilled my blood." These were reasonable apprehensions.

Fearing for his security, he reluctantly concluded that flight to the West was the only way out.

His reflections toward the end of his career as an important Soviet scientific official sum up the major motives accounting for his break with the system:

> I had once been a grimy-handed worker believing in peace and in a future golden age. Again and and again I had been accused of crimes . . . because I had tried to do my duty as a whole man. Now I had risen to honors and position, my brain and my knowledge were valued by the Kremlin. My value to them was not as a man, but only as a brain which could provide them with the weapons of destruction they required.

One need not read between the lines to see that the high position Tokaev reached, and his opportunity to engage in high-level scientific work, provided incentives to keep his objections to the system under control. But when threats to his personal safety combined with the long-standing disaffection and the opportunity to escape, he seized it. In November 1947 he defected from East to West Germany with his wife and daughter. He settled in England and taught at the Cranfield College of Aeronautics and at the Imperial College of the University of London; he was later head of the Department of Aeronautics at Northampton College of Advanced Technology.[26]

Lev Kopelev (1912–1997) was a well-known Soviet dissident, literary scholar, and, late in life, exile in Germany. In his youth and through much of his adult life he was an idealistic, committed supporter of the Communist system. In 1929, at age seventeen, he was arrested briefly for his involvement with the Trotskyite opposition. In the early 1930s he edited the newspaper of the locomotive factory in the city of Kharkov. In 1933 he enrolled at Kharkov University and in 1936 went to the Moscow Institute for Foreign Languages, specializing in German and graduating in 1938; later he taught at the Moscow Institute of Philosophy, Literature and History. In 1941 he volunteered for the army as a propaganda officer and rose to the rank of major.

Kopelev was first arrested in 1945 because of his protest (and attempt to stop) the mistreatment of German civilians by Soviet soldiers in East Germany. Initially acquitted, briefly freed, and rearrested in 1947, he was sentenced to three years of hard labor, a sentence that was subsequently extended. Altogether he served ten years; he was released and rehabilitated in 1956 and reinstated in the Party.[27] Throughout the 1960s and '70s he was among the prominent Soviet dissidents, a supporter and friend of Solzhenitsyn (and instrumental in arranging for publication in the Soviet Union of his *One Day in the Life of Ivan Denisovich*). In 1968 he was expelled from the party for protesting the Soviet invasion of Czechoslovakia. In 1980, while he was on a study trip to West Germany, his Soviet citizenship was revoked—in effect he was exiled. After 1981 he was professor at Wuppertal University. Under Gorbachev his Soviet citizenship was restored. He died in Cologne, Germany.

The seeds of Kopelev's disillusionment are to be found in his early experiences of the campaign to collectivize agriculture, and the resulting famine. In the early 1930s he was among the activists sent to the villages to coerce the peasants to join the collective farms, and he experienced firsthand the sufferings inflicted on them. He recalled with deep regret:

> I was proud of having been part of the events of the 1930s, which I saw as a heroic high tragedy. . . . The action was moved by "historical necessity" in which I believed more ardently than, as a child, I had believed in God. That is why I was proud that I had helped take bread away from peasants; that I, a twenty-year-old city know-nothing, had instructed people who had grown old farming as to how they should live, how they should work, what was good for them. . . . I had looked down on them from the pinnacle of the one, true, all-redeeming social science . . . private property was seen by us as a wretched, despicable sin, the basis of "petit bourgeois outlook." So I was convinced of my ideological superiority to the peasants and was ashamed of feeling pity while we robbed them.[28]

In his second autobiographical book he continued to agonize over his participation in what he also called "the war against the peasants":

> It was excruciating to see and hear all this. And even worse to take part in it. . . . I persuaded myself . . . I mustn't give in to debilitating pity. We were realizing historical necessity. We were performing our revolutionary duty. We were obtaining grain for the socialist fatherland. . . .
>
> Some sort of rationalistic fanaticism overcame my doubts, my pangs of conscience and simple feelings of sympathy, pity and shame, but this fanaticism was nourished not only by speculative newspaper and literary sources. More convincing . . . were people who in my eyes embodied, personified our truth and our justice, people who confirmed with their lives that it was necessary to clench your teeth,

> clench your heart and carry out everything the party and the Soviet power ordered.[29]

More specifically, Kopelev's faith in Stalin legitimated these actions: "He [Stalin] said: 'The struggle for grain is the struggle for socialism.' And we believed him unconditionally. And later we believed that unconditional collectivization was unavoidable if we were to overcome the capriciousness and uncertainty of the market and the backwardness of individual farming." Collectivization was also supposed "to liberate [the peasants] . . . from ignorance and prejudice."[30]

Identification with and submission to the party facilitated these attitudes, though in retrospect they also prompted further questions. Kopelev wrote:

> We were raised as the fantastical adepts of a new creed, the only true *religion* of scientific socialism. The party became our church militant, bequeathing to all mankind eternal salvation, eternal peace and the bliss of earthly paradise. . . . The works of Marx, Engels and Lenin were accepted as holy writ, and Stalin was the infallible high priest.
>
> Factories, mines, blast furnaces, locomotives, tractors, . . . were transformed into . . . sacramental objects. . . .[31]

The self-critical insights found expression only decades later. At the time (in the 1930s) he had no serious moral conflict. He also wrote:

> In the terrible Spring of 1933 I saw people dying from hunger. I saw women and children with distended bellies, turning blue. . . . And corpses. . . . I saw all this and did not go out of my mind or commit suicide. Nor did I curse those who had sent me to take away the peasants' grain in the winter. . . . Nor did I lose my faith. . . . I believed because I wanted to believe. . . .
>
> . . . Such men . . . become unprincipled liars and unrelenting executioners, all the while seeing themselves as virtuous and honorable militants . . . convinced that if . . . they have to lie, it is in the name of eternal truths. . . .
>
> When we saw the base and cruel acts that were committed in the name of our exalted notions of good, and when we ourselves took part in those actions, what we feared most was to lose our heads, fall into doubt or heresy and forfeit our unbounded faith.[32]

Elsewhere he wrote:

> All this was a nasty, rotten business. But unavoidable. For grain and gold were vital to the country. . . . No, I did not fall prey to doubts and

> vacillations . . . we were forced by unfavorable conditions to dissemble, and in some cases even to lie, in order to assert and defend our worldwide historical truth. . . .
>
> I needed no less than two decades before I could begin to distinguish the concepts of *sincerity* and *morality*. The fanatical evildoer may be sincere if his words and deeds match his convictions.[33]

Demystifying Stalin was also a lengthy process. Kopelev wrote: "Several years were required after the first disclosures of 'the cult of personality' . . . before I could finally begin to understand what an ugly little pigmy I had imagined to be a handsome giant, how irremediably disastrous our—my—dialectical illusions and blind faith had been."[34] For another decade Kopelev retained his loyalties, made easier by the Nazi invasion of the Soviet Union.

After collectivization, the next hurdle his faith had to surmount was the purges and show trials of the late 1930s. Once more it was neither the lack of information nor his acceptance of the official version of these events that was decisive in allowing him to retain his faith but the ability to neutralize these outrages with other considerations. By persuading himself that the ends justified the means, he found ways to reduce the moral significance of the unappealing means used in the accomplishment of long-range goals:

> I believed that a real, revolutionary Socialist ethic flowed from "objective historical necessity" . . . *A higher necessity* [my emphasis] could demand the strictest punishment . . . for someone you liked personally, even someone related to you by blood. . . .
>
> I never believed that Bukharin and Trotsky were Gestapo agents or that they wanted to kill Lenin. . . . But I regarded the purge trials . . . as an expression of some farsighted policy; I believed that, *on balance* [my emphasis], Stalin was right in deciding on these terrible measures in order to discredit all forms of political opposition, once and for all. We were a besieged fortress, we had to be united . . . the opposition leaders had to be depicted as deviationists and villains, so that the people would come to hate them.[35]

Even after he was imprisoned (on false charges) his chief concern was "that my sense of personal injury would impair my view of what remained most important to the life of my country and of the world. That vision was essential to me as a source of spiritual strength, of my conception of myself as part of a great whole. Without that conviction my life would lose its meaning. . . ."[36] He recalled that "once I used to think that if I lost my faith in socialism I would immediately kill myself."[37]

These were profoundly and genuinely religious attitudes and beliefs, those of a true believer who consecrated his life to them. Throughout his life, it seems, Kopelev struggled with these conflicting impulses, those of the true believer and the critical skeptic, the true intellectual. His struggles indicate that intellectuals—no less than ordinary people and possibly more so—long for sustaining beliefs. Kopelev's beliefs also provided a sense of belonging to the political community, a self-conception "as part of a great whole." The sanctified political community was the Party.

Even years later, after his first imprisonment, Kopelev continued to combat his "doubts and anxieties" with the "comforting formulas of our 'materialist dialectic'":

> "When you chop down the forest, the chips fly"; "bad means to achieve good ends"; "the road of progress isn't like Nevsky Prospect"; "barbaric means to overcome barbarism" . . .
>
> [Even during almost ten years in prison he] stubbornly believed, wanted to believe, that the cruel baseness and dull heartlessness of our organs of state security, procurators, judges and prison and camp officials, as well as the shameless lies of our press, official propaganda, and official literature—all were merely unnatural, irregular perversions.

He applied to the party for reinstatement as a candidate member after his imprisonment. He wrote sadly:

> With the rest of my generation I firmly believed that the ends justified the means. Our great goal was the universal triumph of Communism, and for the same goal everything was permissible. . . . And to hesitate or doubt all this was to give in to "intellectual squeamishness" and "stupid liberalism," the attributes of people who "could not see the forest for the trees."

He wrote hopefully that after the war "a new system of Marxist ethic has to be worked out"—a task that had been deferred because of struggles for the survival of the system. In the final months of the war he came to the conclusion that "a set of absolute moral norms" was needed, that "relativist morality—whatever helps us is good, whatever helps the enemy is bad . . .—would debase us in the end, and . . . the cause of Socialism. . . ."

Kopelev's experiences in East Germany during World War II led to his most serious collision with the authorities, culminating twenty years later in his final break. Unlike most of his fellow soldiers, Kopelev did not approve of or succeed in rationalizing the officially sanctioned mistreatment of civilians, even if they belonged to the nation that had attacked his country. Unlike most of his fellow countrymen in the army, he was revolted by the raping of women, the casual killing of civilians, the looting and cheerful destruction of property. As an officer he exerted his authority to prevent these atrocities and expressed his disapproval of them. This was an unacceptable attitude and led to his being accused of undermining the troop morale, among other things. Aside from the intangibles of his moral sensibilities, his affinity with and knowledge of German culture probably also played a part in the formation of these attitudes.

Kopelev's wartime experiences had three dimensions. First was the shock and revulsion prompted by widespread brutalities against German civilians; second was his awareness of official encouragement of and acquiescence in these atrocities; third, and probably most important, was his being penalized for taking a stand against the atrocities. First he was expelled from the party, then later arrested and given harsh sentences. Since the system rejected and excluded him, there was hardly any alternative to his rejecting the system, though he tried to retain his loyalty and beliefs even in prison.

He considered himself "a Marxist (though not a Leninist) up until 1968." Thus while in prison he argued with Solzhenitsyn and other fellow inmates, trying "to prove that our internationalism, Soviet, Marxist, Leninist . . . did not suppress national independence . . . that our aim was . . . friendly, equal relations between various peoples." In prison, not "even Stalin's semiliterate thoughts on linguistics" shook his faith as he convinced himself that "Stalin was . . . opening new paths for a new movement toward the creative development of Marxism-Leninism." Kopelev even tried to find some reassuring explanation for the alleged doctors' plot in early 1953 by conjuring up Zionist "terrorist organizations" who "probably also recruited one of the Kremlin doctors." Concurrently he "realized that the MGB [Ministry of State Security] and the Procurator's Office, the courts, and a significant portion of the party and state apparatus were filled predominantly with immoral, cynically conscienceless careerists or conscientious but ignorant, stupid order-followers. Both types were corrupted by privileges, bribes, the tinsel of awards, medals and uniforms." This realization uneasily coexisted with his own efforts to find an acceptable explanation for this new wave of repression and to exculpate Stalin himself. He continued to reflect on these matters:

> The arrest and killing of old Communists, the old friends and comrades of Lenin . . . recent leaders of the Party, horrified me, but at the same time did not seem unnatural. . . . I explained them away as the internal regularity of any postrevolutionary development. . . .
>
> But even before the war I began thinking about . . . the contradiction between historical necessity and moral necessity. I began to have doubts—did Stalin's strategy really correspond with the demands of historical necessity? . . .
>
> After the war, I was convinced that the punishments meted out in the prisons and camps . . . were unfair, cruel, and simply senseless . . . [they] could not be explained by historical necessity. . . . I realized that I could not resolve these contradictions with the familiar methods of dialectical materialism and historical materialism. . . .

These reflections also represent a warning about becoming prey to concepts such as "historical necessity," as if such an idea had an objective existence independent of the fallible, subjective judgments of human beings who decide what does and does not constitute such "necessities."

Kopelev's contacts with other dissidents after his release doubtless solidified his critical attitudes. As always, there were also attributes of personality. By nature Kopelev was a nonconformist—or, in the view of some officials, a troublemaker or softhearted intellectual. One of his military superiors said of him: "He's all mixed up. . . . A real Don Quixote, or a Hamlet"; another considered him a "petit bourgeois anarchist." An official deposition in the judicial proceedings put it this way: "He was always known as an oppositionist. He was always at odds with his immediate superiors . . . morally unstable in his private life . . . made serious political errors . . . [he was] opinionated. . . ."

Authorities both in the military and in the party regarded him with suspicion and contempt because of his intellectual leanings (his erudition was also held against him) and noted with disapproval his "bourgeois humanism"—an especially damning trait in the official view. For the "bourgeois humanist," the identity of victims and victimizers did not determine the morality of particular policies; inhumane policies were rejected even when aimed at the purported enemies of the system.

Kopelev was expelled from the party on grounds of "gross political errors, for showing pity for the Germans, for bourgeois humanism, and for harmful statements on questions of current policy." Later he was indicted for "undermining the moral and political consciousness of the Soviet troops," for "slander," "discrediting the Soviet command," and "propaganda in favor of the enemy." It was also held against him that he had "protect[ed] German civilians and their property." The official attitude toward looting was reflected in the policy of allowing soldiers to send parcels home: "Eight kilograms per soldier per month, twice as much for officers. This was a direct and unmistakable incitement to plunder. What else could a soldier send home . . .?"

Kopelev's disaffection rested on experiences available only to those who lived in a Communist state such as the Soviet Union at a particular period. But these experiences by themselves were insufficient to set in motion the long and torturous process of disillusionment; that was prompted by his unjust arrest and incarceration, in a case decided in part by false testimony based on personal grudges.

Kopelev's attitudes and political evolution confirm that human beings are fully capable of suspending moral judgment of horrendous misdeeds as long as belief in the long-term vindication of suffering is available. These long-term goals may be considered irrational since they were ill-defined, abstract, intangible, and largely unattainable, whereas the costs of seeking to attain them were all too visible, concrete, and readily experienced.

It is not clear to what extent Kopelev's disenchantment extended to the ideals that inspired the discredited practices. Thus he wrote that "while convinced of the falsehood of my former perceptions of Stalin, I still believed in the righteousness of Lenin and felt that the most dependable means for the scientific comprehension of history was the critical method developed by Marx, Engels and the 'real' nondogmatic Marxists: Plekhanov, Eduard Bernstein, Rosa Luxemburg, Gyorgy Lukacs and later Milovan Djilas. . . ." Gradually Kopelev became aware that "the gulf between names and the substance, between words and deeds, continually widened and deepened."[38]

Writing of Kopelev in the 1970s, Robert Kaiser suggested that "his values are the values of the early Marx, the humanist Marx, who has been compared to an Old Testament prophet."[39] While it is not clear whether or not Kopelev had undertaken a thorough reassessment of Marxism and its relationship to the Soviet system, he did conclude that the sufferings imposed by the system were not justified by either its goals or its actual achievements; that the system and its leaders were mendacious and created a huge and widening gap between promises and their realization; and that it was profoundly mistaken for an individual to blindly subordinate himself to any political organization, program, or set of political beliefs.

At the end of his 1983 memoir, Kopelev lists numerous specific events that contributed to the final rethinking of his political philosophy. They included the 1956 revolts in Poland and Hungary, the failures of Soviet agriculture, the massacre of strikers in Novocherkassk in 1960–1961, the end of the "thaw" in the Brezhnev era, the Cultural Revolution in China, the crushing in 1968 of the Czech attempts to humanize the system, the cults of personality of Mao, Castro, Kim Il Sung, Enver Hoxha, and others: "all this proved to me that the forecasts of Marx and Engels were utopian. . . . The principles of their material dialectics apparently did not lead by accident . . . to the inhuman practices of Lenin and Trotsky and the totally unprincipled totalitarianism of Stalin."[40]

These reassessments, prodded by historical events, were also bolstered by Kopelev's readings as he returned to Leo Tolstoy, Korolenko, Schiller, and Herzen and read for the first time Berdyaev, Teilhard de Chardin, Camus, and Sartre. He wrote, "My discoveries astonished me. Probably the students of Galileo experienced the same joy as they escaped the cramped, tightly locked universe."[41]

It is not easy to establish the exact progression of Kopelev's changing attitudes. His memoirs are filled with flashbacks, so it is not always clear *when* he reached particular milestones in his political-philosophical evolution. Many circumstances converged to pave the way to disillusionment: he was an idealistic man who experienced firsthand some of the worst atrocities of the regime; he suffered for his ideas and beliefs, and in prison (and outside) met kindred spirits, many of whom had much earlier lost their illusions about the system and its supporting beliefs; and he also discovered timeless ideas and ideals which further undermined his earlier worldview. Most remarkable about Kopelev's political peregrinations was the durability of his residual loyalties and his almost desperate attempts to cling to ideas and ideals that he himself realized were deeply flawed and crumbling.

VICTOR KRAVCHENKO[42] (1905–1966). Largely forgotten now, Victor Kravchenko was one of the most famous Soviet defectors because of the controversy generated by his revelations about the Soviet Union under Stalin. The Soviet authorities and their Western allies made a concerted effort to discredit him by accusing him of fabrications. He sued his detractors in a French court and won a symbolic victory. Leftists in the West found it particularly hard to stomach the title of his first book, *I Chose Freedom* (1946), which stimulated as much scorn as was heaped decades later on Ronald Reagan for calling the Soviet

Union an "evil empire." On both occasions what critics found most galling was not so much the condemnation of the Soviet system but the suggestion that the United States was better.

Kravchenko came to the United States on a government purchasing mission in 1943 and defected in 1944. At the time and during the following few years, the memory of wartime alliance between the United States and the Soviet Union was still vivid, and Western public opinion was unprepared for his revelations. Little was known about repression and poverty within the Soviet Union; even Hollywood movies idealized and romanticized Soviet reality.

Kravchenko was trained as an engineer in the Soviet Union, rose to high positions (including chief engineer at steel plants and construction projects), and was an enthusiastic supporter of the Soviet system as a young man with a "thirst for a faith."[43] When he was admitted to the party in 1929, "it seemed to me the greatest event in my life. It made me one of the *elite* of the new Russia. I was no longer an individual with a free choice of friends, interests, views. I was dedicated forever to an idea and a cause . . . a soldier in a highly disciplined army. . . ." He now "belonged to the minority that was stirred by the ideas behind the great effort . . . caught up in a fervor of work." As to the sufferings of people around him, "to people like me, possessed by the idea and the faith, today's pain seemed only a necessary payment for the glorious future. . . . Industrialization at any cost, to lift the nation out of backwardness, seemed to us the noblest conceivable aim."

Kravchenko sampled virtually every disillusioning experience the Soviet Union under Stalin offered (short of imprisonment) and sought to neutralize their impact while still a loyal supporter of the regime. They included the collectivization of agriculture and its accompanying sufferings; the fear and terror of the purges; the contribution of political prisoners to the "building of socialism"; the wastefulness and irrationality of the planned economy and the prevailing scarcities and hardships of the vast majority. He was also thoroughly familiar with the privileges of the elite (that he himself enjoyed), which contrasted sharply with the impoverishment of the masses.

Increasingly Kravchenko became disturbed by the pervasive discrepancies between the promises and realities of the Soviet system. Countless other officials had similar experiences which did not lead to disaffection culminating in escape and public revelation. Defection, he wrote, "was not a step any Soviet Russian, especially a Communist of long standing and fairly advanced in the ranks of the bureaucracy, took . . . on a sudden impulse. It was an act that had its beginnings somewhere far down, in the substratum of his mind; that grew slowly and could not be smothered."

Several aspects of his biography, taken together, help explain his political evolution culminating in his flight. His youthful idealism eventually made it difficult and then impossible to accept and rationalize the painful experiences noted above. Further, he himself suffered indignities as a suspect interrogated and beaten during the purge. Finally, and perhaps most important, was the influence of his parents. His father belonged to the prerevolutionary working class and participated in the October Revolution in 1917 but later became critical of the system; he readily shared his disillusionment with his son, even during those years when the son's commitment was unwavering. His mother was religiously observant and equally vocal in her critique of prevailing conditions, and freely expressed her contempt for the official rhetoric.

Kravchenko witnessed the impact of the collectivization campaign when he was sent to the countryside with other party activists to assist the authorities. These experiences may have been most wrenching for him, and the beginning of disaffection:

> What I saw that morning making the rounds of houses was inexpressibly horrible. . . . I saw people dying in solitude by slow degrees, dying hideously without the excuse of sacrifice for a cause. They had been . . . left to starve, each in his home, by a political decision made in a faroff capital. . . .
>
> The most terrifying sights were little children with skeleton limbs. . . . Starvation had wiped every trace of youth from their faces. . . . Everywhere we found men and women . . . their faces and bellies bloated, their eyes utterly expressionless.

He also wrote:

> We saw long trains of cattle cars filled with peasants . . . presumably on their way to the tundras of the North. . . . The railroad stations of the city were jammed with ragged, hungry peasants fleeing their homes . . . homeless children were again everywhere. . . . Beggars, most country people . . . again appeared on the streets. . . . Which was the reality, which the illusions? The hunger and terror in the villages, the homeless children—or the statistics of achievement?

Looking back, he believed that he "must have begun the break with the Party at this time. The village horrors left psychological lesions which never healed." But in order to survive and function, "compromises with conscience" were unavoidable. He could not denounce these policies and leave the party without disastrous consequences. "It was imperative to squelch those emotions, to drive them into the underground of my mind. I labored to repair my loyalties." Immersion in work was a major escape from these dilemmas and conflicts.

The scenes of suffering and especially starvation were all the more difficult to rationalize since Kravchenko knew well that party and state officials in the same rural areas enjoyed special food rations. On another occasion, seated in a well-stocked dining car at a railway station, he was "startled by several little faces peering through the window with sad, hungry, envious eyes. These were . . . homeless boys and girls . . . staring at one of their 'socialist uncles' at lordly ease under the dictatorship of the proletariat."

As he rose in the hierarchy, Kravchenko gained access to the "special stores . . . as well as shoemaking and tailoring establishments reserved for the *vlast* [the powerholders]. . . . Not one Russian in a thousand suspected that such abundant shops existed."

These inequities and privileges became a major source of his questioning of the moral foundations of the system. He himself was a beneficiary of these privileges but apparently could not enjoy them with an untroubled conscience, unlike "men [other functionaries] who could eat ample and dainty food in full view of starving people not only with a clear conscience but with a feeling of righteousness, as if they were performing a duty to history." Kravchenko, by contrast, professed to be uneasy: "Sometimes alone in my fine house, with the buxom, ruddy-faced Pasha preparing a good meal for me in the kitchen, with a state gardener watering my garden, with the icebox full of fresh vegetables, melons, caviar and sour cream, I felt guilty." His mother's shocked surprise on one of her visits to his spacious house contributed to these feelings; she was especially amazed by his exclusive access to a bathroom. In turn, during his visits home "father sometimes told me about the arrests and 'disappearance' of men we had both known for many years at the Dniepropetrovsk factory. I felt as if he were holding me personally responsible, as a Party member, for every injustice."

Another memorable and traumatic experience was the spectacle of forced laborers at work:

> The sight of the haggard, scarcely human creatures in their filthy rags . . . The awareness of these millions of slaves working and suffering, dying like flies all over Russia was so painful that I kept pushing it into

> the background. Every direct confrontation with the cruel facts was . . . a new shock.

On another occasion:

> . . . while on a day's outing with a colleague, we came across a dismal stretch of marshes where perhaps three hundred prisoners, mostly women, were at work. All of the unfortunates were indescribably dirty and grotesquely clad and many of them stood up to their knees in muddy water. They worked in absolute silence, with the most primitive tools. . . .

The divergence between appearance and reality intensified each disillusioning experience. The mendacious official rhetoric made a substantial contribution to such feelings. Thus "'the liquidation of the kulaks as a class' amounted to a lot of simple peasants being torn from their native soil, stripped of all their worldly goods, and shipped to some distant lumber camps or irrigation works." With seeming enthusiasm, workers endorsed measures reducing their income and increasing their workload, resulting from the upward adjustment of work "norms." Production figures were routinely misrepresented. As the famine coincided with the completion of the first Five Year Plan for the nation, there was much boasting in the press about the achievements of the system. Kravchenko felt that "the shouting about the new 'happy life' seemed ghoulish, more terrifying than the famine itself." In a prison camp he visited (which supplied workers for the industrial enterprise where he worked), on one wall he noticed a frayed strip of red bunting "on which I read the slogan . . . WORK—THE ROAD TO REHABILITATION." As Kravchenko summed it up: "Nowhere in the world was there such a fearsome concentration of . . . suffering and political despotism, nowhere else was misery so cynically disguised with 'advanced' slogans."

Kravchenko's final emotional break with the system followed his roughing up by NKVD men for refusing to sign a confession of sabotage—but miraculously he was not arrested. As he recalled, ". . . I knew that never, never again would I feel the same about the Party, the Leader, the Cause. The umbilical cord that had so long bound me to these ideas and symbols, despite everything, was finally and forever cut. I would work for the government . . . accept important Party assignments . . . make speeches. But it would all be play-acting . . . while waiting patiently for the chance to escape."

Kravchenko's life and political evolution, culminating in defection, suggest that experience must combine with opportunity to act on disillusionment, and that such action also needs at least implicit emotional legitimation from important people who are close to the individual in question. In Kravchenko's case it was his parents.

Arkady Shevchenko (1930–1998) was an adviser to Foreign Minister Andrei Gromyko (a hard-liner in the Soviet leadership) and subsequently undersecretary-general of the United Nations, among other positions he held. Like Kravchenko, he took advantage of being posted to the United States in order to defect. Before that, for several years he successfully played the part of the loyal and devoted servant of the system and guardian of Soviet interests at the UN Secretariat. He defected in New York in 1978.

A member of a younger generation, unlike those figures already discussed, Shevchenko had no personal experience of the horrors of the Stalin era, such as the collectivization, the purges, or the Gulag system. At the Institute of International Relations in Moscow, where he trained for his career in the diplomatic service, "none of us knew about the Gulags. . . . For us . . . there was no choice except that which had been chosen by Stalin, whom we idolized. It was not Stalin or the system that was responsible for wrongs or mistakes but individuals. We were sure that mistakes would be corrected."[44]

His career proceeded smoothly. Shevchenko was an authentic product of Soviet society; his parents did not seek to enlighten him about the evils of the system, and his later rejection of it is not easy to explain. His disaffection was certainly unrelated to any personal disadvantage, deprivation or threat to his or his family's well-being, or to any traumatic experience such as Kravchenko and others of an earlier generation had suffered. He wrote:

> I should not have had any real reason to hate or even dislike the Soviet system. It had given me . . . a high position in the ruling class, complete financial security, privileges and the prospect of further advancement.
>
> I did not suffer during the Stalin period. . . .
>
> Occasionally, one or another dark side of Soviet life irritated me or aroused indignation at the gap between theory and practice. But there were always sufficiently convincing explanations for all the shortcomings: the Soviet Union was the brave land where a golden age was being built, and the new is never born without struggle, and errors are the result of human nature.

He entered service in the Ministry of Foreign Affairs in 1956, when Khrushchev was in power and de-Stalinization his policy. Initially he was favorably impressed by Khrushchev, on account of both his policies and his boisterous and accessible personality. It was a period of official soul searching, though there were clear limits to asking what went wrong under Stalin and why. Khrushchev's revelations about Stalin wounded Shevchenko "deeply" and "almost" destroyed his faith in the system. But these revelations also restored the legitimacy of the system for him, and he was "inspired" by Khrushchev. He became a part of the nomenklatura, the party elite, after his appointment as adviser to Gromyko.

In his new position Shevchenko learned about the lifestyle and privileges of the political elite.

> While condemning consumerism . . . [it] valued above all else the consumer goods and comforts of the West. I was not immune. The gulf between what was said and what was done was oppressive. . . . Unlike ordinary mortals members of the elite have . . . high salaries, good apartments, dachas [vacation homes in the country], government cars with chauffeurs, special railway cars and accommodations, VIP treatment at airports, resorts and hospitals off limits to outsiders, special schools for their children, access to stores where consumer goods and food are available at reduced prices. . . . They live a rarefied existence far removed from the common man. . . .
>
> When we became part of this class, we regarded the luxuries and special courtesies accorded us with delighted wonder. All too soon the garnering of more and the deference by others became something that we treated as if it were a birthright.

Shevchenko believed that his promotions "propelled" him "toward defection" by allowing him to discover "what went on behind the scenes, how the system really worked and what were its unwritten laws." The contrast between appearance and reality disturbed him most. At the same time, it is important to emphasize, from childhood on he learned (with the help of his parents) that it was important to keep unorthodox political feelings and questions to himself. Such discipline was second nature to people who grew up in the Soviet Union under Stalin. As he later observed: "Millions upon millions of Soviet citizens conceal their true feelings about the Party line and policy. I knew that many officials . . . held deviant opinions, hidden for years, lifetimes. . . . Nearly everyone in the Soviet Union must be at all times alert and cautious."

These habits help us understand why and how even disaffected members of the elite maintained a façade of loyalty and conformity.

The possession of privileges was also strong motivation, and most of the elite enjoyed it without compunction or sense of guilt.

In most cases the privileges by themselves did not stimulate fundamental questioning let alone rejection of the system. Other sources of disaffection and of weakened ideological conviction usually came into play, which made the privileges morally problematic. In the case of Kravchenko it was his exposure to the ravages of collectivization and the sight of slave laborers. In the far more placid Brezhnev era—when much of Shevchenko's political life unfolded—members of the nomenklatura were not exposed to such experiences; repression was more restrained, and no major coercive social-political transformations were under way. On the other hand, the Brezhnev period was one of widespread and growing corruption, stagnation, and loss of idealism among the elite, resulting in part from the percolating, subterranean influence of Khrushchev's revelations.

Shevchenko believed that his political journey was accelerated by his familiarity with the personal qualities of those in the highest echelons of the political elite, including Brezhnev and Gromyko, and his resulting disenchantment with them. He found them hypocritical, corrupt, smug, resistant to new ideas, and totally isolated from ordinary citizens. Gromyko had not set foot on the streets of Moscow for some forty years, having been driven around in official limousines. Shevchenko also observed that "The Kremlin was the last place on earth where one might expect directness, honesty and openness. The falsity of these men was everywhere, from their personal lives to their grand political designs."

There was, of course, as always, the matter of personality. Shevchenko avers that he found a life of dissembling increasingly intolerable, and "the prospect of living as a mental dissident while maintaining the posture of a bureaucratic 'yes man' in practice was terrible to contemplate. . . . As I approached the pinnacle of influence I found it a desert. By continuing to serve the Soviet regime I would be helping to support and promote what I hated." He did consider resigning and becoming a dissident, but the prospect of being jailed or placed in a mental institution was difficult to contemplate.

Shevchenko's disenchantment was further stimulated and strengthened by contact with Western ideas, by "the wealth and volume of every imaginable kind of newspapers, magazines, books, television and radio" that he found upon his arrival in New York and during his several years at the UN. He was astounded and impressed by "the incredible openness of American society." He felt comfortable and at home in it.

There is no reason to believe that Shevchenko's defection was motivated by a desire for a materially more comfortable life or enhanced social status; his American contacts also made it clear that such expectations would be misplaced—"no car and driver, no government-supplied home. None of the luxuries that the Soviet government showered on its favored bureaucrats." Those official privileges were, in any event, tainted by the requirements of conformity and the need "to parrot whatever they wanted me to say at meetings," by KGB surveillance (notwithstanding his high position), by the obligation "to be a moral watchdog over my fellow Soviets in New York." In short, he wanted a new and free life, apart from the system he had come to detest.

The weight of nonpolitical, personal motives and family ties should also be considered in trying to understand Shevchenko's decision "to break with Moscow." As a matter of course, Communist systems used family ties to prevent defections: entire families were rarely allowed to go to Western countries together. Shevchenko's case was different since his assignment was to last for several years, hence his wife accompanied him, though not his young daughter and his adult son. He was strongly attached to his daughter but apparently less so to his wife. He did not expect that his wife would join him in exile, though he attempted to persuade her in a letter left in their home after he fled. Earlier conversations with her indicated that she would not be receptive to the idea of staying in the United States. While she enjoyed and took full advantage of the bounty of America, she was a genuine product of the Soviet system and could not envisage living in the West permanently. Shevchenko had reason to believe that she "would not come with me willingly." Moreover the marriage was hardly a focal point of his life: "When we were poor, struggling, miserable in that awful communal apartment . . . then we had been truly happy. But over the years, I had been absorbed in my work. We had grown apart. Lina [his wife] also had been obsessed with my getting to the top. . . . Perhaps it was only the weight of years." They had been married since he was twenty-one; when he contemplated defection he was forty-eight.

These circumstances made the break with the system easier. As was customary on such occasions, his wife returned to the Soviet Union surrounded by numerous escorts, and wrote to her husband, as did their son (both doubtless inspired by the officials), imploring him to return. She committed suicide shortly after her return to the Soviet Union.

Shevchenko defected in April 1978 and in December of the same year married an American woman he had met at a dinner party in the home of friends. When he wrote his book he had been happily living with her for seven years.

While the foundations of Shevchenko's estrangement from the Soviet system were deep and political, and nurtured by a thirst for a free life, his defection appeared to result from a combination of political and personal motives. He sought and found both political and personal liberation in the United States.

ALEXANDER YAKOVLEV (1923–2005) presented one of the most striking reversals of faith. He was neither a defector nor a dissident but a former high-ranking Soviet official who lived in Russia until his death. His life was devoted to the Soviet system, and he served as head of the propaganda and ideology department of the ruling Communist party under Gorbachev and was a major architect of perestroika and a Gorbachev ally. He was ambassador to Canada from 1973 to 1983 and, much earlier, a student at Columbia University in New York.

Yakovlev's disillusionment found expression during *perestroika* when the new political conditions encouraged the questioning of the system and reflections on Soviet history. The elaboration and expression of this disillusionment continued after the collapse of the Soviet Union. New opportunities for free (or freer) expression under and after Gorbachev encouraged the reexamination of deeply buried experiences, which for a long time had been compartmentalized and quarantined. Yakovlev's reflections and sentiments found expression in two major books. In the first he addressed the part played by Marxism in the shaping and degeneration of Soviet communism; in the second he provided an inventory of the major misdeeds of the Soviet system and its victims.[45]

Yakovlev's first doubts appeared during World War II when he learned of the official policy of treating Soviet soldiers who had been taken prisoners as traitors, regardless of the circumstances of their surrender. His doubts intensified after the war when he saw former Soviet prisoners of war being transported, once more as prisoners, at a train station in Yaroslavl:

> I was still on crutches but I went with others from the city to watch. Railway cars, small windows with iron bars; thin, pale, bewildered faces at the windows . . . on the platform, women weeping and wailing. Tossed out through the bars, rolled-up scraps of paper with the names and addresses of relatives and appeals to let them know that so-and-so was alive. And the women running back and forth between the cars looking for their husbands, brothers, sweethearts. . . . The people

> on the platform waited and waited. They could not understand why these boys from the Nazi camps were being transported like criminals to the Urals and Siberia. I remember the tortured faces, the total incomprehension, theirs and mine, as to what was going on.[46]

This was a potentially transformative, traumatic experience, yet Yakovlev somehow absorbed it and set it aside for decades. It did not interfere with his subsequent career as a high-ranking party functionary.

The Khrushchev speech he himself heard in 1956 at the 20th Party Congress was a major blow: "The shock had been indescribably severe, especially since this was the first time we'd been told officially of the crimes of Stalin. . . . I was crushed. . . . I sensed that Khrushchev was telling the truth, but it was a truth I was afraid of."[47]

The third crucial experience occurred in 1968 in Prague, where he visited with Soviet journalists covering the Soviet invasion. He was at the time deputy head of the propaganda department of the CPSU Central Committee. It came as a shock and "had a great sobering effect" to learn firsthand that the Czechs did not regard the Soviet troops as rendering "friendly assistance," as the official propaganda had it.[48]

On the other hand, as of 1989 Yakovlev averred that "It was not until 1985 that we learned just how bad things really were, particularly in our economic and financial affairs."[49]

Although not discussed in his writings cited here, his exposure to Western values and institutions while in Canada and the United States probably influenced his eventual detachment from the system and its legitimating ideals, even if their impact was delayed and indirect. Presumably these experiences provided a yardstick, a basis of comparison with the far better-known realities of his own society.

A further possibility, indeed a likelihood, is that his disaffection was also accelerated by conflicts with hard-liners in the party. In 1973, after decades of working in various positions in the party's Central Committee, Yakovlev was appointed ambassador to Canada, "a form of political exile for having offended the increasingly conservative Brezhnev leadership."[50] During the perestroika period he was under attack by conservatives because of his far-reaching critiques of the system. He recalled: "A great deal of this attack fell on my head. Someday I will publish the articles, flyers and excerpts from speeches that demonstrate so well the methods of the Bolsheviks."[51]

As Yakovlev himself put it, for a long time he "lived a double life of agonizing dissimulation. I conformed, I pretended, trying all the while not to lose my bearings and disgrace myself." His soul searching led him back "to the original sources"; he reread the classics: Marx,

Engels, Lenin, the German philosophers, the French socialists, "fountainheads" of his worldview. During his immersion in such studies (at the Academy of Social Sciences attached to the Central Committee of the party) he began to reexamine his views of Marxism:

> It was at the academy, while immersed in studying primary sources, that I became fully conscious of the hollowness and unreality of Marxism-Leninism . . . the deeper I explored the theoretical rantings of the Marxist classics, the more clearly I saw the reasons for the dead end at which the country had arrived.[52]

This was an unusual path to disillusionment, or to the legitimation of disillusionment. Yakovlev was among the few who explicitly held the theoretical-ideological foundations responsible for what had gone wrong. By contrast, after the collapse of Soviet communism, leftists in the West insisted that the Soviet system had little to do with Marxism, that it was the *discrepancy* between the ideals of Marxism and the practices of "actually existing" socialist states that was responsible for the deformation of the system. Very few disaffected Western supporters of Communist systems came to conclusions such as Yakovlev's, or if they did, they refrained from making them public. Before the collapse, Communist authorities would ritualistically affirm that the excellence of their social system was based on faithful applications of the Marxist legacy.

Yakovlev examined the relationship between theory and practice and found congruence. He came to regard Marxism as "a neo-religion," "a deluded faith," and compared it to traditional religious beliefs which thrive on "a deeply seated habit of relying on an authority that . . . is capable of releasing us from responsibility for our own thoughts and actions." He faulted Marx for his simplistic view of human nature and for his conviction that it can be easily modified by changing the social environment; he was also critical of his determination "to reduce all contradictions of human existence to the contradictions of the economy." He pointed out that

> the individual suffers not only from economic inequality but also from spiritual and bodily vulnerability, from fear of death, from the inherent solitude of human beings. The world and life create a multitude of problems . . . that cannot be fixed by achieving an equal relationship to the means of production. . . .
>
> The whole fulness of life disappears from such economic narrow-mindedness. The family disappears, as do love, power . . . heroes,

> myths, the crimes of the Spanish Inquisition. The tragic disappears. . . . Everything that is sublime disappears. . . .[53]

Yakovlev superbly identified the fatal paradox of an official optimism about human nature (rooted in Marxism) and the repressive practices that accompanied it: "The harsh attitude toward the individual [in Marxism] was caused . . . by his [Marx's] optimism, his belief that human nature could be easily changed."

Marx was similarly optimistic about industrialization, provided it was dissociated from capitalism, from the profit motive. Yakovlev wrote: "Marxism did not understand the tragedy of industrialism. Industrial civilization erodes . . . spiritual culture. A severe price must be paid for . . . a strictly technocratic treatment of the individual as an instrument of production—all of those collective farms, labor camps, slave labor. Everything is permitted that is economically useful."[54]

The importance of these insights cannot be overestimated. Yakovlev grasped the deepest sources of the failure of the "Soviet experiment" (and other, similar undertakings elsewhere): a misguided optimism about the promised fruits of a repressive modernization, resting on fundamentally failed assumptions about human nature and human needs, encouraged and sanctioned by Marxism.

Yakovlev located the roots of Soviet Communist political violence in the Marxist rejection of universal moral norms and its attendant embrace of moral relativism that supposedly benefited the revolutionary struggle:

> This special "class" morality, which flouts universal human norms, leads to indulgence of any action. . . . Moral criteria . . . are "revoked" by the brutality and directness of class warfare. . . . The idea that one should not fear creating victims in the course of serving the cause of progress . . . is very characteristic of Marx. . . .
>
> . . . Belief in the inevitability of the coming Communist world served to justify the numerous and senseless victims of the class struggle . . . terror is the way of remaking human material in the name of the future.[55]

It is again important to stress that Yakovlev's disillusionment, while initially stimulated by the specific policies and practices of the regime he served, was solidified by the realization that these policies were products of a flawed belief system, a wrongheaded philosophy and its conceptions of human nature. He came to embrace a tragic view of life, recognizing that the radical, romantic notions of improving the human condition embedded in Marxism are unrealizable, and that their attempted political realization, such as he observed in the Soviet Union, could lead only to vast accumulations of unanticipated human suffering and degradation.

While the sources of disillusionment in Eastern European Communist states had much in common with their counterparts in the Soviet Union, there was one important difference: the discontents of East Europeans with their political systems were not homegrown. These systems were imposed by the Soviet Union which occupied Eastern Europe after World War II and installed governments dominated by Communist functionaries loyal to Moscow. East European discontent had a powerful nationalistic and ethnic ingredient. Czechs, Hungarians, Poles, and East Germans considered themselves more Westernized and culturally superior to Russians and other Soviet nationalities, which made their domination by the Soviet Union even more intolerable.

WOLFGANG LEONHARD (1921–). Wolfgang Leonhard's case is particularly instructive because of his unusual life history and his preoccupation with the questions this book seeks to answer: how is political commitment maintained and finally eroded, how are conflicts between ideals and reality handled by the believer, and which experiences are critical in the process of disaffection? His case is also unusual because he experienced life in two Communist states, the Soviet Union and East Germany.

Leonhard defected initially not to the West but to another Communist state, Tito's Yugoslavia. This choice was a reflection of his hope at the time to find another Marxist-Leninist society more faithful to the ideals of socialism than the Soviet Union under Stalin. He refers to his political-ideological transformation as a "break with Stalinism,"[56] not with communism, socialism, or Marxism. Whether or not his departure from Yugoslavia after nearly two years reflected disappointment with the Yugoslav route to socialism or a desire to return to his country of origin is not clear.

Wolfgang Leonhard was born in Germany, schooled and trained in the Soviet Union, and sent to East Germany as a functionary after World War II. He escaped from East Germany in 1949 and later settled in West Germany. His positions in East Germany included deputy head of the press office of the Central Committee of the East German Communist party, and later the editor "responsible for the Party's educational material."

Unlike many of the disillusioned, Leonhard was anxious to understand the processes that allowed him to remain loyal over a long period of time despite experiences that tested his commitment and raised serious questions about the cause. He wrote about this process: "Such decision [the defection] is the outcome of a painful process extending over years—taken up with doubts and recantations, and pangs of conscience and fabricated theories to set conscience at rest. But once the process has begun, there is no going back."

Leonhard arrived in the Soviet Union in 1935 at age fourteen with his mother, a German Communist fleeing Hitler's Germany. Like many such political refugees, she was—incomprehensibly enough—placed in a Soviet labor camp where she was to spend twelve years. Following his mother's arrest, Leonhard was educated in various Soviet boarding schools and was subsequently groomed for the role of a future functionary in East Germany. At age twenty-four he was in the first group of German emigré Communists (led by Walter Ulbricht) sent back to East Germany to spearhead the establishment of the pro-Soviet regime. When he defected in 1949, he still thought of himself as a Marxist-Leninist. At the time he did not see a connection between the nature of these ideas and ideals and the difficulties of their attempted implementation in the Soviet Union and elsewhere.

Leonhard's disciplined political loyalty was all the more remarkable since the morally problematic features of the system he encountered included the arrest of his mother when he was fourteen. Over time he developed a loyalty based on the core belief that the fundamentals of the system—its key values, basic theoretical propositions, and validating intentions—remained intact notwithstanding the numerous departures from its avowed ideals, including the groundless mistreatment of particular individuals. These supposedly intact fundamentals legitimated the moral-ethical compromises, the amoral means used in the struggle to attain the great goals. This belief was identical to Koestler's "doctrine of unshaken foundations . . . the last line of defense of the sophisticated apologist."[57]

These attitudes also resembled those of religious believers who, while unable to deny that bad things happen in this world, manage to reconcile them with their faith in God on the grounds that ordinary humans cannot grasp his will. Such unconditional belief is compatible with admitting that God does not necessarily protect good people from incomprehensibly horrible events. (On the other hand, such is the elasticity of faith that when something fortuitously beneficial happens—for example, a person misses the connection to a plane that later crashes—the religious true believer will credit divine intervention.) Neither the believing Communist, as Leonhard used to be, nor the religious true believer feels the need to understand everything.

Leonhard excelled at an early age in learning how to neutralize morally and emotionally dissonant experiences which could have undermined his beliefs. But such experiences also planted the first seeds of doubt, which was to reach fruition ten years later, summoned up, as it were, in the wake of other disillusioning phenomena. The key to maintaining loyalty and living with unanswered questions was dissociation, or compartmentalization, in particular the separation of factual matters from their moral significance or evaluation. This could be accomplished by "form[ing] radically different judgments on . . . phenomena . . . which at first sight appeared similar. All depended on whether the context was capitalist or Soviet." Dilapidated housing in the West was "proof of the miserable standard of living of the workers," but similar housing in Moscow was "a relic of the past."

Leonhard and his peers rationalized the arrest and disappearance of their parents in the following manner:

> Each of us knew . . . that his mother or father was innocent of the charges. But our Soviet indoctrination had progressed so far that we did not base our judgment on the fate of individuals, even when those individuals were our parents. . . . We instinctively recoiled from the thought that what was happening . . . was in diametrical opposition to our Socialist ideals. We still went on trying to convince ourselves that what was happening was no more than an exaggeration of measures which were in themselves both necessary and justified. . . .
>
> To many of us these events had the appearance of historical necessity—perhaps serving purposes which were unknown to us, but which were so important that they could not be sacrificed by those in position of higher authority.

It should be kept in mind that these children were in a strange country, totally dependent on the authorities and especially the benevolence of the party, which in effect was a substitute or surrogate parent. They were not in a position to bite the hand that fed them, literally or figuratively. Moreover it was a period when disturbing events became mundane and ordinary. Leonhard recalled: "I no longer found it extraordinary when I visited a friend to find the door sealed. . . . A few years before, the idea of being under arrest meant something exceptional and terrible. . . . Now it was commonplace."

Leonhard's lapse of faith crystallized after his return to Soviet-occupied East Germany as it became clear that, contrary to his hopes, a different, more humane form of socialism was not emerging in Eastern Europe, East Germany included ("the last link that still bound me to the Party was snapped—the theory of a separate German road to Socialism"). Nor was there a decline in repression and regimentation in the Soviet Union following victory in World War II. Even more consequential was the erosion of Leonhard's ability to tolerate and rationalize officially sanctioned inequalities and privileges, such as he observed in East Germany. To be sure, he had observed similar inequalities in the Soviet Union as well. During the war, in Central Asia he was astonished by the poverty he saw, including "housing" consisting of holes in the ground covered with cardboard and layers of dirt. By contrast,

> the standard of living of the staff of the Comintern was as discriminatory as their accommodation. . . . The most senior officials, apart from living in splendor in the Bashkiria Hotel, also had large parcels of what was called *payok* brought to their homes: . . . the regularly distributed packets of food over and above the normal ration. . . . All Comintern workers were graded according to their political usefulness in a carefully constructed hierarchical system. . . .

Leonhard was also aware of the "reserved" shops and restaurants "limited to a particular circle of people. . . . Even in times of difficulty such as these . . . every kind of good was to be found in abundance in the 'reserved' restaurants and shops." Such privileges multiplied when he was admitted to the Comintern school in which he was "released from all the burdensome difficulties and adversities I had experienced before."

In East Germany after the war he found the privileges of the nomenklatura more irksome perhaps because they were juxtaposed to the mistreatment of the civilian population, including mass rapes and widespread looting by Soviet troops. In a conversation with a senior party official he raised the issue of the misbehavior of Soviet troops only as a matter damaging the reputation of the party and the Soviet Union; but he was told that Stalin himself took a tolerant view of these depredations and that the matter could not be discussed publicly. Leonhard tried to consider these incidents "regrettable isolated cases" (which they clearly were not), but presumably his own national origin made it more difficult to overlook them with an untroubled conscience.

He reports a particular incident that had a far-reaching impact on him. It occurred when he met a visiting West German Communist party official in the Central Committee building of the party. The West German official was looking for the dining room, and Leonhard responded to his inquiry:

> "That depends on what sort of ticket you have . . ."
>
> It was Category III—a ticket for the less important members of the staff. I showed him the way.
>
> "But tell me—are the meals different for different members of the staff in the Central Committee?"
>
> "Yes, of course. There are four different kinds of tickets, according to the class of work one is doing. . . ."
>
> "Yes but . . . aren't they all members of the Party?"
>
> "Yes, of course . . ."
>
> He looked at me in astonishment and said: "Different tickets—different meals—and they are all members of the Party!"
>
> He turned and went without another word.
>
> For the first time I had an uneasy feeling as I opened the door into the dining room reserved for our category. Here, at a table covered with white cloth, the senior members of the staff enjoyed an excellent meal of several courses. . . .
>
> My thoughts turned to the luxurious villas . . . where Pieck, Grotewohl, Ulbricht . . . and others lived.

Leonhard broached the subject of such housing privileges with one of the senior officials who "grew serious" and said, "I should never have expected such antiquated ideas from you. . . . Why shouldn't our leading comrades live in these villas?" Leonhard suggested that at a time of widespread scarcities, and when officials of other parties had far more modest residences, this was perhaps not such a good idea. Whereupon his interlocutor observed that "Sometimes I have the impression that in spite of your responsible position you are something of a starry-eyed revolutionary idealist."

The event of incalculable emotional importance was the reunion with his mother when she was finally released from Soviet captivity, an event that in all probability provided the final push for Leonhard's distancing himself from the system. Her haggard looks and bewildered, intimidated attitude testified to her sufferings:

> At first we could hardly find a common language, so different had been the twelve years which we had passed, she in a concentration camp, and I in the Komsomol and Party. At first, I sharply rejected

> the expressions of opposition to the regime. . . . I was determined in no circumstances to allow my mother's fate to influence my political reasoning.

His mother had concluded that the Soviet Union was not a socialist country, but her son had not yet done so. In the end his mother's experiences did have an impact on his political reasoning.

Leonhard's political thinking was also influenced by unorthodox reading. While at the Comintern school in Karaganda in Central Asia, he came upon and eagerly read an article by Trotsky, which he compared to "a packet of dynamite." Subversive readings and sources of information multiplied when he was in East Germany. They included Western newspapers and Arthur Koestler's essay "Soviet Myth and Reality," in which he introduced the notion of "the doctrine of unshaken foundations" which for so long had characterized Leonhard's thinking as well. Leonhard also listened to Western broadcasts, which included a dramatization of Koestler's *Darkness at Noon*; he read Yugoslav publications challenging Soviet claims and accusations, leading to the split between Tito and Stalin. Such readings helped solidify his disaffection. But it is important to point out that similar readings a few years earlier would have had a far more limited impact. When the unorthodox writings reached him, he was receptive to their messages; earlier he had not been.

The final event that accelerated Leonhard's transformation and decision to escape was the public rebuke he received for insufficiently embracing Soviet policy toward Yugoslavia. It was made clear to him that the Soviet leadership would not tolerate "the creation of a socialist society independent of Moscow"—the possibility cherished by Leonhard. He was accused of "a failure . . . to adopt a clear and frank attitude"; "a frank and unequivocal self-criticism" was demanded. He expected that "further measures" would be taken against him if he did not make a declaration unequivocally supporting the Comintern resolution against Yugoslavia. At that point he decided to escape to Yugoslavia.

Leonhard could control and compartmentalize his doubts before his return to East Germany in 1949, but once there his capacity to do so weakened for the reasons noted above. The most important among them were the encounter with his mother, the latent sense of solidarity with German civilians brutalized by Soviet troops, and the personal danger he suffered as a consequence of his questioning of Soviet policy toward Yugoslavia. Quite possibly his determination to escape and break with the Soviet and East German systems was made easier by continuing to believe, at the time of his defection, that he remained an idealistic supporter of the cause of socialism, yet to be realized somewhere.

ANDRAS HEGEDUS (1922–1999). The disillusionment of Andras Hegedus, former prime minister of Hungary, paralleled the gradual unraveling of Communist systems as their elites lost their sense of legitimacy.[58]

Hegedus came from a rural, peasant family and was one of the few high-ranking Communist leaders who during the war had been in the Hungarian Communist underground rather than in exile in the Soviet Union, returning to Hungary with Soviet troops who liberated the country from German occupation. He wrote: "My generation was not so cut off from Hungarian society as those who returned from Moscow. We had many ties of kinship and friendship to those who either directly experienced or had a feel for the grievances of various social strata or those of the nation as a whole."

His transformation was all the more remarkable since in October 1956, as prime minister, it was he who summoned Soviet troops to crush the revolution and thereby provided legitimacy for their intervention. His disillusionment stretched well over a decade. His curious career included temporary exile in Moscow in the aftermath of the 1956 revolution. After his return to Hungary the new Kadar regime treated him as an embarrassment (a former hard-liner), and he was not given further opportunity to participate in political life; he was, however, permitted to join a sociological research institute with the warning that "if I intend to work as an empiricial sociologist I will get all assistance from the Academy, but if I intend to engage in the sociological criticism of the official ideology I should expect nothing good." He was expelled from the party in 1973, branded a "revisionist"—that is, an advocate of a more liberal, reformist approach to economic and cultural policies.

Hegedus was sufficiently reflective (at any rate, by the time he wrote his memoir) to realize that his attraction to the system was based on both belief in the party's idealistic goals and the pleasure of exercising power to implement them. Hence the title of his memoir: *Under the Spell of History and Power*. The "spell of history" he alludes to was the belief of having been engaged in the historical task of building socialism in Hungary with the help of the Soviet Union:

> It was the combination of a sense of historical mission with the need for power that made it possible [to persist in his commitments] . . . but the internalized role of the party functionary also played a part. . . .

> My generation was born into a historical turning point and many of us became active participants in the great social transformations. We quickly got used to the possession of power and the privileges which went with it, and it became one of our basic needs.

These attitudes were bolstered by a belief in the historical laws postulated by Marx and Engels and the conviction that Hegedus and his fellow functionaries were merely validating and helping to implement these laws.

His initial attraction to the movement grew out of his experiences of rural poverty and the inequalities that prevailed in pre-1945 Hungary. Participation in the Communist underground further cemented these commitments; in 1944 he was arrested by the pro-Nazi authorities and sentenced to two years' imprisonment. He escaped from a moving train while being shipped westward with other prisoners and continued his illegal work in the Communist youth movement, printing and distributing anti-Nazi leaflets; he joined the party in late 1944. This youthful involvement and risk-taking became a foundation of his enduring commitment.

After the war he spent six months at a party school established to train functionaries and party members for important administrative positions in various institutions and organizations. Attending these schools was a badge of honor (those selected were judged to be reliable and promising candidates for high positions in the political or economic hierarchy, or already occupied such positions) and a precondition of further advancement. These schools sought to forge devoted loyalists willing to subordinate personal to political interests, and exposed them to large doses of Marxism-Leninism as interpreted by the instructors. These ideas were not debated but were presented as the exclusive road to truth, social justice, and desirable social change. Criticism and self-criticism sessions were used to extinguish any trace of individualism or deviant social-political attitudes. At the time Hegedus attended, he accepted the demands made upon him and did not rebel against the ethos of the school that helped him become a loyal functionary.

Like some other high-ranking officials, Hegedus was ambivalent about the privileges he and his family enjoyed, but these reservations were by no means critical in his disenchantment with the system. Initially Hegedus was uneasy about these privileges.[59] When he was first served a special meal delivered to his office at party headquarters, he protested to a higher official in charge of these services. He was told that, "given my capabilities which are of great value for the Party," the good meals were justified. "I was embarrassed but later on ceased to protest the special meals." In all probability, the deprivations and risks Hegedus experienced while in the Communist underground made it easier to accept the new privileges, which at some level must have been felt as hard earned and well deserved.

Numerous "prestige symbols" were available to Communist functionaries. They were highly valued not merely because they made life more comfortable and enjoyable but because they were tokens of the trust that the party's highest leadership bestowed on their recipients. They included curtained black cars of Western manufacture for high-level functionaries and armored ZIL limousines, made in the Soviet Union (a copy of the American Packard), for top leaders. These vehicles came with special horns and lights; different colors signified different positions in the hierarchy. Another "prestige symbol" was the number of telephones and phone lines available in one's office. Housing was also a major status symbol. The villas allocated to high-level functionaries were located in the most desirable neighborhoods, and the most luxurious had their own swimming pool. These same functionaries had access to the luxury items of the period, such as lemons, salami, and veal provided by special shops. The nomenklatura (high-level party functionaries) also had at its disposal (as in all Communist states) special resorts or rest homes and superior health-care facilities.

Looking back, Hegedus reflects that "the privileges which came with power deepened the spell of power." They also had an insidious impact: "All these [privileges] were supposed to insure that we perform our duties without petty distractions, but in fact they removed us from the daily life of the population, from standing in line for various scarce commodities, from the world of low incomes and standards of living. These privileges made us largely deaf and blind about the cares of the nation." These insights came later. Initially Hegedus could also accept the imposition of the Soviet patterns of government: "We copied mechanically the Soviet-type social institutions and we strove to turn the traditional . . . Western European orientation of the country, completely toward Eastern Europe, that is to say, toward the Soviet Union. . . . These policies offended national sentiment."

The combination of early idealistic motivation, underground experiences, elevation to high office, and privileges that confirmed his importance together provided strong defenses against disaffection, even in the face of problematic events and experiences. The strength of his faith was demonstrated by his response to the major Hungarian show trials in 1949 of Laszlo Rajk and his fellow "conspirators." The rationalization of the show trials by party functionaries occurred in stages: "First we recognize the necessity of the Party purge, based on biographical data; suspicion will suffice for the decision to expel those selected from the party. We accept the necessity of the campaigns of vigilance under critical historical conditions even if the price paid is our own victimization."

These attitudes persisted up to the time of the execution of Imre Nagy in 1958, which Hegedus learned of during his exile in Moscow: ". . . I was deeply shocked by the human tragedy involved yet felt no moral revulsion against those who made the decision. I knew well that all of us in Moscow . . . due to the logic of the situation could not have avoided rendering a similarly harsh verdict, even if all our feelings had protested against it." This was still the loyal fuctionary who considered the 1956 revolution a "counter-revolution."

In retrospect Hegedus also asked himself how he could have avoided the fact that "many of my old friends were at Recsk [the notorious Hungarian labor camp], others were in prison, often under worse and more humiliating conditions than the political prisoners experienced in the jails of the Horthy regime" [the right-wing anti-Communist government that preceded 1945]. But as long as the fundamentals of his political beliefs were in place, such questions and conflicts could be silenced, deflected, or neutralized.

Two major historical events accelerated the process of his disenchantment. One was Khrushchev's famous speech of 1956, which made Hegedus realize "how many innocent people were murdered in the Soviet Union during the tyranny of Stalin." At the time, he recalls, "strictly speaking" he was

> no longer an orthodox Marxist-Leninist, most of us were guided by the practical considerations of retaining power. Nevertheless, our faith in the validity of our ideology played a great part in our thinking. . . . We failed to take into account the obvious fact that the ideology we regarded as infallible was severely damaged by the revelation and condemnation of the crimes of Stalinism that were performed at the 20th Party Congress.

He was among those at the time who blamed the deformations of the system on the "cult of personality," on subjective factors, individual shortcomings—that is, on Stalin.

Khrushchev's revelations compelled Hegedus to confront the crimes committed by Hungarian Communist authorities and in early October 1956 led to the rehabilitation and reburial of Laszlo Rajk. As prime minister, Hegedus was obliged to attend the reburial ceremony with other dignitaries and functionaries; standing in the front row of the mourners, he sensed the hatred of the crowd. By then he felt estranged from the old hard-line leadership and was "tempted by the idea that people of my generation [in the party elite] could join together to take power and cleanse the situation. . . . I was also well aware that we too were tainted and unsuited to introduce new and genuinely moral political practices."

The second historical event that led Hegedus toward disillusion was the Hungarian Revolution itself, which erupted in the wake of the Rajk reburial in late October. Its deeper significance eluded Hegedus for some time. While it was happening he still wished to defend the status quo, as reflected not only in requesting the help of Soviet troops but in his objection to the suggestions of other Politburo members to dissolve the Hungarian political police, the AVH. As he recalled, "I protested with some passion the idea since disbanding the AVH would have meant sacrificing the defenders of our system and politics to the lynching mob." Since Hegedus was widely considered one of the hardliners associated with the Stalinist leadership, during the revolution both Imre Nagy (then prime minister) and Yuri Andropov, the Soviet ambassador, proposed that Hegedus and his family be moved to the Soviet Union with other former leaders for reasons of safety.

His two years of exile in Moscow allowed him time for reflection and provided a period of incubation for his desire for independence and personal autonomy. He decided later to become a sociologist in part because he thought it would help him better understand the events which led to the revolution and because he still had hopes that the practice of sociology might pave the way for his return to the higher echelons of the political elite. It took him another decade to renounce such aspirations.

Upon his return to Hungary from Moscow, a party official informed him that he no longer enjoyed the trust of the authorities but would be given an opportunity to regain it; he was allowed to engage in scientific activity. Hegedus was given a choice between two agricultural research institutes and one engaged in economic research. He chose the economic enterprise in the hope it would allow him to pursue his sociological interests. In the decades that followed, he gradually regained a capacity for independent thinking, a development helped by the supportive, unorthodox subculture of the sociological research institute he later became affiliated with. When he wrote his memoirs he still had an ambivalent affinity with Marxism, which he treated as "a spiritual legacy" and used in a somewhat eclectic manner, without surrendering his newfound autonomy. He continued to embrace socialist values perceived as instrumental in the struggle against inequality and in the shaping of economic conditions that would nurture democratic institutions and help develop authentic communities or communitarian institutions and the rise of civil society. Nonetheless he categorically rejected the much-quoted proposition of George Lukacs that "the worst socialism is better than the best capitalism." In 1968 he lost his job as head of the Sociological Research Institute for his critique of the invasion of Czechoslovakia, and was pensioned in 1975.

At the very end of his memoirs, Hegedus reaffirms his independence and commitment to his role as critic of the system, but he also reveals some reluctance to renounce all possible connections to power.

ZDENEK MLYNAR (1930–1997) is not well known in the West, but he is among the high-ranking former Communist functionaries who engaged in prolonged and thoughtful reflections about his disenchantment with "actually existing communism" and the abandonment of his hopes for the prospects of a "humane communism" or "socialism with a human face." It took him twenty years to complete "the slow and painful process" of reassessment that continued even after his expulsion from the Czechoslovak party in 1970.[60]

His background was particularly relevant and helpful for a moral reassessment of Communist systems, for he studied law in the Soviet Union and worked as a trainee in the public prosecutor's office in Moscow. He spent five years in the Soviet Union, which came to constitute the incubation period for his subsequent doubts. After his return to Czechoslovakia he became a department head in the Office of the Public Prosecutor in Prague. In this capacity he was intimately involved in the machinery of repression that included the confiscation of property of people convicted of political crimes and the coercive collectivization of agriculture.

Mlynar joined the Czech Communist party at age sixteen in 1946 and was a member for twenty-five years. He was an avid reader of Marxist-Leninist literature, which helped implant and bolster his ideological convictions; he recognized in the course of his disillusionment that these ideas provided a sense of privileged access to truth and were the source of much arrogance and paternalism in the exercise of power he assisted.

Mlynar is among numerous functionaries who for lengthy periods recognized many defects in the system they served but dismissed their importance or moral-ethical significance. His case also confirms that knowing about morally problematic matters was by itself not decisive in the process of disaffection. It was not so much an avoidance of or insulation from unpleasant and ideologically incongruent facts that made a difference but the handling of such information. The interpretation of such facts, the capacity to redefine whatever was morally unacceptable—this was the key for the retention of beliefs. Commitment rested on a single-minded focus on ends and intentions.

Mlynar's reflections suggest religious analogies (as do other similar writings examined on these pages). He wrote: "It was faith that kept me from drawing normal, logical conclusions from all those occasions in everyday practice and experience. After all, we committed young communists were living in the same reality as everyone else, but that reality spoke to us in a different language." That such beliefs and attitudes were shared by a closely knit group made their maintenance easier:

> We were a very specific sect, and we shared the traits common to all sects: we treasured the strictness of our values and morality, and in guarding and preserving them we were reaffirming our sense of being superior to the world of unbelievers . . . who did not see things as we did.

There were, generally speaking, three major ways for supporters of these regimes, including Mlynar, to explain away their questionable positions and diminish personal responsibility for the misdeeds of the system they served. One was to claim unfamiliarity with the specifics of the most indefensible policies or their consequences. For example, Mlynar wrote that while present at the interrogation of common criminals in Moscow jails, he "never dreamed that in another wing of the very same prison things were taking place that Solzhenitsyn afterwards wrote about."

The second way was to shift responsibility to the higher authorities—a particularly appealing and plausible option in a highly centralized political system run by a supposedly infallible political entity, the ruling Communist party, and the similarly (or even more) infallible supreme leader.

Third, the sufferings imposed by the system could be justified by falling back on the appropriate interpretation of the relationship between ends and means. In addition to overvaluing the ends, the justification of tainted means often also rested on exculpation by "difficult historical conditions" (especially in the case of the Soviet Union) and the associated inadequacies of the "human raw material" (as Trotsky put it) at the disposal of the ruling elites who undertook these momentous social transformations.

The decisive importance attributed to the ends was often also associated with a preference for the "whole" or the "organic whole" over its parts.

The erosion of Mlynar's beliefs probably began in the Soviet Union. He later wrote, "Our experience of everyday life in the Soviet Union mercilessly shattered all our preconceptions about the Soviet man." While he did not expect to find "a consumer's paradise" in the early 1950s, he was disturbed by the apparent absence of any political idealism among the Soviet citizens he observed and by his frequent encounters with excessive drinking and "the significance vodka has in the life of Soviet people." He also learned about the oppressiveness of the bureaucracy and witnessed instances of ordinary people acting as humble supplicants facing indifferent or arrogant officials. It was not supposed to be the way the relationship between ordinary Soviet people and "their" officials worked.

Mlynar recalled that "Most of the young [Czech] communists who studied in Soviet universities in the first half of the 1950s returned home with their ideological faith shaken . . . yet our communist faith still refused to yield to our experience." A major reason for this refusal was the conviction that what really mattered, as far as the Soviet Union was concerned, was that it had abolished capitalism—a conviction Mlynar shared with many Western sympathizers. He wrote: "Whatever faults the Soviet Union may have had, there was no private capitalistic exploitation." At the same time he claimed that despite five years in the Soviet Union and fluency in Russian, he "had no idea whatsoever of the extent and forms of Stalinist political terror."

As is often the case, it is difficult to establish the importance and chronology of particular experiences or incidents in the process of Mlynar's disillusionment. But it is clear that besides the drawn-out, percolating impact of the Soviet experiences there were others in his own country that proved significant. One was his learning about the personality and personal morality of the individuals in charge of the political system. Antonin Novotny, head of the Czechoslovak Communist party during much of the 1950s and '60s and deeply involved in the preparation of the Slansky trial (the major Czech show trial in 1951–1952), was one of them. Mlynar observed that Novotny "may well have been born without some basic human qualities." Mlynar also learned from official documents that after the execution of the defendants in the Slansky trial, some of the personal property of the executed ended up in the households of high-ranking officials, including Novotny's: "The thought that the first secretary of the ruling party and head of the state slept between the sheets belonging to a man whom he had helped to send to the gallows is something incredible," he wrote. Another incident of similar impact occurred when Antonin Zapotocky, another party leader, "invited Slansky to his home for a party, knowing that on his way home Slansky would be arrested. When Slansky was getting into his overcoat after the party, Zapotocky telephoned the police officer responsible for making the arrest and according to a prearranged agreement told him: 'He is on the way.'"

Finally there was the continuing spectacle of elite privileges—the usual assortment of special shops, clinics, schools, recreational facilities, vacation homes and substantial inequities of income—that came to trouble Mlynar. Apparently for a long time he accepted them without misgivings, but at last he concluded that such privileges "always spoil people, particularly when they are associated with power."

Conceivably he could have lived much longer with these doubts and conflicts if it had not been for the Soviet invasion, the Soviet crushing of Czech efforts in the "Prague Spring" of 1968 to reform and humanize their system. The Soviet intervention, he wrote, was "the ultimate debacle of my life as a Communist . . . this was the irrevocable ruin of everything I had devoted my life to . . . and in particular of reform communism." It became clear that the Soviet Union was not about to tolerate a more humane and pluralistic form of socialism within what Brezhnev called the "Socialist Commonwealth," that is, the countries under Soviet control in Eastern Europe. The new repressive measures, including occupation by Soviet and other Warsaw Pact troops, confirmed and finalized the misgivings Mlynar had accumulated but kept in check over decades.

Following the intervention he was first expelled from the Central Committee of the party and then from the party itself, a quarter-century after he had joined it. He lived "seven more years in Czechoslovakia, not among the privileged but in the ghetto of the outcasts." He was among the founders of Charter 77, a dissident group. He went into exile in Vienna in 1977.

JULIUS HAY (1900–1975), a prominent Hungarian playwright and friend of Arthur Koestler, was almost as fluent in German as in his native language. He spent much of his adult life outside Hungary, mostly in exile in Germany, Austria, the Soviet Union, and finally Switzerland. He came from an assimilated liberal Jewish family; his father was a landowner as well as manager and chief engineer of a flood-control company in a Hungarian country town.

Hay's leftist sympathies first found expression in his support of the short-lived (four months) Hungarian Communist government in 1919, when he worked in the commissariat for education. At that time, being a socialist meant for him "To put an end to war forever by removing its causes. To make work a pleasure. To give each according to his needs . . . all the things that should make mankind irrevocably happy including the equality of all nations."[61]

At the time Hay was already a believer, though not ignorant of the failings of the new political system:

> Why did Bela Kun [head of the Hungarian Soviet Republic in 1919] not go on with the redistribution of the land begun by Karolyi [head of the previous government]? The question left me no peace. . . . Although not once during those 133 days [the duration of the Hungarian Soviet Republic] did it occur to me to doubt that Bela Kun's policy was right and in the people's best interest. I *wanted* to believe that it was so, and I succeeded. . . . In later years . . . it became more difficult. Even so I went on. . . . Not believing was for a long time an even greater strain.

Here in a nutshell was the dilemma faced by many believers who could not fully extinguish their capacity for critical thinking. In their lives they sought to balance the emotional imperatives of belief with an awareness of the realities that challenged the foundation of this belief.

In the 1920s Hay lived in Germany for six years, beginning a playwriting career with several pieces performed in major theaters. During his stay he joined the German Communist party ("I wanted to be the member of an international revolutionary organization and create a new world in place of a world gone rotten"). After the Nazi seizure of power he escaped to Austria, where he was briefly imprisoned as a Communist; later he was invited to the Soviet Union where he spent a decade before returning to Hungary in 1945 with Soviet troops. After enjoying privileged status as a prominent, award-winning writer in Communist Hungary, he became a critic of the regime following Stalin's death and was an active supporter of the 1956 revolution. In the wake of its defeat he was given a six-year sentence but was released during an amnesty in 1960. In 1964 he went into exile in Switzerland, where he died.

While writing plays was the major focus of Hay's life, it was also "quite clear" to him from early on that he wrote in order "to change the existing social order." But these political goals had a distinctly religious quality. Upon rejoining the Communist party in Germany (he first joined it in Hungary in 1919), and after putting away "lovingly and reverently" his membership card, he reflected: "I have learned that man needs redemption. He needs to be redeemed from wholesale slaughter, from hunger, from immorality, from his neighbor's hatred and from hatred of his neighbor, from being exploited and from being driven to exploit in his turn. . . ."

Upon his arrest as a Communist in Austria he declaimed to a skeptical police officer:

> I became a Communist in order that I might assist in making everybody in this world happy; in abolishing war for ever; in securing equal rights for all peoples . . . in bringing prosperity to the whole of mankind; and in depriving everyone once and for all of the possibility of exploiting others, of oppressing others, and of making others unhappy.

Like many artists and intellectuals, Hay was deeply convinced that the sacred duty of the serious artist or intellectual was to use his talent in a good cause: the perfection of social institutions and human beings and relationships. Later on it was precisely as an artist safeguarding his creative autonomy and freedom of expression that he came into conflict with the requirements of politicized literature codified in the precepts of socialist realism. Thus while he was in Moscow one of his plays "met with . . . Walter Ulbricht's unqualified disapproval" because it was "at variance with the rules of . . . 'socialist realism' in that it had no 'positive hero.'" (Ulbricht later became the East German party leader.) Hay's idealistic artistic-literary commitments came to play an important part in distancing himself from both the Soviet and Hungarian embodiments of Communist ideals. In an article written shortly before the Hungarian Revolution, he declared:

> . . . the writer, like any other person, must be unconditionally allowed: to tell the truth; to criticize anything and anyone . . . To believe in God's omnipotence; not to believe in God's omnipotence; . . . to think un-Marxistically; to think Marxistically . . . to expose injustice even in places where the official opinion is that only justice is to be found . . . to condemn the way in which certain of our leading figures live, speak, go about their business . . .

Hay scorned the abdication of autonomy and critical impulse among his fellow writers, prompted by their zealous ideological convictions more than the coercive pressure of the authorities. Lion Feuchtwanger, at the time a famous German writer and fellow traveler (whom he met when Hay lived in the Soviet Union), was a case in point. Hay was given by Alexander Fadeyev, head of the Soviet writers union, the task of persuading Feuchtwanger of the need for the ongoing purge trials. As it turned out, Feuchtwanger "arrived in Moscow more convinced than I was myself and glided with surprising ease over every absurdity" of the proceedings. Hay also wrote of Feuchtwanger's visit:

> Accepting gifts and hospitality, making public appearances, going shopping, being received by Stalin in person, paying his respects to Lenin's body in the mausoleum, visiting factories. . . . He was completely wrapped up in his political gesture of having come to Moscow and bearing witness to Communism . . . on the basis of superficial impressions and with the assistance of party hand-outs. . . .

Bertolt Brecht, the famous German writer whom Hay knew well from his years in Germany, was for Hay another example of the writer transformed into a party hack. Brecht criticized one of Hay's plays for being insufficiently inspired by Marxist theory. Worse, Brecht provided a rationale for the Moscow Trials which in effect the Soviet authorities embraced.[62] Brecht wrote: "It is necessary to bring to light behind the deeds of the accused a political concept that can credibly be attributed to them and that has led them into the swamps of common criminality."

Hay's loyalties were severely tested during his long stay in the Soviet Union, a period which included the purge trials, the mass terror, and the mandatory worship of Stalin. He had the first inkling of the terror while still in Germany after the Kirov assassination in 1934.[63] In the repression that followed, Hay was ". . . tormented by the feeling that this was no due process of law any more. . . . A massacre [had] been going on for months . . . and showed no signs of coming to an end. This prompted . . . gloomy feelings—feelings, however, that never managed to assume the form of thoughts." That is to say, the misgivings were not confronted or articulated at the time.

Later it became impossible to ignore the terror when close friends and acquaintances disappeared daily; nor was it possible to find justifications for these events:

> At the beginning we still tried to find reasons and connections, but as the arrests went on we gradually got used to the fact that it could happen to anybody. Even to people who only just escaped the clutches of

> the Fascists, for the appalling, scarcely credible fact . . . was that the NKVD had even been known to hand over German anti-Fascist militants to the Gestapo. Any one of us could disappear any time, never to be seen again. . . . There was no moral context any more.

Not all of the difficulties of life in the Soviet Union were life threatening, but they too created dissonance between high expectations and daily realities. Hay wrote:

> Somewhere in the depths of my tiredness . . . a vague and barely perceptible sense of unease began to make its presence felt. . . . I had come to this capital of every international revolutionary movement in order to find something I had never experienced before. . . . Gradually, however, I had to get used to the fact that everything I needed I could obtain only in the form of laboriously preserved but none the less decayed relics of an earlier bourgeois existence.

This referred to the trivial and more than trivial hardships and scarcities that even relatively privileged Communist exiles like Hay had to contend with. The difficulties of satisfying simple needs were closely linked to the political control of one's life: "A further feature of such a system is that in the end no one has the right to own a thing simply because he needs it. Everything comes as a gift, a mark of distinction, an indication of rank. And as a result of right-mindedness and good personal contacts." Here Hay put his finger on the key attribute of socialist inequalities, namely their purposeful political determination: the allocation of privileges was carefully calibrated as a reward for supporters of the system, depending on their importance.

It did not take him long to discover the specific patterns of these inequities:

> The food and consumer goods available in public shops were insufficient for the daily needs or far beyond the means of the average family. Once Micky [his wife] discovered a particularly well-stocked grocer's and shopped there with such naive assurance that at first she was served with no questions asked. Only when we had both shopped there on two further occasions did it emerge that we had hit upon one of these special shops that were only open to the employees of a particular institution. The particular institution happened in this case to be the so-called Lubyanka, the much feared secret police. . . .

After the war in Hungary, Hay continued to learn more about elite privileges, such as the "Party bigwigs' summer colony on Lake Balaton. . . . A luxurious settlement . . . sealed off with barbed wire, guarded by the AVO [the Hungarian political police]. Service by nimble waiters—everywhere, even in the water. No food might be set on the table without first having been examined by the doctor." When an excursion boat was driven by a storm to the barbed-wire fence in the water, the guards drove it back into the stormy lake.

An experience on the streets of Moscow provided a particularly disturbing reflection of the system:

> One day . . . I saw in the street a man who often returned afterwards to haunt my dreams. . . . This man was a middle-aged peasant. . . . His peasant shoes looked as ancient as the earth. . . . He held a small, flat lunch-bag pressed between his knees. One had the impression that everything he owned in the world he had on him. He was staring fixedly at a slip of paper in his hand. . . . In fact he was staring beyond the paper into nothingness—perhaps into the nothingness that the paper had made of his future. . . . Over and over again his silent lips repeated the words that were written there. And sweat, the cold sweat of fear, streamed down his face. . . .

For Hay the peasant symbolized misery created by official callousness and high-handedness. Whatever the slip of paper contained—a summons, an eviction notice, an order or demand of some kind—it had apparently devastated the life of this peasant. Later Hay had an opportunity to see for himself what the rural areas looked like. He was commissioned to contribute to a film scenario about the German Volga Republic, whose residents were descendants of ethnic Germans settled by Catherine the Great. He was shocked by the poverty and starvation in the fertile area they inhabited:

> . . . here were these peasants offering a wide variety of objects in exchange for bread. . . . There was something preposterous and unnatural about it all. One was used to the *town* having no bread. . . . But this was the case of the *country*, of a tract of land celebrated for its fertility, without bread. The villages were plundered. . . . They were compelled to get their own food from the towns as and when they could.

How did Hay manage to preserve his political loyalty and commitment given the iniquities and adversities of Soviet life he came to see? His total dependence on the system must have been a factor at a time when he would have faced persecution in those countries he had lived in earlier. The Soviet Union took him in when he had nowhere else to go. And there was nowhere to turn for explanation or rectification of the evils witnessed: "With whom should one argue? Whom implore? Whose name abominate and curse? The system of impersonal repression wore one out, exhausted one's moral reserves, ushered in despair. . . . One sank into stupor. One learnt to be a vegetable. The human values one bore within one went into decline." This was a time-honored if extreme response to the apparently overwhelming power of a totalitarian state.

After the Nazi attack on the Soviet Union it was easier to come to terms with the Soviet system that now confronted a genuine, foreign enemy. Of this period Hay wrote:

> . . . let them give us a rifle . . . and we'll defend Moscow to the death. . . . The many abominations of bureaucracy . . . the incompetents' lust for power, the preferential treatment offered to drones . . . the meaninglessness of life and death . . . the self-perpetuating massacre . . . all the evil that one had come to accept as the essential component of socialism, of Communism—our generation would forgive and forget it all. . . .

There was also the hope, later on, as Soviet troops advanced, that in a liberated Hungary a socialist system different from and superior to the Soviet version might be constructed: "Hungary must become a democratic republic. . . . The first task of any new government in Hungary must be to distribute the land among the have-nots." Hungary was not to follow the disastrous path of Soviet collectivization. Hay also felt that "From this point of view it mattered little whether Russia was already socialist or only called itself such. What was still wrong in Russia we would put right in our country." In spite of his experiences in the Soviet Union, Hay imagined that the Kremlin would consent to the creation of a free, democratic Hungary.

After his return to Hungary in a Soviet military plane, "it was impossible to spend a day or even an hour in Budapest without hearing of the brutalities committed by [Soviet] soldiers." Nonetheless he still managed to keep faith, or his reborn faith. In this period between 1945 and 1953, Hay belonged to the officially indulged elite of politically correct Hungarian artists and intellectuals. His plays were performed in the National Theatre, he was awarded the prestigious Kossuth Prize and appointed chairman of the Hungarian-Soviet Cultural Association—the regime treated him like the trusted and loyal supporter he still was. The horrors of the Soviet purges were apparently forgotten, the experience of Soviet-style scarcities replaced by the privileges reserved for artists and intellectuals who supported the party. Even in retrospect, in these memoirs, Hay appears to believe that at least initially the Hungarian Communist party was a great force for good: it made "a tremendous impression on the population," and its leaders "enjoyed a quite extraordinary prestige." These were questionable assertions, especially in light of the results of the first and only relatively free election in which the Communist party won only 17 percent of the vote—and even that was achieved with some electoral fraud. Subsequently the Communist takeover of Hungary in 1948 was accomplished with the active help of the AVO, the Hungarian KGB that remained the essential basis of Communist power. Hay wrote:

> Whatever the Hungarian Communist Party and its leader Matyas Rakosi wished to accomplish, they had . . . at their disposal the AVO. . . . The AVO grew steadily in size, strength, unscrupulousness and cruelty. . . . Its task was to impose upon a vast majority the commands of a tiny minority—and it fulfilled it.

The Hungarian trial of Laszlo Rajk in 1949 followed the pattern set by the Soviet show trials of the 1930s: "Phoney charges, false witnesses, wrongful sentences, mistaken self-accusations. . . . Torture by hunger, by light, by sleeplessness, by electricity—under the supervision of the top expert, General Belkin."

In 1955 Hay joined other writers in their increasingly vocal protest of the abuses of power and mismanagement of the economy by the party. As an outspoken supporter of Imre Nagy (prime minister of the revolutionary government in 1956) and a leader of the Hungarian Writers Union (a major source of dissidence before the revolution), Hay was arrested as a counterrevolutionary after the defeat of the revolution.

Hay's privileged status and personal success did not hinder his eventual realization that socialism in Hungary failed to better the Soviet model. The moderate liberalization that followed Stalin's death, both in the USSR and in Hungary, made it easier for Hay to confront and articulate his newfound critical sentiments about the system. We have no way of knowing when he first reached these conclusions about conditions in Hungary:

> We had an organized state and called it socialist or at least believed it was on the way to socialism. It mirrored ever more precisely its archetype in the East and everyone was somehow a prey to a deep feeling of unhappiness. . . .

> . . . Workers and peasants [were] forced to live in an aimless and illusory life in this world of illusion. . . .
>
> A nation was compelled to raise three cheers to its own destruction.

It is not easy to determine what if anything remained of Hay's political beliefs after the defeat of the Hungarian Revolution and his own imprisonment. His principled defiance of an oppressive and mendacious political system confirmed an undiminished idealism now turned against his earlier ideals. The final remarks of his memoirs suggest that he had no high hopes that "a socialism with a human face" would make its appearance at some future date:

> For decades I had walked . . . and hurried along the same path . . . the one I knew as the path of socialism. Other men, though, who called themselves the Party . . . opted for the high road of power and dominion and they said that high road led to socialism, to Communism.
>
> Our sort was reviled, put in prison, and threatened with death because we had tried to continue along the path the others had abandoned.
>
> They have failed to reach their goal and I have failed to reach my goal. The difference is that I admit the goal is unattainable. For my dreams to find their realization the world must look for a new path, a path as yet unknown.

Hay began his memoirs with the question that is also at the heart of this study: whether or not it is possible to discern and isolate some fact, event, or circumstance in the life of an individual to account for the shift or total reversal of his political beliefs and attitudes. As he put it:

> As I embark upon these memoirs at the age of almost seventy, it is with the intention . . . of tracking down an answer to this question: will I, somewhere along the meandering line of my narrative, stumble across some Damascus road where as a result of a spectacular volte-face I became a different person? Or will I, despite the evidence of abrupt reversal, be unable to pin down either a place or a time at which I switched directions?

At the end of the book he does not return to this question; the reader is left to draw his own conclusions. I, for one, failed to discover "a spectacular volte-face," either in regard to his early involvement with the Communist movement or his later disenchantment with it. Rather, his disillusionment (the primary concern here) resulted from a lengthy accumulation of experiences which ultimately could not be explained away. These experiences, and especially those in the Soviet Union and Communist Hungary, made it increasingly clear to him that the political systems and ideologies he was allied with did not measure up to his idealistic expectations. The process was drawn out because for a long period of time the movement and the system sheltered him, and because the risks he had taken while in the Communist underground appeared to validate his commitment: "Little by little one forgets to ask how far the cause that one holds to be good still in fact is a good cause. One finds sufficient confirmation in the danger to which one is exposing one's life."

The honors showered on Hay by the Communist government in Hungary presumably also halted or slowed the process of questioning that began in the Soviet Union. But in the post-Stalin ferment his idealism returned in full force, culminating in his unqualified support of the revolution. His imprisonment after the revolution put the final seal on his break with the system and its unfulfilled promises.

MIKLOS GIMES (1917–1958), a Hungarian journalist, is the only individual discussed in this book who paid with his life for his disillusionment with communism. His life and beliefs provide an exceptionally illuminating case study of the relationship between belief and behavior, both during the years when Gimes was a true believer in communism and later when he became its equally sincere critic and opponent. His biographer wrote that "his transformation was the most far reaching" and his "critiques of the regime were most consistently determined by the criterion of freedom." A Hungarian contemporary observed that

> . . . his career . . . exemplifies the similar trajectory of the generation hopeful of a new, redemptive world after 1945, one which went astray and recovered its sense only after Stalin's death. He differed only insofar as he was more impassioned, committed more serious crimes, but also repented more deeply. . . .
>
> . . . The example and horrific mistakes of the unusually intelligent, erudite, and well-meaning Gimes offer an excellent introduction to understanding that insane period and its fanatical Stalinist intellectuals, barely comprehensible for the present generation.[64]

Gimes, as a journalist-functionary, worked for the cultural propaganda apparatus of the Hungarian Communist party between 1945 and 1955. He was a combative, dedicated supporter of the regime installed by the Soviet Union and was widely considered a fanatical, ruthless Stalinist. He was also a faithful servant of the literary policies of the authorities, a point man in the campaigns to impose socialist realism on Hungarian writers. For his efforts he was awarded in 1950 and 1952 various medals by the government. He used to be a close associate of Joseph Revai, one of the four top party leaders who was in charge of Hungarian literary life and the arts.

Gimes came from a liberal, assimilated, highly educated Jewish family: his father was a medical doctor, his mother a psychoanalyst; the family converted to unitarianism. Jewish identity played no part in his outlook, though the anti-Semitic aspects of the Slansky trial in Czechoslovakia in 1952 alerted him to the questionable nature of these proceedings. Under parental influence he enrolled as a medical student but gave up and later gravitated to literary studies. He was a voracious reader drawn to Goethe, Shakespeare, Tolstoy, Dostoevsky, and Thomas Mann. In 1942 he was among Jewish men aged twenty-four to thirty-three who were conscripted into labor battalions established by the right-wing government allied with Nazi Germany. He served in and finally escaped from Transylvania and eventually made his way to the partisans of Tito in Yugoslavia, and from there back to Budapest as the war ended. His father died in a German concentration camp.

The post–World War II career of Gimes paralleled those of many others of similar talent and disposition: it was a period of new opportunities and accelerated social mobility for those with the requisite political attitudes; it was possible to combine self-interest with political virtue. Journalistic opportunities suited him both ideologically and as a source of livelihood; he became an influential correspondent and editorial writer for the official daily newspaper of the Communist party.

Gimes was a resolutely nonpragmatic, idea-driven man in the grip of an impassioned idealism that found fatal and final expression in his refusal to escape from Hungary after the defeat of the revolution, even after the government made clear its determination to capture him. His biographer saw him as possessed of a contradictory duality: on the one hand there was in him "a demand for the intellectual ordering of the world, for finding . . . explanations for everything in a comprehensive, coherent, rational system. On the other hand there was an inclination to give priority to feelings, to follow impulses in opposition of life's demand for order." Contemporaries also recalled two Miklos Gimeses during the Stalinist period. One was "charming, friendly, good-natured, open, kind-hearted and gentle"; the other was "despicable, pompous, much feared by literati and editors, a man . . . who would later describe himself as 'insane, evil and idiotic.' In an obituary written by two well-known anti-Communist exiles, he was remembered as "propagating communist myths for years with extraordinary intolerance."

Gimes had an undisciplined, bohemian streak, a certain naiveté, or lack of calculation, and "an underdeveloped sense of danger" framed by a somewhat disorderly way of life. He would easily have fitted into a Western countercultural setting of the 1960s. Choosing a profession or occupation did not come easily to him. As a young man he wrote of himself: "I feel helplessly that there is something I ought to accomplish but I don't know what it is. I am incapable of sustained work that is its own reward. . . . I am 27 and I have always felt a strange superfluousness, aimlessness, wasting time." He went into analysis but ended it after finding not only a job but a calling as a journalist. In the same year, 1945, he joined the party, as did his mother, sister, and brother-in-law.

Gimes's political career and his ultimate fate were seen by contemporaries as influenced by his passionate, uncompromising temperament, by a "capacity for indignation and anger that defied the limitations of rational calculation." It was further observed that "many emotional, sentimental elements blended into his political attitudes which interfered with his sharply observant and coldly analytical persona." There seemed to be a moral and compensatory element in his subsequent risk-taking, in the wish to make amends for his earlier aggressive championing of a bad cause.

Being a hard-core, committed Communist in Stalinist Hungary between 1945 and 1953, in the expectation of contributing to grandiose social improvements, seems to be the counterpart of Gimes's later, correspondingly unrealistic and hopeless stand against the reimposition of Communist rule after the repression of the Hungarian Revolution. He was among the few who seriously tried to organize some sort of resistance after the military defeat, bringing together different political groups, publishing an underground newspaper, distributing leaflets restating the goals of the revolution, questioning the legitimacy of the authorities and advocating nonviolent resistance.

In a candid and revealing memorandum written to the party early in his career, he characterized his political attitudes:

> . . . I don't have a place in capitalist society. The birth of a classless society, the victory of communism for me is an existential question. The future of the communist movement is my own future. . . .
>
> It was not my class position that made me a communist, nor a pure, rational conviction. I was a rebel and revolutionary well before

> I learned anything about Marxism. I had good housing, proper clothes. I cannot and won't forget that it was my inability to fit in that made me a communist; my revolutionary disposition has an emotional origin. . . .

It would be difficult to find a clearer recognition of the connections between the personal and the political. Whatever the precise origins of his devotion to the party, Gimes's subservience was unrivaled while it endured; as a party journalist he accepted every propaganda assignment. In 1950, on Stalin's birthday, he wrote in the party daily, among other things, that Stalin's name equaled "human liberation and the conquest of nature," that Stalin's life was dedicated to the struggle for peace. As Revai's point man in the campaign to regiment writers, he severely criticized those who failed to present in their writings "true workers" and "communists of a highly developed political consciousness." He rebuked Tibor Dery, one of the best and most respected Hungarian writers of the period, for creating appealing characters who should not have been portrayed as appealing given their "class position." He criticized literary characters who were shown as capable of loving one another notwithstanding their divergent positions in the class struggle. He was no less radically judgmental in foreign affairs, suggesting, for instance, that "American imperialism descended from German fascism but it was actually worse." He claimed during the anti-Tito campaign in 1951 that the leaders of the Yugoslav partisan forces were "agents of the Gestapo and deliberately sent to their death the best of the Yugoslav people."

As a full-time propagandist-journalist, Gimes came to experience especially sharply and painfully the divergence between theory and practice, promise and reality. There was a symmetry between the intensity of his early devotion and the bitterness of his disillusionment. It was in the wake of Stalin's death in 1953 (but before Khrushchev's revelations in early 1956) that his outlook changed and that he became an increasingly impassioned, uncompromising critic of the regime. As in many other cases, the new, more liberal ideological currents encouraged his political awakening. He ceased to be an isolated soul searcher, a closet critic struggling with inner doubts. The post-Stalin revelations and rehabilitations of those innocently imprisoned and executed led him to conclude that the theory that underlay his support for the regime had no empirical foundations.

While no single event or experience can be pinpointed as decisive, several contributed to a prolonged process of disenchantment. One was the major Hungarian show trial of Laszlo Rajk in 1949. Like other brooding and apprehensive loyalists at the time, Gimes thought "the proceedings were neither wholly truthful nor wholly false, but in all probability appropriate . . . demanded by the struggle." He succeeded in calming these apprehensions by falling back on a version of Koestler's "doctrine of unshaken foundations." He reassured himself by the apparent material-economic accomplishments of the system which legitimated, for the time being, phenomena such as the police terror and show trials. His biographer wrote: "For many, the material advances of the system provided a refuge for their faith: maybe the arrests and the trials were a bit fishy, but from a historical perspective the lives of some wretched individuals were of little importance. What mattered was the great progress of the country, growth and development, the creation of the foundation of the future."

There was another line of defense against doubt: the fatalistic reliance on and irrational belief in the great leader, Stalin, who provided the guarantee that despite all appearances, progress was being made. Loyalty also rested on the conviction that if "the individual comes into conflict with the Party, it will end in his disappearance, it will be the end." The latter recalled the reasoning of the Bukharin-like character in Koestler's *Darkness at Noon*.

The anti-Communist uprising in East Germany in 1953 was another pivotal event seen by Gimes as "a fissure in the structure of the Empire." Nonetheless he commented on these events in the party newspaper as was expected of him, characterizing them as a Western provocation, a "fascist putsch." Another important source of his misgivings was the French translation of the transcript of the Bukharin trial of the 1930s, which circulated among some Hungarian intellectuals at the time. Coming to doubt the credibility of the charges against Bukharin and the legitimacy of the proceedings as a whole led to the further questioning of the charges against Tito, as well as the policy of rapid industrialization in Hungary and, most of all, the Rajk trial. The Slansky trial in Czechoslovakia was another turning point, the beginning of the collapse of his Stalinist beliefs, so designated by Gimes five years later while under arrest.

His travels in Western Europe also undermined the official view of the world he held (with minor reservations) until then. His visit to Geneva in particular, while covering the 1954 Geneva conference of Soviet and Western foreign ministers, made a deep impression, providing "immediate, experiential refutation of the worldview he held and was committed to." In Switzerland Gimes discerned "the small miracles" of a society where things worked, not plagued by endemic shortages. He also found manifestations of democracy and free expression, including the availability of books not to be found in Hungary; he bought many, some banned in his native country. Upon his return to Hungary he reportedly suggested to close friends that the concepts of socialism and capitalism needed reexamination. In the summer of 1954 he struck an observer in Paris as "a tormented, doubt-ridden person, overwhelmed by a sense of guilt." He considered staying in France but decided against it because he felt he should not abandon the struggle to change the system at home. After his return he apologized individually to many of those he had attacked or hurt while he had been a fanatical supporter of the regime. He was the first to demand the rehabilitation of Rajk. In early October 1956, before the outbreak of the revolution, he published his reflections on the conditions that stimulated the journalistic misrepresentations and misperceptions of reality:

> Gradually we came to believe . . . that there are two kinds of truth, that the truth of the Party . . . could possibly be different and more important than objective, factual truth, that truth and momentary political expediency are identical.
>
> . . . If there is a truth higher than factual truth, if the criterion of truth is short-term political expediency, then lies can be "true," since lies can be useful in the short run; a fabricated political trial can also be "true" since it may yield political benefits. Suddenly we are transported to the outlook which infected not only those who devised the show trials but often their victims as well, which poisoned our public life . . . paralyzed our critical faculties and finally prevented many of us from perceiving basic facts of life.

Between 1954 and 1956, Gimes belonged to the circle surrounding Imre Nagy, in and out of power during that period. Prime minister of the short-lived revolutionary government in 1956, Nagy was arrested after its defeat and executed in 1958. Gimes was somewhat isolated during much of the revolution, lacking a substantial, satisfactory role; he was positioned between those on the left who wished to resuscitate the party and those on the right, the fighters on the street, relentlessly opposed to it. He was visible and active but held no major position and did not participate in the armed struggle. Nonetheless, and not fully explicably, he ended up in the small group executed with Nagy, at age forty-one. He found his place only at the end, after the Soviet troops crushed the revolution, when he became "the most active and conspicuous figure" in the doomed resistance. He was in charge of producing an underground paper which appeared just five times. He was also an outspoken supporter of the general strike that lasted a few weeks.

Gimes came to be treated by the authorities as a dangerous opponent because of his activities in the short-lived and ineffectual underground resistance. Even Malenkov, at the time Soviet premier and head of the party, considered him "a major ideological leader of the uprising," and Janos Kadar, prime minister of the new Soviet-installed Hungarian government, singled him out in a speech as a dangerous counterrevolutionary leader whose capture was a high priority. After his arrest, Gimes was charged with "initiating and leading an anti-state organization."

In the course of his prolonged interrogation he was asked to confess his alleged attempts to revise aspects of Marxism-Leninism. This is the gist of what he said:

> . . . In a sense "I still hold Marxist-Leninist views" but see certain problems which are not resolved by the tenets of Marxism-Leninism. Up till 1953 I believed that the works of Marx, Engels, Lenin and Stalin provide resolution for every important problem of our times and that each and every major proposition of their works is correct. I no longer believe this. My views had gradually undergone change from the end of 1952 to the summer of 1956. During the Slansky trial, due to the unmistakable antisemitic aspects . . . I felt that something was wrong. My doubts intensified following the exposé of the doctors' plot in Moscow and the Beria affair [his arrest, that is]. The 20th Party Congress strengthened my conviction that major errors were made during the building of socialism.
>
> What were these errors? . . . it was the neglect or underestimation of matters having to do with political freedom. . . .
>
> My readings led me to believe this underestimation . . . began with Marx and that Lenin only paid the attention to this matter it deserves in the last few months of his activities. . . .

As Gimes's biographer rightly argues, self-interest had little to do with the services Gimes rendered to the Communist dictatorship. Rather, he embarked on a path paved by good intentions; it was a case of secular messianism characteristic of our times but with an unusually tragic outcome for the true believer. The Gimes case indicates that the political systems that produced many of the catastrophes of the twentieth century cannot be understood without an awareness of "the eruptions of the passionate pursuit of brotherhood and truth" at work during their emergence and consolidation. The final meaning and message of Gimes's rebellion was the resounding denial that ends sanctify means. He was a genuine idealist in both his embrace and his disavowal of communism.

The major common denominator of disillusionment and moral indignation among the defectors, exiles, and dissidents behind the Iron Curtain was a sense of betrayal—all the more intense since these individuals were idealists, at any rate when they were initially attracted to these systems. The sense of betrayal was stimulated by a series of experiences which highlighted the gulf between ideals and realities, and by the official mendaciousness that unsuccessfully attempted to bridge the gulf. Thomas Aczel and Tibor Meray, the dissident Hungarian writers who escaped after the 1965 revolution, wrote:

> . . . Most intolerable was the simulation of virtue, the endless proclamation of good intentions: everything was taking place on behalf of "the people," in the name of the workers' power. . . . The writers knew very well that there were great social contradictions in Western capitalist systems: an American automobile manufacturer or a British oil tycoon commanded a far greater income than Mathias Rakosi or Erno Gero [Hungarian Communist leaders]. But in those capitalist societies at least they did not insist that everything belonged to the masses . . . workers on the assembly line or those drilling in the oilfields were not told that they must guard each and every tool they used or every drop of oil they extracted because they all belong to the People.[65]

THREE

In the Third World: Vietnam and China

While there is a substantial literature of disillusionment with Soviet communism, produced by former Western sympathizers as well as defectors and exiles, it is far more difficult to find published writings about similar disaffection with Third World Communist systems. The reason for such scarcity cannot be found in the greater popularity or success of these systems, which also generated huge outpourings of refugees whenever possibilities for escape opened up. Although millions of refugees left countries such as Communist Cuba, Nicaragua, Cambodia, Vietnam, and China, there are few accounts by their former officials who were disenchanted with these systems—unlike books by ordinary people who describe their suffering.[1]

Little is known and has been written about political-social conditions in Communist Vietnam in particular, and its levels of repression and popular discontent following the war with the United States. Some public awareness can be found in the United States of Vietnam's economic reforms and growth of its market economy, but on the whole Communist Vietnam has receded from American and Western consciousness and public interest since the mid-1970s. Waves of refugees, the boat people, continued to flee for a while, but even their dramatic escapes and subsequent settlement in Western countries (mostly the United States and France) failed to raise questions about the political system they were intent on leaving behind. In later decades erstwhile American supporters of North Vietnam and the Vietcong retained, largely unrevised, the heroic, revolutionary images of these two entities.

Considering these conditions, BUI TIN's (1927–) account is revelatory and its significance magnified by the evident integrity and idealism of its author. Early in the book he writes:

> When I joined the Communist party at the age of nineteen, I swore an oath . . . always to be loyal to the idea of liberating the people and the whole of mankind. Oh, what joy and happiness to take part in the struggle for such beliefs! Lacking education, I knew little about political theory. I had read a few Communist manifestos but did not really understand them. I equated joining the Party with patriotism and gaining independence. A life full of activity . . . beckoned; it would be bright and glorious without a ripple of concern discernible in the future.[2]

But there was a personal motive as well: Bui Tin's mother was killed in 1948 by a French soldier, having been pointed out as "the wife of a high-ranking Viet Minh official," that is, his father. "After that it was impossible not to feel vindictive. Whenever I went into battle, behind every opposing gun was the enemy who killed my mother."

It is a matter of conjecture how Bui Tin's social background may have influenced his becoming a revolutionary fighter, and much later the development of his misgivings about the system. His great-grandfather, grandfather, and father were distinguished public servants in the colonial era. His grandfather was a provincial governor, his father "earned degrees in classical literature and French before starting a public career as a provincial judge," eventually rising to the rank of minister of justice. In October 1945 he joined the government of Ho Chi Minh as inspector general, at Ho's personal request. "Such was the esteem in which my father was held," Bui Tin writes, "that when he died . . . in . . . 1955 he was accorded a state funeral."

Bui Tin became an early participant in the guerrilla war against South Vietnam, joining the North Vietnamese army at age eighteen and eventually rising to the rank of colonel. In the army he directed a divisional political school in 1952, became a regimental commander at age twenty-two, and in 1959–1960 was in charge of the political training of groups organized to infiltrate the South. Between 1958 and 1962 he was in charge of political indoctrination in a large military zone, lecturing the officer corps about dialectical and historical materialism, among other things. He was a member of the Vietnamese Communist party for forty-five years. After his military service he became a journalist, reporting on the war with Cambodia, and later served as editor of an official publication. In the late 1970s he was assigned to help establish the new Cambodian national news agency following the defeat of Pol Pot.

In the early 1990s Bui Tin visited France at the invitation of the Communist newspaper *L'Humanité*, and decided to stay in order to be able to make public his critiques of conditions in his native country. His writings are among the few sources in English about these conditions and the only account I know of the political disillusionment of a former high-ranking Communist Vietnamese official. While his book does not make clear when precisely his doubt and criticism began to emerge, they clearly multiplied and intensified following the Communist victory in 1975. His decision to accept the invitation from the French Communist newspaper was not easily made since he had to leave behind his family, country, and a "stable occupation" as editor of a magazine. Probably helping his decision was the fact that his son was among the boat people in 1989, a mechanical engineer who "became fed up with the way people of talent were treated and wanted to improve his educational qualifications." He and his wife (who graduated in English at Hanoi University) fled to Canada.

The first impression to strike the reader is how remarkably and unexpectedly similar Bui Tin's critiques of the Vietnamese system and social-political conditions are to those expressed both by disenchanted officials and by ordinary citizens in the Soviet Union and East European Communist states. What sets Bui Tin's critiques apart from many others is that he belonged to a generation of genuine revolutionaries who fought and risked their lives for the cause; there is no doubt about the seriousness of his original commitment. He writes: "I am writing it [this book] as a result of the pain felt by somebody who has been a member of the Vietnamese Communist Party for forty-five years before being expelled in March 1991." He recalled:

> In early 1975 I was nearly fifty years old and had spent the major part of my life serving the Revolution. I had fought against the French and the Americans. . . . On several occasions I had fallen ill and thought I would die. . . . I had also been wounded three times by mortar shells and artillery. So the first days of May that year [of 1975] were overflowing with the elation of victory. Then I began to ponder and became uneasy.

By the time he reached this stage in his life he harbored a wide range of misgivings about the system, which he could not publicly express.

> . . . I felt a deep sadness for the country and the people who were in such a state of poverty and despair from which there seemed to be no way out. I wanted to play a part in rescuing Vietnam from its misery and isolation. Yet if I went abroad I might have to face many difficulties in getting my ideas accepted. Would I be wasting my time and

> bringing misfortune on myself and my family? However, I could not just sit back and do nothing. . . . I decided I had to act.

He reached the conclusion that

> There is a crisis . . . which affects every level of society. . . . Everybody dreams . . . of a change that will help Vietnam escape from its poverty and the stagnation of its political and economic life. . . . Walking around the streets of Hanoi in recent years, I have felt continuous mental torture. The children look thin and frequently speak in obscenities. The women are gaunt and anxious. Sewage spills here and there. Sometimes arguments explode, abuse is hurled and knives are brandished. The city teems with gamblers, thieves, pickpockets, prostitutes and opium smokers.
>
> So what was all the sacrifice of the Revolution about? Was it so that our people would suffer more hardship after our victory than during the war?

These are not the images that used to be associated in the West with a Communist or socialist society. The social pathologies noted above were for a long time thought to be peculiar to decaying, amoral capitalist systems. Their emergence in Vietnam (and other state socialist states, among them most recently Cuba) indicates that Communist systems are not immune to them; their proliferation following the political-military victory in Vietnam suggests that these systems are more efficient at waging war than creating equitable social-economic conditions in times of peace.

The major thrust of Bui Tin's critiques is aimed at the party and its leadership and what he saw as their degeneration after the 1975 victory: "In the old days, the Party was clean and the people had a high sense of self-respect. But when greediness ran riot and the whole system became rotten from top to bottom, morality became nonexistent and there was no law to exercise restraint. . . . All this stemmed from a lack of moral values, the inhumanity and blindness of a Communist leadership which had become arrogant and lost touch with the people."

He finds an interesting and somewhat unexpected connection between these developments and the Confucian tradition, which apparently nourished the elitism of the leadership:

> Following our victory in 1975, our leaders had virtually no experience in democracy because they had never lived in such a society. If they traveled abroad, it was mostly to Communist countries. They had escaped from a feudal and colonialist society to become revolutionaries,

> but their conduct clearly remained Confucian, given the way they deferred to one another to preserve harmony and discipline, as was done within a traditional village or family hierarchy.

Bui Tin, while appreciative of Ho Chi Minh's personal qualities, is also critical of some of his policies. In particular he disapproves of his cult of personality. He is also critical of his praise for Mao and, following the Soviet line, his denunciation of Tito. He believes that Ho's "ability to develop democracy and legality, and his understanding the need for it, were limited, not to say, defective."

Another explanation of these autocratic practices is that because

> the Vietnamese Communist Party learned its Marxism-Leninism by taking a shortcut through the works of Stalin and Mao Tse-tung, its ideology is strongly imbued with the traits of those two discredited leaders.

Bui Tin is highly critical of his government's dependence on and emulation of Mao's China: "Having just escaped from the long night of being slaves to the French, we were dazzled by the new light of the Chinese Revolution which was acclaimed as our role model. We accepted everything . . . without any thought, let alone criticism."

Another major theme of Bui Tin's critiques is the new inequalities and privileges, the shameless greed of the Vietnamese nomenklatura. He associates these attitudes with the abandonment of traditional values (which in another context he blames for the ready acceptance of the privileges of the ruling elite). Thus he observes:

> For many years the *Nomenklatura* has engaged in a frenzy of dispossessing and splitting society into the "haves and have-nots." . . . Every day they become more like the Mafia, Red Capitalists who have emerged from the jungle. . . . Thanks to those in power, Vietnam is losing its traditional values and being overwhelmed by robbery, gambling, prostitution, drug addiction and the spread of AIDS, while the health and education systems continue to decline.

He also points out that while the rapaciousness of these elites increased after the military victory in 1975,

> there had always been special shops in Hanoi for the top leadership or *Nomenklatura*. . . . When food was in extremely short supply in the North and severely rationed with many children suffering from malnutrition, there was a store . . . in Hanoi where the families of the Politburo and their cronies could always obtain top-quality fragrant

> rice. It was carefully grown without the use of fertilizers on 100 hectares of collectivized farmland near Hanoi specially reserved for the "old men" of the Party, just as in former days certain fields were earmarked for royalty. There were other special shops in Hanoi . . . providing clothing and international goods for the *Nomenklatura*.

These shops were managed by relatives of high-ranking functionaries. Such special shops (first introduced in the Soviet Union) were established in every Communist state and became symbols of the new inequality.

An incident that made a deep impression on Bui Tin occurred when Truong Chinh, chairman of the National Assembly, invited him to his holiday villa in Dalat, which had previously been a residence of the Emperor Bao Dai:

> One day . . . Truong Chinh asked me to come to his bedroom. There he pointed out the bed with sheets of gold brocade embroidered with dragons . . . and asked whether I was aware that the bed and bedclothes had belonged to Emperor Bao Dai and Empress Nam Phuong. . . . He was now . . . proud and emotional about sleeping in a room where he could use sheets and pillows embroidered with the symbols of royalty!

The elite privileges were all the more repugnant since they were enjoyed by leaders supposedly devoted to the creation of an egalitarian society. The lifestyles of the new rulers increasingly resembled those of the old:

> Special privileges became very evident. To the north of Ho Chi Minh City . . . Song Be province has a lot of rubber plantations intermixed with cashew trees. This became a hunting ground favored by officials from the Ho Chi Minh City administration. Whenever guests from the Central Committee traveled south, the whole area started to bustle. The director of the rubber plantation had to mobilize two to four production brigades to abandon their work in order to drive wild game into a "trap" for the "old men" to shoot. The high-ranking officials sat in small huts providing shelter from the sun and raised their guns between sips of expensive liquor and puffs of fragrant cigarette smoke to kill wild boar, sambar deer, civet cats and monitor lizards. . . . It is a very aristocratic way of hunting. One can imagine how the workers in the production brigades felt when they lost their earnings in order to serve those who style themselves "servants of the people."

As to housing, "in 1975 the Party committee responsible for its financing and administration collected a lot of data about public buildings and villas in the South. The most luxurious villas . . . were allocated to the members of the Politburo and their families." Much of the year these houses stood empty, having been used only for holidays; air force planes and helicopters were pressed into service to transport their occasional occupants.

Bui Tin also revealed that "Each home [of Politburo members] consists of a private villa which has been expanded to accommodate the family, offices, secretaries, chauffeurs and security guards. . . . Then there is the personal photographer and majordomo who organizes the domestic household, the cook and the servants." Summing up:

> the higher the rank . . . the more privileges, both conspicuous and discreet, he enjoys. They include housing and transport as well as food and drink, plus priority medical treatment at hospitals such as the one equipped in Hanoi by the Soviet Union where the most modern techniques and drugs are available. . . . These privileges extend to wives, children, grandchildren and in-laws. . . . Then there are the gifts, presents and . . . rewards like traveling abroad on duty. . . .

Bui Tin is not entirely consistent in explaining the moral decay and corruption he witnessed. On the one hand he blames the abandonment of traditional moral standards and restraints, but on the other he writes that "there was another form of privilege which became common, stemming again from Confucian custom [surely part of tradition], whereby gifts are conveyed upwards in the hope that power and prestige will subsequently flow downwards." Thus at the end of the visit of the party general secretary and his entourage at the mountain resort of Dalat, each of them was presented by the provincial party committee "with a rather large package containing . . . tea, coffee . . . medicinal liquor and herbal balm." The ladies, children, and grandchildren received similar packages. Likely that the traditions of past inequality helped legitimate the new practices (such as gift giving), both in the eyes of those who enjoyed them and among the rest of the population, while the weakening of traditional restraints made it easier to indulge the new appetites without embarrassment.

While the allocation of elite privilege in Vietnam did not differ from similar practices in other Communist states, it has been far less familiar partly because of the long wars for independence which left behind an impression of revolutionary purity among North Vietnamese and Vietcong leaders. Bui Tin knew well that such purity was a thing of the past: "It really makes my blood boil when I see people in power using their positions . . . to profiteer, coin money and build large houses where they live extremely comfortably . . . and over-indulge themselves day and night . . . while the war-wounded are left to survive in destitution." He concluded that Vietnam too had a "New Class" of the kind described in the 1957 book by Milovan Djilas.

The new inequalities also found expression in the military campaign against Pol Pot's Cambodia: "It turned out that the burden of this war was being borne by a section of society beyond the fringes of power." It was "the children of peasant families . . . or ordinary townspeople . . . who had been forced into military service" while the children of the political elite "went abroad to study or work irrespective of qualifications. . . . And at home it was also the sons of the political 'elite' who got the easy jobs and perks."

A remarkable manifestation of official corruption was the widespread smuggling by Vietnamese diplomats abroad. When the "diplomatic bag" of a Vietnamese diplomat posted to Eastern Europe was opened while in transit in Moscow, it was found to contain eight hundred pairs of jeans and two thousand digital watches. Bui Tin observed: "There are no limits to the . . . scope of corruption. Party cadres could argue that . . . they had sacrificed nearly their whole lives to the struggle, so it was only right for them to enjoy a little comfort. They deserved it. But how much?"

Bui Tin seems to believe that in the final analysis the flawed human qualities of the leaders best explain the country's moral decline after 1975:

> The basic fact is that in 1975 the leadership became lax, intoxicated and dizzy with victory. Most of the top leaders were in their sixties and thought increasingly about their families, their children, their homes and property. . . . They were human beings, not saints. Few of them could resist the lure of materialism because they lacked the education which forms the basis of human dignity. Therefore there was nothing to control them and they let themselves go. . . . This was the beginning of our real cultural crisis.

These sentiments may have been influenced by the author's social origins. Time and again he laments the lack of qualifications and the poor quality of the leaders and elites, juxtaposing the "revolutionaries" to the "intellectuals." A similar dichotomy was also prominent in Mao's China where the officialdom contrasted "red" with "expert," favoring the former. Official incompetence was also responsible for large-scale mismanagement, such as the construction of the Hoa Binh hydro-electric power station which, as a result of a political decision, was "tunneled through rock to avoid nuclear attack. The project was wasteful and extremely expensive, taking over fifteen years. . . . The same was true of the Thang Long bridge . . . near Hanoi. Le Duan wanted it to be the longest bridge in South East Asia, but it became a white elephant and hardly anybody used it." Similarly ill-conceived and wasteful projects abounded in Communist East Europe and the Soviet Union as well as in Cuba.

The repressive character of the Vietnamese system was another major source of Bui Tin's disaffection. It was already manifest in the 1954–1956 land reform which "caused the deaths of more than ten thousand people. . . . They were shot having been condemned by . . . kangaroo courts." Bui Tin found unacceptable the classification of people (for purposes of social control) based not on their actual behavior but on their social background or former class membership. Like the so-called kulaks in the Soviet Union, those in Vietnam who owned small amounts of land were similarly persecuted. Even "capitalist" children "were forced to . . . work either in factories or in the countryside. It was difficult for them to get higher education. . . ." Victimization extended to "thousands of ordinary people . . . detained in a whole network of prisons, sometimes for decades. There they exist in unsanitary conditions and have been ill-treated, oppressed and dishonored . . . their families and friends have suffered discrimination. . . ."

The mistreatment of intellectuals was another manifestation of the repression: ". . . gradually the role of the intellectuals and technocrats within the Party and the government was eliminated. . . . Many of them had already been abused, belittled and humiliated during the Land Reform campaign by having to confess that they had been brainwashed by imperialist education." Shunting aside the intellectuals and technocrats greatly contributed to rising levels of incompetence and mismanagement, Bui Tin argued.

As in other Communist states, the political police or "public security force," the Cong An, carried out these repressions. "Together with the army, [the Cong An] has always been considered the most important branch of the regime, providing it with stability." Like the army it was bloated, "overmanned." Its members were often totally uneducated, as reflected in the joke asking "why the Cong An always went around in groups of three. The reply was that one could read, another could write and the third was there to control these two intellectuals."

These security forces were trained by and modeled on the Soviet KGB and the East German Stasi. In this as in other respects, the regime closely followed the Chinese and Soviet models (at least before its 1975 victory); "there was even the saying: 'What the Soviet Union and China are today, Vietnam will be tomorrow.'" Bui Tin bitterly remarks that "lack of respect for human rights makes natural allies of the leaders in Hanoi and Peking."

He also criticizes the so-called reeducation camps ("which in reality were prisons") established after the Communist victory. He visited them and found the conditions inhumane. ("I still shiver when I think about the hundreds of camps set up along Stalinist lines after 1975.") Coercive policies included the expulsion of people mostly of Chinese origin ("over half a million people were forced to leave . . . so that the authorities could lay their hands on the property of these families"). Those expelled included simple people like fishermen, coal miners, and pottery workers; it was a "campaign . . . motivated by xenophobia rather than anything else." The repressions in the newly occupied South especially disturbed Bui Tin: ". . . to impose strict political views as well as heavy and lengthy punishment on so many members of the former regime was unnecessary and contrary to our proclaimed policy of national concord and reconciliation." Again, reality and the promises of propaganda diverged.

As in other Communist states, the chronic, institutionalized mendaciousness of the authorities made the other flaws of the system harder to bear; in Bui Tin's words, "mendaciousness became almost a way of life." The practices of criticism and self-criticism were an example: ". . . criticism and self-criticism were just something we had to cope with. There was no sincerity involved. You criticize me so I criticize you . . . you forgive me so I do the same. . . ."

It should not be surprising that the realities of the postrevolutionary consolidation of power and privilege did not measure up to the high expectations generated by the long and arduous revolutionary struggle. If many shared Bui Tin's feelings, few had the will and the opportunity to express them; he had the will and created the opportunity by going into exile. His uncommon idealism intensified his disappointment over the familiar features of Communist systems: abuse of power, intolerance of free expression, discrepancy between social realities and political rhetoric, corruption of the ruling elite, and loss of original idealism. He believed that his becoming a critic was fostered by his travels abroad, "and not only to communist countries . . . all these travels opened my eyes."

Another important factor in the process of his disaffection was the Vietnamese leadership's apprehensive response to Gorbachev's reforms. There was little hope for the rise of "socialism with a human face" in Vietnam; "there was no Gorbachev or Deng Xiaoping in the Vietnamese Communist Party." Stalin's works were "printed and reprinted in Vietnamese long after he was discredited in the Soviet Union. . . ."

The reforms of the 1980s were limited and grudging:

> . . . when it comes to individual freedoms, Doi Moi [Renovation] is very slow and extremely apprehensive. A market economy and freedom of enterprise have been adopted, but these are not accompanied by personal real estate property rights. . . . The Communist party of Vietnam carries a big burden from the past. Its members still repeat the Marxist-Leninist scriptures, proclaim absolute loyalty to socialism, and observe solemn celebrations in Hanoi on the anniversary of the October Revolution in Russia.

Elsewhere he observes that "many of the top leaders in Hanoi continue to believe that the collapse of Communism in the Soviet Union and Eastern Europe is only a temporary phenomenon, a storm which will soon pass."[3]

Bui Tin refrains from speculation about the causes of the degeneration of the system other than repeatedly noting the part played by universal human attributes such as greed, selfishness, corruptibility, and concern for one's family. He says next to nothing about the part played by ideology in the developments and failures he describes. His disillusionment came about over a long period of time—a product of experience, frustrated expectations, and high moral standards which survived decades of participation in the brutal military and political struggle.

Truong Nhu Tang was minister of justice in the Provisional Revolutionary Government (PRG) of South Vietnam established in 1969, and one of the founders of the National Liberation Front (NLF), established in 1960, the political arm of the Vietcong. Both these entities were supported and controlled by the Communist authorities of North Vietnam. In the early 1970s he was a prominent representative of the NLF and PRG, seeking international recognition for the PRG. In this capacity he visited the Soviet Union as well as Eastern European and Third World countries supportive of the Vietcong, and met heads of state and high-ranking officials. He returned to Saigon after the Communist victory in 1975 and became rapidly and deeply disillusioned, leading to his escape by sea in 1978.

Truong came from an upper-class, Francophile, French-educated family. His father "had come from wealth and had married wealth."[4] He owned a rubber plantation and a printing house and was also a professor at a French college. Six Chinese nurses looked after the six sons of the family, who later attended school at a French lycée "reserved for the children of French colonial administrators and the most privileged Vietnamese." The sons completed their higher education at European universities.

Despite his close ties with France and French culture, Truong as a young man began to develop a strong sense of Vietnamese identity and came to reject his country's colonial status. While pursuing pharmaceutical studies in Paris he met Ho Chi Minh, who made an enduring impression on him. Ho "combined ardent and idealistic nationalism with a moving personal simplicity. Ho had created for us [the students who met him] an atmosphere of family and country and had pointed to our own role in the great patriotic endeavor. . . . From that afternoon I was [his] fervent partisan. I had been won by his simplicity, his charm, his familiarity. . . . The force of Ho's personality had by itself created a turning point in my life."

While in France he began to attend meetings of the Association of Vietnamese in France and became involved in political activities; his reading also came to reflect his growing concern with the colonial status of Vietnam. He found allies in the French Communist party. His academic focus changed, and in 1951 he earned a master's degree in political science. In the same year he returned to Saigon and found a teaching job in a new secondary school in a small town on the Cambodian border. He made his first contact with the guerrillas and realized that while he would "never make a soldier" he "could play a role in the propaganda and psychological war." Subsequently he was drafted and chose naval training, which once more took him back to France. Discharged, he returned to Saigon in 1955 and took a job as chief comptroller for the Industry and Commerce Bank of Vietnam. Increasingly he found himself "part of an informal network of people who opposed Diem. Slowly we were beginning to form the underground resistance that would eventually evolve into the National Liberation Front, the political organization of the Vietcong." While working for the Vietcong he changed jobs and became director general of Vietnam's national sugar company.

In 1962 he was elected a "secret member of the Central Committee" of the NLF. He was twice imprisoned and tortured by anti-Communist authorities and finally released as part of a prisoner exchange. After his release he joined the Vietcong resistance full time and spent six years in the jungle, which included establishing the ministry of justice in the PRG, affiliated with the Vietcong. During these years there was much contact and growing friction with Northern Communist party officials seeking to mold the Southern NLF and its officials to their image. Truong wrote:

> Many of us were from well-to-do families and had been used to the good life before we enlisted in the revolution. . . . We all regarded ourselves as people who had already sacrificed a great deal for the nation and were quite ready to sacrifice everything. Many of us had struggled . . . against the French, and in moving to the jungle all of us were decisively committed against the Americans. . . . We were not touched by guilt about our class background, and we felt that our motives were every bit as pure as those of our ideologically minded colleagues [from the North]. . . . Some of the cadres [party officials] regarded our previous, citified lifestyles as a subject for mockery and contempt. . . .

These frictions and disagreements increased over time as "the Party leaders, glimpsing a vision of armed triumph," came to view the political aspects of the war and the role of the PRG as less important: ". . . the course of the war had put us in an uncomfortable position, progressively diminishing our real power while at the same time emphasizing our propaganda function." These trends intensified after the death of Ho Chi Minh with "the ideologues . . . firmly in control not inclined to waste effort on their junior partners." In the summer of 1970 "the Party's manipulative heart began to reveal itself."

From the beginning the conflict between Truong and party officials from the North was rooted in his conviction that the liberation of South Vietnam was primarily a matter of nationalistic self-assertion rather than a social-political transformation modeled on the system in the North. For a long time he succeeded in viewing these disagreements "as an argument between brothers."

These differences flared up in the course of a three-month seminar in 1971 organized by the North Vietnamese authorities for the benefit of NLF leaders, to acquaint them with "the fine points of Marxism-Leninism" and "educate South Vietnam's revolutionary bourgeoisie to the truth of dialectical materialism." The French-trained Southerners who "had imbibed Buddhist and Confucian spirituality with their mothers' milk" were not receptive to such indoctrination:

> . . . the air grew thick with invective and acrimony. Those who spoke for the primacy of nationalism also espoused democratic freedoms and

> national independence. The party cadres flung back the tenets of international class struggle and the dictatorship of the proletariat. National independence or the class struggle, which was it to be? . . .
>
> The nationalists were infuriated at the cadres' narrow-minded bigotry.

The Southerners "were to 'come forth,' to capitulate and renounce . . . [their] 'class of origin,' rallying wholeheartedly to the proletarian revolution." On the occasion of this seminar, a rupture was avoided and difficulties were papered over:

> It was not until five years later . . . after the Great Spring Victory of 1975 brought the Party to power that I was able to fully appreciate fully the brilliant choreography. . . . Whipsawed into anger and tears by the cadres' frontal assault on our principles, our dignity and our self-worth, we had been well prepared to embrace the reassurances extended to us by the COSVN [Communist Party Branch for South Vietnam] leadership. None of us had recognized the classic interrogation technique for what it was: brutal softening up followed by the kindly offer of friendship and accord.

The indignation occasioned by the experiences of duplicity and deception was the chief source of Truong's disillusionment. In his case as in some others, objective conditions were less important in the unraveling of political convictions than the extended, gradual or dramatic (as the case may be) frustration of expectations, the sense of betrayal, the feeling of having been deceived. In the case of Truong and other leaders in the NLF, the experience of having been deliberately deceived, of promises being violated, was profound and tangible. Most important, he and his fellow NLF leaders were led to believe that the NLF and the PRG would play an important role in the governance of South Vietnam after the military victory, and that their views would be given substantial weight by the Northern leadership. In contrast, "We all began to note the extent to which the Northern cadres were filling positions of responsibility on our staffs and handling business of every variety. . . . As the weeks slid by it became impossible to shut our eyes to the emerging arrogance and disdain of our Party staff cadres—almost as if they believed that they were the conquerors and we the vanquished." These developments and attitudes were in sharp conflict with official rhetoric of years past, when the PRG was designated as "the sole genuine representative of the Southern people."

Truong and his associates were also led to believe that social, political, and economic arrangements and institutions in the South would not be copied from those of the North, that the unique cultural and historical differences between North and South would be preserved. However,

> with total power in their hands, they [the North Vietnamese officials] began to show their cards in the most brutal fashion. They made it understood that the Vietnam of the future would be a single monolithic bloc, collectivist and totalitarian, in which all the traditions and culture of the South would be ground and molded by the political machine of the conquerors. . . . All of the NLF and PRG emphasis on civil rights, land reform and social welfare was "no longer operative."

The duplicitousness and cynicism at the core of these policies were hardest to swallow: "With North Vietnam's Army firmly in charge, there was . . . no further need for any of the techniques of seduction or covert control that circumstances had previously called for." Truong was shocked to discover "the duplicity behind the Party's relationship with us over so many years."

Idealistic Southerners such as Truong were led to believe that their desire for national reconciliation and unity would be respected, that political revenge and punitiveness would be averted or minimized. "Our Party comrades, however, were not to be persuaded by arguments either of compassion or reason. They had . . . given up both their consciences and pragmatic sense in return for the certitudes of their political religion. Among their steely and arrogant convictions, compromise could find no room. . . ."

A sweeping and fraudulent "reeducation" program was imposed on the South, which was supposed to last for at most thirty days. Truong, as well as the entire population of the South, was spectacularly deceived. He drove his brothers who had worked for the previous government to their reeducation points: "Like hundreds of thousands of others they had convinced themselves that the public announcements were sincere and after a month they would be welcomed back into a society desperately in need of people with their considerable talents."

In the first year after the North Vietnamese victory, 300,000 people who used to be officers, state officials, and party leaders under the previous government were summoned for this "brief" reeducation program; none of them returned after a month or even after a year. Many more were arrested "in the sweeps of governmental organs and military authorities." Months and years passed, and the "reeducation" continued. When Truong complained about the deception to the PRG president, who also happened to be "one of the Politburo's chief agents" in the South, the president told him: ". . . we never said the term would be limited to thirty days. All we said was that they should report with thirty days' worth of food and clothing."

Aside from these deceptions, Truong found the severe repression imposed on the population abhorrent:

> Everyone had some family members or others in camp and even those with the strongest revolutionary credentials were coming up against a wall of silence when they tried to find out anything—where they were being held . . . when they would be home. . . . The wave of arbitrary arrests . . . scythed through cities and villages. . . . It was a year that had seen outrages of every description perpetrated by a government whose priorities called for the ruthless consolidation of power. . . .

The "breathtaking rapacity" of the Northern soldiers and political cadres sent by the thousands to the South to govern further deepened Truong's bitterness and disillusionment.

> Accustomed to the extremes of austerity, they [the cadres] seized voraciously on the opportunities offered by westernized and decadent Saigon. They fought each other over houses, cars, prostitutes and bribes. Soldiers and officials brought up in the bleak poverty of North Vietnam and subjected for years to the rigors of military life were suddenly confronted with what seemed to them an almost fairy-tale richness, theirs for the taking. It was as if the city had been invaded by a swarm of locusts.[5]

Truong's return to Saigon and his reunion with his family was far less joyous than anticipated. His father had died a month earlier after a long illness; his mother was in distress; his wife, "unable to endure the separation of so many years, had obtained a divorce and was now living in the United States. My children too had left the country. . . ." These personal, familial losses converged with Truong's growing disillusionment over the nature of the "liberation" visited upon the South. Thus, aside from "objective" factors, Truong's break with the system also had familial roots and components, which upon his return to Saigon reasserted themselves. In the end his father, who had disapproved of his political involvements when he was young, proved to be right. Truong now recalled his father's warnings when he last saw him:

> I had last seen my father in late 1967 while I was still a prisoner of the National Police. Emaciated and half-blind I had tottered uneasily . . . to the visiting room, where he was waiting. His expression as we embraced was one of bottomless grief. His words had burned themselves

> in my memory. "My son," he said, "I simply cannot understand you. You have abandoned everything. A good family, happiness, wealth—to follow the Communists. . . . They will betray you, and you will suffer your entire life." I had answered him then, "My dearest father, you have six sons. You should be content to sacrifice one of them for the sake of the country's independence and liberty." Now, though I had returned as a minister in the government of the new, liberated South, the sorrow of that last parting could not be erased.

There was increasing sorrow and guilt as he confronted the results of the policies of the system he had supported for much of his life: "What had possessed me to inflict this misery on my family and my people?" Although given an opportunity to work in the new "unified" government as vice minister of food and supply, he was unwilling to participate in a regime "after the betrayal of so many promises." In the "throes of a devastating disillusionment," he sought to retire from politics. In 1976 he remarried and moved to a small cottage in the countryside. His retirement was not viewed favorably by the authorities, so he accepted a position as director of the National Rubber Industry, "a position that provided a degree of protection from unwanted scrutiny and also allowed me to intensify my search for a way out," that is, to escape, joining the ranks of the "boat people." In 1978, after many difficulties and adventures, he landed on a small Indonesian island and eventually he made his way to France where he currently lives.

It is not surprising that Truong's youthful idealism collided with the realities of a ruthless North Vietnamese exercise of power and the subjugation of his homeland, accentuated by the circumstances of deception. But other NLF and PRG functionaries had similar experiences and managed to collaborate with the occupiers, or in any event did not seek to escape. It is a commonplace that people often respond to similar or identical experiences in different ways. Truong's response may have been influenced by a resurgence of familial beliefs and traditions vindicated by his father's death, and by recollections of his past beliefs which clashed with new political realities. Most important and irreducible, his personality and moral sensibility made it impossible for him to work with and acquiesce in the new system, given its "ideological ruthlessness and contemptuous disregard for human dignity and rights . . . attitudes firmly embedded in the mental world of the Party leaders."

LIU BINYAN (1925–2005), in the scholar Merle Goldman's words, is "regarded as China's preeminent intellectual exemplifying in his words and actions the traditions of the courageous literati of independent conscience who criticized China's political leaders when they did not live up to their ideals."[6] Liu spent much of his life trying to improve the Chinese Communist system by publicizing its shortcomings, reminding the rulers and lesser officials of their declared ideals they failed to live up to.

He joined the Communist underground movement as a teenager, first fighting the Japanese occupiers, later the Nationalists. Eventually he became a prominent, muckraking journalist, but he suffered for his beliefs and was sent to rural areas to be "reeducated through labor." Subjected to various humiliating work assignments, he was expelled, readmitted, and once more expelled from the party. He ended up in exile in the United States in 1989, following his second expulsion from the party, and died there.

Liu Binyan's idealism was nourished by his father, who worked as an interpreter on the Central Manchuria Railway in Russia from 1914 to 1921 and "brought back the seeds of Russian liberalism from the Soviet Union."[7] He was a man lacking in formal education but eager to study, and he encouraged his son to do likewise. But "it was his yearning for social justice that had the greatest impact on me," Liu recalled. As a youth Liu learned both Russian and Japanese and was a voracious reader of both Western classical literature and the classics of Marxism.

From an early age he showed a rebellious, independent streak that helps explain why he became a leading dissident, unable to tolerate the mendaciousness of the authorities. He recalls that while in school "the aridity of the traditional teachings ran completely counter to my yearning for freedom and my spirit of rebellion." Also at an early age, "the first question that arose in my young mind was, Why was there such injustice in life? Father said it was not so in the Soviet Union . . . [and] often told stories about Lenin and the Russian Revolution. . . . In the Soviet Union there were neither rich, nor poor, he said, and the Soviet Union became a symbol of utopia in my dreams."

Liu's political commitment had a pronounced individualistic ingredient uncommon in the society he was born into:

> . . . I had joined the revolution mainly to liberate myself, to realize myself. I could not say precisely what this "self" was. . . . From my teens until the age of thirty, I had the conviction that although I was nobody at the time, someday I would be somebody. . . . I have never been truly content with myself or my environment. . . .

His nonconformism found further expression in his aversion to the dress code promoted by the party, which was "an expression of the uniformity that was imposed on our lives." In defiance he sometimes wore his father's Western-style suit at the training center for young cadres. Later in life he considered his outspokenness an "old weakness" which repeatedly got him in trouble; his "emotions were hard to control." In 1957 he wrote a letter to Mao pleading with him not to reverse the apparent trend toward more liberal policies, or what was called at the time "rectification." Mao was not impressed.

While he was in the underground, Liu's

> sentiments clashed with the dictates of the revolution. Of course, after the liberation, these clashes occurred more frequently. I had to remind myself continuously to keep my distance from "bourgeois" sentiments, to keep from becoming alienated from the dictatorship of the proletariat. . . . I laid down a rule for myself: save your love and sympathy for the entire working class, rather than wasting it on individual suffering; beware of the words of any individual, but have absolute faith in the Party. In the coming years I found myself at war with this rule.

It was not only his personality and capacity for critical thinking that made for recurring conflict with the authorities and undermined his political faith, but a wide range of specific experiences as well. To be sure, his particular sensibility made these experiences troubling and significant; many individuals of a different disposition were able to overlook them. One such early experience was the behavior of Soviet troops who entered northern China in pursuit of Japanese forces at the end of World War II: "The looting and raping . . . came as a great shock. At first I refused to believe it. It was impossible, I told myself; the Soviet army was a socialist army helping to free us from Japanese occupation. . . . After learning [of] eyewitness accounts I was obliged to believe. . . ."

In 1946, as a party functionary, Liu had to make speeches mitigating these atrocities:

> I had to sing the praises of the first Communist state even though its army pillaged our towns and violated our women! . . . The best I could do was contend that the atrocities had been committed by an army of convicts and not the real Soviet Red Army! At the time I did not know what the real Soviet Red Army was doing in Germany and Eastern Europe.

This was the beginning of his lifelong learning process about the system's chronic divergences between political ideals and social realities, between the world as portrayed in official propaganda and that experienced by individuals living in that world.

In 1947, working with land-reform teams, Liu witnessed the brutal treatment of landlords and the false accusations made against them. In one instance (his first such experience), a landlord was accused, among other things, of hiding weapons, and "beaten to a pulp" since he would not confess: "The landlord was just a miserable wretch who owned about an acre of land. But every village had to have its target of the class struggle in order to arouse class consciousness, and that landlord served the purpose." In the Soviet Union, such landlords were called "kulaks," and their persecution served a similar purpose. Liu found it difficult to support these policies:

> I thought it was important to divide the land among the peasants—but not the family possessions, and especially everyday household goods. . . . I felt that if Marx had been there, he would not have approved.
>
> Again I had nagging doubts about the Party. In theory, landless peasants surely had a right to land. But there were also landowners who had, through a lifetime of hard work, scrimped and saved to buy up small plots of land.

Also in this early period he had his first experience of the privileges of the new political elite and the "status consciousness that pervaded the Communist Party. In the dining room of the Party offices, there were three areas—a small one for the top cadres, where the food was specially cooked, a middle one, and a lower one. Such rankings made me uneasy." (It was at about the same time, in 1946, that Wolfgang Leonhard in East Germany discovered a similar stratification in the dining rooms of the East German Communist party headquarters.) On his trip to the Soviet Union in 1949, as a member of the Chinese delegation, Liu once more experienced discrimination based on political status: the Soviet passengers "not eligible" for the same kind of food, "jammed against the glass doors" of the dining car to watch what the Chinese visitors ate. Later in life he was critical of the extra housing space "Party cadres" received and "the special privileges of the officials' children." The corruption of officials he later came to expose was another important illustration of the inequalities he deplored.

Liu also objected to the empty slogans of official propaganda and the tireless self-glorification of the regime.

> In July 1951 a huge meeting was held . . . to commemorate the thirtieth anniversary of the founding of the Chinese Communist Party . . . a huge red banner spanning the width of the stadium was un-

> furled, reading: "Long Live the Glorious, Great and Correct Chinese Communist Party of China!" It suddenly occurred to me that it was perhaps too early to make such a statement. Shouldn't such statements be left to others? I realized that my thoughts bordered on the seditious. . . .

Elsewhere he wrote: "'Give yourself to the Party!'—'Give All to the Party!'—'Follow Party orders in everything!'—these are the slogans that governed people's lives for the last forty-odd years." More fundamental to the growth of his critical sentiments was the realization that

> In our everyday lives, there were no opportunities to participate in the process of decision-making. . . . Our role was to listen to orders . . . and act accordingly. . . . There were no truly independent groups or organizations; every single aspect of one's social life was supervised by the Party. . . . How far, I asked myself, could the individual go to protect his or her rights? Politics had seeped into every aspect of our lives. . . . Withholding anything from the Party—one's private history, family connections, or misguided thoughts—was the most dangerous form of individualism. . . . To express a desire for more education, to ask for a change in job assignment . . . or to request a workplace so that one could be reunited with one's family—all of these were viewed as displays of individualism.

Nonetheless Liu and his wife, whom he married in 1950, remained a "model revolutionary couple." Their only wedding presents were a pair of pillowcases and a copy of *The History of the Soviet Bolshevik Party*. Working as a journalist and still seeing himself as a loyal party member, he wrote critiques of red tape and wasteful production practices but often could not publish them.

In the mid-1950s he came under attack for an article in which he criticized the callousness of doctors toward their patients, and was rebuked for "smearing" a socialist society where the relationships among the citizens, including doctors and patients, were (as if by definition) "close and warm." Increasingly he was criticized and came under suspicion of being "a counterrevolutionary . . . because my ideas seemed subversive in a time of rampant political conformism"; his probing of the darker aspects of the society certainly were.

In 1956, in the wake of de-Stalinization in the Soviet Union and unrest in Eastern Europe, Liu hoped that similar trends would emerge in China, but they did not. During his trip to Poland in 1956 he was impressed by the relative openness of Polish society and its media compared with conditions in China. Doubtless these trips and his exposure to more liberal political alternatives also fueled his expectations and impatience with conditions at home.

A notable instance of confronting the gap between ideals and realities occurred when in Poland Liu observed prostitutes plying their trade; at the time he still believed that "prostitution should never exist in a socialist country." (Carlos Franqui, the Cuban revolutionary, ran into the same phenomenon in Prague, and had similarly negative reactions—see below.) While prostitution was not a major problem in China, widespread corruption was, indicating that living in a socialist society by itself made little difference to personal morality or to how people treated one another.

Then came the explosion of Khrushchev's 20th Party Congress speeech:

> I have never been as shocked as I was when reading that secret report. I trembled as I read about the mass murders committed twenty years earlier. I cried . . . I read the report twice; my outlook on many things was forever changed. Now I knew why after my visits to the Soviet Union I always felt a strange sense of depression. . . . Now I understood why the Soviet people who met with us, or worked with us . . . never gave us their addresses. They had drawn lessons. . . .

The impact of such major historical revelations reinforced Liu's seemingly trivial daily experiences, such as encountering a beggar on the street though China was supposed to be a "beggar-free country after liberation." He spoke to the young man from the countryside and learned that excessive official demands on the peasants to deliver grain had "left the people without enough to eat. In the general lethargy resulting from forced collectivization of farms, they had no desire to work and no choice but to go begging." It would be interesting to know how much the Chinese leaders and planners of collectivization knew about corresponding Soviet practices and experiences of the 1930s and what if any lessons they learned from them.

Instances of grotesque discrepancies between theory and practice multiplied. Liu writes:

> I was astounded by the news that my friend at the Youth League passed on to me. "We kept telling the workers that they were the owners of the country. But when we would visit the factories, we saw that the workers did not behave like masters at all. They stole public property all the time . . . because they were so hard up. They were full of resentment. . . . I had never expected the Party to lose the confidence of the workers after so few years in power."

Family circumstances also had an effect on Liu's political outlook. His sister's husband committed suicide during the 1955 campaign against counterrevolutionaries and Liu sent half his salary to her to help her support five children on her salary as a schoolteacher.

In 1957 Liu was expelled from the party as a "rightist." Public denunciations in the press followed; people stopped talking to him. (His older sister was also labeled a "rightist" for defending him.) He responded to the expulsion with perplexity: ". . . part of me could not accept the reality. I thought, 'It is a misunderstanding. . . . How could I be an enemy?'" He was accused of vilifying the party and its leadership and denying its achievements in guiding art and literature; of spreading slanders about human rights violations; of rejecting official policies concerning *China News Youth* (the publication he worked for), of opposing the Party's political indoctrination of the young, of trying to stir up unrest, and of unspecified anti-party activities. The system had obviously rejected him, but at that stage he did not completely abandon it. He remained classified as a rightist for twenty-two years. The so-called anti-rightist campaign intensified: "From then on, intellectuals and ordinary cadres no longer dared to raise their voices in criticism of the Party or the government. . . . The adulation of Mao grew out of bounds."

Expulsion from the party had tangible consequences: Liu was suspended from his job and given twenty yuan a month for living expenses, barely enough to pay for food and cheap cigarettes. He was sent to a remote area in the countryside for "reform through manual labor." It was the first time in his life he had performed manual labor. He spent thirteen years separated from his family as a laborer in the countryside.

The policies (and "colossal mistakes") of the party failed to "reform" Liu's thinking. While laboring in rural areas he learned about the government's irrational agricultural policies that he found an insult to the common sense of the peasants, whose "last inch of freedom" was invaded by being forced into the communes. There was also an absurd campaign ordering peasants to build makeshift backyard furnaces to melt iron while their crops were left to rot in the fields. Between 1958 and 1969 he experienced firsthand the disastrous consequences of Mao's economic policies aimed at overtaking the West in productivity.

In another remarkable similarity to Soviet conditions and responses to collectivization, "the starving peasants resorted to the only legal form of protest in China—a work slowdown—and they would continue to do this for the next thirty years." Also, as in the Soviet Union, "from this universal lethargy and depression, the Chinese character has deteriorated into one of submission to order and hostility toward all initiative." But these policies had a weaker impact in China than in Russia as indicated by current Chinese economic expansion and the rapid growth of private incentives in the 1990s and the new century.

In the spring of 1961, Liu was sent back to Beijing and given a new assignment: "to cart night soil [human excrement] from the city to a farm run by the *China Youth News*, the publication he had once worked for." Later in the same year he was given a lowly job in the library at his old place of work, but his "rightist" classification was not rescinded until 1966. With the start of the Cultural Revolution in the same year, he was "relabeled" as a rightist and assigned to "labor under surveillance." The "relabeling" took place in an auditorium in front of a large gathering and in the presence of his wife and son. Later his wife was compelled to write "a big character poster, ordering me to confess my sin."

In the summer of 1968 Liu was once more sent to the countryside and detained in "a small, crude hut for the worst offenders" for further investigation. More demands for confession followed, and he was sent to another rural area "to spend eight years planting rice, making adobe bricks and raising pigs." In rural exile he experienced an upsurge of interest in the political theories that were in some measure associated with his bitter experiences: "After work every day, in the heat of the summer night, I would sit in the dorm, take out my magnifying glass, and pore over the works of Marx, Engels, Plekhanov and Lenin, in search of answers. I asked myself how China had ended up in such an appalling situation?" This preoccupation resembles that of Alexander Yakovlev, who sought answers to similarly nagging questions in the classics of Marxism-Leninism. Unlike Yakovlev, Liu Binyan apparently did not conclude that the theories were responsible for the practices; it is not entirely clear from his writings what conditions or circumstances Liu came to hold responsible for the deterioration of the Chinese system, other than particular individuals at the top, including Mao.

He continued to be labeled a rightist for twenty-two years. This period included a period of "reeducation" in 1969 at a so-called May Seventh Cadre School. In 1972 he was returned to his newspaper with reduced responsibilities. It was only in 1979 that he was finally rehabilitated and allowed to resume his investigative journalism. One scandal he encountered led him to reflect: "How could this case of embezzlement, record-breaking in terms of the sums involved, take place in a land under thirty-three years of Communist rule? How was it that these criminals were so free to act after thirty-three years of class struggle and political campaigns? I was looking for the historical and social roots of this evil. . . ."

The many cases of corruption confirmed the most critical failure of the system: its inability to improve human nature and inspire idealism and selflessness. It was actually worse than that: ". . . our special kind of socialism not only created a housing shortage, but also bred thugs . . . who accumulated power and wealth under the guise of the Party line." As to the impact of political practices on other groups:

> With time, a segment of the population . . . deteriorated into a set type, with a smirk on their faces, rote words on their lips, a noncommittal stance on issues for which they have responsibility. They simply carried out their daily work according to routine, choosing their words carefully . . . and taking every precaution to ensure their own political safety.

Such behavioral changes were characteristic of all Communist systems where people learned to carefully separate the public expressions of their beliefs or sentiments from their private thoughts in all matters that had the slightest political relevance.[8] In the Soviet Union this behavior used to be called "wearing the Party mask."

Corruption and the planned economy converged: "'planned economy' was in practice but a continuous flow of public resources into the private pocket of the power-holders," Liu wrote. His most famous exposé, of corruption, "People or Monsters?" (available in English), was published in 1979 in a magazine with a circulation of 1.4 million and had a huge impact; it was reprinted in many papers and broadcast over the radio. Afterward Liu became a popular speaker but also the target of criticism of various local officials who had much to hide. Ordinary people came to visit him "to report theft of public property and the general lawlessness" from all over the country. He also discovered and investigated the incarceration of political offenders in psychiatric wards, dissent being diagnosed as a mental illness, as in the Soviet Union. He received more than ten thousand letters reporting specific instances of corruption.

He came to see that even after Mao's death in 1976, "the political and social atmosphere of the Cultural Revolution [was] preserved unchanged. The people who had come to power during the Cultural Revolution were still in charge and the people who had been victimized were still oppressed. . . ."

Liu explains his persistent defiance of the authorities by saying that he did not share "values generally held by intellectuals. I did not hope for favors from those in power. Honorific titles . . . were beyond me." He would not be silenced. A visit to Germany in 1985 provided an opportunity, in an article, to reflect on the differences between West Germany, which was determined to confront and eliminate the Nazi legacy, and China, which preserved discredited political institutions and practices from the Mao era.

In early 1987 Liu was expelled from the party for the second time. In both instances the reason was his criticism of "abuses within the Party." From an official point of view, he was a disruptive element, undermining stability and order. His books were banned, though available in private bookstalls. In 1988 he was allowed to visit the United States; the visit stretched into 1989 when the protest demonstrations in Tiananmen Square were brutally crushed. Liu felt this was the ultimate betrayal by the regime: "I gave up my youth for the Communist Party in its struggle to seize state power. And now a handful of tyrants betrayed the Party. . . ." He stayed in the United States where he died.

Endless humiliations and escalating mistreatment led to Liu's rejection of the Chinese system but failed to erase completely his hopes that a more humane form of socialism could yet be created. His memoir does not offer a clear answer why, in his view, the Chinese system degenerated. Was it the backwardness and traditional character of Chinese society that frustrated the application of the Marxist ideals? Or was the degeneration inherent in the attempted application of certain Marxist ideas and propositions, for example the belief that private ownership of the means of production is the source of all injustice and evil? Was it the personality of Mao? The authoritarian structure of the party taken from the Soviet model? Was it the inherent flaws of human beings who are incapable of creating a utopian society?

Although he does not explicitly confront these questions, Liu's numerous critical references to various party leaders and officials suggest that he blames them rather than the nature of the ideals to be realized or the historical and cultural legacy of Chinese society.

Fang Lizhi (1936–). Sometimes referred to as the "Chinese Sakharov," Fang Lizhi emerged as a major critic of the regime in the 1970s and '80s. He was an astro-physicist and at one point vice president of the University of Science and Technology in China. Widely traveled abroad, he was well known both in China and around the world for his scientific work as well as his steadfast critiques of the system. These first found expression in 1957 when Fang made highly unorthodox criticisms of the Chinese system of higher education and science policy.

After the Tiananmen Square demonstrations in 1989, he sought asylum at the U.S. embassy due to a well-founded fear of impending arrest. In the arrest warrant issued after he sought asylum he was accused of committing the crimes of "disseminating counterrevolutionary propaganda and inciting counterrevolutionary activities. . . ."[9] In fact he headed the "most wanted list" at the time. A year later, due to U.S. pressure, he was allowed to come to the United States and has lived there ever since, working at an astronomical observatory in Arizona.

Unlike many other critics of Communist systems who had lived in them, Fang was capable of articulating and disseminating his critiques while still living in China; most native critics were only able to do so after their defection or exile. Fang was not an isolated critic but part of the vanguard in a broader movement of protest and dissent by intellectuals.

His critiques of the system gained strength during the post-Mao period of reform which encouraged and legitimated, to a point, such critiques. It was a period of rising expectations and diminished repression. The post-Mao leadership was anxious to modernize the country and realized that encouraging the development of science was essential for accomplishing this task; it did not realize, however, that free and fruitful scientific investigation also required political reform and greater freedom of expression and inquiry than the regime was willing to grant. The political system, as it became more permissive, stimulated unanticipated critiques: "In co-opting science and its ideals in service of the reforms, the Deng leadership opened the way for scientists to judge the regime itself according to those ideals." Dissenting scientists like Fang Lizhi directly linked their dissidence "to their identities and self-conceptions as scientists."[10] This was a new point of departure in questioning the system, and had few parallels in other Communist states. Fang's travels in the West (made possible by the post-Mao reforms) were an important influence in the development of his worldview.

In 1958 Fang was expelled from the party for critiques that he refused to retract. Readmitted in 1978, he was again expelled in 1987. According to the relevant party resolution his "main errors" leading to the second expulsion included his proclaiming Marxism "obsolete" and repudiating the "guiding role of the Party"; he was also charged with propagating "wholesale Westernization" as well as "advocat[ing] the capitalist road." He wanted independence for the universities and the elimination of party leadership over them; he called for "bourgeois democracy and 'freedom.' . . . "

Throughout the late 1970s and '80s, both at home and abroad, Fang unhesitatingly criticized the system and its founding principles. In 1986 he "began to project his views of science and the political implications he drew from them outward into the larger political arena, attracting the attention of both the international media and domestic political authorities." His demands for democracy allowed him to find "common ground with social scientists and literary and artistic intellectuals voicing the same demands." These shared sentiments found expression in 1989 in open letters by intellectuals supporting Fang's earlier letter to Deng in which he called for the release of political prisoners. More generally speaking,

> In calling for political guarantees against a recurrence of party intrusions into science, for arenas of public debate in which science could be defended against antirationalist intellectual trends, and for freedom from the hegemonic associations of science with Marxism-Leninism, scientific liberals such as Fang Lizhi and Xu Liangying found common ground with the critical and humanistic intellectuals from the social sciences, literature and the arts.[11]

The major theoretical foundation of Fang's critiques was his belief that the unfettered pursuit of science, liberalism, and political democracy were inseparable.

Given his long record of vocal criticism of the Communist system and its rulers, it is not easy to conceive of Fang as a past supporter of the system, especially in light of his strong commitment to rationalistic, scientific values which were incompatible with the policies of an intolerant, obscurantist, secular-religious regime such as the Chinese under Mao. Yet, he wrote, "Immediately after liberation [in 1949] and in the 1950s I firmly believed in Marxism. When I entered the Party in 1955 I was convinced that Marxism should show the way in every field and that the Communist Party was absolutely good." Even after the 1957 anti-rightist purge, he still thought of himself "as a believer or semi-believer in Marxism and felt that the criticism of free thought, including my own free thought, was not entirely unreasonable. But what worried me, what I just couldn't figure out, was why the Communist Party . . . would want to use such cruel methods against intellectuals who showed just a tiny bit . . . of independent thought." (He refers to a purge that led to the persecution of half a million people;

some were killed, some committed suicide, others were imprisoned or subjected to "reform through labor.")

Fang's early beliefs notwithstanding, he grew to become a vocal critic of Marxism, asserting in 1980 that "Marxism has become ossified. . . . We have admitted our failures and our backwardness when it comes to the material aspects of our society, but it seems that we are either afraid or unwilling to acknowledge that our failings along cultural-spiritual lines are just as bad, if not worse." He held Marxist orthodoxy responsible for stagnation and backwardness, for the "numerous anti-intellectual political campaigns fostering suspicion and hatred of learning. . . . These pogroms seemed bent on eradicating any kind of intellectual endeavor."

Perhaps most telling was Fang's 1990 critique of Marxism for its contribution to the lowering of moral standards. These critiques may remind the reader of another great dissident and critic, discussed earlier, Alexander Yakovlev:

> I disagree with this idea that Marxism brought morality to China. Especially during the last forty years the moral standards in China have been declining. . . . Rather than the so-called morality of Marxism-Leninism, we will have the morality of humanism . . . mutual respect among the people and not class struggle. . . . Any principle of morality has to conform with those of human rights, because the principles of human rights are universal. Those of Marxism-Leninism are not.

Yakovlev too insisted on embracing universal moral standards.

Besides the influence of Marxism, Fang also held Mao Zedong's anti-intellectualism and his "erroneous theories" responsible for the many disastrous developments in Chinese society. He came to the conclusion that both Chinese and Soviet socialism were resounding failures in achieving their egalitarian ideals. He did not hesitate to compare these socialist systems to Western countries and found them wanting in most respects. He believed "the self-imposed isolation of Marxism" to be the prime reason for these countries falling behind the West.

Among the major and most tangible economic and humane failures of the Chinese system were the famines of the early 1960s. Fang wrote: "In the three years between 1960 and 1962 approximately twenty-five million people in China died of hunger." He was also well aware and properly critical of the denial of the famine by Western authors such as Edgar Snow, whose "books have adopted too much of the viewpoint of his old friend, Mao Zedong, which is to say, the viewpoint of official communist propaganda."

Fang was a firm believer in the link between modernization and democracy, as well as modernization and freedom of inquiry and expression. He himself appears to be highly Westernized in the best sense of the word. He had no patience with the views of some Western politicians and intellectuals who took a tolerant view of human rights violations in non-Western countries because of their allegedly "unique" character:

> The theory of China's unique characteristics . . . is the basis of the double standard for many Western politicians. . . . Because of this double standard, human rights violations by China's rulers are frequently ignored, tolerated, even covertly encouraged. An oft-heard proposition is that "China has a unique history and culture and therefore it should be judged according to its own standards." Violent and repressive encroachments on human rights are thus "understandable," and rulers who . . . slaughter innocent people are "acceptable."

But his rejection of the system did not rest on purely rationalistic grounds. There was also a sense of moral violation and a resulting moral indignation that he once revealed to an interlocutor:

> After the Cultural Revolution started everything became much clearer. I realized that the Party had not been telling the truth, that they had in fact been deceiving the people, and that I should not believe them anymore. You see, sense of duty, responsibility and loyalty to the country had been inculcated within me as a youth, but what I saw around me made me feel that the leaders weren't similarly concerned about the country and weren't shouldering responsibility for its people.

Although his scientific values and knowledge of the Western world were crucial factors in Fang's rejection of Communist totalitarianism in China, in the final analysis his sensibility and his intolerance of mendaciousness and injustice determined his positions.

WEI JINGSHENG (1950–). The political attitude formation and transformation of Wei Jingsheng are among the most remarkable discussed in this book. From a "fanatic Maoist"—as he called himself[12]—he became a committed and uncompromising critic of the system, willing to face lengthy and repeated imprisonment for protesting the inhumane and irrational policies of the authorities. Imprisoned first in 1979, he refused to plead guilty; the prosecution demanded a severe sentence: it was fifteen years, and Wei served much of it in solitary confinement.

While in prison he was subjected to many restrictions and harassments: the electric light was always on in his cell, interfering with his sleep; he was allowed fewer visits than common criminals; he was deprived of recreational activities that other prisoners enjoyed; he was denied adequate medical care for his growing number of ailments.

Wei's political evolution culminated in his famous statement, "The Fifth Modernization: Democracy," presented in poster form during the Democracy Wall Movement in December 1978. In it he spelled out the need for a "fifth modernization"—that is, democratization—to supplement the other four types advocated by the Deng government (in agriculture, industry, science, and technology). He argued that "the old political system so despised by the people remains unchanged . . .," that the reforms were insufficient. His criticism of Deng and his reform program led directly to his arrest and imprisonment. Released in 1993 (when China sought to improve its human rights record to make itself more eligible to host the Olympic Games), he was rearrested in 1994 and subsequently sentenced to another fourteen years' imprisonment. In 1997 he was released and allowed to emigrate to the United States.

Two major influences converged in the formation of Wei's political personality: the first was his family, the second was a series of observations of the living conditions of ordinary people (the supposed beneficiaries of the system), especially those in rural areas. Both his parents were party members and functionaries. His father was an old revolutionary who had worked for the party underground from the 1930s and later fought in the Red Army. His mother became a Communist as a student during the 1940s. His father was "devoted to his Marxist and Maoist ideas and did his utmost to instill" them into the minds of his children. His efforts, Wei wrote, turned his son "into a staunch believer in Marxist–Leninist–Mao Zedong Thought." It is likely that Wei's early familiarity with these ideas and ideals sharpened his perception and awareness of the contrast between existing social realities, as he discovered them, and their official representation, or rather misrepresentation—that is, the divergence between promise and reality, or theory and practice, became the the major stimulus of his critiques of the system and its leaders.

It was "the emotional education" his mother provided that seems to have been the major influence on Wei's moral development. Apparently his mother, despite her political loyalties and values, entertained ideas about morality and moral standards that transcended ideological criteria. She believed, for example, in the importance of siding "emotionally with the people" and in "understand[ing] the people's suffering." He wrote:

> The emotional education my mother gave me was to have a decisive influence on the development of my later thinking. Had it not been for her effort to cultivate my revolutionary devotion by imbuing me with a sense of "sacrifice for those who are suffering," I might have ended up like the children of other cadres, shrugging off the reality of the living conditions of Chinese workers and peasants. . . .

What these parental and especially maternal influences added up to was an unusually developed capacity for compassion and moral indignation when confronted with suffering, injustice, and hypocrisy. Wei also came to embrace a view of human nature radically different from the official Marxist one:

> Class is only one aspect of humanity. . . . Even the mother of "public enemy" Chiang Kai-shek was from the "poor middle peasant" class. . . . Class is a matter of status and interest and doesn't determine a person's morals or personality. . . . The goodness or badness of a person's character, the nobleness of his feelings, his integrity and sense of justice are not absolutely determined by what class he was born into.

Elsewhere he wrote:

> Man is not a product of his social relations. . . . He is not a robot. . . . Rather, he is a product of nature. . . . His essential qualities are "instinctive" and very basic, and they constitute a human "commonality." . . . Human rights and basic freedoms refer to the satisfaction or realization of this part of human nature.

These ideas, while not appearing strikingly original to those who grew up in Western societies, were highly unorthodox coming from a man raised in a Marxist, collectivist society. They are also strikingly reminiscent of Alexander Yakovlev's critiques of the limitations and shallowness of the Marxist view of human nature and relationships.

A further influence on Wei's political outlook was what he learned about the Chinese repression of Tibet from a Tibetan girlfriend whose father spent eighteen years in prison. As one commentator put it, "Wei became fascinated by the tragic history of his girlfriend and her homeland. . . . Wei gained an understanding—unusual even among the dissidents of today—of the brutality of Chinese rule in Tibet."[13]

Despite their loyalty and dedication to the system, Wei's parents were not spared "the savagery of the Cultural Revolution." His father was sent to the countryside "to 'reform his thinking' through hard labor" while his mother was demoted from her earlier position and forced to write "endless self-criticisms." She died of cancer in 1976, in part due to inadequate health care.

Wei was among those of the disillusioned whose change of heart (a highly appropriate designation in his case) was as intense as his earlier convictions: ". . . right up until my illusions were later shattered by the reality I witnessed, you could say I was a fanatic Maoist."

What were these realities? In the course of his travels as a Red Guard he encountered, among other disheartening sights, "an extraordinary number of beggars" in rural areas, many of them young. He was particularly shocked by some who wore hardly any clothing. He recalled: "For the remaining two days of the trip, I could not put the scene at that nameless little [railway] station out of my mind. Was this the 'fruit' of socialism? Or was it the evil doings of a few bad local leaders?" Seeking an answer, he visited "the lower echelons of a production and construction corps in Xinjiang, a remote border region. . . ." It was an area where many former urban dwellers, students, demobilized soldiers, and "exiled old rightists" had settled. He "discovered that, despite their divergent aspirations, experiences and circumstances, they all shared one common attitude . . . dissatisfaction. The former city folk, students and army veterans all felt that they had been deceived." This was a basic animating and defining feeling of Wei's evolving outlook: a sense of betrayal, a nagging awareness of promises not kept; it became the emotional foundation of his rejection of the system.

Following his experiences in the countryside, "whenever I read glowing praise in the newspapers for the 'superiority of socialism' or heard people brag about how socialism was better than capitalism, I would swear silently 'Bullshit!'" He was appropriately indignant about the contrast between "peasants without a morsel to eat or a stitch to wear" and the wastefulness of "sending rockets and satellites into the sky."

Wei had particularly strong objections to the violence and cruelty associated with the "class struggle." Such feelings were strengthened by his visit to his father's ancestral village at a time when movements such as "cleansing the class ranks were going strong." While he believed that "former landlords and rich peasants should not hold any special place in the economy after the revolution" he also felt that "ordinary workers and peasants had no special right or need to oppress them either." During his stay in the village he also learned about the horrific results of the "Great Leap Forward" in 1958, which threatened the very survival of these peasants. He "began to realize that there was nothing 'natural' about the period known as the 'three years of natural disaster' for it was actually caused by misguided policies." He wrote: "During the more than a year I spent in the countryside, I saw for myself how Mao's theory of 'class struggle' was actually played out in real life. . . ." Again, his moral indignation was fueled by the discrepancy between misguided theory and the visible results of its attempted realization.

Time and again his frustrated hopes and betrayed expectations were more powerful incentives to political disenchantment than the actual damage to human beings and the larger society. To be sure, these two phenomena were linked, but if the damage and destruction had occurred without the barrage of false promises and the fraudulent claims of propaganda, his moral revulsion might have been more circumscribed.

By the early 1970s little if anything was left of Wei's support for the regime and his reverence for Mao. In his prison letters he matter-of-factly refers to "the fascist dictatorship under Mao Zedong." He also concluded that it was quite appropriate to consider Mao an "executioner . . . masquerading as the leader of the people." He was puzzled by the support he had earlier enjoyed.

Finally—we do not know the precise chronology—he came to feel "as if I had suddenly awakened from a long dream. . . . I began to feel that all my previous views and political notions were no longer reliable and needed to be completely rethought and reexamined"—an accurate and memorable summation of the experience of political disenchantment. At this stage he proceeded (making use of "the quiet of the village" where he was staying) to "immerse" himself in the texts of Marx, Engels, Lenin, and Stalin. Marx and Engels "inspired the most trust," and he considered their work "far more scientific than that of the others." Of Lenin's writings he liked only *State and Revolution*. We do not know whether or not he retained these positive sentiments about the ideas of the founding fathers in more recent times.

While Wei's political transformation was nourished by a combination of family influences, personality, and distinctive personal experiences (of the consequences of official policies), it should also be noted that at the time he became a political activist at Democracy Wall, a social-political movement supportive of his beliefs and endeavors already existed; he was no longer an isolated protester but belonged to an active group of like-minded young people. In his "Fifth Modernization" he went further than most critics of the regime; he was in the vanguard of protest and uncommonly willing to risk his personal safety and welfare. During his long years of imprisonment

> his health declined precipitously. His teeth began to fall out as a result of severe gum disease, and he could barely chew the coarse grains that were his main food. The poor diet also caused serious digestive problems. He developed high blood pressure and rheumatoid arthritis . . . doctors diagnosed him with heart disease and apparently said that the conditions under which he was imprisoned were "life-threatening."[14]

His long imprisonment and accompanying mistreatment were bound to confirm his beliefs and solidify his opposition to the system.

SIDNEY RITTENBERG (1921–). The history of Sidney Rittenberg's political attitude changes is among the more unusual. An American, in his early twenties he decided to spend the rest of his life in Communist China, inspired by a profound admiration for its political ideals and practices. He spent thirty-five years of his life there, sixteen of them in prison notwithstanding his devotion and loyalty to its government. He was released from his second imprisonment in late 1977 and three years later resettled in the United States with his Chinese family. He then founded a consulting business and became a prosperous liaison between American corporations eager to do business in China and the Chinese government. As described in the *New York Times*: "Like the Chinese officials who were once his junior comrades, [he] does not seem to waste much time wrestling with his conscience over his new role helping those who in the past he might have described as imperialist forces seeking to exploit China's vast resources and downtrodden masses for personal gain. 'I don't think a lot in ideological terms of capitalism vs. socialism, and neither does the leadership in China' he said."[15]

Is there much to explain about the political disillusionment of an individual who was twice imprisoned for lengthy periods by the authorities he used to revere, and whose cause he wholeheartedly embraced? Disillusionment under such conditions is hardly remarkable; rather, it is the nature of the initial attraction to the political system that stimulates curiosity. It is remarkable that after his first spell in prison—consisting of six years in solitary confinement—Rittenberg emerged with redoubled zeal, determined to prove his loyalty to his jailers. In the end, after the second imprisonment lasting almost a decade, even a true believer like him learned his lesson and parted, not without pain, with his deeply held convictions. The prime interest of Rittenberg's story lies in the insights it provides into the prolonged and difficult struggle between deeply religious impulses (folded as they were into political values and objectives) and the experience of discrepant realities.

Rittenberg was the only son of a well-to-do Jewish family in Charleston, South Carolina. His father was a prominent lawyer, his mother the daughter of a Russian immigrant. He attended prep school in Charleston and later studied languages at the University of North Carolina at Chapel Hill.[16] He learned Chinese in the U.S. Army during World War II. He had joined the American Communist party in 1940 while in college, because the Communists were opposed to the war [before the German attack on the Soviet Union] and, more important, because the party offered "a hope of righting the injustices I saw all around me." He spent two years in the party organizing workers: "I felt that in the left-wing labor movement I had at last found a force for good, multitudes of organized, dead-serious men and women who shared my vision but who were determined where I was faltering, clear-eyed where I felt confused." These feelings were replicated later in life in Rittenberg's attitudes toward the Chinese authorities.

Where precisely these early longings for social justice and political community originated is not clear, but their setting and circumstances resemble those of young American radicals in the 1960s with similarly privileged backgrounds, who found different organizational outlets for expressing their longings. The young Rittenberg may also remind the reader of the sixties activists for another reason: the flickering individualism they shared, which came into conflict with their communitarian longings. Rittenberg's lingering individualism earned him the suspicion and disfavor of Chinese authorities, with far more drastic consequences.

Rittenberg offers few clues as to what stimulated his political impulses. But there was a connection (as there was at other times and places) between being Jewish and the pursuit of social justice and leftist ideals. He recalled:

> It was the [U.S.] Communist Party that had come closest to helping me love my fellowmen the way I wanted to. And it was in the party that I had felt the most loved and accepted. Growing up Jewish in South Carolina, I had never felt completely accepted. . . . I remember being snubbed and shut out of places. When I had worked as a labor organizer . . . I was really proud to be accepted as an equal by workers, who didn't usually like college boys. And when the Chinese Communists accepted me as one of them, it made me more than proud.

This desire for love, acceptance, and community remained a lifelong impulse and driving force.

When he was drafted in the army in 1942, Rittenberg had to give up his party membership since "the party didn't want to be accused of infiltrating the military." But "even though I was no longer a party member, I hadn't given up my ideals. I still wanted to work for a new society. And leaving the party behind left a big hole in my life." Feverish involvement in political activities in revolutionary (and postrevolutionary) China came to fill this hole. If he had come of age in the United States in the 1960s it might have been not China but Castro's Cuba, Students for a Democratic Society (SDS), the Weathermen, or a similar cause offering political-communal redemption. He wrote: "I never meant to go to China. . . . True, I was a reformer, a revolutionary, almost a zealot for the social causes of the day. But China wasn't one of them. . . . I was . . . preoccupied with the social problems of my own country." While serving in the army he was initially sent to a Japanese-language training course; after the defeat of Japan he managed a transfer to a Chinese course since he did not wish to go to Japan with the U.S. occupation forces.

Serving with a U.S. military mission in post–World War II China, Rittenberg encountered social injustices and miseries far more degrading than anything he observed in American society. He began to feel "dirty and corrupted" from "living side by side with misery and evil and not doing anything about it." He came upon underground Communist publications and began to feel "a kinship with these strange and exotic Chinese Communists." He made contact with them and made arrangements to visit Yenan, a liberated area where his involvement deepened. He now had no desire to return to the United States: "I didn't want to go. I was enthralled with my newfound friends, excited by what I was learning about the Communists." He felt alone in the world after his American wife divorced him during the war. There is no previous or subsequent reference to this marriage in his memoir. Likewise there is only a brief reference to his sister at the end of the book, when he notes their reunion after his return to the United States.

In China after the war, "surrounded by millions of people in one of the most crowded cities on earth," he "wanted companionship . . . affection . . . love." His disposition exemplified the convergence of unmet personal needs with political motives—the merging of the personal with the political. He decided not to return: "There was really nothing to go home to. . . ." Party work, such as he did before the war, did not seem viable, "nor were there strong family ties pulling me home. Violet had divorced me and we had no children. My father had died before I left the States and my mother and I were not close. I was angry with her. . . . My mother's love of money and fine things had made my father's life miserable." During his second imprisonment he reflected revealingly about the circumstances that early in his life had influenced his personality, emotional needs, and hunger for approval and acceptance, suggesting that unhappiness as a child (or adolescent) had predisposed him to the pursuit of happiness in the political sphere:

> I thought all the way back to my lonely, unhappy childhood, terrified of my mother's incessant quarreling with my father and her hunger for fine things and social position. I was always trying to find some meaning in a short life that ended in oblivion, always hovering on the edge of depression. . . . I thought of how happy my life had become when I realized that human happiness comes from contributing to the freedom and happiness of other people, and that the greatest joy—and obligation in life—was the pursuit of truth.

After his tour with the U.S. military ended, Rittenberg found a job with UNRRA, the United Nations relief organization, which was distributing food in both Communist- and Nationalist-controlled areas of China during the civil war that followed World War II. He was impressed by the Communist troops he encountered: "This was a people's army, and these were peasant boys . . . fight[ing] their own battle for their futures and their families." He found no corruption and no beggars in the Communist-controlled areas and came to see the civil war as one "between the oppressors of the half-starved workers, beggars and prostitutes in Shanghai on one side and the clean-living revolutionaries . . . on the other."

Upon reaching the Communist-controlled area of Yenan (he calls it Yanan), he

> felt a strange exultation. Everything around me seemed clean and pure [an empirically doubtful observation]. The people. Their clothes. The music. Even the fierce winds and bleak landscape of Yanan seemed unsullied. . . . I was in a place far from the naked greed and corruption I had already seen too much of. . . . Yanan was not just a place where people were trying to live virtuous lives. It was the crucible in which the New China would be forged, and with it, the new world.

In Yenan he met Mao: "I could scarcely believe my good fortune . . . here I was 25 years old . . . sitting and chatting with Mao Zedong as an equal." Subsequently he became an adviser in Yenan at the English broadcast section of the Communist news agency. Like the rest of the staff, he lived in a cave—"a wonderful and strange place"—and "felt a great sense of peace and contentment," though "like the early Christians our lives were circumscribed by our caves, our catacombs." He was "intensely proud of . . . [his] role in this revolution. It was one that could only be played by someone like me, an American and a Marxist, who knew the Chinese language and agreed wholeheartedly with the beliefs and goals of the Chinese Communists." He felt he was continuing the same fight he had waged as a Communist labor organizer in the South.

In Yenan as elsewhere in the party hierarchy there were several levels of food service, depending on the rank and functions of the staff. This stratification did not seem to disturb Rittenberg especially since "it had been decided that I would eat, not with members of my own section, but with much higher officials. That meant not only a better grade of diet for me, but access to top secret information." It was during this period that he applied for admission to the party as it was "clear that everything good that was happening in China came from the party." He was admitted despite being a foreigner, with the special approval of five members of the Central Committee secretariat that included Mao. Being a party member meant "being a part of a movement, a cause, a revolution—almost a religion. . . . It was an utterly joyous self-abnegation . . . every party member was expected to achieve. . . ." This sense of belonging "overrode any worries or personal problems that might occur in our everyday lives. . . . The party satisfied my every need."

Even by Rittenberg's own reckoning, this belief fell short of reality: when the party pressured him to marry a woman he had a brief affair with, he refused. This was a serious mistake, a reassertion of Western individualism: "Had I obeyed the party . . . and agreed to marry the woman, the problem would have vanished. But I had refused to do so, and thus had called into question not only my moral character, but my political character as well."

After his first marriage to a Chinese woman in 1947, he had trouble accepting the housing arrangement which "required all [radio] announcers to live in isolation in a village about two miles away. All married couples thus separated were allowed to sleep together just one night, on Saturday. In defiance, I began a regular evening trek to [his wife] Wei Lin's new home, walking back in the morning in time for work."

In 1948, as the civil war drew to an end, the organization he worked for was moved to a "cluster of hamlets" which included Mao's headquarters. "There in the tiny village I felt most strongly the feeling of belonging that I had all along wanted. It seemed that my transgressions had been forgiven and forgotten and I was one of them again. . . . No one seemed special, no one was too high or too low to mingle together."

In January 1949 while en route to Beijing on a new assignment, his jeep and escorts stopped to return for what was supposed to be a forgotten thermos bottle. While waiting to be served tea, he was arrested on the order of the Revolutionary Military Commission for having "accepted instructions from U.S. imperialism to sabotage the Chinese Revolution." The deceptive aspects of his arrest resembled similar techniques used in other Communist states in the arrest of high-ranking functionaries. As in the Soviet and East European purge trials and during the associated waves of arrests, it was demanded that he confess to political crimes he did not commit. And like many loyal Soviet functionaries unexpectedly detained, he too thought at first that it was a simple mistake:

> How could they arrest me? How could they accuse me of being a spy? How could they keep me here in this dark room? . . . How could they hate and fear me? Hadn't I been completely open and honest with them? Hadn't they seen the love, the ardor I felt and demonstrated toward them? . . . It was all a big mistake, I told myself.

He was going to do his best to dispel the misconceptions about him and bare his soul to his interrogators. But it didn't work; the interrogators insisted that he tell them how he became "an enemy agent" and who his accomplices were. To please them he agreed that he was an agent but then broke down and admitted he had made it up because it was expected of him to make such a confession.

He was crushed by the "suspicion and rejection" of the people whom he considered his "friends, people [he] dearly loved, admired, respected and wanted to serve." He was determined to convince his captors of his love and loyalty to "make it impossible for them to reject me"; he would shed his leftover American individualism and transform himself "into a seasoned Marxist revolutionary." He resolved "to study the behavior of real revolutionaries to find role models. . . ." In search of such inspiration, he reverently read the grotesque socialist realist classic by the Soviet author Ostrovsky, *How the Steel Was Tempered*, trying to model himself on the young hero whose life, as detailed in the novel, was a chain of self-sacrifices in the service of the cause. There were also real-life Chinese role models, such as the soldier in the Korean War who preferred to burn himself to death rather than betray the location of his comrades' position.

He succeeded in generating in himself such self-critical remorse that when reading in the paper about the alleged crimes of foreign missionaries he "wept copiously. How could I fault the Chinese authorities for suspecting me when other foreigners did this kind of thing to them?"

Six years after his arrest in April 1955, he was informed that, after all, the authorities found him to be "a good person . . . wrongfully charged and imprisoned." He was offered an apology that he rejected: "No, no," he insisted. "Don't apologize! It was right to investigate me, because the organization did not know who I was. . . ."

Upon his release Rittenberg was assured that he remained a party member in good standing. He was given "superior grade housing" as well as "a better, more elaborate diet" and a new, higher position at the Broadcast Administration as an esteemed "foreign expert." He was also provided with an official car and driver; he was "being taken into the inner circle of the party." He rejoiced in his new acceptance by the authorities of this "wonderful country," contemplating "how freely young people can use the well-kept parks and playgrounds without charge . . . go to the movies and eat delicacies in little restaurants. I was pleased at the signs I saw all around me that showed I had been right to throw my lot in with the Communists, and to wait patiently through my time in prison to rejoin them." Following his release from prison, he wrote:

> . . . Everything I did was colored by one furious urge: to prove myself a loyal Communist. I emerged from those six years in solitary wanting nothing more than to show party authorities that I had changed. I wanted them to see that I was no longer a flawed and faltering weakling, but a true party stalwart. . . . I wanted to belong. My need to be accepted had not been stanched by my imprisonment, but rather intensified by it.

Having regained the apparent trust of the regime, Rittenberg was now included in a high-level team which translated Mao's work into English, a project he worked on for two years. He flourished as a devoted, busy party activist in a "system that seemed close to the ideals I had fought for back in the labor movement in the South." It was a land where the downtrodden of the past "were now masters." He believed that "a golden age of democratic socialism had begun in China."

Like all good party cadres, he volunteered for tasks outside his regular job, teaching evening classes in political economy and coaching his pupils individually after class. In his new broadcasting position he had "significantly more power and authority." At his new place of work he met his second Chinese wife, a fellow worker whom he married in early 1956 and who became an important influence on his political outlook and evolution. She had a remarkably independent mind and "unlike me did not believe everything she was told" by the authorities.

In 1957 began the campaign to encourage criticism of the shortcomings of the system among intellectuals (broadly defined), called "Let a Hundred Flowers Bloom." But it soon became clear that the regime did not embrace a new tolerance for different points of view. "This wasn't going to be a democratic debate at all. . . . We weren't going to be settling contradictions among the people . . . because Mao had decided that the party critics weren't people at all, but enemies." The critics were dubbed "rightists," and every organization had to find some to be singled out, "debated," and crushed. Rittenberg too was enlisted to persuade one of these "rightists" at his organization to confess his errors; he did confess and was sent to a farm. Rittenberg himself had been in exactly the same situation earlier: charged with a crime he did not commit. In another demonstration of political conformity, Rittenberg refused to visit a friend disgraced in the same "rectification" campaign. Having internalized the official norms, Rittenberg argued that "you can't visit with a rightist just because he is your friend." His wife strongly disapproved. Rittenberg also found himself "trying hard to toe the party line" at a public meeting when he joined the criticism of another close friend accused of being a rightist: "For the first time I was going along with the persecution of someone—and a friend at that—who I couldn't really believe was disloyal to the party." His moral impulses were stifled by his political loyalties and fears. In retrospect it appeared that "the nastiness of the campaign against the rightists opened a little crack in the armor of loyalty I had forged around myself in prison."

Next came the "Great Leap Forward" campaign in 1958, promising a new, better, Chinese way to rapid modernization. Once more Rittenberg was enthusiastic and ready to believe that "the many years of class struggle had been for a purpose after all. . . . I had wholeheartedly supported the idea that individuals should subsume themselves in the collective. Here was a signal from Mao that the collective would now, in turn, support the flowering of the individual." There was a wave of volunteering for extra work, including "productive physical labor." The "stultifying division of labor" was to be overcome: "people would rotate by turns as doctor, bookkeeper, worker, farmer, teacher." Supposed miracles of production were taking place everywhere, but as it later became apparent, some of them were as counterfeit as the record coal production of the Soviet miner Stakhanov in the 1930s, after whom a new movement to raise production was named.[17] In the Chinese campaign, peasants as well as office workers were urged to set up "backyard furnaces" to increase steel production. In the course of this truly lunatic program, much useful metal equipment was melted down and peasants were diverted from agricultural work, many sent to prospect for iron ore. By 1961 the results of the Great Leap became apparent—famine instead of bumper harvests. Rittenberg wrote:

> Few in China knew the truths until decades later. The Chinese were not just hungry, they were starving to death in the countryside by the tens of millions. Fewer still knew the main cause: not bad harvests, not the Soviet debt . . . but the Great Leap Forward itself. The same enthusiasm and all-out effort that had built the roads, the dams . . . the Great Hall of the People, the backyard steel furnaces . . . had also devastated China's agriculture. The ill-conceived hunt for ore that had pulled able-bodied peasants from the field had ruined the harvests.

The catastrophic results of the Great Leap were not easy to shrug off, not even for a true believer like Rittenberg, especially as he and his family were "forced to confront the painful reality of the hunger close up." More than two-thirds of the people working at the Broadcast Administration, including his wife, suffered symptoms of protein deficiency. They were foraging for leaves as substitutes for vegetables. By 1963 conditions improved.

Meanwhile Rittenberg's career took another, new turn. It became his job "to nurture the loyalty of the foreigners who chose to stay in China, whatever their nationality." His "star was rising," and he was "more and more at the center of things," "everywhere . . . in great demand." He became "not only a celebrity in Beijing, but a bit of a gourmet and theater buff as well." He had "intimate knowledge of Beijing's attractions," including the best restaurants. He was invited to the eightieth-birthday celebration of Anna Louise Strong attended by the highest-ranking officials and most prestigious foreigners, and presided over by Mao himself. His admiration of Mao knew no bounds: "Meeting Mao wasn't like meeting the President. It was like meeting God. When you met Mao, you were meeting the father of the country and the liberator of mankind."

At the same time he was beginning to feel that the Chinese system was growing corrupt—"and I had allowed it to corrupt me," as evidenced by his own "big belly protruding over my belt, the product of the last few years' good living." Under these conditions he welcomed the cleansing Cultural Revolution in 1966 and was "eager to participate." Once more he was "ecstatic. The people were going to be free at last." Moreover, "we promised to end bureaucracy, waste and mismanagement, to listen to people. . . ." In retrospect he saw that

> We were caught up in a shining and powerful drama. Our hopes . . . blinded us to the realities around us. . . . It seemed like the birth pangs of a new world. . . .
>
> . . . The applause thundering in my ears had deafened me to something I should have been listening to. . . . Mao had said it was right to rebel but only under conditions he had set—to serve his purposes.

He was named the new head of the Broadcast Administration. He also became "a public speaker, a mover of masses, a stirrer of souls."

Rittenberg's career in the Cultural Revolution abruptly ended in February 1968 when he and his family were arrested at night in their home. In a matter of hours he was "again locked away in a kind of prison I didn't think still existed for a crime I had not committed." Thirteen years had passed since the end of his first imprisonment. Abandoned by his highly placed friends (Mao and Zhou Enlai included) who signed his "detention order," he still believed in "the cause of democratic socialism." Once more he had no idea why he was in prison and for how long. He was "ordered to bow to Chairman Mao's portrait on the wall and ask for forgiveness." He heard the sounds of torture around him and wondered, "How could such things be happening to anyone, enemy or not, criminal or not?" He himself was not tortured, but sleep and food deprivation, as well as endless interrogations, were used to break him down and extract a confession. This went on for three years. He was initially accused of being a spy and a foreign agent, but later it transpired that it was his interpretation of the goals of the Cultural Revolution that had landed him in jail. He had "fundamentally misunderstood Mao's real intention in the Cultural Revolution." It dawned on him at last that "Mao's point in the Cultural Revolution wasn't . . . to destroy restrictions on civil rights, blind obedience to party discipline, thought control over the masses and arbitrary one-party dictatorship. It was to strengthen these things."

During this second and, as it turned out, much longer imprisonment, Rittenberg engaged in a great deal of soul searching about his life and his political beliefs and activities. He was reluctant to conclude that all his efforts had been wasted: ". . . I had not been wrong to throw in my lot with the party" which, he still thought, brought great improvements to the lives of the Chinese people. He wondered if he had "lost the battle for a meaningful life?" He still felt that "If I could only put one drop in the long river of human progress, then my purpose would be fulfilled."

But during this second imprisonment he "realized for the first time that those in power didn't think the way I was thinking." As to the source of his "major political mistakes," it was his unquestioning loyalty to the party and its leaders, as well as, in his youth, his "blind acceptance" of the notion that the Soviet Union was "a workers' paradise." Whatever his apprehensions had been about specific policies or methods of their implementation, "in each case . . . [they] had been overruled by my belief in Marxist theory and in some great authority." He was particularly tormented by the idea that the sacrifices were in vain: "The worst thing, I thought, would be to have gone through all this pain and suffering only to find—if and when I was ever released—that socialism had failed."

After Mao's death, Rittenberg was released and "rehabilitated" in 1977. The authorities concluded that "the spy charges were unfounded. It was a mistake. I was a good comrade. All possible restitution would be made." He had spent close to a decade in prison. After his release he learned about the mistreatment his wife and children had suffered, but he continued to resist the idea that his suffering and those of the millions of Chinese people were pointless:

> In prison my worst fear was that I would come out and find that my suffering and loneliness had all been in vain, that socialism had failed. I pushed away with both hands the evidence Yulin [his wife] and the children brought to me that my worst fear had come true. . . .

He was shocked to hear from his wife that "nobody cares anymore what the paper says, or what official Central Committee documents say. . . . They told me tales of . . . corruption, low morale and seedy ethics that I found hard to believe. 'These must be individual cases . . .' I said." But when he and his wife toured the country, he "found the same wherever I went. Corruption had seeped into the marrow of the party structure. . . . There was so much pain . . . disillusionment . . . sense of betrayal. . . . No one believed in it [the party] anymore, including those who were using it to advance their own power and comfort." In the families around him he saw "wrecks of the Cultural

Revolution . . . children who had denounced parents, wives who had divorced husbands, husbands who had reported on wives." As a free man he continued "the painful process . . . begun in prison: a deep reexamination of my belief in Communism." He reread the official texts and concluded that "the major problems were in the Communist doctrine itself." He had "vastly overestimated the degree of truth any . . . social ideology can hold and the capacity of human planning to determine the development of society." He also realized that it took him so long to see these errors "because of the stake I had acquired in the system and the life I had lived in China, a life of perks, privilege and deluded complicity." The final blow to his beliefs came when Deng Xiaoping shut down the Democracy Wall and arrested some of the poster writers. Rittenberg had come to China "to serve humanity . . . to change the world." He had no desire to spend the rest of his life "serving those whom power had corrupted." In March 1980 he and his wife left for the United States; his children followed later.

Few people have been more deserving of the label "true believer" than Rittenberg. In his concluding reflections he designates, as key to his lifelong attitude, the desire and determination "to believe what I saw, what I wanted to see, ben[ding] reality to fit my own notions." Late in life he came to accept with "great relief," he writes, that his "life's vision was flawed." He was able to make a fresh start with his "mind now unleashed from the rigors of dogma." He reevaluated Mao and his numerous, profoundly flawed "key theoretical assumptions."

Running his consulting company in the United States has provided Rittenberg with a new, if less exalted, sense of purpose, including the belief that he is of some help to the people of China. He came "light years from my old party days when I believed that the world was divided into angels and devils . . . capitalist . . . villains pitted against the common people as victims." He settled in Seattle, ". . . a sage and guide to the capitalist class . . . in relative splendor . . . on a 3-acre site that includes an outdoor hot tub and a gazebo [and] affords . . . dreamy views of Puget Sound." He enjoys a secure, prosperous, apolitical life at an advanced age, thanks to flourishing trade relations between the United States and China. With the crucial help of his wife, he has recovered from his consuming political preoccupations. (Having grown up in China, she had a far better intuitive grasp of the unbridgeable gap between political ideals and social realities, and of the limitations human nature imposes on the pursuit of utopian schemes.) Finally, Rittenberg's American persona, including an ingrained cultural belief in the individual's capacity to remake himself, helped change his life fundamentally.

FOUR

In the Third World: Cuba, Nicaragua, and Ethiopia

Throughout its existence, Communist Cuba, like China and Vietnam, has been a major exporter of refugees and exiles. They have included many former supporters of the revolution and the political system subsequently established; many of them have written memoirs. Many former Communist Ethiopian officials had also defected before the overthrow of the Mengistu regime in 1991, but they failed to publish their recollections, at any rate in English. The same applies to Nicaragua. Fortunately the writings of Davit Wolde Giorgis and Gioconda Belli provide revealing accounts of political disenchantment in Ethiopia and Nicaragua, respectively. I begin with the Cuban accounts.

CARLOS FRANQUI (1921–) experienced a disillusionment that was not quite as prolonged a process as those reported by numerous high-ranking officials in other Communist states. Franqui's objections to the system were freely expressed even while he was serving it. His disaffection appears to have been more significantly shaped by his personality and proximity to the leader than was often the case. He wrote:

> I knew where I stood. As a socialist who believed in democracy and human dignity, I was declared enemy of the Cuban Communists and the Soviet Union. All my actions and the policies of *Revolucion* [the paper he edited] at least had the virtue of clarity: we were antimilitarist, proculture, proart, in favor of free labor unions, tolerant of homosexuals, and totally opposed to terrorism of any kind.[1]

Heberto Padilla, the famous Cuban writer, discussed below, who knew Franqui well, wrote:

> Franqui was always a radical, and although bitter experience has led him to make a clean break with his political executioners, he has not totally abandoned his faith in "the midwife of history." . . .
>
> Franqui believed . . . that ethical questions must take precedence over political exigencies; for that reason, he was unable to accept the iron discipline of the Communist party. . . . [He] was the spokesman of the antisectarian, democratic spirit which the world outside saw in the Cuban Revolution in its initial stage. . . . Revolution and poetry were synonymous for Franqui.[2]

Franqui came from a poor peasant family; his father was a sugar cane cutter. He had ample revolutionary credentials—he was a fighter as well as an organizer and propagandist. He created Radio Rebelde, the radio station of the Cuban revolutionaries, and the underground newspaper *Revolucion*. During Castro's imprisonment in the early 1950s, the guerrilla years, Franqui was appointed national head of propaganda for the 26 July movement, the major organization of resistance to the Batista government. He joined the Cuban Communist party at an early age and later Castro's underground. In 1947 he participated with Castro in an aborted military expedition to overthrow Trujillo, dictator of the Dominican Republic. Arrested by the Batista police, he was jailed and tortured. Later he joined Castro and his guerrillas in the Sierra Maestra Mountains. Padilla wrote:

> Carlos Franqui is the victim of chronic hope. He was a militant member of the Popular Socialist party, perhaps its poorest adherent. He was born into a peasant family and attained a secondary education against enormous odds. . . . The social injustice of which he was victim and witness led him, while still young, to identify with Marxism.[3]

Political disaffection in Communist Cuba had two major generic and two more specific localized sources. The former included elite privilege and repression; the latter the personality, political role, and impact of Castro and the growing influence of the Soviet Union and the Soviet model.

Since the Cuban Revolution was indigenous and authentic, it generated high hopes and expectations—and later, deeper and more impassioned rejections of the system (when it failed to realize its high hopes) than was the case in other settings where the new system was imposed by external force, as in Eastern Europe. Such disappointment was reflected not only in the attitudes of former revolutionaries such as Franqui, but even more spectacularly in those of more than a million ordinary citizens who left Cuba, legally as well as illegally. Franqui wrote: "Originally only the Batista supporters had fled, then the middle classes went; now people of every class who had sympathized with the revolution were emigrating." To this day the outflow has not stopped: people still take their lives in their hands attempting to cross the sea to Florida on primitive rafts.

It is not easy to establish the precise chronology of Franqui's political-ideological journey and the major milestones of his disenchantment. While at the time he supported the postrevolutionary executions of former Batista henchmen, *in retrospect* he had second thoughts: "The problem is not who gets shot, it's who does the shooting. When you execute someone in cold blood, you are learning how to kill. That's how human beings are turned into murder-machines, and those machines are unstoppable. . . ." It was the beginning of institutionalized repression in Cuba.

Later Franqui learned from former revolutionaries of many atrocities, of degrading prison conditions, of peasants who were accused of crimes they did not commit (and were told to confess) and who were often shot. He found out about the specifics of torture, including the "apple bobbing" technique whereby the prisoner's head was immersed in a barrel of water until he almost drowned. Just when he was about to die, he was pulled out. He either talked or drowned. He acquired photos of "Commandante Escalona and his thugs beating and torturing prisoners" and showed them to Castro, "thinking I was giving him some terrible evidence of which he was ignorant. To my shock, Fidel showed not the slightest surprise. . . . How could Fidel condone Escalona's methods?" It was not the only occasion on which he protested "Party terrorism." At a meeting of Castro and the Council of Ministers, he "listed persecutions, arbitrary imprisonment and other outrages. My statements were met with silence and with countercharges. . . ."

"Operation P" in 1961 was, according to Franqui, "the first massive socialist raid of the Cuban revolution," a coercive attempt to cleanse Cuban society of undesirable elements; it involved an extensive police sweep of the "bohemian sections of Havana and other cities." Those arrested "were made to undress and put on a uniform, a striped suit with a huge P across the backside. Capital P: pederast, prostitute, pimp." This too he protested, arguing that those arrested "were nothing more than victims of the old society," as Marxist theory would have it.

After learning of such atrocities, "something inside me broke down. It was impossible to pardon crimes like that in the name of the revolution, and every day more stories . . . came in." Elsewhere he wrote:

> Three or four kilometers from Varadero [a famous beach and luxurious resort area for foreign tourists], there were other incredible things to be seen: persecuted people, peasants whose land had been given them and then taken away, jailed revolutionaries, and fishermen who refused to change their lives. They were used to fishing alone, in the style Hemingway describes in *The Old Man and the Sea*, but the revolution had other ideas. First it gave the fishermen new houses . . . then it took away the fishermen's boats and tried to make the men work in teams—they would stop being fishermen and become sea workers. This the fishermen refused to do, so Security [the political police] stepped in to harass them and stop any mass migrations to the north.

As these examples suggest, the coercion and terror were rooted in a doctrinaire concept of how people should live: fishermen should fish together, forming a collective; peasants should work on collective farms and, if unwilling, should be forced into them as in every Communist state. In Cuba a fetishized notion of "The Revolution" provided legitimation for the party/state to intervene in people's lives and force them to act in ways the leaders deemed desirable. The idea of "The Revolution" stood for everything sacrosanct about the system and its goals. Raymond Aron's observation about the idea of revolution in Communist states applies here: "The myth of the Revolution . . . fosters the expectation of a break with the normal trend of human affairs. . . . [It] seems capable of changing everything. . . . Revolution provides a welcome break with the everyday course of events and encourages the belief that all things are possible."[4] The Cuban Revolution in its early phases encouraged such beliefs, at any rate among its committed partisans and sympathetic observers in Western societies.

Contary to widespread impressions abroad, there was much popular dissatisfaction with the system even in its earlier days, and not only among those who chose to depart. As Franqui wrote in 1961, the Escambray Mountains "were full of rebels . . . peasants, workers, the common people. They weren't Batista supporters. . . . The rebels were all individuals . . . unjustly persecuted by the revolution." In his offensive against these rebels, Castro had the entire peasant population of the area deported, "no matter what their politics might be."

The personality and charisma of Castro provided the decisive and direct legitimation for everything done in the name of "The Revolution," which he personified; he also determined to an extraordinary degree the shape of the political system. Thus Franqui's rejection of Cuban communism was in a large measure a rejection of Fidel Castro—his absolutism, intolerance, power hunger, and ruthlessness, all inspired by a sense of mission and historical destiny. Franqui saw him as the prototypical totalitarian ruler:

> . . . Fidel is a calculating man who believes in terror as a means of government. He responded to a critical letter of mine saying: "All criticism is opposition. All opposition is counter-revolutionary." Then he repeated his definition of Stalinism as the dictatorship of a revolutionary minority during difficult times, a minority that functions like a father who must deny his children something he has promised them. . . . Fidel always thought of himself as the revolution. . . .

Castro's personality was congenial with some of the classical attributes of a totalitarian state, especially the initial puritanical orientation:

> What Fidel has done is to impose on Cuba all the punishments he suffered as a boy in his Jesuit school: censure, separation of the sexes, discipline, thought control, a Spartan mentality. He hates culture, liberty. . . . All sensuality . . . is anathema to him. We used to have one main prison . . . now we have many. We used to have a few barracks; now we have many. We used to have many plantations, now we have only one and it belongs to Fidel. . . .

Castro was also "fond of biblical parables and always spoke of the Twelve"—the supposed original twelve revolutionaries—"and a Christ-Fidel who had gone out in the wilderness. . . . Twelve barbudos [bearded ones] and a good hero, coming down from the Sierra, were offering us salvation."

The mandated worship of a supreme leader[5] (designated in the Soviet Union by Khrushchev as "the cult of personality") and the associated concentration of power were not peculiar to Cuba, as Franqui was well aware: "How did it all happen? It happened because all power was concentrated in one man. Socialism became dictatorship; socialism became Stalin, Mao, Kim Il Sung, Brezhnev, Husak, Fidel Castro. . . ."

Doubtless Franqui arrived at such conclusions much later, after the erosion of his commitment and the opportunity to reflect upon his activities and experiences in Cuba. The influence of specific experiences (some of them noted above) also steered him to these conclusions, some of them acquired while on official visits to other, more established socialist states. Socialist prostitution was one of them:

> When I got back to my hotel [in Prague] I was surrounded by my colleagues, each of whom wanted twenty dollars. When I asked why each wanted the same amount they told me that that was how much the girls charged. I was flabbergasted that there could be prostitution under socialism. But there was. . . . The girls had government-owned—and bugged—apartments and would accept only dollars or coupons. These coupons they later turned in at the State Bank, where they were given vouchers . . . they used at a special store. We visited it and found, to our surprise, that it was crammed with the best consumer goods from the West—all the things no ordinary Czech could buy. . . . We saw lots of high-ranking Czechs there. . . . We had discovered a side of socialism we didn't like.
>
> Later on we would find that the same corruption existed in Moscow. . . . It was apropos this corruption that I had a run-in with Che Guevara when I got back to Havana. I told the story of the socialist prostitutes in Prague and the special stores, and Che called me a liar.

Two years later Che Guevara, Castro's revolutionary comrade, apologized to Franqui when he himself discovered the phenomena he had earlier denied. Franqui could not have dreamed, when he wrote the above, that in the 1990s Cuban prostitution would become a major growth industry and a foundation for the improved living standards of large numbers of Cuban women (and their families), servicing foreign tourists and enlarging the flow of foreign currency to the economy.

These were important sources of disillusionment, both because the phenomena in question—prostitution and special stores for the privileged—were undesirable in themselves and because they were not supposed to exist in socialist countries like Czechoslovakia and the Soviet Union. It was a galling instance of the gulf between theory and practice, ideals and realities.

The Soviet influence in general was a vexing problem for idealists like Franqui. His visits to the Soviet Union and his observations of Soviet citizens in Cuba helped him realize that the Soviet model was not to be embraced. He saw the Soviet system "mummified" and afflicted by "bureaucratic malaise." But Castro was impressed by Soviet power and the techniques that Soviet rulers had used to stay in power: "A fusion of the Russian model and the new dictatorial militarism of Fidel Castro was taking place. In a casual conversation with him, in which

I expressed my concern with the course of events, he made a statement which shook me to the core: 'Only the old Communists and the Soviets know anything about communism. We must be patient and learn from them.'"

New, institutionalized inequalities were another major source of disenchantment for Franqui. Shortly after the victory over Batista,

> Some rebels began to "requisition" cars that belonged to Batista supporters, to take over the houses of the rich. "Now there is a great idea," Raul Castro said, "the barbudos living in the mansions of the rich." Great, I said, but dangerous, because men think the way they live.

"What was really happening," Franqui wrote, "was that we were creating a new elite." He was led to ask and to ruefully conclude:

> . . . did the revolution change anything? Yes, everything in the highest echelons of Cuban society changed: the Party-state was the new ruling class. But nothing changed below. . . . The word [socialism] just has no meaning any more . . . "the proletariat," "popular democracy," "communism" . . . No one believes these words any more because everyday reality gives them a lie. The socialist world is . . . a world where the people are forced to work and to endure permanent rationing and scarcity, where they have neither rights nor freedom. . . . There is no equality in education, because the new elite gives special attention to the children of party members and state officials. The same applies to labor. There is no unemployment, because people are made to work at forced labor. . . . Salaries are not equal and are insufficient. This goes as well for housing, medical attention, transportation and food.

Perks for the elite included even wedding presents: "When a certain commandante-minister got married, he was given a house in the Miramar district, a new car, assorted whiskies, dishes and perfume for the blushing bride. . . . As an old veteran of Prague and Moscow remarked, 'Only the best for the proletariat.'"

Ordinary citizens were forbidden to keep pigs or chickens in their houses, but the second in command of the political police, Manuel Pineyro, "had a huge house surrounded by a huge piece of land, a farm right in the city . . . a real farm with all kinds of chickens, pigs, ducks—all taken care of by army personnel. It was kind of conspicuous consumption by a new class. . . . I remembered that Fidel had denounced Batista's officers for using soldiers as farm laborers and now both the army and police were doing the same thing."

Franqui's rejection of the system and his departure from Cuba were also furthered by the authorities' negative view of him—Castro in particular—and by the likely consequences of this view. From the time he became a vocal critic and refused to muzzle his objections, the authorities were ready to silence him. Up to a point his critiques were tolerated because of his revolutionary credentials and perhaps also because of his early personal association with Fidel, but not indefinitely. As he recalls, "I was identified as the intellectual chief of the group [those critical of the Soviet influence and other matters] and Huber Matos as its political leader. We were all marked men." Matos was arrested and tried for conspiracy in 1959 and sentenced to twenty years, which he served.

An interesting and unusual aspect of Franqui's memoirs is that he makes no reference to Marxism-Leninism—neither as a source of his original attraction to the system and its ideological foundations, nor as a set of ideas whose influence might help explain the system's flaws and deformation. Nor does he dwell on the obvious contradiction apparent in every Communist system between ostensible faithfulness to Marxism, which deemphasizes the role of the individual in the historical-political process, and the cult of personality of the supreme leader to be found in all these systems.

Among the strength of Franqui's critique of Communist Cuba is his understanding that "revolutionary Cuba" shared all the major, defining weaknesses and moral flaws of other Communist states in different parts of the world: "Any opposition was automatically considered counterrevolutionary . . . automatically dismissed as Yankee. This pattern clearly emerged after Playa Giron [the failed invasion at the Bay of Pigs by anti-Castro forces, aided by the United States, in 1961] but it is visible throughout the supposed socialist world, from the Soviet Union to China, from Vietnam to Cuba. In the world where the state is supposed to disappear, a monolithic party emerges to oppress, to suffocate all liberty, to repress the people and to create a privileged bureaucracy to enjoy wealth and power."

HEBERTO PADILLA (1932–2000) was one of the best-known contemporary Cuban writers whose fame, in part, was due to his arrest in 1971 and his forced confession of counterrevolutionary attitudes and political errors. The arrest led to widespread protest among Western intellectuals, many of them former friends of the Castro regime, including Jean-Paul Sartre, Simone de Beauvoir, Gabriel García Márquez, and Susan Sontag. It is important to note that Padilla's rejection of the system predated by several years his arrest and personal mistreatment; the arrest eliminated whatever residual affection he might have harbored toward "The Revolution." In 1980 Castro allowed him to leave for the United States.

Padilla was among the supporters of the anti-Batista revolution led by Castro. At the time of the revolution he lived in New York, teaching Spanish at the Berlitz School. A few weeks after Castro's victory, another well-known Cuban writer, Humberto Arenal, who also lived in New York, asked Padilla to join the new Cuban news agency, Prensa Latina, he headed; Padilla accepted the offer. He did not stay in the job for long, preferring to return to revolutionary Cuba in the early spring of 1959 "since all signs pointed to the fact that a splendid political transformation toward good government had begun. I wanted to be part of it in any way I could."[6] In the early years of the new regime he believed that Cuban exiles were unworthy enemies of the revolution. He wrote: "The years between 1959 and 1962 were crucial ones. Although in reality the country was splitting apart, with ever increasing numbers choosing exile . . . this meant nothing to us. We believed that they were simply members of the privileged classes. . . ."

Padilla's political disaffection followed, gradually, with the decline of political and intellectual freedom and Cuba's growing dependence on the Soviet Union. Much of Padilla's memoir treats this political disaffection matter-of-factly, as something quite natural and almost inevitable, a state of mind shared by many Cuban intellectuals and especially writers as the Castro regime grew more repressive. He does not indicate how his political estrangement began, nor does he systematically examine its various sources or stimulants. What stands out is the conflict between the creative writer and the political authorities, their intolerance of the autonomy of writers and their ideological as well as bureaucratic determination to subordinate literature and the arts to political goals and requirements. Padilla strenuously resisted official pressures to produce socialist-realist works and was incautiously critical of the regime; he also shared his views with other intellectuals similarly inclined as well as with some foreign visitors and diplomats such as Jorge Edwards of Chile, whom the authorities suspected of hostile attitudes toward the Cuban government.

The second major source of Padilla's disillusionment was the inimitable personal dictatorship and duplicitous personality of Fidel Castro, his oppressive interference with every aspect of Cuban life, including literature and the arts, and his barely concealed contempt for intellectuals. Arguably Castro personified everything that was objectionable about the political system. Padilla believed that "there was a human quality missing in him"; his megalomania and sense of mission were such that he would regularly inflict on his audiences, in person or television, speeches which might last up to nine hours! Castro's authoritarianism, Padilla believed, had "nothing to do with the CIA," that is, it was not primarily a response to external threat but rather self-generated, a matter of personality, power hunger, and extreme intolerance of those seen as interfering with his political ambitions and favored ways of exercising power. In these endeavors he was ably supported by his brother Raul, of whom it was said by an American writer, Waldo Frank (a sympathizer with the Cuban revolution), that "there is some deep abnormality in Raul. He's cold and cruel and is capable of any crime."

In justification of his repressive policies, Castro said (as Padilla quoted him): "It is better to sin through excess than through default . . . a few months of terror were necessary to do away with terror which had lasted for centuries. We need many Robespierres in Cuba." Padilla knew Castro personally and had several one-on-one conversations with him, including one before his final departure from Cuba. On that occasion Castro said, "Even though you will never admit it publicly, I know that this revolution will grow in your memory." But this was wishful thinking; Padilla's potentially nostalgic, youth-affirming recollections did not prevent him from wholeheartedly rejecting the regime, which became thoroughly totalitarian notwithstanding its early, idealistic goals. Under this system, anyone was "an 'objective counterrevolutionary' . . . [or] an enemy . . . who displayed the merest disagreement with his [Castro's] ideas." Such intolerance was fostered by the persistently mendacious official propaganda. Padilla endorsed the observation of the German author Hans Magnus Enzensberger that "a Communist lies with the total conviction of a man who knows he is lying."

While some Soviet officials "were saying that they had found again 'the youth of the October Revolution'" in Cuba, that is, in Padilla's opinion "the same authoritarianism had taken hold." It was not just a matter of literary policy and censorship. The repression was broader and deeper: homosexuals and "people disaffected with the systems because of their beliefs such as Jehovah's witnesses" were sent to newly established concentration camps where homosexuals were subjected to Pavlovian deconditioning that "drove many people mad." Padilla's arrest and forced confession provided an authentic insight into the policies of repression; at the same time they also "opened up a breach . . . between the repressive policies of the Cuban government and . . . writers and artists around the world, who until that moment could not imagine that Fidel Castro would reproduce the methods of Stalin in such a distant different country."

Padilla's travels in both Western and Eastern Europe also made a distinct contribution to his disillusionment, offering further bases of comparison. His lengthy stay in the Soviet Union and visits to Eastern European Communist states helped him better understand and abhor more deeply the direction Cuba had taken under Castro. He was among the few individuals in a position to learn firsthand about the unappealing attributes of several Communist systems, not only those in his own country.

Padilla chose to go to Moscow to work for the Spanish-language edition of the *Moscow News*, "convinced at the time that in this far-off land I would be able to glimpse the outlines of Cuba's future." This anticipation proved to be correct to a point in regard to repression and doctrinaire economic mismanagement, but it did not take into account the unique historical role Castro was to play in resisting the kind of liberalization Gorbachev introduced much later.

In 1962 when Padilla arrived in the Soviet Union, revelations of past horrors were permitted within limits, and Solzhenitsyn's short novel about the Gulag (*One Day in the Life of Ivan Denisovich*) had just been published. A longtime resident in Moscow of Spanish Republican parentage told him that "Cubans deserve to know that the Soviet people have suffered this political experience as has no other, and they should avoid the repetition in Cuba of the errors of those times." Padilla correctly foresaw and feared the applications of the Soviet model to Cuba; some Soviet intellectuals, notably Yevgeny Yevtushenko, also warned him about the possibility. Yevtushenko told him: ". . . Your Cuban leaders are not interested in knowing the historical truth about Stalinism. Any time I mentioned it in Havana or in any other Cuban city or town, they listened with only half an ear."

While in the Soviet Union, Padilla came to the conclusion that ". . . Communism, or whatever one wants to call it, can no longer be the challenge of our times. Communism remains a prisoner forever of those astonishing revelations of Khrushchev. . . . The reality I came in contact with had been subverted, poisoned: this was a nation given over to rites of burying and exhuming bodies. . . ." Czechoslovakia was no better: ". . . In Prague I found the same bureaucratic authoritarianism, the same political espionage, the same censorship, the same fear, the same nihilistic resignation." Later he wrote: "If there was a difference between Cuban society and its 'fraternal equivalents' in the Soviet Union or Czechoslovakia, it was the cheap, crude tone which in Cuba dominated everything."

In the end Cuba turned out to be one of the few Communist states that resisted reform, refusing to moderate its harsh repression and relax the doctrinaire ideological determination of its economy, which, along with Castro's personal mismanagement, remains to this day the major source of Cuba's endemic scarcities and stagnation.

It is not clear when precisely Padilla's doubts began. Following the 1962 Cuban Missile Crisis he "began to keep a lower profile in Moscow." He and other Cubans in Moscow were increasingly unwilling to share "private thoughts." During a visit to Paris he unburdened himself to a friend, the Spanish writer Juan Goytisolo, telling him "of all the worries and uncertainties" his life in Moscow stimulated and describing "what the Communist world, the one we had given our allegiance to, was really like." He was obviously shaken by his Soviet experiences, but "at the same time, you could not be anti-Communist because that would mean acquiescing in the shameful history of Western colonialism. So it was the duty of the supporters of the Cuban Revolution to prevent it from repeating the same errors the Soviets made. But our criticisms should be made from within."

For Padilla this was a period of fluctuation between doubt and affirmation; he drew strength from and was comforted by the nationalization of "powerful sugar plantations," by the "gigantic literacy program," by the conversions of "barracks into schools," the establishment of "hospitals in every corner of the country," and the ending of unemployment. But even as he reviewed these accomplishments he was "prey to long bouts of depression. *More and more had to be explained away*" [my emphasis]. This need is characteristic of the drawn-out process of disillusionment. At this earlier stage the believer registers some dissonant, disillusioning phenomena but he is not ready to come to far-reaching conclusions because of them. He is not ready to give up; he is still eager and able to "explain them away," to reevaluate these phenomena in order to diminish their importance in light of the supposedly more important accomplishments of the system and his own deeply felt commitments; at this stage his long-term hopes are still intact. Padilla wrote:

> My allegiance sanctioned each step of the process; rejection would mean turning my back on the most ambitious transformation ever undertaken in my country. . . . To accept everything was like swallowing

> live toads. . . . Those of us who had to swallow live toads will have with us for the rest of our lives an inescapable sensation of nausea and a loathing of our very act of hope.

Padilla was arrested in 1971 for "'having plotted against the power of the state.'" He later wrote:

> I realized that Castro was looking for the opportunity to liquidate the first wave of intellectual dissidence in his regime. . . . This kind of purge is frequently instituted when criticism or discontent appears within the Communist state. But I had only known of purges as an intellectual possibility. I never imagined that I would be given the opportunity to observe the careful organization of such a farce. . . . Moreover it was inconceivable that I would head the list.

During his detention he discovered "the socialist world's outstanding contribution to jurisprudence," namely that "policeman, detective and examining judge are one and the same person." It was held against him that he expressed doubt about the charges against Pierre Golendorff, a French citizen arrested for spying. Padilla's unpublished novel, *Heroes Are Grazing in My Garden* (the manuscript of which was seized), was regarded as proof of his intention to "spread poison" about the revolution. It was demanded of him that he confess "step by step" all his "activities with the enemy," writing on his own typewriter. In his confession Padilla admitted to "act[ing] in an irresponsible manner in . . . dealings with foreigners," and acknowledged that his "literary ambitions were . . . out of sync with our political responsibilities. . . ." His association with Jorge Edwards was a source of official displeasure as was his "deviation from correct opinion" and his "ungrateful attitude toward Fidel and the Revolution." Under pressure he repented. He had to memorize his confessions and self-criticisms so that he could recite them at a closed meeting of the most important members of the Writers and Artists Union. He did so; the transcript was distributed internationally by Prensa Latina since "Castro wanted to make known to the world that Padilla and his friends had acquiesced in the ceremony of self-degradation."

During his thirty-seven days of detention during which the public confession of errors was demanded and prepared, Padilla's genuine remorse for his past support of the regime deepened:

> I cried from shame. With the passing of years, I realize all too well that I was a privileged witness to horror, as well as its accomplice. . . .Whether or not I was conscious of what was going on in Cuba at

> that time, I had never taken the trouble of finding out for myself that in Cuba people were being tortured on the most preposterous pretext.

He also noted that numerous outstanding revolutionaries "who were with Fidel from the first days of the insurrection . . . were later beaten, tortured, even executed with a degree of sadism more refined and monstrous than in the worst tyrannies." As his "complicity with an authoritarian regime became evident," he recalled Koestler's warnings in 1943: "There is no excuse for you—for it is your duty to know and to be haunted by your knowledge."

It is perhaps not surprising that Padilla's remorse deepened in captivity; it was a forceful reminder of the ruthlessness of the regime, and his mistreatment contributed to a depressed, self-punitive state of mind.

Unlike many Western intellectuals who "were too taken with the delirium of a revolution" and for whom "all Cubans were inferior to Commandante Castro, the only man able to converse with history," Padilla was not beholden to such delusions. He became a critic of the regime because, unlike foreign sympathizers, he had overwhelming evidence and abundant personal experience of its brutal and confidently wrongheaded policies, and he knew personally the megalomaniacal leader who made such a favorable impression on so many. Padilla came to reject the system because as a true intellectual and writer he could not excuse or mitigate the extinction of free expression.

RAFAEL DEL PINO (1938–), who defected by plane to the United States with his family in 1987, was probably the highest-ranking Cuban defector. He left behind a distinguished military career, a status of "a national hero, with all the comforts and perks granted a General,"[7] and thirty years of service in the Cuban air force.

His career in the air force began in 1959 at an early age. Trained in the Soviet Union to fly Soviet aircraft, he played an important role in repelling the Bay of Pigs invasion in 1961. In 1966 he was appointed general director of Cubana de Aviacion, the state airline; in 1968 he was reassigned, at his request, to military duty and soon thereafter appointed second in command of the air force. In 1971 he was sent to Vietnam to observe the air war between North Vietnam and the United States. This was followed by two more trips, the last in 1975 to study American armaments and technology from the equipment captured by the Vietnamese. In 1975 Del Pino was appointed chief of the air force in the Cuban expeditionary force sent to Angola; in 1977 he became deputy commander of the Revolutionary Air Force and Anti-Aircraft Defense in charge of Cuban air space safety and control.

While loyal to the revolution and trustful of the Castro brothers, Del Pino was primarily a professional military man, not an ideologue, and had little interest in the writings of Marx: "As far as I was concerned, any direction Fidel and Raul decided to take was fine by me." Early in his career he avoided political discussions and was "naively confident that Fidel Castro would not lead the country into a totalitarian regime." He concentrated on mastering his professional training and qualifications; he saw his life as "totally devoted to perfecting my military career." It was in part this devotion to professional, military values which led to conflict between him and the political system—which for all practical purposes meant Castro, devoted to micromanaging every aspect of the government, the economy, and the military forces. Del Pino was dismayed that considerations of personal and political loyalty often trumped professional qualifications and determined personnel policy and professional advancement. He also objected to the mindless imitation of Soviet military doctrine, training, and methods. More generally he developed serious reservations about the increasingly political uses of military force motivated by Castro's desire to project his power globally.

Notwithstanding his commitment to strengthening the military forces, Del Pino grew critical of the huge investments made in building up the military: "There could be no reason for such an unbridled arms buildup when people lacked the basic necessities of life." He considered the intervention in Angola, beginning in 1975, a particularly costly and mistaken adventure, serving no Cuban interest but only those of the Soviet Union and Castro's ego.

His experiences in Angola may have initiated and deepened the process of disillusionment stretching over many years; his memoir abounds in critiques of both the purpose and conduct of that campaign:

> . . . the air force became the favorite instrument of terror of the Cuban commanders. The Angolan people were subjected to the most criminal and merciless treatment by all the high-ranking officers that paraded through the higher echelons of the Cuban forces in Angola. . . .
>
> . . . We did become a mercenary army serving the interests of Soviet imperialism. . . .

Del Pino saw the intervention in Angola and later in Ethiopia (in its war against the Somalia) equally reprehensible:

> We were to use our powerful war machine to smash an enemy that was far weaker in every sense, and then to loudly proclaim a hard-won victory, pulling wool over the eyes of our people and glorifying

> a supposedly invincible army . . . to subdue what was . . . a fairly primitive force. . . .
>
> Our military intervention in Angola ranks as one of the greatest crimes committed by Fidel Castro, not only against the Angolan people but against our own Cuban youth, whom he sent to the slaughterhouse, for no other reason but to satisfy the Napoleonic airs of his schizophrenia.

Del Pino was also scandalized by the behavior of the Cuban troops abroad, "who swept away everything they came upon, ransacking estates and towns. If there is one thing for which History will not forgive us . . . it will be for having inoculated the gentle and noble people of Angola with the poisonous viruses of pilfering and corruption."

As the intervention continued into the 1980s, he had the disturbing experience of seeing young enlisted men being flown to Angola on a troop transport plane and, barely a week later on a return flight, encountering the dead bodies of many of the same young men he had earlier seen alive:

> I was shocked to realize they were sending raw recruits into battle. . . . Now their lifeless bodies were riddled with bullet holes. I wondered how much longer the senseless killing would go on. . . . I returned to Luanda despondent, unable to think of anything during the two hours' flight back to the capital except the young boys who had been sent to their deaths.

In this case it was the visual experience that made a great and lasting impact, even on the professional military man.

It is difficult to establish exactly when the process of estrangement from the system began and how Del Pino developed ways to cope with it. Apparently for much of his highly successful career he was immersed in discharging his military duties, overlooking (or unaware of) the accumulation of evidence of corruption, incompetence, and repressiveness around him. But occasional incidents intruded and made detachment difficult, as for instance a conversation with an air force mechanic who told him he was barred from becoming a pilot because when he was five years old his parents had applied for a passport to leave Cuba, even though they changed their mind and stayed. Del Pino recalled, "What really got to me was that this kid, just as many others in similar circumstances, came to me with the conviction that I could do something to help. . . . He was far from realizing how much I hated those methods, how much it hurt me to see the hope and future of our youth dashed by that absurd, inhumane system."

One of the more unexpected of his critiques was that under Cuban communism human relationships, and the moral standards underpinning them, deteriorated in a manner far more commonly associated with the ravages of capitalism:

> . . . It is appalling to see a whole generation lost to the most insensitive individualism, an alienated generation to whom the common well-being of society means nothing. For the Cuban people, the State is Public Enemy No. 1., the one from whom to steal and the one to cheat, deceive and swindle. In their eyes, the State is responsible for their frustrations and their lack of breathing space . . . at the hands of an insane, arbitrary power structure managed by a corrupt and inefficient governing elite. . . .
>
> Theft and embezzlement within the Armed Forces have reached skyrocketing levels. The chiefs of military units have had to reassign the bulk of security personnel and now, instead of preventing uprisings and enemy attacks, they must prevent the theft of toilets, wash basins, light switches, doors, windows, tools and all kinds of government assets.

Similar manifestations of disrespect for "public property" were endemic in virtually every socialist state, especially the Soviet Union and those in Eastern Europe.

Del Pino's memoir reaffirms (if more affirmation is needed) that Castro's Cuba has maintained a high level of repression longer than many other Communist states—an important point, given some lingering Western illusions about the popular support his regime enjoys. Del Pino wrote:

> When I first read his works, I failed to realize just how accurately George Orwell had predicted . . . the catastrophic impact of totalitarian regimes on humanity. Only Fidel Castro's regime has been able to exceed the horror and despair so magnificently portrayed in . . . "1984." . . .
>
> . . . The enormous repressive apparatus created by the dictator . . . has surpassed all imaginable extremes—surprisingly enough, even those of the Soviet Union itself.
>
> For those of us who refused to continue to be accomplices . . . there remains the inescapable duty of revealing to the world the true dimensions of Castro's repressive apparatus. . . .
>
> Only North Korea, Romania and Albania come close to the Caribbean Alcatraz.

To be sure, such rankings are difficult to make. Many, including this writer, would question that Cuba has surpassed North Korea in repressiveness.

Del Pino proceeds to describe in detail the many branches, sections, and affiliates of State Security, the network of informants, the Committees for the Defense of the Revolution, the special squads and organized mobs of muscular assault troops dressed as civilians "used to repress the people while pretending to be part of the people." These groups were used, for example, to attack and beat up former political prisoners and others waiting in line for a U.S. visa.

Del Pino reproduces the questionnaire (or "informer's guide") used by informers, containing fifty-five questions. They include: the kinds of electrical appliances used by the parties spied upon, the names of friends who visit, contacts abroad, religious beliefs, whether or not the informer heard "the characteristic beep of our interference [jamming] on Radio Marti" [broadcast by anti-Castro Cubans from the United States], complaints about rationing, criticism of government figures or the telephone system, counterrevolutionary jokes, attendance at "government ordered mobilization meetings," praise for the American way of life, and many other potential indicators of political disloyalty.

The deceptiveness of the system is a recurring theme in Del Pino's memoirs. Not only did the propaganda apparatus bombard the citizens with falsehoods, strenuous efforts were also made to mislead public opinion abroad, far more vulnerable to such deceptions:

> For years it has been Castro's systematic practice to prepare internal conditions and display a "truth" for foreign visitors which differs greatly from the reality suffered by our people. On many occasions this practice has been successful, and many delegations which have visited the island for a week have returned to their respective countries preaching the wonders of the Cuban miracle.
>
> What those delegates don't know is the monumental government apparatus that pulls the strings behind the curtain to make a reality of the mirage.

Elite privilege and associated corruption further prompted Del Pino's sputtering moral indignation. For one thing, Castro treated the entire country as his personal fiefdom; he had numerous residences and his own recreational island, Cayo Piedra. In its vicinity he and his brother regularly used military aircraft to assist in their duck hunt: "the military planes had to come in low and buzz the areas where the birds were located in order to force large flocks toward the location where the elite hunters were ready with their shotguns." The practice led to a fatal crash when the birds collided with one of the planes, but public reporting of the incident was forbidden and the file of the official investigation destroyed.

Like an old-fashioned monarch, Castro was in the habit of generously rewarding his loyal officials, or he might induce loyalty by handing out expensive cars and luxurious residences.

As time went by Del Pino increasingly recognized the huge part that Castro played in the degeneration of the system: "In Cuba, the influence of Latin American caudillismo . . . compounded by the colossal ego of a man like Fidel Castro, came to worsen the totalitarianism of the system." He provides many examples of Castro's insatiable thirst for power, duplicitousness, and vindictiveness. Much of Castro's relentless anti-Americanism has been nourished by the conviction that Washington did not give him sufficient respect; but Del Pino points out that his need for respect, admiration, and submissiveness has been bottomless. In an incident in 1980 when he ordered Cuban planes to sink a Bahamian vessel (with the loss of lives of the crew) to revenge the detention of Cuban boats illegally fishing in Bahamian territorial waters, Castro said: "I want that ship sunk now! Let all those lackeys of imperialism . . . know that they can't play around with me! . . . What's important here is the political significance—let everybody know they'd better give us some respect. Plus, this is a subtle message to the Yankees to give them a taste of what to expect in case they want to tangle with us. . . . This alone is worth the cost, if any, that we might pay as compensation. . . ."

In addition to his pursuit of glory and a grand historical role, Castro's foreign adventures and interventions played an important part in maintaining his power:

> The only way to deal with the utter economic, political and social failure of the regime and avoid a catastrophe, was to maintain the extremely heavy flow of economic aid from the USSR. . . . In exchange, Cuba would, of course, have to provide more of the only thing it had been able to come up with in nearly 30 years of communism: guerrillas and full-fledged armies to carry out military operations on a worldwide scale to seize strategic positions and outposts for Soviet imperialism.
>
> After three decades of socialism, Cuba was incapable of manufacturing a simple razor blade, and its economy was practically unchanged from its 1959 sugar dependency. It had, however, been able

> to build up a vast and powerful army, ten times the size called for by its real requirements.

Del Pino was no less critical of the Soviet model, in part adopted by Cuba. His experiences in the Soviet Union made him realize the profoundly corrupting influence of the Soviet example. He wrote:

> When we Cubans first arrived in the Soviet Union early in the sixties we were very adversely affected by that society . . . it was too much of a cultural shock to watch the abysmal difference between the unproductive military breed and the rest of the population. The salary of any given member of the military surpassed by three or four times the salary of a physician, an architect or an engineer. . . .
>
> Teachers would twist history and lie to us . . . they would explain . . . that the airplane had been invented by the Russians, like the telephone, telegraph and the radio. . . .
>
> . . . Also it bothered us to be constantly spied on and that we could not move around without flashing the damned passport. . . . We could never understand why a citizen could not travel from one city to another within his own country without a passport. . . .
>
> We were extremely upset at the rampant corruption. . . . A two-star general and the Hotel Ukraina doorman would likewise trade . . . rubles for a dollar. We . . . found ourselves living in a State where the precept "every man for himself" could be Article I of the Constitution.
>
> In those days, we were far from the realization that all the madness which was enveloping us, thousands of miles from home, had already been injected into our own society.

The long inventory of iniquities raises the question—as in other cases—of how Del Pino reconciled these realizations with his long and conscientious service, and what finally led to his decision to sever all ties with the system in the only possible way, by escaping.

His memoirs suggest that a handful of incidents that created intense moral indignation and anguish triggered his decision to break with the system. Once, visiting Soviet cosmonauts were provided with "special entertainment," that is, teenage Cuban girls assigned by the authorities to prostitute themselves. Upon expressing his disgust to a high-ranking official of the Ministry of the Interior who made these arrangements, Del Pino was told that the girls were "militants of the Young Communists Union" and regarded as "ideologically advanced persons" for their cooperative attitude:

> That evening [he recalled] I realized for the first time the enormous frustration of my life. I had given up my entire youth, long years of struggle and sacrifice hoping for a more just society and the only thing I achieved was the enslavement of my people—I had simply helped deliver them to ruthless and exploitative masters. That night I could not sleep a wink. . . .

Quite possibly the most decisive incident was the unexpected revelation of his older son's disaffection in 1984, himself an air force fighter pilot, after his second period of training in the Soviet Union. This filial disenchantment may have helped confirm his own feelings, which led to Del Pino's own high-risk defection. His son reached exactly the same unspoken conclusion his father had: that the system was corrupt, repressive, and unjust, that a "new class" headed by Castro "has turned the country into their personal fiefdom." His years in the Soviet Union made him recognize that "socialism has proved to be an experiment that didn't work out." His son's disclosures made him feel "like a coward" and led him to decide that he could no longer "aid and abet those who had turned our country into their personal fiefdom."

He had to come to terms with the notion that socialism was a failure: "After years of faithfully struggling for what was believed to be a just cause, it was not easy to conclude that it had been all in vain." The sheer investment of time and energy obstructed the process of disillusionment and especially the existential conclusions to be drawn from it—a common pattern among all those who had a long-term commitment both inside these systems and abroad.

One more incident involving his fifteen-year-old son "pushed me to the brink." The boy was beaten up by an infuriated army officer for not getting inside the crowded school bus (which would not leave because the door could not be closed), but the officer was not held responsible for his behavior.

There was also his continued and "firm opposition to our military intervention in Angola [which] created problems for me with my superiors." In June 1986 he was relieved of his duties and named deputy commander of the Anti-Aircraft Defense and Revolutionary Air Force.

The decision to break with the system took several years to ripen and was, evidently, helped along by official responses to his perceived wavering and critical disposition: ". . . My refusal to attend the 25th anniversary of the Bay of Pigs victory, in protest of the absence of plaques to commemorate the 'heroic aviators who had given their lives at the Bay of Pigs,' and my open opposition to the war in Angola, were reasons more than sufficient to be labeled as 'problematical' and therefore to come under the watchful eye of military counter-intelligence." Here was a convergence between his rejecting the system and the system rejecting him—an important circumstance leading to defection and the risks it entailed for him and his family.

As is always the case, many factors combined to bring about the disillusionment of Rafael Del Pino. As a high-ranking member of the political-military elite, he acquired intimate personal knowledge of the behavior, personality, and moral transgressions of Cuba's rulers, including preeminently the Castro brothers. As a professional military man trained in the Soviet Union, he had learned about the failings of the Soviet system and the profound error of grafting its policies and institutions upon Cuba. His exposure to the war in Angola provided concrete and searing experiences of needless and pointless suffering and the waste of resources that the regime imposed on its own people and those of Angola. The disillusionment of his son, an idealistic member of the younger generation, confirmed and validated his own feelings. The growing suspicion of the authorities toward him made living with his doubts and criticisms dangerous.

Del Pino's memoirs say next to nothing about his family background and its possible influence on the development of his moral sensibilities. In the final analysis, these too were most important factors in his inability to accommodate to the misdeeds of the Cuban system.

GIOCONDA BELLI (1950–) came from a wealthy, upper-class Nicaraguan family and became a member of the Sandinista underground during the Somoza dictatorship. She spent several years in exile, mostly in Costa Rica, working for the Sandinista cause. In 1975 she was given a seven-year jail sentence in absentia by the Nicaraguan military tribunal. After the Sandinista victory in 1979 she held various positions connected with the press and mass communications and belonged to the political elite. In the end she became a resident in the United States.

As a child she was a "demure, sweet proper girl." While an adolescent she was devoted to reading, and "revolutionary dreams found fertile ground" in her mind. She finished high school in Spain and afterward took a one-year course in the United States in advertising and journalism.[8] She became an idealistic, romantically inclined woman burdened by "the guilt of privilege." Trying to recall the beginnings of her involvement in politics, she could not tell "what came first—poetry or conspiracy." Domestic life as a married woman she found "suffocating." She read a great deal of feminist literature before her political engagement: Germaine Greer, Betty Friedan, Simone de Beauvoir. "The more I read," she later recalled, "the less I was able to stomach the prospect of years and years of discussing recipes, furniture, interior decorating. . . . Saturdays at the country club bored me to tears—we were turning into our parents. . . ." She also read Fanon, Marcuse, Chomsky, and Che Guevara.

Her first marriage brought her deep dissatisfaction almost from the beginning. She had her first child when she was nineteen. Although she enjoyed motherhood, she felt the need to return to her advertising job. Her social circle consisted of bohemian free spirits with whom she shared literary interests; she was also influenced by their political attitudes: "In the artsy circles, the Sandinistas were regarded with admiration and respect." She also read books that convinced her that armed struggle and revolution were "Nicaragua's only chance." A poet friend asked her to join the Sandinistas.

One may speculate that if Belli had lived in the United States in the same period, and had a similar social background and marital experiences, she would have become a militant, radical feminist, possibly a member of a radical fringe group such as the Weathermen. But in Nicaragua at the time there was no feminist movement, and the major and obvious source of repression was the Somoza dictatorship, not the "patriarchy," not racism, sexism, or capitalism, though she was also shocked by the poverty she occasionally observed. Having joined the Sandinistas, she was "no longer a transient observer, contemplating the misery from the comfort of my car. I was now one of the people fighting it. I cared about how the people of Managua were suffering . . . and I would prove it by doing something to effect a change."

For those of a rebellious disposition, such as Belli, working with the Sandinistas to overthrow the Somoza regime was both a compelling political priority and a "way into a more meaningful existence"; it meant leaving behind her upper-class lifestyle, a stultifying marriage, and uncertainty about her role in life. The personal and the political were intertwined. She was also captivated by the romance of "the secret, quixotic life of the guerrilla"—an attraction she shared with many Western intellectuals.[9] Participating in the struggle against Somoza was not merely an undertaking to rid the country of a corrupt dictator: "I was exhilarated by the vision of our country transformed—into a land of harmony rather than great gulfs separating one man from the other."

She became intoxicated with the vision all revolutionaries share, one that combines personal and political liberation: "We couldn't help but mix the political with the personal—. . . you couldn't commit to the cause of freedom unless you freed yourself first." Throughout her involvement with the Sandinistas, both before and after they took power, there was an undercurrent of preoccupation with her identity as a woman and with the limitations imposed upon her both by a traditional society and by the Sandinista movement and government. Her refusal to accept these limitations was fueled by an ingrained rebelliousness which led her to question and reject not only the traditional social arrangements of the prerevolutionary society but also the unembarrassed sexism of the Sandinistas. She was dismayed to learn that the first Sandinista cabinet included only one woman (the minister of social welfare); she was among the women who expressed disappointment "and protested the absence of women on the list, but our objections went unheard." Later she complained about the relegation of women to administrative posts in the military forces. She was among "most of Nicaragua's revolutionary women [who] ultimately broke with the top Sandinista leaders."[10]

In 1979, on an official trip to the Soviet Union and Eastern Europe, she was struck by the fact that these socialist political systems were not eager to equalize the distribution of power and status among men and women. At the lavish Moscow mansion for her delegation, "the men were given rooms on the upper floors while I was assigned a small room on the ground floor as the 'secretary.'" During the visit she also learned about persisting inequities in the Soviet domestic division of labor. On the same occasion she visited East Germany and Bulgaria hoping to find "in the socialist systems the humanistic utopia . . . an egalitarian, just society, moved by values such as solidarity and mutual respect." While she thought people's lives were not "particularly adverse," on the other hand "the total lack of markets, shops, billboards . . . did lend a flat, shabby quality to the atmosphere." She preferred to think that "the absence of market and consumerism allowed people the freedom to dedicate their time to more transcendental pursuits," but she found herself "doubting that it was possible to be happy" in such a tightly controlled environment. Again she comforted herself with the belief that in Nicaragua it would all be different, that a formula would be found "to achieve the balance between the individual and community."

Belli's political disenchantment was furthered by unpleasant personal experiences with individual Sandinistas. Thus she wrote: "Of all the Sandinista leaders I had met, Humberto Ortega was the first who really troubled me. Without blinking an eye, he manipulated reality to suit his needs. And he did it with such conviction that sometimes I wondered if he actually believed what he was saying." On one occasion Ortega agreed with her about the poor human quality of a particular functionary and added (reminiscent of similar attitudes on the part of Lenin): "I know he is a piece of shit. . . . But if shit is what we have to make the Revolution happen, shit is what we'll use." The incident led her to conclude "that a war can be won with any class of people, but a fair, ethical system of government cannot be put in place if the people who take it upon themselves to do it lack those qualities or sacrifice those values along the way."

Her impressions of Castro, whom she met several times, were also ambivalent. While she was excited about meeting him in Cuba, "it disturbed me to see that Fidel was so inclined to meddle, so intent to playing a leading role in our revolution." She thought it was "most inappropriate of him to use his authority and prestige to induce me" to take a particular position regarding internal disputes among the Sandinistas. Castro "acted like our grandfather. We were the triumphant guerrillas that he had so often dreamt of for Latin America. . . . We sat around him . . . listening to him philosophize. . . . He felt a kind of calling to be our mentor, to guide us down the arduous path of governing a nation."

A genuine idealist, Belli repeatedly reaffirms her conviction that ends do not justify all means and that "The Revolution" is not only about political change but should also instill higher ethical values. She writes: "Remembering these events after 20 years, I realize those were the first signs of the unscrupulous political methods that later on damaged the ideals and mystique of the Sandinista cause and, in the end, led the Ortega brothers . . . not only to political but moral defeat." She recalls that "coming to power with . . . popular support . . . gave us a sense of absolute entitlement which presented a myriad of temptations." She observed the regrettable effect of power on people's behavior at the lower echelons as well, including the obsequiousness and docility of the bodyguards of the Sandinista leaders.

Gradually the temptations and corruptions of power became manifest and disturbing:

> . . . these men had been seduced by the spell of their own self-image. . . . They felt eminently astute and capable, a cross between political bright boys and heroic, strapping knights-errant. That was the attitude with which they confronted dangerous challenges that deserved . . . more cautious judgment and a maturity that the spell of power placed beyond their grasp.

The dreams of "a new kind of socialism—Nicaraguan, libertarian . . . a new kind of revolution . . . original and open, the product of a tropical, irreverent left-wing movement," receded. "With time the Revolution . . . grew more and more rigid." She also began "to question the wisdom of the Sandinista leadership" on more pragmatic grounds, and especially their bellicose anti-American rhetoric and policies. The conduct of the war disturbed her: "too many young people were forcibly recruited into the army and sent off into battle. The poor were paying the highest price. . . ." Peasants were barred from selling their products in the open market.

Belli's feelings, and her moral scruples, raise the question whether or not, and to what extent, being a woman contributed to her higher moral standards, to her heightened abhorrence of unscrupulousness. To be sure, among disillusioned men similar feelings had also surfaced, but there is nonetheless something stereotypically and honorably feminine in her reflections and soul searchings.

Belli's attitudes toward political and personal infatuations were strikingly similar. She wrote: "Because of my romantic nature and my desire to find the 'perfect man' I was easily swept off my feet, seduced by the intensity of unbridled passions." This was precisely the case during her early worship of the revolution and the perfect society it was supposed to usher in. Underlying these beliefs and hopes was "a fervent belief in the inherent nobleness of the human species." At the same time the personal and political sadly collided in her doomed relationship with a high-ranking Sandinista leader for whom matters political took precedence over the personal and emotional.

Despite her ample underground revolutionary credentials, Belli's upper-class background was held against her, it was a liability: "People like me were subtly made to feel the burden of their class origin. It was a shame . . . a primeval sin, pardoned but never fully erased from the record."

The system crudely intruded into her personal life when she was told to break off her affair with an American journalist. At the same time the love affairs of male functionaries with foreign women were condoned. She refused to comply and eventually married the American and followed him to California.

The 1990 electoral campaign of the Sandinistas was a final source of dismay and disappointment for Belli: an "incredibly tactless, obnoxious campaign." In the end she concluded that "the obsession to redeem humanity can be just as dangerous" as many other, more common obsessions and "quest[s] for immortality." She also came to recognize that "any model of society must be based on absolute respect for individual freedom."

The loss of popular support for the regimc, clearly evident in its 1990 electoral defeat, made it easier for her to find a new and less politically centered life in the United States. She maintains close personal ties with her native country and visits several times a year. Her sense of identity as a writer has also made it easier to escape her political roles and preoccupations. In Belli's case, the personal apparently trumped the political.

DAVIT WOLDE GIORGIS (1943–), a high-ranking official in the government of communist Ethiopia, defected in 1985 after serving the regime in various capacities for almost twelve years. He summed up his involvement as follows:

> I was at first an enthusiastic participant in the 1974 Revolution. I was caught up in its emotions, excited by its potential for improving life in our country. . . .
>
> The men of the Coordinating Committee of the Armed Forces gathered for the first time in June 1974 . . . with a sincere desire to bring genuine, desperately needed changes to Ethiopia. . . . I feel proud and honored today to have been a part of that beginning. . . . We worked for justice, equality, freedom and independence. . . .
>
> The stirring beginning, the blind idealism, the power struggles and manipulations, the executions, and the final sinking into a tyranny far worse than that with which we began—all these events and developments need to be recorded and critically analyzed for posterity. . . .
>
> After emotions subsided, many of us saw the impracticality of our ideals. . . .[11]

Little known in the West, Communist Ethiopia was one of the most repressive, dysfunctional, and monumentally mismanaged of all Communist states, comparable only to North Korea, Albania, and the Soviet Union during the worst years of Stalinist terror and deprivations in the 1930s.[12] Not incidentally, Ethiopia copied some of the most destructive Soviet policies, preeminently the coercive collectivization of agriculture. It also shared with North Korea, Albania, and the Soviet Union the misfortune of being ruled by an exceptionally ruthless, brutal, and megalomaniacal leader. In Ethiopia he was Haile Mariam Mengistu.

The miseries of the Ethiopian people were multiplied under Communist rule by the combination of natural disaster (drought); profoundly mistaken, doctrinaire agricultural policies (collectivization and forcible resettlement); domestic terror, and a heavy burden of wasteful and pointless wars. In fact the Communist regime was at war during most of its existence against its neighbors and ethnic minorities seeking independence. While Ethiopia received huge amounts of military assistance from the Soviet Union and Cuba, including thousands of Soviet advisers and Cuban troops, these wars were spectacularly mismanaged. Giorgis wrote: "The armed forces have been in combat for 13 straight years. The toll has been terrible. . . . The only way to get back from the front lines alive is by being wounded or captured." In 1988 in Eritrea, the demoralized, poorly led army suffered its most humiliating and costly defeat in fifteen years at the hands of a much smaller force, with ten thousand soldiers killed and five thousand surrendering, and vast amounts of equipment lost.

The price paid for the policies of the regime was staggering. Giorgis noted in 1989, "In the last 10 years, 2.6 million people have died as a result of war and famine; over 3 million have been made refugees . . . 6 million have been displaced internally; 500,000 children have been either abandoned or orphaned; and more than 400,000 people disabled, while the entire population lives in permanent poverty, fear and terror." Under these circumstances it is hardly surprising that even members of the ruling elite became disillusioned: "In the last 13 years 21 ministers, 18 deputy ministers and 26 ambassadors defected."

Why an idealistic supporter of the system such as Giorgis continued to serve it as long as he did may be more difficult to explain than his eventual disillusionment. The explanation he offers is not entirely convincing: "The question is not . . . why I or other officials stayed with the government so long, but why we had to leave it. I could have left Ethiopia earlier; but when there was still a possibility of influencing policies and decisions, I felt it would be wrong to abandon my people in their time of distress. My tragedy is that I can no longer help my people from within."

Given the wide range of inhumane and failed policies available to inspire moral revulsion the key question is which among them had the most shattering emotional impact leading to the break with the system? What particular personal experience was the most decisive in the process? The reflections of Giorgis provide partial answers.

As a young man Giorgis served in the prerevolutionary Ethiopian army between 1962 and 1968, eventually reaching the rank of major. His father was a member of Emperor Haile Selassie's government, vice minister in the Ministry of Information, and retired just before the revolution in 1974. He had worked his way up "from simple clergyman to vice-minister. . . . On his death in 1980 he was mourned in the government media as 'the father of Ethiopian journalism' and a true patriot. . . . The entire cabinet . . . came to his funeral." But after Giorgis defected, his father too was denounced as "a reactionary."

In 1969 Giorgis enrolled at Haile Selassie University where for the first time in his life he was exposed to radical political views. He graduated with a law degree, and his thesis on land reform "reflected the radicalism" he absorbed at the university. In 1975 he enrolled at Columbia University in New York in a master's program[13] where he also was influenced by the highly politicized, leftist Ethiopian student movement that advocated the overthrow of Haile Selassie and the radical transformation of Ethiopia into a socialist society. For these students "Marxism was . . . an unchallengeable truth, even if it was not understood. It generated a mass hysterical loyalty . . . every element of youth discontent was defined in Marxist terms." Giorgis observed of his time at Columbia: "I was a product of that time. I blamed the West, and especially America, for all the problems of the third world. And I saw revolution as a shortcut to development."[14]

Upon his return from the United States in 1974, after the revolution, he became close to the new Military Council in Ethiopia because of his connections with both the military and the student movements. He was appointed by the new authorities to launch a program mobilizing university and high school students to go into rural areas, educate the peasants, and "explain the benefits of the revolution." Subsequently he became deputy foreign minister. In 1979 he was sent to Eritrea as the chief political representative of the head of state and governor of the rebellious province. Between 1983 and 1985 he was head of the Relief and Rehabilitation Commission, an organization set up to deal with natural disasters. This position proved to be probably the most consequential in the evolution of his critical attitudes toward the regime. It was in this capacity that he learned firsthand of the dimensions of the famine and the scale of human suffering. In 1984 he was also appointed to the 120-member Central Committee of the ruling party. From the earliest days of the Communist government he had close ties to the supreme leader Mengistu, who personally appointed him to his various positions.

The confluence of three sets of experiences undermined his commitment: the personal qualities and governing style of Mengistu, the famine and policies associated with it, and widespread repression.

Mengistu personified everything that was wrong with the Ethiopian system and was directly responsible for its disastrous and inhumane policies. As to what conditions allowed such a repellent human being to seize power and hold it for so long (1974–1991), it is a question Giorgis does not address, except by dwelling on Mengistu's exceptional ruthlessness. He writes:

> Mengistu . . . began to manipulate events from the day the Emperor was overthrown. . . . [He] maintains his power like Stalin, through force, intrigue, and manipulation. He rules by decree, enforcing his will through small groups of loyal henchmen, secret police and terrorist squads placed in nearly every government agency. Many of his actions are motivated by a burning desire for vengeance for past wrongs, real or imagined. . . . The remotest hint of dissent is taken as a direct threat against him and dealt with at once.

These characteristics strikingly resemble those of Stalin (whom Mengistu admired), as does the personality cult Mengistu created. Officials were expected to quote his pronouncements; his speeches were printed up "in little books like the Quotations of Chairman Mao." He also loved titles: he was chairman of both the Provisional Military Administrative Council and the Council of Ministers; commander-in-chief of the Armed Forces, and general secretary of the party as well as president of the "Democratic Republic of Ethiopia." He enjoyed presiding over "forced rallies" and, according to Giorgis, persuaded himself that "the coerced cheers are the genuine sentiments of the people." It was widely known that security people watched those who were not cheering loudly enough. His political style was influenced by a 1982 visit to North Korea.

Mengistu even had to win the tennis games he played with members of his government who let him win; he expected and received "rounds of applause" from the officials who gathered to watch these games. Like Stalin, he personally corrected the final version of his biography written under his direction, which "made his life sound like the second coming of Christ."

In addition to megalomania there was also a pronounced streak of cruelty in Mengistu. Giorgis recalled that "Mengistu once confided to me that he enjoyed chairing meetings in this hall [where the former emperor used to give banquets] because he was able to sit right above the basement where all the former aristocrats, whom he despised, were imprisoned." He consolidated his power by participating in the execution of members of the steering committee of the Military Council whom he considered his enemies. They were dragged out of a meeting he himself attended, taken to the basement by his bodyguards, and shot.

On the reviewing stand "at a May Day rally he shouted: 'Death to counter-revolutionaries! . . .' He suddenly produced two bottles of blood (actually colored water) and smashed them to the ground to show what the Revolution would do to its enemies." He also ushered in the "Red Terror," which involved "arbitrary executions, lynchings, street massacres . . . many high school students were among the dead. Bullet-ridden bodies were left in the streets, or publicly exhibited. . . ."

After Mengistu ordered the execution of his former friends and associates, Giorgis "realized how excessively cruel and vengeful [he] had become. . . . From then on we feared [him]." Elsewhere he recalled that "none of us felt we were able to tell him the truth. It is a guilt that I and other public officials must live with."

The impact of repression was twofold. In the personal dimension it led to fear for one's safety and possibly one's life, a fear shared by even highly placed officials, exactly as in the Soviet Union under Stalin. There was also the suffocating awareness of living in a society dominated by fear: ". . . There is no escaping terror in your day-to-day life. At any time it could be you who is dragged out and shot, as many of my friends and acquaintances have been." The high levels of violence were especially dismaying since "the Revolution began with a famous slogan and song: 'without blood, without blood.' It was what nearly everyone sincerely wanted—a bloodless revolution."

Mengistu bore a heavy responsibility for the Ethiopian famine, not merely by introducing the disastrous policies of collectivization and forced resettlement that greatly diminished productivity, but by denying the magnitude of the problem and his initial reluctance to seek famine relief abroad. At one point he responded to Giorgis's reporting of the severity of the famine: "'You must remember that you are a member of the Central Committee. Your primary responsibility is to work toward our political objectives. Don't let these petty human problems that always exist in transition periods consume you.'" Mengistu rebuked Giorgis for his report to the UN about the famine, considering it "exaggerated" and showing "Ethiopia in a bad light because it told only of disaster and nothing of governmental . . . efforts to overcome the crisis." He and the "hard-liners toward the famine . . . either refused to believe it existed, implying that it was an insult to suggest that such a thing could happen in a Marxist-Leninist society; or they asserted that if it did exist, it was best to let nature run its course." A primitive belief in Marxism encouraged such attitudes as Mengistu observed that "the tide will turn . . . Marxism will overcome nature."

Giorgis found Mengistu "detached from reality, living in a world created by his own illusions . . . there was no place in his world for famine." For the leader, organizing and funding the immense celebration of the tenth anniversary of the revolution took precedence over the famine. These celebrations were a remarkable illustration of the gulf between official make-believe and reality:

> Four days of ceremony, banquets, elections, celebrations and parades. Four days of pageantry in the midst of horror. Everyone was forced to celebrate. . . . The people detested this show, this piece of theater that mocked their suffering. . . .
>
> People asked themselves, was all this pomp really necessary? . . . Starvation was rampant within the city. Bread lines had been getting longer every day . . . until, miraculously the arrival of foreign dignitaries brought simultaneous plenty into the capital. . . . No one was deceived, however. Everyone knew the senseless celebration was costly.

The causes of the famine were quite straightforward, as Giorgis pointed out: "the natural environment and government policies. Nature can cause food shortages, but it is often the reaction of society that creates the famine." As in the Soviet Union, "collective farming [was] the biggest reason for the national underproduction." These policies and the resulting hardships were also stimulated by the anti-religious policies of the authorities, which "in accordance with their Marxist doctrines . . . do everything possible to cut them [the peasants] off from their sources of spiritual comfort." The program required "a complete change of attitudes and values" on the part of the peasants and the destruction of their traditional communities and religious institutions: "Demoralization has been the biggest harvest. None of the 'collectivized' peasants showed enthusiasm for their land or their work. They felt they had been snatched from their homes and herded into slave camps." The state farms were also a failure, employing an "undisciplined and unmotivated workforce." Thus was the Soviet model and its disastrous consequences faithfully reproduced.

The combination of collectivization with resettlement was especially destructive. Giorgis wrote: "Perhaps the cruelest chapter of the entire famine was the resettlement program initiated by Mengistu in late 1984. This program . . . executed by Legesse Asfaw with no compassion or human decency, was aimed solely at fulfilling callous political objectives . . . another example of the regime ignoring the human factor." The resettlement program did not aim at economic development but served political and national security purposes. "Resettlement programs became our Siberia" and were "equated in the minds of people with concentration camps." An estimated 700,000 people were relocated, and in the process half or more were separated from their families. The program also served to destroy traditional religious beliefs and practices:

> There are no churches or mosques on settlement sites. The whole idea of these settlements was to create the New Society without that "opium of the masses," religion. . . . But in a country where faith is so much a part of the people's lives, they feel demoralized without it. The peasants will never be productive in the settlements. They are lost souls. They miss their communities, their land and tools, their churches and mosques, their family members.

For Giorgis, the errors and misdeeds of the regime were not abstractions or matters of hearsay but human realities he personally witnessed and experienced in various official capacities. He traveled widely in the country, organizing the famine relief and on other political missions, and he personally knew not only Mengistu but other perpetrators of terror as well, including Colonel Asfaw Zenebbe, the army officer in charge of securing Asmara in the province of Eritrea, which sought independence or greater autonomy. Giorgis called him "only one of several pathological killers who were able to rise to the top under the system of terror instituted by Mengistu."

Early in his career Giorgis learned of the brutality that became the hallmark of Mengistu's exercise of power. A group of "former officials" was under arrest in the basement of the former royal palace when Mengistu decided to execute them without judicial procedure: "The Legal Committee . . . was horrified at this turn of events" as they wished to continue with legal procedures against the prisoners. But Mengistu could not be swayed, and

> that same evening the condemned men were dragged from the Palace basement and loaded into military trucks . . . at Mengistu's order. What particularly angered many of us later was the cruel way the prisoners were executed. . . . As the first resisting prisoners were pushed down from the truck, the soldiers opened fire with machine guns. Many of the victims were still alive after the first volley . . . the wounded . . . were sprayed with bullets again and again until all were dead. They were buried in a mass grave. . . .
>
> Most educated people and revolutionaries believed that these people committed serious crimes and wanted them tried . . . but were shocked at the announcement of their sudden execution. As a young

> lawyer I was being considered for the post of one of the judges at their trial. I was terribly depressed by this event. I felt we had missed an opportunity to establish the rule of justice at the outset.

Giorgis's comment is of particular interest as it indicates the long-standing conflict between his idealism and his commitment to serve the regime notwithstanding his awareness of its crimes. While governor of Eritrea, Giorgis witnessed widespread hunger and suffering and felt especially strongly the conflict between playing the part of the loyal official and his full awareness of the living conditions of the people:

> I was expected to address the people. I got up on the podium, took the bullhorn, and tried to speak. As I saw the crowd in front of me, their faces dulled with sorrow and hunger . . . I thought: "What am I going to tell these people? The usual empty statements about the Revolution? About the bright future?" These people had no future. They did not even have a today—no food, no work, no shelter. . . . A lump came into my throat and . . . I was overwhelmed with grief . . . all I could manage to say was "My dear friends, I'll talk to you under better circumstances. . . ." I left the podium in tears. It was one of the saddest moments in my life.

In 1983, when he was head of the Relief and Rehabilitation Commission and touring the northern provinces hit by drought, it became clear to him that "Ethiopia was facing a national disaster. . . . But the political cadres I met in the villages . . . did not seem worried. These were young men between 17 and 21 who had been sent to proclaim the superiority of Marxism-Leninism and to indoctrinate the peasants. . . ." Giorgis observed the actual indoctrination session and "could see that the peasants were disgusted. Most of them were eating only once a day. . . . It made me tremble with anger to see this arrogant boy with his half-understood teachings, smugly lording it over his elders. He was blind to their most basic human needs." So was the entire political system. In the scene described, Giorgis was also offended by the disrespect shown toward the traditions and traditional beliefs of the rural population. Although he himself was a highly educated revolutionary, he apparently respected and understood the strength and virtues of a traditional society. He wrote: ". . . I learned how difficult it was to alter the life-styles of traditional societies. It is not something that can be accomplished by official fiat. . . ."

In the end it was the combination of revulsion from the policies and practices of the system *and* concern with his own safety that impelled him to leave his country:

> The thought of leaving my country had always been there, but the decision is a very painful one. If it had been possible to resign and stay . . . to contribute to the nation in a different way, I and many others would have done so. But dissenting opinions were answered by jail or execution. . . .
>
> I wasn't safe anywhere. I could be pulled out of my office or my bed at any time . . . and never heard of again. . . .
>
> . . . Something happened that finally forced my decision. I went about my job in the capitals of Europe signing agreements and meeting with donors. Then, at the end of my tour I called . . . and I was told that people had been in my house. It had been searched. . . .
>
> I had tried to put off the decision because of what it meant: the pain of exile, the status of second-class citizen in a foreign country, giving up the Revolution I had been so much a part of, living with the guilt of what I had helped bring about.

Like several other high-ranking officials discussed in this book, Giorgis managed for a long time to strike an uneasy balance between his moral impulses and misgivings on the one hand, and his commitment to the revolution and its unrealized ideals on the other. Prudential fear of betraying his feelings and antagonizing the authorities helped maintain this equilibrium. Given his opportunities for travel in Western countries, he could have defected earlier. Finally he came increasingly under suspicion and fell into disfavor; Mengistu himself accused him of various failings, even sabotage by allowing the CIA to infiltrate the relief organization he headed. The threat to his personal safety finally tilted the balance and led to his escape and open break with the system.

FIVE

Disillusionment in the West: I

As might be expected, the relationship to Communist systems and their supporting beliefs is different when sustained from a distance. Under such conditions the attraction is likely to be more idealistic, uncontaminated either by personal interest (such as sheer survival or a politically based career) or by personal experience and knowledge of the shortcomings of the system. By the same token, disillusionment too has somewhat different sources: secondhand information about formerly admired countries, particular historical-political developments affecting their political systems as well as social-political circumstances in Western societies. Sometimes the same historical event hastened or precipitated the process of disillusionment in both settings, as for example the 1956 Khrushchev speech did both in Soviet Bloc countries and in the West. Most decisive, as we shall see, were the experiences of individuals in their own Western societies, which conditioned their attitudes toward the idealized political systems or movements abroad.

While it is easier to break with a system or movement that has no control over one's life, and under circumstances when the disillusioned enjoys considerable freedom of political choice and expression, at the same time the lack of concrete, personal experience of the failings of these systems makes it more difficult to reach the breaking point. Likewise, the existence of adversarial subcultures in the West since the 1960s has made it easier to cling to beliefs and loyalties that have been discredited or undermined by historical events and experiences elsewhere.

Although for different reasons, disillusionment in the West with communism was also a lengthy, gradual, and painful process, facing as many obstacles (of a different kind) as in Communist societies. The disillusionment of Westerners has been a more complex process and requires more probing explanations. As will be seen below, personal and political circumstances are more closely intertwined in these cases than in the lives and political evolution of those who grew up in Communist states.

HOWARD FAST (1914–2003), a prolific, popular writer, was a member of the Communist Party of the United States between 1943 and 1957. He was also a regular and frequent contributor to the party paper, the *Daily Worker*; his books were translated into Russian and other languages; he was lionized in Soviet Bloc countries and received the Stalin Peace Prize. He was a major organizer of the Waldorf Conference in 1949 in New York, a large gathering of Western fellow travelers, sympathizers, and Soviet Bloc delegations. In the McCarthy era he was briefly imprisoned.

He broke with the party in early 1957 after Khrushchev's revelatory speech, but there had been other factors that had begun to undermine his relationship to the party. Before his disenchantment he exemplified the true believer:

> I came to the left-wing movement out of my own poverty and hunger and despair in the early 1930s and I came to it out of a working class background, but I joined the Communist Party in 1943 because I could no longer see any future as a writer unless I was able to wed my principles to action. . . . I felt that I had now become part of an edifice dedicated singularly and irrevocably to the ending of all war, injustice, hunger and human suffering—and to the goal of the brotherhood of man.[1]

Fast's disaffection had numerous sources. One was a long-standing reluctance to accept the party's demand for unconditional subservience and the suspension of independent, critical thinking. Like many others who eventually became disillusioned, Fast harbored a non-conformist streak; even while in the party he was considered difficult and not fully trustworthy: "During my time in the Party I had the reputation as an undependable and uncontrollable element. . . . Charges for expulsion were brought against me twelve times. . . ." He was considered by party officials as "a good front . . . an able public speaker . . . but not 'politically developed.' . . ." His relationship to the party was further exacerbated by his being a writer; he never fully accepted the party's right to censure his writings, to instruct him in matters literary, which it regularly did. Many of his books were severely criticized by the party hacks.

Because Fast was Jewish, learning about official Soviet anti-Semitism created further unease, especially Soviet denials that any specific individuals were being mistreated on such grounds. At a Soviet diplomatic reception when he inquired about the fate of the poet Itzik Feffer, a *Pravda* correspondent said to him, "Howard, why do you make so much of the Jews? That is all we hear from you! Do you think Stalin murdered no one but Jews?" The conversation took place after Stalin's death but before the famous Khrushchev speech. On another occasion Fast discussed the fate of another Jewish-Soviet writer, Leyb Kvitko, with his supposed friend Boris Polevoy, head of the Soviet writers union, on a visit to the United States. Polevoy assured him that stories about the arrest and death of Kvitko were "the usual anti-Soviet slanders." He said he was in an excellent position to refute these slanders, having lived in the same apartment house as this writer. He further reported that he had seen Kvitko before leaving for America and that he was finishing a translation; Kvitko asked him to convey "his very best regards to friends in America." After the 20th Party Congress, Fast had "learned, via a Jewish-Polish Communist paper, that Kvitko had been dead for years, beaten and executed . . . as Feffer had been." To make matters worse, Polevoy's brazen lie was told at a party Fast gave for him, one which he had characterized as suffused with "warmth, closeness and openness." Fast sadly concluded that "it was not merely that he told a tragic and grotesque lie; his invention was the summation of what the Communist Party does to a writer."

The Soviet writer's obligation to mouth official propaganda was illustrated by an incident that occurred during the Waldorf Conference. When American women who helped organize the conference demanded an explanation from the head of the Soviet delegation, the writer Alexander Fadayev, why there were no women in the Soviet delegation, he responded, "But we have solved the women question. So you see, for us it no longer presents a problem."

Another "sickening" incident occurred when the Romanian ambassador invited Fast and other editorial board members of *Mainstream* magazine (a party publication) to a stylish restaurant in New York. To Fast's consternation, the driver of the ambassadorial limousine was told to wait outside in the car; the ambassador was "horrified" at the suggestion of Fast and his comrades that he should join them.[2] In time Fast learned more about elite privileges and attitudes—and much else that was extremely disturbing—from conversations with East European diplomats and journalists in the wake of the 20th Party Congress:

> They talked. They spread . . . such a picture of terror, injustice and sheer nightmare as to make Khrushchev's secret speech appear to be a moderate outline of a never-to-be-itemized whole. . . . One of them . . . told about how the Communist leaders . . . lived—their sleek black limousines, their servants, country homes, bejeweled wives, their mistresses. . . . He talked about the crumbs left to the people. And, because he was a Jew, he talked about antisemitism.

From a Russian diplomat Fast learned of "Beria's record as a womanizer," from a Communist journalist about "Khrushchev's record of butchery," and from a foreign minister of an East European country about the brutal torture and death of old Communists.

Preceding these revelations it was Khrushchev's secret speech in 1956 that dealt the major blow: "With the appearance of this 'secret report,' the edifice I had become a part of thirteen years earlier came crumbling down in ashes—ashes of grief, horror and hopelessness." The speech became the "pivot" of his thinking and a major determinant of his subsequent behavior. He had described it as "a strange and awful document, perhaps without parallel in history. . . . It itemizes a record of barbarism and paranoiac bloodlust that will be a lasting and shameful memory to civilized man." Following the report and Fast's break with the party, "he lived with the feeling of a man who has come out of a deep and distorted dream. After long years, I have found myself. . . ."

There is a curious sequel to these confessions and soul searchings in *The Naked God*. In his much longer and more broadly autobiographical book *Being Red*, Fast's emphasis shifts from a narration of conflicts and disappointments with the party and the Soviet Union to a portrayal of his mistreatment and persecution as a Communist in the United States. This shift is further underlined by the surprising omission of *The Naked God* from the list of his previous books provided at the beginning of *Being Red*. The exclusion, combined with the main thrust of *Being Red* (indeed the title itself), suggests that by 1990 Fast might have come to feel that in *The Naked God* he went too far in rejecting his past beliefs and alignments. This is all the more likely given his later conviction that "the notion of Communism and Communists in recent years has been so maligned and distorted." Retroactive complaints about American anti-communism abound in *Being Red*. In the United States, Fast writes, "the stream of anti-Communist lies and slanders and hatred never ceased and Communists were persecuted and imprisoned." He vigorously protests the "pervasive and unending slander" that the party wished to overthrow the government "by force and violence,"[3] but he has nothing to say about the spying the party undertook on behalf of the Soviet Union. He claims that the Communist Control Act of 1954 (never implemented) "legally turned America into a police state." He even asserts "that under Truman seven very large internment camps had been built—hidden from media notice. . . ."

In *Being Red*, unlike his 1957 book, more bitterness is directed at the American authorities than at the party or Soviet authorities. In 1990 he writes: ". . . our government had turned all that we were into its opposite, and defined us as a set of murderous villains or puppets on strings held by Moscow." In the same book he habitually refers to "government terror" exercised by American authorities in the McCarthy period, and goes as far as to suggest that "the Rosenberg case had been orchestrated to an anti-Communist frenzy that matched the exuberant hysteria of the Nazi horror."

In *Being Red*, descriptions of the party and its newspaper are also far more positive. Now Fast feels called upon to defend the party against "all the lies and slanders." Party members were "brave and incorruptible" though also "rigid, insensitive and stupid." But "cruelty [and] harm to other human beings" was always alien to the party. He recalls that "when I found the Communist Party, I joined the company of the good"; the members were "priests of the brotherhood of man." In these more recent recollections, the *Daily Worker* becomes "a newspaper of courage and independence unmatched on the American scene, and for all the . . . accusations that we merely echoed the Soviet line, was independent." In the same sentence he characterizes the *Daily Worker* as both "a small and gallant newspaper . . . [that] fought for the poor and the oppressed" and one that "had slavishly supported every action of the Soviet Union." In effect he proposes that fighting against oppression in the United States was compatible with supporting it in the Soviet Union. The Waldorf Conference is described as by no means a pro-Soviet undertaking; the Russians "had no part in it."

Unlike in *The Naked God*, here Fast emphasizes his desire "not to be overjudgmental." Thus the recollection of a corrupt party official gives way to reflections about general corruptions of power or "the rot of people who possess power." The United States and the Soviet Union under Stalin (and after) become morally equivalent in matters such as the character of the KGB and the FBI, travel controls, and the unfortunate qualities of people in power in both Moscow and Washington.

Fast also adds a new dimension to Khrushchev's secret speech (absent from his comments in 1957), seeing it as a manifestation of "courage and integrity." He contrasts it favorably with post–Nazi Germany, which produced no such document "and lacked the will and courage to do so." Here he overlooks (or is unaware of) the enormous efforts of the German Federal Republic to make amends for the Nazi past, including compensation to Jewish survivors of the Holocaust, memorials to its victims, and the continued ample documentation and teaching of the evils of Nazi Germany—efforts which had no parallel in the post-Stalin Soviet Union or even in post-Communist Russia regarding the evils of Stalinism and communism.

He is reluctant to dwell on details of the Khrushchev speech ("there is no use in trying to sum up the contents of the speech; it is an awful and terrifying list of infamies, murders, tortures and betrayals") while inching closer to a less judgmental view of the Stalin era itself. Thus he writes that "today, I look back on it [the speech] with great sorrow, but with some understanding of the forces that created the situation and some knowledge of what an awful price mankind pays for a small step forward. . . ."

In the end Fast sees himself as maligned both by his former Soviet friends and American comrades and by the authorities and media in his own country. He is not sure if he regrets "those years in the Communist Party" or whether he would do it again. He found in the party "ambition, rigidity, narrowness and hatred" as well as "love, dedication and high courage and integrity."

Howard Fast's drawn-out grappling with his past political beliefs and commitments and his back-pedaling from the unqualified rejection of 1957 to the more ambiguous rethinking of 1990 is a reflection of the difficulty of making a total, definitive break with a cause and belief system which has demanded an enormous emotional investment over a long period of time. Howard Fast remained (or became, with the passage of time) eager to reclaim his old idealism and the purity of its goals even while admitting that the means of achieving them were flawed, as were the human beings who devised them. Apparently too much of Fast's life was devoted to the party, the support of the Soviet Union, and the ideals these two entities were associated with to allow for an unconditional break. He could not purge his life and past of these commitments without, in effect, acknowledging that a large part of his life had been wasted and misspent in the service of morally repugnant forces and organizations, in the thrall of ideals that were either unattainable or altogether wrongheaded, or both.

Fast's reconsideration and modification of his earlier rejected beliefs reflect the understandable desire of an individual to find in his past some vindication for his life as a whole and for the choice of the causes he once embraced. He could no more completely expunge aspects of his political commitments than the Soviet system after Stalin could truly and thoroughly de-Stalinize itself. In one case the unrestrained admission of past criminal policies was incompatible with preserving the legitimacy of the system, in the other with preserving the meaning, integrity, and sense of identity of the individual believer.

DAVID HOROWITZ (1939–) is the rare 1960s radical who has made a complete and public break with his political beliefs and attitudes and become a vocal anti-radical, in a manner somewhat reminiscent of Arthur Koestler. He has also become, as he puts it, "the most hated ex-radical of [his] generation,"[4] having earned the enmity of his former fellow radicals and all those who harbor sentimental recollections of the 1960s.[5] A generation earlier Koestler experienced similar disapproval: "I remember how at a New York cocktail party . . . a lady journalist of obvious sincerity attacked me with some vehemence. . . . The gist of it was that people who had once been Communists should shut up or retire to a monastery or a desert island instead of going 'round teaching other people lessons.'"[6] Kingsley Amis (*before* his own conversion from fellow traveler to vocal anti-Communist) memorably articulated the contempt and the stereotype the anti-Communist convert inspired:

> To have been a Communist and to have served the Soviet Union and to have turned against it, are, in themselves, passwords to fame and fortune. Announce that you have repented and are prepared to reveal the horrors of Communism, and a swarm of journalists will be on your doorstep . . . lucrative invitations will reach you from glossier magazines, and the FBI will seek your cooperation in rooting out spies and traitors. Your past sins will be forgiven; safe from prison yourself, you may play your part in destroying your old friends. No wonder that thoughtful people tend, on principle, to dismiss the testimony of informers. . . ."[7]

Horowitz aggravated these hostile preconceptions by taking an aggressive, confrontational stance: ". . . By the time I reentered the political battle, I had made a decision to speak in the voice of the New Left—outraged, aggressive, morally certain. I would frame indictments as we had framed them, but from the other side." His polemical style was the lesser provocation compared to what he stood for—the uncompromising rejection of all that a generation of radicals and leftists cherished: a highly flattering self-conception of youthful idealism and compassionate commitment to social justice and solidarity.

Like Koestler, Horowitz engaged in prolonged and highly personal political soul searching, and he too felt marginalized. There have also been important differences: Koestler's allegiance was to the Communist party and the Soviet Union whereas Horowitz (like other sixties radicals in the United States) considered himself a "new leftist." These radicals bypassed the Communist party and the Soviet Union and turned their attention to other, Third World Communist countries such as Cuba, China, and Vietnam, which they regarded as more authentic revolutionary societies than the Soviet Union.

Horowitz, unlike Koestler, came from a leftist family. He was a typical "red-diaper baby," the child of a generation of American Jews who fervently embraced Communist beliefs in the 1930s and joined the American Communist party.

Horowitz's thorough disenchantment with leftist beliefs may also be plausibly attributed to a delayed rebellion against his parents, his father in particular, and the subculture they belonged to. It was a highly structured, rigid subculture, something very tangible to rebel against. Horowitz writes: "Looking back I see that there is a way in which my entire youth was a form of quarantine. There was the protective environment of our political community. . . ."

He was raised by parents as zealous and dogmatic in their beliefs as some Christian fundamentalists. He recalls:

> What my parents had done in joining the Communist Party and moving to Sunnyside [a New York City neighborhood] was to return to the ghetto. There was the same shared private language, the same hermetically sealed universe, the same dual posture revealing one face to the outer world and another to the tribe. More importantly, there was the same conviction of being marked for persecution and specially ordained, the sense of superiority toward the stronger and more numerous goyim outside. And there was the same fear of expulsion for heretical thoughts, which was the fear that riveted the chosen to the faith.

He understood early in life that his parents' "political religion was really the center of their moral life." At home "the dinner table was a zone of political engagement."

The parental subculture required frequent meetings ("my parents attended four and five political meetings a week for as long as I could remember"), summer camps for the children, and politicized entertainments. Young Horowitz attended "Sunnyside Progressive School . . . a Party creation" and belonged to the "Sunnyside Young Progressives" club in junior high school. He went to the Wo-Chi-Ca summer camp (an acronym for "Workers Children Camp") "for children of the Communist Party," where the children were entertained by Paul Robeson and Pete Seeger. There were "ritual family outings" to a movie theater that showed the latest Soviet films, including one that "documented" American germ-warfare atrocities in Korea. At home the *Daily Worker* was delivered and bookshelves were filled with the likes of *Stalingrad*, *Scottsboro Boys*, *The Plot Against Peace*. He recalls that "almost all conversation in our household was political."

His father had the prototypical attributes of the true believer:

> He was a Marxist, and apparently could not face the possibility that life might be a puzzle without a solution. . . . Having embraced the truth of Marxism, he was convinced he had discovered the key to life's important questions. . . .
>
> Political utopians like my father had a master plan. They were going to transform the world from the chaos we knew into a comfortable and friendly place. In the happy future they dreamed about there would be an end to grief from life out of control grinding you down. . . . Human cruelty would go out of style and become a memory. . . . In my father's paradise there would be no strangers. No one who felt like an outsider, *alienated* from others and at odds with themselves. . . . Fusion and unity—this was the cry of my father's Communist heart. His unquenchable longing to belong.

After the death of Stalin, Horowitz's father felt compelled to summarize the great man's achievements.

As has generally been the case, the rejection of political faith and commitment for Horowitz was gradual and proceeded through several fairly distinct stages. First, Horowitz rejected his father's rigid, conspiratorial old-leftism or pro-communism—doubtless as part of a generational conflict. At the same time, as was the case with other "red-diaper babies," the family political background predisposed him to turn to the New Left. Old and New Left did share several basic postulates and ideals of Marxism; most important, both abhorred capitalism, were suspicious of liberals, and entertained great hopes for a sweeping transformation of human societies and beings. Marxism, or at any rate its most general ideals and aspirations, appealed to both generations. As Horowitz noted, "The secret of Marxism's appeal was, ultimately, its conjuring power, its fantastic vision that there could be a world different from the one we inhabited."

The New Leftists' social backgrounds and positions greatly differed from those of the old left: they were far more privileged than their parents, let alone their grandparents. Consequently they were also far more individualistic, undisciplined, and hedonistic, and more inclined to believe that revolutionary social-political change was easy to accomplish if only it was desired strongly enough.

The second stage of Horowitz's political disillusionment was much longer and more difficult than the first as it entailed a slow and painful disengagement from the New Left and a way of life with a community of like-minded people. During this phase he still tried to cling to socialist ideals while dissociating them from the movements and the individuals he became intimately familiar with during his years in London and in Berkeley, California.

In the final stages of his disillusionment he gave up on socialist ideals and theories altogether and concluded that Marxism shared responsibility both for what happened in the "actually existing" socialist states and for the degeneration of leftist movements and ideals in the West.

Arguably the single major trauma of Horowitz's political engagement resulted from his long and close association with the Black Panthers and from his gradual realization that they were, for the most part, a gang of thugs engaged in a wide variety of criminal activities, especially drug dealing and pimping (for example, "the pimps had taken out a contract on Huey's [Newton] life because he was shaking them down"). There was also a "disturbing revelation concer[ning] a school benefit night. . . . Afterward a group had been invited to the penthouse to snort cocaine. When a dealer was summoned to replenish the supply, Newton gave him $3,000 in cash—the entire proceeds of the benefit." Several times Horowitz had seen Newton and other Panthers stoned on drugs.

As is always the case during the process of political reassessment and disenchantment, past events and experiences are seen in a new light. Horowitz "began to review events of the past to which . . . I paid little attention before, like the expulsion of Jews from the civil rights movement in 1966." The Panthers, like many black radicals, were anti-Semitic, and Horowitz was now more aware of this.

Despite their liabilities, the Panthers capitalized on the prevailing political ethos (especially of campus communities) and the sympathy and support of white liberals and radicals. As Todd Gitlin (another former sixties radical who has retained some of his past beliefs) wrote, "The Panthers were streetwise, disciplined, fearless, Marxist-Leninist, revolutionary and, most miraculously of all . . . they welcomed white allies." Whether or not they were all this, they were certainly *seen* as having these attributes by their white admirers. They also skillfully manipulated white guilt over racism.

What finally put an end to Horowitz's romance with the Panthers was his discovery and accumulating circumstantial evidence that they, his "political comrades," murdered a decent woman (Betty Van Patter) who worked for them at his recommendation. The murder not only ended his involvement with the Panthers, it also deepened his disillusionment with the left as a whole when it remained profoundly indifferent:

> This silence was more than unusual for people who normally felt compelled to protest injustices—even those which took place at the far ends of the earth. In the past they hadn't hesitated to identify good and evil in regions they could hardly locate on the map. Or to express indignation, if only the political symbolism was right. . . . There were no protests for Betty. No one called for an investigation. . . . A political activist working for the Black Panther Party had been murdered but because the suspects were the Panthers themselves, it didn't matter. . . .

There was another explanation for this indifference. The Panthers were the enemies of the government, and the government—the authorities, the police—represented self-evident evil: "This idea of government evil was even more important to the self-image of the Left than was the preservation of the Panther legend. The specter of the oppressor was what kept the Left's innocence intact and fed its indignation."

After the murder, Horowitz "ceased to be politically active" and began to ask himself "whether there was something in Marxism, or in the socialist idea itself, that was the root of the problem." In this inquiry he was influenced by the writings of Leszek Kolakowski as well as Solzhenitsyn. His emerging critique of Marxism combined with the unraveling of his faith:

> If it was necessary to "seize power" and "smash the state," the individuals who rose to the fore in revolutions were likely to be fanatics with an aptitude for violence. . . . My own political experience con-

> firmed the rule. In volatile situations the momentum was always seized by those most certain of their conviction, least impressed by ambiguity and most ready to take risks or manipulate facts to achieve their objectives.

Horowitz arrived at the classical anti-utopian position resting on the recognition that human nature imposes significant constraints on all highly ambitious and idealistic projects of social-political transformation: "Betty's death killed this fantasy in me. There was no revolutionary community. There would be no redemptive future. THERE IS NO ONE TO SAVE US FROM WHO WE ARE. . . . For the first time in my conscious life I was looking at myself in my human nakedness, without the support of revolutionary hopes, without the faith in a revolutionary future."

Another traumatic event capped his estrangement from the radical left: the suicide of Fay Stender and the left's reaction to it. Stender had been an attorney for Huey Newton and George Jackson but was expelled from the defense team by the defendants and other black radicals. Years later she was "shot by a member of Jackson's prison gang and paralyzed from the waist down" for allegedly betraying Jackson and the prison movement. Those attending her funeral service resolutely refused to reflect on the larger political meaning of her death and its connection with the character of the black radicals she had been involved with.

Other experiences and incidents further eroded Horowitz's beliefs but lay dormant until the more traumatic experiences noted above. For instance, in his late teens Horowitz had been troubled in reading a passage by Lenin which proposed that "it was necessary to lie in order to advance the revolutionary cause." The issue was of particular relevance since at the time the Rosenbergs insisted on their innocence, though there was nothing reprehensible from the point of view of Communist morality about spying in the interest of the Soviet Union. It was a classical dilemma of ends and means which at the time did not detain the young Horowitz for long but was recalled much later.

Khrushchev's 20th Party Congress speech was not only a milestone in the history of Soviet communism but a major occasion for soul searching among all supporters of the Soviet system inside or outside the Soviet Bloc. Many American Communists, including Horowitz's parents, left the party as a result while continuing to nourish varying amounts of residual commitment. Horowitz came to see the humiliation of his parents by the speech as his "formative" political experience, which made him determined "never . . . to be involved in a similar complicity." Horowitz and his cohort believed they "could create a new socialist vision free from the taint that Stalin had placed on the movement our parents served." Likewise he felt obligated—like one of his early intellectual-political mentors, Ralph Miliband—to embark on an "intellectual mission . . . to rescue Marxism from the Stalinist debacle." While Horowitz abandoned this effort, Miliband persisted till the end of his life.

Horowitz records numerous other reservations he had about the Movement which did not decisively affect his commitment at the time. Among them was the widespread use of "pigs" applied to policemen. He "had an uneasy feeling about the term" but "forced" himself "to take the hard line defending its use, convinced that this was the mark of a serious revolutionary. If the police were the armed forces of the class enemy, to shrink from calling them 'pigs' was to shrink from the task itself." It was another example of overcoming moral reservations while his political commitments and convictions were still largely intact.

He also found "alarming" the "uncritical admiration" of the Vietnamese Communists and other Third World radicals and was made "uncomfortable" by Tom Hayden, Jane Fonda, and Ralph Schoenman urging American troops to desert. In retrospect he recognized that hostility toward the United States and the desire for revolution were intertwined: "Vietnam served to justify the desire; we needed the war and its violent images to vindicate our destructive intentions."

As an editor of *Ramparts* magazine, he commissioned a review of Solzhenitsyn's *The Gulag Archipelago* and was taken aback by an incensed letter from Saul Landau (a major and durable supporter of Castro) who reproached him for giving space to Solzhenitsyn and for allowing the Russian's "'sensational' claims to distract attention from America's atrocities in the Third World." There was also the matter of the lifestyle of some of his comrades in the movement, as for example Warren Hinckle, editor-in-chief of *Ramparts*, and Robert Scheer, the editor, who paid himself a salary three times that of the staff writers and "five times what the black receptionist made." *Ramparts* editors enjoyed "six-martini editorial lunches at Vanessi's restaurant in San Francisco, junkets at the Algonquin in New York and first-class airfare. . . ." The extravagant lifestyle of Huey Newton and other Black Panther leaders he also found distasteful.

Horowitz's explicit "farewell to the left" was conveyed in a December 1979 article in *The Nation*, much of which dealt with his loss of belief in the "Marxist promise" and his rebuke to his fellow radicals for their double standards and refusal to confront and condemn the "catastrophes" created by various leftist regimes around the world. He was no longer "guided by a vision of the future in which an unjust world would finally be put to right. It was the prism through which I judged the reality around me, and whose spectrum provided the justification for everything I did."

In several passages in his autobiography, Horowitz raises the question of the relationship between the "personal and the political," more specifically between personal grievance and the embrace of radical politics:

> If radicalism was a displacement of personal grievance, it was not surprising that radicals could not confront their interior lives. New Left radicals favored the slogan "the personal is political," but the intention behind it was not introspective. The phrase expressed, rather, their totalitarian agenda to CONTROL the personal in order to make utopian politics work.

Tom Hayden, a largely unrepentant sixties radical, apparently exemplified the displacement noted above. His "radicalism seems to have sprung full-blown from what Irving Howe described as 'an obscure personal rage.' The son of an alcoholic father with whom he was not on speaking terms, Tom was indeed an angry man who seemed in perpetual search of enemies." Howe further observed of Hayden that "if he had the power and believed it necessary, he wouldn't hesitate to put me against the wall and have me shot. That done, he might shed a tear for my miscreant social democratic soul."[8]

Writing about another radical, Horowitz suggests that "Whatever rage was rolling inside him came from psychological layers so deep that he himself had lost contact with them. As in Bernardine's [Dohrn] case the bitterness he felt had little to do with anything that could have been inspired by the world outside." This of course is the key question: was the great bitterness felt by these individuals inspired by the world outside, and if so, by what particular injustice? Horowitz observes:

> If the Left was primarily motivated by the desire to "make the world better," why was it so indifferent to the consequences of its efforts? What else could explain its lack of concern about the deeds of its liberators in Indochina, or its Panther vanguard at home? Its disinterest in whether socialism WORKED or not? The more I thought about the moral posturing of the Left, the more I saw that its genius lay not in reforms but in framing indictments. Resentment and retribution were the radical passions.

Those characterized in this passage would argue that they were not indifferent to the consequences of their efforts, whether in Indochina or the United States, but were more concerned with the crimes of their government than the policies of the Communist authorities in Vietnam.

Since Horowitz is one of only a handful of prominent disillusioned sixties radicals, it is not easy to link his case with larger patterns of behavior. "Defections" of his kind were unusual. Most "red-diaper babies" did not reject the politics of their parents or their peers and retained varying degrees of loyalty and reverence for their youthful political beliefs. Many *moderated* their beliefs, but few rejected them categorically and publicly as Horowitz did. What made the difference in his case and the handful of others here discussed?

Essentially the question is why human beings of apparently similar backgrounds, educational attainments, and social locations turn out to be different. It is a question similar to that which seeks to explain why among the many slum-dwelling young males brought up in impoverished broken homes by an uneducated parent, most will not become a juvenile delinquent or professional criminal. Sociologists can suggest only probabilities or tendencies in group behavior, not individual causation. The latter is the domain of psychologists.

There are probably three explanations of why so few sixties radicals renounced their political beliefs. First, because their political activism and their youth overlapped; discarding their political ideals and activities would have amounted to renouncing their youth and youthful idealism. Second, this was a genuine mass movement, nurtured by well-defined, supportive settings (the campus), which made it easy to cling to old, shared ideals and beliefs. Third, the social and cultural sources of adversarial attitudes and sentiments persisted after the Vietnam War, benefiting from their association with the civil rights and women's liberation movements.

Aside from the intangibles of personality, some specific explanations may be suggested for Horowitz's attitude change. The most obvious are his experiences with the Black Panthers and the fact that they were responsible for the murder of a person who was close to him. Moreover it seems that he had an unusual amount of experience of the thuggishness and corruption of the Panthers.

The troubled relationship with his father is another likely though more indirect source of his attitudes. This relationship might have contributed a readiness to question authority and doctrinaire dispositions, including those associated with the radical movements and their ideologies.

In a private communication[9] Horowitz disputed the notion that the Panther experience was especially important. He did not comment on the suggestion that his relationship to his father played a part. He did, however, write that "maybe I was more religious in my commitment to the radical faith than others (but I don't think so) and therefore felt more betrayed when it failed." But there were many people with similarly strong beliefs who did not feel betrayed when these ideas failed, or refused to conclude that they had failed. Moreover a persuasive counterargument could be made that the stronger the faith and commitment, the harder and more painful it is to abandon them, and the deeper the emotional investment, the more compelling the need to persevere in support of the cause.

RONALD RADOSH (1937–) was also among the handful of sixties radicals who undertook a full-scale political soul searching which he combined with a demystification of the period.[10] Among the recent generation of true believers, very few have been willing to engage in the kind of public confession and unhesitating disavowal of political misjudgments that an earlier generation of pro-Soviet intellectuals and fellow travelers were capable of.

The darker sides of the 1960s remain to be fully chronicled and explored.[11] Radosh's searching self-examination[12]—against the background of the political struggles in which he participated—sheds light on what went wrong, notwithstanding the high levels of idealism that burst forth at the time. In particular Radosh helps us understand why so many of the beliefs and attitudes of the period survived and found their way into major cultural, educational, and political institutions and the mind-set of educated Americans. These overlapping phenomena include political correctness, racial preference, radical feminism, identity politics, the cult of victimhood, postmodernism, critical legal theory, grade inflation, the dumbing-down of the curriculum, and a primitive hostility to science.

Radosh's account illuminates not only his own unusual political journey but also the stubborn persistence of political commitments and attitudes among his former comrades in arms. As co-author of the study demolishing the myth of the innocence of the Rosenbergs,[13] Radosh was in a unique position to learn firsthand the fury of true believers when their articles of faith are called into question. He sheds further light on the emotional determination of political attitudes and on their adversarial roots: the simpleminded "Which side are you on?" mattered far more for most of the protagonists he describes than truth or falsehood, reality and illusions. This mind-set was strikingly revealed in the refusal of people who agreed with him in private to support him in public, especially in regard to the Rosenberg affair. Not only was Radosh vilified by radicals, but "democratic socialist intellectuals" too refused support when he asked for their comments for the jacket of his book. Michael Harrington, whose organization Radosh belonged to at the time, said: "I always knew they were guilty . . . but we are trying to get former Communists . . . into our organization and I can't do anything to alienate them." Irving Howe turned him down saying, "I can't get involved in that."[14]

Radosh traces the evolution of his political attitudes from early childhood. He was a bona fide "red-diaper baby," born to parents of strong leftist convictions. Many readers will be surprised to learn how highly structured and well defined a political subculture the old Communist left created. Besides the American Communist party and its numerous front organizations, there were party-controlled schools, summer camps, unions, and cultural-recreational organizations that created and sustained this subculture. Radosh went to one of them, Camp Woodland, as a child and later worked there as camp counselor. Among his fellow campers were the two sons of the Rosenbergs. Later on he was an activist in the "Labor Youth League," a major front organization. He also attended what was then known as "the little Red Schoolhouse," a high school in Greenwich Village which had on its faculty a high concentration of teachers who were either Communist party members or committed fellow travelers. A list of the graduates of the school "reads like a Who's Who of the Children of the Old Old Left."[15] They include Victor Navasky (former publisher of *The Nation*), Angela Davis, Kathy Boudin, the Rosenberg sons, and other eminent figures of what became the New Left in the 1960s and '70s. Radosh also took a course given by Herbert Aptheker ("dean of the party historians") at the "Communist Party's educational institution named—of course—the Jefferson School of Social Science."[16] In the course of his involvement with radical movements and causes, he came to know many prominent activists and leftist political figures of the period, including Paul Berman, Eric Foner, Abbie Hoffman, Tom Hayden, Bianca Jagger, Saul Landau, Herbert Marcuse, Bertell Ollman, and I. F. Stone.

Radosh's recollections also help identify the often overlooked connections and continuities between the old and New Left. While organizationally much of the New Left did move away from the American Communist movement, there remained an unmistakable political affinity between the generations; for example, Bettina Aptheker, the daughter of Herbert Aptheker, the prominent ideologue of the American Communist party, became a prominent West Coast radical student activist in the 1960s. She also boasted in the Berkeley student newspaper (*Daily Californian*) of her membership in the party: "I have been for a number of years, I am now, and I intend to remain a member of the Communist Party of the United States. . . . It is time to affirm the right to be a Communist."[17]

Vivian Gornick's *The Romance of American Communism* (cited earlier) exemplifies the sentimental reaffirmation of a bond between old-line American Communists and the sixties generation that Gornick represented. Even those among the sixties radicals who did not follow in their parents' footsteps retained a sentimental appreciation of the party and what it stood for (as, for example, Eric Foner, the historian).

Once more the question arises, Why have there been so few people like Radosh (and David Horowitz, Peter Collier, Eugene Genovese, or Julius Lester) who have succeeded in divesting themselves of these beliefs and willing to admit this in public? Why have so few chosen to examine the evolution of their political identity and the roots of their disillusionment? It is far less mysterious why so many became radicalized in the 1960s than why so few made a public break with these attitudes in the decades that followed.

Besides acknowledging that human behavior is generally hard to explain and predict, there is a plausible sociological explanation of the persistence of the sixties worldview. Unlike earlier periods when pro-Soviet and pro-Communist sympathies were far more often emphatically abandoned (as chronicled, for example, in *The God That Failed*), the beliefs of the 1960s were far more widespread. They were supported by a critical mass, especially on and around college campuses; it was more comfortable and less problematic to maintain wrong-headed political beliefs when they were widely and vocally shared by like-minded people (often of the same generation) living in close proximity. No similarly extensive and entrenched subcultural, communal group support existed for the pro-Communist commitments of the 1930s or early '40s; party loyalists were a much smaller and more isolated group. Moreover these earlier beliefs were easier to discredit because of their close association with a hostile foreign power, the Soviet Union. While many among the radicals of the sixties idealized Mao's China and Castro's Cuba, those systems were not as widely and profoundly discredited as the Soviet Union became after Stalin's death and later, after the continued revelations during Gorbachev's *glasnost* and finally in the wake of the Soviet collapse in 1991.

Preserving the sixties worldview (to which an increasingly reflexive rejection of American society was central) was also easier because it was bolstered by idealistic beliefs and movements: anti-war, civil rights, women's liberation, and later environmentalism.

Why did Radosh become disillusioned when most of those around him did not, or not to the same degree? Broadly speaking, political disillusionment originates in perceiving and being troubled by a discrepancy between idealistic expectations and their flawed fulfillment. Many individuals become aware of such discrepancies but succeed in convincing themselves that they do not undermine or taint the great goals pursued, that even a flawed movement, cause, or ideology is preferable and deserves support.

For reasons hard to detect and explain, some people are more sensitive to such disparities than others, who feel that preservation of a political commitment at all (moral) costs is more important and central to their sense of identity. People also differ in their capacity to withstand the social pressures of their setting or community toward commitment and conformity. There is also the matter of experience: some succeed in sheltering themselves from disillusioning experiences more ably than others. But most important is the apparently widespread determination to preserve important, long-held, identity-giving beliefs and worldviews. Conversion experiences are rare and usually occcur under highly depriving conditions and pressures, as in the case of inmates serving long prison sentences in the United States who come to embrace fundamentalist religious beliefs (Christian or Muslim).

Several events and experiences led to the erosion of Radosh's political beliefs. As in other cases, the process was halting and gradual, extending over years. The beginnings of his doubts were apparently stimulated by the extreme, shrill, and less than fully rational attitudes and behavior of many radicals he knew: "We [including his wife] seemed to find shrill and almost pathologically crazy behavior wherever we looked on the left."[18] It may be recalled here that the political currents of the sixties merged with apolitical and self-indulgent thrill-seeking attitudes and activities involving drugs, promiscuous sex, and mind-numbing music.

Radosh's trip to Cuba in 1973 was the first important and specific stage in the process of his disillusionment. Like most of those associated with the New Left, Radosh revered Castro and believed that Cuba represented an authentic socialist revolutionary system, embodying all the attractions the Soviet system had lost. But as happened to André Gide during his visit to the Soviet Union—but to hardly anyone else well known on similar conducted tours—Radosh found unexpected blemishes and flaws in Cuba. Like Gide, he noted with dismay the difference between the way he and his fellow political tourists were fed and accommodated and the more typical diet and housing of Cubans. He was also horrified by the working conditions and neglect of worker safety in a refrigerator and cigar factory where he and his group were taken. He was not convinced by the manager's response: "If it [working conditions] were dangerous, Fidel would have informed us. Masks would cut down production, and we are certain that what we are doing is safe." Radosh was further disturbed by learning about production quotas determined by the authorities without any input from the workers. He was shocked to learn that homosexuals were confined in a mental hospital and that lobotomization was widely practiced. He was not reassured by the explanation of the tour group leader: "We have to understand that there are differences between capitalist lobotomies and socialist lobotomies."[19]

But the group leader quoted above put her finger on something important concerning the attitude of the true believers on conducted tours (and in general): they were capable of a reflexive reinterpretation of social and empirical realities, evaluating the same phenomena differently depending on their context—a process also observed by other former true believers and sympathizers such as Arthur Koestler, Wolfgang Leonhard, and Malcolm Muggeridge.[20] The historian Gertrude Himmelfarb has written of this mentality: "The marvel was not that there should be parks, hospitals, factories [in the Soviet Union]; after all these could be found in England as well. The marvel was that they should all . . . be inspired by a collective ideal, a single moral purpose."[21]

Radosh's fellow tourists in Cuba found ways to explain away whatever might have seemed problematic or disturbing: the lack of affirmative action to correct past racism (no need for it in a socially just society); the dilapidated buildings of Havana (they had charm); what in the United States would have been sternly condemned as the sexist display of female bodies when it occurred in a Havana nightclub ("What's wrong with a woman showing her body and moving it on stage?" a feminist in his group said).[22]

Radosh was also disturbed by Castro's support of the Soviet invasion of Czechoslovakia in 1968, and that too isolated him from his fellow tourists who could not bring themselves to condemn it. The trip prompted him "to rethink . . . my most fervently held assumptions. It was an accumulation of small things that began to push doubts into the forefront of my thinking."[23] Subsequently he wrote an article about his experiences and impressions in Cuba which prompted a flood of "bitterly hostile" letters to *Liberation* magazine where it was published. These hostile responses to the article and to other expressions of his increasing doubts within the radical-left subculture helped distance him from his earlier beliefs and the people who upheld them.

Radosh began a search for more moderate political positions "working for incremental change" and joined various organizations before his complete break with earlier beliefs and goals. It was his involvement with the Rosenberg case, also in the early 1970s, "that began my slow motion exit from the left." When he began a book about them, he was as much a believer in their total innocence as the rest of the old and New Left; as a child he had attended their funeral with his parents. He joined the movement to rehabilitate them (in particular the National Committee to Reopen the Rosenberg Case) in the same frame of mind as other true believers in their innocence and in the good of their cause. (It was a peculiarity of the Rosenberg supporters that they at once indignantly rejected the charges of spying while tacitly taking the position that spying on behalf of the Soviet Union, and helping it equalize its position with the United States by acquiring the atomic bomb, was a good cause.) While Radosh "hoped and expected that the files would provide enough hard data to prove a frame-up" and "a major miscarriage of justice," the opposite occurred: it became clear that they were guilty as charged. He revealed these findings first in an article in the *New Republic* and later in a book. It was the end of his acceptance by his former political community, even by friends who "made it clear that that they were shocked by what I had done." One of them suggested that he should have written "a book that would show Julius Rosenberg to have been a spy, while at the same time explaining 'sympathetically' that the Rosenbergs saw their espionage as 'entirely in the best interests of the American people.' . . ." Another good friend told him: "'Even if it was true you should not say this, because you're helping the other side.' And others would say quite bluntly: 'The facts are irrelevant. We need the Rosenbergs as heroes.'"[24]

The Rosenberg case and the left's response to his findings led him to "the ultimate heresy: perhaps the Left was wrong not just about the Rosenberg case, but about most everything else."[25]

With the Rosenberg book Radosh became "the new enemy" of the left. From then on it was no longer only his own attitudes that determined his affiliations and beliefs but the rejection by his critics and adversaries as well. The most deeply felt reproach had little to do with the facts of the matter (the guilt or innocence of the Rosenbergs) but with his providing ammunition to the enemy.

There was still Nicaragua to come—the final, confirming experience of his disaffection. Initially, as with Cuba, he hoped "that what was taking place in Nicaragua was something different. . . ." Several visits during the 1980s disabused him of this hope. For example, it gave him pause that during the Somoza period there were no refugees pouring out of Nicaragua whereas under the Sandinistas hundreds of thousands fled. Again, his critiques of the Sandinistas were dismissed with the same arguments and emotional disposition that had met his Rosenberg book; political expediency was everything: "Your timing is wrong. The Sandinistas are under attack, and we have to support them." As Radosh paraphrased the prevailing attitude: "Whatever the sins of the Sandinistas, since the U.S. is opposing them, they had to be supported." An editor of the "democratic socialist" magazine *Dissent*, Debbie Meier, put it this way at a meeting called to discuss Radosh's views of Nicaragua at a time when he was still on the magazine's editorial board: "You may be right about what you say about the Sandinistas, but while they are under attack by the American empire, we have a responsibility to extend our solidarity." Irving Howe, *Dissent*'s editor, informed him that he would not be allowed to write about Nicaragua in the magazine.[26]

Although Radosh did not inspire the kind of hostility David Horowitz had, he too paid a price for his political transformation and its candid public expression. Not only was he excommunicated from a social-political community and rejected by many former friends, but he found it difficult to obtain academic employment commensurate with his seniority and scholarly work. This was not surprising at a time when white males, even without the stigma of political incorrectness, had trouble getting teaching positions in the humanities and social sciences.

Radosh's political journey is an important contribution to understanding the incompatibility of truth seeking and realizable social ideals with political causes and movements that thrive on the mistaken notion that complete self-realization can be achieved by political means.

EUGENE GENOVESE (1930–). Eugene Genovese's abandonment of both Marxism and Soviet communism has been highly significant given the depth and history of his past commitments and his position in American academic-intellectual life. A widely respected historian of black slavery and author of many books, Genovese also edited and served on the editorial boards of journals such as *Marxist Perspectives*, *Studies on the Left*, and *Science and Society*.

In 1998 he founded the Historical Society to provide an alternative to the politically correct ethos of the American Historical Association.[27] He noted that while they routinely passed resolutions critical of U.S. foreign policy, "none of our leading historical associations have thought it intellectually challenging to devote sessions at their enormous annual meetings to frank discussions of the socialist debacle. We of the left are regularly invited to give papers on just about any subject except this one."[28]

Genovese's reassessment of his political beliefs and commitments converged with his distaste for the histrionic politics and "cultural radicalism" of the New Left. He was particularly incensed by what he called "the toxic slogan of the period—The personal is political! . . . [which] spread like a weed. . . ."[29] The mounting reign of political correctness in academic life further estranged him from what used to be the New Left and its "tenured radicals." He could not, for example, accept that it was bad form (if not altogether impermissible) for a white person to write about black affairs, and in 1968 he publicly defended William Styron who was subjected to abuse and accusations of racism for his novel *The Confessions of Nat Turner*.[30]

After his departure from the ranks of the left, Genovese rejected not only the policies and practices of "actually existing socialist systems" and left-wing movements but their goals and ideals as well, in particular the pursuit of radical egalitarianism. His objections to the New Left and its remnants concentrated on their contradictory and unrealistic embrace of both radical egalitarianism and radical individualism. It was a combination he considered a species of irresponsible utopianism, resting on ignorance of and indifference to the historical record. In his critique of "critical legal studies" (which often reflect these attitudes), he wrote: "They wish to tear down liberal society and its legal system in the hope that whatever replaces them, if guided by an egalitarian ethos and sensitive to the demands of participatory democracy, would probably be better. . . . A long and depressing history tells a different story, which is full of murderous attempts to realize the beauties of egalitarianism and a world without hierarchy."[31]

Genovese's sense of reality and knowledge of history set him apart from the sixties generation of leftists imbued with utopian impulses conditioned by their generally privileged background and unfamiliarity with history, especially its most murderous chapters in recent times outside the United States. These radical egalitarians, Genovese wrote, "invoke no history at all in their support of their contention that civilized life would be possible without some form of hierarchy";[32] nor did they grasp the pervasiveness of the conflict between community and personal autonomy confirmed by the breakup of countless short-lived communes created in the 1960s (as well as others of earlier times). The fragmentation of the political movements of the sixties and seventies indicated to him the difficulty for large numbers of people to agree on and work together for idealistic political goals.

It was Genovese's no-holds-barred dismissal of "utopian egalitarianism" and its naive views of human nature that his former colleagues on the left found most unpalatable, for it entailed the rejection of lifelong identity-giving convictions and their ongoing efforts to salvage them. His indictment of these longings was far-reaching as he dared to hold the idealistic theories themselves responsible for unwelcome consequences:

> The horrors did not arise from perversions of radical ideology but from the ideology itself. We were led into complicity with mass murder and the desecration of our professed ideals . . . by a deep flaw in our very understanding of human nature—its frailty and possibilities—and by our inability to replace the moral and ethical baseline long provided by the religion we have dismissed with indifference, not to say, contempt. . . .
>
> Our whole project of "human liberation" has rested on a series of gigantic illusions. The catastrophic consequences of our failure . . . cannot be dismissed as aberrations. . . . They have followed in the wake of victories by radical egalitarian movements throughout history, from ancient times to the peasant wars of the sixteenth century to the Reign of Terror and beyond, social movements that have espoused radical egalitarianism and participatory democracy have begun with mass murder and ended in despotism. . . .
>
> The allegedly high ideals we placed at the center of our ideology and politics are precisely what need to be reexamined.[33]

Elsewhere he wrote: "A requiem for Marx cannot ignore the iniquities of his offspring—prophets and messiahs must share the blame for the excesses of his followers."[34]

Genovese's abandonment of Marxism was further reflected in his willingness to submit it to a psychological critique, pointing out that "Marx was a man of strong hatreds and loves—mostly hatreds—which deeply conditioned his thought." Genovese agreed with the contention of Frank E. Manuel that Marx can be held responsible "for much of the criminality that subsequently occurred in his name. In doing so Manuel exposes self-hatred and projected self-hatred as at the root of much of modern radicalism."[35]

Not being attracted to "autobiographical mea culpa," as he puts it, Genovese has written little about the circumstances that led to his political reassessment. He has refrained from confessional revelations as to when, how, and why his views of the political world changed and especially why they had endured for so long unchanged. The discussion that follows is, for the most part, based on my conversation and correspondence with him.[36]

Genovese was born in 1930 and belongs to a generation very different from that we associate with the 1960s. His social background may have been the most important influence on his political attitudes, including the repudiation of a left-wing worldview. He came from a working-class family and grew up in Bensonhurst, Brooklyn. His father was a dock worker of Italian descent, endowed with an old-fashioned class-consciousness, some of which he imparted to his son; he also encouraged him to go to college. This background apparently provided a substratum or reservoir of common sense which survived long periods of ideological intoxication and eventually reasserted itself.

Genovese joined the Communist Party of the United States, the pivotal organization of the old left, at age seventeen, under special dispensation since eighteen was the age requirement. As a young man he seriously considered becoming a full-time party functionary or union organizer. At age fifteen he had joined the American League for Democracy, a front organization of the CPUSA; at seventeen he was its local secretary in Brooklyn. Around the same time he began to read the *Daily Worker* and Marxist literature, and stopped attending church. The high school he attended was about equally divided between Jews and those of Italian origin. Genovese was drawn to the bookish Jews and their leftist beliefs. He went to Brooklyn College, majoring in history and graduating in 1952. While in college he worked full time as a copy boy at a New York newspaper. He was drafted in 1952 and discharged after nine and a half months as a security risk. Benefiting from the GI bill, he enrolled as a graduate student at Columbia University and in 1959 he received his Ph.D. in history. In subsequent years he taught at the Polytechnic Institute of Brooklyn, Rutgers University, George Williams University in Montreal, the University of Rochester, and finally at the Atlanta University Center in Georgia, from where he retired in 1995.

In 1950 he was expelled from the party not because of major theoretical disagreements but for specific criticisms he made of policies he considered sectarian.

Genovese was never drawn to the cultural radicalism of the New Left and has been critical of both multiculturalism and radical feminism as institutionalized in the framework of political correctness. Even during the turbulent sixties and early seventies he remained a supporter of academic freedom and the autonomy of universities, and strenuously objected to the narrowing of freedom of expression on the campuses; he defended the rights of conservatives to be heard. Although a vocal opponent of the Vietnam War in 1969, he opposed the American Historical Association's decision to take a position on the war on the ground that this was not the job of a professional association. Throughout his life he refused to choose his friends according to their politics; at the personal level he found people on the left more difficult, sour, and humorless than their counterparts of conservative or traditional persuasion.

Despite the strong and doctrinaire old-left beliefs he used to hold, he had never subscribed (among other things) to utopian ideas such as the withering away of the state under communism; nor did he accept the scenarios of the Moscow Trials of the 1930s, though he managed to keep his revulsion about them under control for a long period of time. He entertained the possibility that socialism need not be democratic; he used to admire Stalin and accepted the idea of sacrificing one generation for other, future generations. Unlike many other true believers of his generation, he was not shattered by Khrushchev's revelations in 1956 because they did not surprise him. He believed at the time that the Hungarian Revolution of 1956 was a counterrevolution and had to be suppressed, especially after Imre Nagy announced his intention to take Hungary out of the Warsaw Pact. In the same year he briefly rejoined the Communist party and then the Progressive Labor party, staying in it for six months as a member of its Central Committee. He remained a supporter of the Soviet Union well into the 1980s.

In Genovese's own opinion, the seeds of his disillusionment are to be found in his long-held views of human nature, which were never optimistic; throughout his life he had "a deep sense of human depravity." Although he was an atheist for much of his life, he believed in original sin. (". . . I reject the liberationist philosophy of humanity that Marx arbitrarily imposed upon his great interpretation of history. Thus, although a non-believer, I accept much of the Christian view of man's fallen state and inherent tendency toward depravity."[37]) A decade later he became a religious believer.

These views of human nature had two paradoxical consequences. On the one hand they made him more a Leninist than a Marxist, that is, they inclined him to voluntarism (which emphasizes the importance of will and organization in political action) and elitism. Underlying these dispositions is a low estimate of the intelligence, political consciousness, and maturity of the "masses." At the same time such beliefs made him less susceptible to the utopian promises of the Marxist project that was based on a rather optimistic view of human nature, at least in the long run. These utopian promises have always been used to excuse and legitimate the political errors and suffering of the present on behalf of the glorious accomplishments awaiting in the forever receding future. Thus Genovese was also immune to the wishful beliefs of many of his former comrades who convinced themselves that "the collapse of the socialist countries . . . has little to do with socialism per se; indeed it opens the way to 'true' socialism freed of Stalinist perversion. That no socialist regime—no regime of the radical Left at any time in history—has ever avoided political tyranny and mass murder goes unremarked."[38]

Genovese never visited the Soviet Union, China, Cuba, North Vietnam, or any other putatively socialist state, though he had been sympathetic toward them while aware of their flaws. He was "appalled" by the "Great Leap Forward" in China and the economic irrationality it entailed, and was totally unsympathetic to the Cultural Revolution there. Unlike much of the New Left, he was not inclined to idealize the Third World. As a Marxist he understood that a high level of economic development is a prerequisite of a civilized and democratic society and democratic socialism: ". . . a socialist society would out-produce its capitalist rival and thereby provide the material foundation for an unprecedented human liberation."[39]

He wished to contribute to the building of an American socialist system that would incorporate "the great social achievements of the West" and be free of the flaws of existing socialist systems. In line with these inclinations, he became a hopeful supporter of Euro-communism in the late seventies. He recognized the corruptions of the Soviet Union under Brezhnev and had hoped that his successor, Andropov, would be able to reform it. Later he had similar hopes about Gorbachev's reforms. When these reforms turned out to undermine the institutional structures of the system, leading to its collapse, his remaining hopes for a successful socialist system came to an end.

It is not quite clear how far back the roots of Genovese's change of heart reach. Like many former supporters of socialist systems—especially those who had lived under them—he was well aware of their flaws and failures but for a long period of time succeeded in preserving his basic loyalty to them, notwithstanding this awareness. Apparently it was a sense of realism and recognition of human frailties (including the low levels of political consciousness of the masses) that allowed him to take a more tolerant view of repression in the Soviet Union under Stalin and after. But such tolerance was predicated on the belief that the system was moving in the right direction and would deliver great material benefits.

He experienced no major shift or reexamination of his attitudes until the mid-eighties. It is noteworthy that, as with many other Western sympathizers, he was more capable of accepting and supporting the Soviet system when it was far more oppressive and mendacious than during its milder but more corrupt phases, when it was no longer engaged in major social transformations.

What mattered most for Genovese and led to the fundamental rethinking of his beliefs—and here again his Marxist training and mindset exerted a strong influence—was that the system, and especially the Soviet one, did not deliver economically. In our conversation he recalled his shock in the 1980s when he learned about the low level of public health in the Soviet Union. He used to believe, and had hoped, that if economic conditions improved, repression would be reduced or eliminated and the system would become generally humanized. But the longer these conditions persisted, the harder it became to expect that they would change. He was finally led to ask to what degree these deficiencies were systemic and had some connection to their legitimating ideals and theories; thus he began to doubt that the system could be reformed.

Admittedly it remains difficult to fully understand how and why he managed to sustain his loyalties to the Soviet system almost until its extinction, or why, knowing all he knew before its collapse, he did not declare his moral responsibility earlier, as one of his critics demanded. Another of his critics wrote:

> . . . although expelled from the Communist party in 1950, he "remained a supporter . . . of the Soviet Union until there was nothing left to support." An extraordinary statement in view of the vast array of known Soviet transgressions to which Genovese does not plead previous ignorance. . . .

> . . . Why did he and countless others maintain their faith in the face of such known brutalities and why did they continue to believe in the ultimate validity of "socialism" in the Soviet Union? . . .
>
> It seems to me that the persistence of support for such a horrifying structure, one that destroys the very values that the believer professes, can be explained only by a psychological need to believe in a system that provides all the answers. . . .[40]

Aside from the possibility of such a need to believe, it may also be that Genovese's dissociation from the radicals of the 1960s—who rejected the Soviet Union as insufficiently revolutionary, among other reasons—played a part in stubbornly preserving his pro-Soviet loyalties (as did his friend and role model Eric Hobsbawm, who was also somewhat critical of the new radicals). He may have felt that remaining loyal to the Soviet Union was an assertion of consistency, tough-mindedness, and moral seriousness.

The next step was his rejection of the materialistic worldview, the realization that the Marxist premises themselves were flawed, and not merely the manner in which they were applied. In this regard his political evolution closely resembles Alexander Yakovlev's, whose disenchantment with the system (based on specific personal experiences) also led him to the explicit questioning and rejection of its Marxist foundations and of the Marxist worldview.

Genovese's personality and his nonconformist, anti-authoritarian streak predisposed him to come into conflict with groups and organizations requiring unwavering loyalty and conformity. Despite his early, fitful affiliation with the American Communist party, he retained an anti-authoritarian disposition which often led him into conflict with the party and later the Progressive Labor party he briefly joined. These personality traits, however, are less helpful in explaining his conflict with various groups and communities associated with the protest movements of the sixties, which were far less structured and demanding of conformity than the Communist party. In all probability, Genovese's difficulties with the counterculture and the protest movements of the sixties had more to do with matters of class, taste, and cultural interests. As an old leftist-Marxist, he was not a "cultural radical" or an aging groupie of the youth culture. Nor did he share with them the obligatory rejections of the nuclear family. His ties to the New Left were too weak to cushion him against a critical reexamination of his earlier beliefs and commitments. Most important, he could not embrace the hostility of the adversary culture toward Western values which became especially pronounced after the collapse of communism:

". . . unable to offer a coherent alternative to capitalism . . . and with no socialist countries left to identify with, many left-wingers now wallow in a mindless hostility to Western Civilization and to their own identity as Americans. . . ."[41]

The attacks that his wife, Elizabeth Fox-Genovese, was subjected to by radical feminists (because of her pro-family and Catholic beliefs) might have been another factor to further estrange him from the left and its academic representatives.

His pessimistic view of human nature, conditioned by his early and revitalized religious beliefs, was the other major determinant of the evolution of his political outlook and of his estrangement from the sixties left. Given a skeptical view of human nature, he could not share the shallow optimism and uninformed utopian egalitarianism prevalent among the sixties radicals, and their inclination to believe that all things highly valued (e.g., freedom and equality, individual self-expression, and communitarian solidarity) are compatible.

Genovese was able to fall back on the Catholicism of his family and childhood as he renounced his radical left beliefs and connections. He could reach out to another emotionally fulfilling belief system that helped bypass, or reduce the void and isolation resulting from the far-reaching reassessment of his lifelong beliefs, commitments, and social roles. Disillusionment with Soviet communism and with much of the American left made it possible to reconnect with the values and beliefs of his past.

SIX

Disillusionment in the West: II

Doris Lessing (1919–). The transformation of Doris Lessing's political beliefs was not limited to her abandoning support for the British Communist party and the Soviet Union. A much broader attitude change occurred over time which also led her to cease being a feminist[1] (or at least cease being preoccupied with the problems of women) and to the conclusion that "the salvation of this world cannot lie in any political ideology."[2] Even more far-reaching has been her recognition that the pursuit of personal fulfillment through public or political means is a futile undertaking—the central theme of her novel *The Sweetest Dream*.[3] In a related and similarly enduring insight, she wrote:

> There are certain types of people who are political out of a kind of religious reason. . . . It is fairly common among socialists: They are . . . God-seekers, looking for the kingdom of God on earth . . . trying to abolish the present in favor of some better future—always taking it for granted that there is a better future. If you don't believe in heaven, then you believe in socialism.[4]

Both her attraction to communism and the Soviet Union *and* her disenchantment with them were well founded, that is, there were good reasons for her to be drawn to these causes as well as for later finding them unworthy. The questions are when, how, and why her dedication and commitment became unsupportable, why her perceptions of phenomena that she earlier found so inspiring became drastically and radically transformed and reassessed?

Lessing's autobiography answers some of these questions and offers further evidence that political attitude change is a lengthy and difficult process, especially for those whose beliefs run deep. Christopher Hitchens has observed that "in order to be a 'radical' one must be open to the possibility that one's core assumptions are misconceived."[5] It is precisely such openness that is rarely within reach of the committed. As Lessing put it: "There are people . . . who have a sudden, reverse conversion, shedding Communist ideas (perhaps the right word is emotions) overnight. They are few. Most dawdled and drifted out of Communism, out of 'the Party.'"[6] The process is lengthy because the committed seek to avoid or postpone a confrontation with the pain of far-reaching attitude change. Lessing also observed: "Losing faith in communism is exactly paralleled by people in love who cannot let their dream of love go. Now [after the 20th Party Congress and its revelations in 1956] I knew that everything I had been clinging to was nonsense." She left the party the same year. The blow of these revelations was not as severe in her case as it was for those "who had invested everything, heart and mind . . . who had lived openly for the golden communist future. . . ." Her "psychological eggs were not all in that basket and never had been."[7] Her sense of identity rested more on being a writer than on being a devoted supporter of a putatively great cause.

Lessing recalled that well before Khrushchev's revelations, "something like 'an alternative reality' was building itself slowly, in my mind. . . . If there is no such thing as a sudden 'conversion,' that is, a sudden reversal of opinion, without a lot of little impressions accumulating . . . then there is no sudden reverse conversion." She recalled that "We felt reading Kravchenko as if our brains were being turned inside out. I remember exactly . . . how I felt: if what I was reading was true then *nothing at all* of what I believed to be true, could be true."[8] Yet disaffection was hard to confront because "to leave 'the Party' was to give up the greater truth, give up being an initiate into understanding the real processes of life."[9]

Another major impediment to political disaffection and especially its public revelation was her fear of ostracism by the (formerly) like-minded. Lessing wrote: "What I suffered from mostly was fear of epithets like 'turncoat' and 'renegade.' . . ."[10] From Arthur Koestler to David Horowitz, the disillusioned were showered with contempt and hostility and rapidly lost the supporting community of congenial fellow idealists. George Orwell earned the lasting resentment of many on the left for committing "the ultimate sin of 'giving ammunition' to the enemy."[11]

Lessing became involved with leftist causes and a self-styled Communist movement in Rhodesia as a young, rebellious woman during

World War II. The involvement was part of her assertion of autonomy, of distancing herself from her family and the prevailing colonial mentality and way of life. At an early age she came to reject the pervasive racism of her social setting and also found morally unacceptable the poverty of the nonwhite majority. She had the "vague but strong feeling [that] there was something terribly wrong with the System. For one thing, why were all these people working for so little money on our farm?"[12] She "hated" what she saw around her. "I was a part of this white oppressing elite," she wrote.[13] Aside from being drawn to kindred spirits similarly repelled by racism, she "became a Communist because of the spirit of the times . . . we were part of a family that covered the world."[14]

In an early demonstration of independence, she left home in her teens to work as a nursemaid. This was followed by secretarial jobs in Salisbury, where for the first time she met similarly disposed young people who gravitated toward left-wing groups and causes, including the Communist movement. She explained their diverse motives:

> People became Communists because of cynicism about their own government. . . . Because they had fallen in love with a communist. . . . Because they were taken to a Party rally and were swept away by mass emotion. Because they had been taken to a Party meeting and found the atmosphere of conspiracy appealing. Because of the idealism of the Party. Because they had a taste for heroics or suffering. In my case it was because for the first time in my life I was meeting a group of people . . . who read everything . . . and among whom thoughts about the Native Problem I had scarcely dared to say aloud turned out to be mere commonplaces. I became a Communist because of the spirit of the times. . . .[15]

Later in life, after she moved to London, Lessing became aware of some of the paradoxes in the idealism of the people attracted to the movement:

> All over Europe . . . it was the most sensitive, compassionate, socially concerned people who became communists. . . . These decent, kind people supported . . . the most brutal tyranny of our time—with the exception of Communist China. . . . This was a religious set of mind, identical with that of passionate religious true believers. . . . We inherited the mental framework of Christianity. Hell: capitalism; all bad. A Redeemer, all good—Lenin, Stalin, Mao. Purgatory: you can't make an omelette with breaking eggs (lagers, concentration camps and the rest). Then paradise . . . then heaven . . . then Utopia.[16]

Political participation provided the incidental benefit of a lively social life: "From four until two or three in the morning we were at every kind of meeting, study group, seminar, or engaged in starting yet another organization. . . ." While "fighting apartheid and standing up for the blacks" was central to these activities, there was also a group called Friends of the Soviet Union. Lessing and her comrades took themselves very seriously: "Ours was the authentic flame, the Spirit of Lenin lived in us, we lived and talked as if tomorrow we might face the firing squad." She and her group believed that in a decade or two "the whole world would be Communist, from free choice, because of the manifest superiorities of Communism. There would be no race prejudice, oppression of women, exploitation of labor—no snobbishness or contempt for others." There was a strong and agreeable sense of belonging to a selfless, idealistic elite:

> We despised anyone who did not believe in Revolution. . . . It was morally superior to believe in Revolution. . . . We were united with each other by superiority of character, because we were revolutionaries. . . . People who did not believe in socialism were not credited with good intentions: a set of mind that continues to this day. It is satisfying to believe in the moral inferiority of opponents.[17]

Elsewhere she wrote about "unchallenged and undiscussed sentimental certitudes," which preeminently included the conviction that "Socialists are [morally] better than non-Socialists"[18]—a powerful stimulant for retaining left-wing beliefs given the association of the socialist outlook with generosity and kindness, as opposed to greed, competitiveness, and profit hunger, supposed hallmarks of the capitalist mind-set. In more recent times, especially the last decades of the past century, anti-capitalism increasingly took a characterological turn: the worst sin of capitalism apparently became its capacity to stimulate and legitimate greed.

In London, Lessing's intense social-personal and political involvements continued: "I lived in a pack, was one of a pack." The "social life of the New Left" too was vibrant and enjoyable.[19] It was both difficult and unnecessary to separate the personal from the political, the pleasures of belonging to a close-knit community from the satisfaction of holding lofty beliefs and participating in principled political activism.

If meeting and keeping the company of congenial people can be a source of attraction to a political cause or movement, by the same token disillusionment may also be stimulated by encountering unappealing human beings who personify the darker side of the same movement.

Lessing discovered in due course that her second husband (whose name she took and who had been a major political influence on her) belonged to "a common type in revolutionary, or left-wing . . . circles. These men find it hard to have simple, ordinary, easy friendships and loves and retire behind walls of cold authority."[20]

Ralph Schoenman, a prominent American radical and anti-nuclear activist, and secretary to Bertrand Russell during the 1960s and 1970s, was another such impersonal, politicized individual whom she knew: "he . . . spoke in that style perfected by History itself, combining idealism with a cold, clipped precision, and full of contempt for opponents, who were by definition cowards, poltroons, and morally defective. . . . What he said was untrue and yet he was radiating sincerity." Paul Robeson and his wife also made a negative impression on Lessing, talking as they did "entirely in communist jargon: capitalist lies, fascist imperialists, running dogs, democratic socialism (the Soviet Union), peace-loving peoples. Not one word was said in normal speech."[21]

At the Soviet embassy in London, during one of the many functions she attended while she was in the ranks of the "faithful," she was introduced "to a very important visitor from Moscow," a KGB general "with eyes like ice . . . [who] was talking entirely in communist jargon. . . . I think this was where I came closest . . . to the murderous horrors of the Soviet Union. I didn't discuss the incident with anyone. It was too 'subjective,' as the comrades said about anything not at once explainable. . . . I did not go to one of these big receptions at the Soviet Embassy again."[22]

In her novel *The Sweetest Dream* an extremely unappealing human being, "Comrade Johnny," combines several repugnant human qualities—irresponsibility, hypocrisy, manipulativeness, exploitativeness, lack of consideration for others—with a totally politicized personality; his sense of identity rests entirely on political values and postures; he cannot and would not separate the personal from the political. He is the prototypical political activist and aspiring revolutionary who loves mankind but is incapable of warmth or concern for his family or other proximate, specific human beings.

Following the 1956 Khrushchev speech, Lessing noted, "having shed all faith in the Soviet Union, and in communism, did not mean relinquishing revolution. Implicit was the idea that revolution was necessary to save us all." The surviving "left-wing romanticism" in her circles focused less on the wonders of existing or emerging socialist states (though they too were supported); rather, it was animated by a generalized belief in revolution "as an article of faith."[23] The myth of the revolution, that is, the glorious end to which means had to be subordinated without hesitation, was part of a broader revolutionary romanticism which enshrined and sanitized violence, an outlook that assumed "revolution is a nobler thing than the ballot box." In recent times, Lessing wrote,

> hundreds of young people with the highest possible motives supported murder for political reasons. Most of the Red Brigades were not deprived people . . . these were the "tender-hearted," dreaming of gentle, fruitful, noncorrupt futures. Those that remained in the organization became merciless, brutal killers. . . . They were and are still sometimes admired precisely for their brutality. There are people on the left who still defend them. Why? I think the reason is, again, revolutionary romanticism.[24]

This romanticism was bolstered by taking "for granted that when the working class—or the blacks or any other disadvantaged people—took power, they would be inspired by only the purest and most disinterested ideals. Of all the absurd things we believed this was probably the worst."[25]

Lessing's journey to the Soviet Union as member of a British literary delegation also took its toll on her political beliefs. On a visit to a collective farm (part of the guided tour), an old farmer startled and defied the official interpreter (and was understood by a Russian-speaking member of the British delegation) by telling the visitors, "You must not believe what you are told. . . . You must not believe what you are shown. Our lives are terrible." The incident was followed by a "long toast-filled meal . . . there is a long, loaded table, flowers, wine, a banquet. There, the special people chosen from the farm to represent the Soviet farmers. There, we happy delegates, elated and pleased with ourselves, the way you get on such trips. There, the party officials, all affability." Lessing also realized that the summer holiday camp for children they were taken to "was a showplace."

On the same trip a more dramatic incident occurred on the drive to the airport at night when a drunk staggered onto the road and was hit by the car in which the delegation was riding. "A peasant lay bleeding, spread-eagled." The interpreter furiously scolded him and was prepared to leave him on the road, but the visitors demanded that he be taken into the car and carried to a hospital.[26]

It took Lessing five years, she wrote,

> . . . from my first falling in love with Communism . . . in 1942, to become critical enough to discuss my doubts with people still inside the

> Communist fold. In another two or three years I discussed with other Communists facts and ideas for which in a Communist country we would have been tortured or killed. By 1954 I was no longer a Communist, but it was not until the early 1960s I ceased to feel residual tugs of loyalty, was really free. That is, it took a good twenty years for me to no longer feel guilty, to shake it all off. I remember with shame how difficult it was to say what I thought with people who were still the Faithful.[27]

It was not only the old-style pro-Communist attitudes and beliefs that Lessing had rejected but the New Left of the sixties as well. Unlike most novelists writing about that period, she portrayed sixties characters critically and sardonically in novels like *The Good Revolutionary* (1985) and *TheSweetest Dream* (2002). She gave a new meaning to the sixties slogan "The personal is political" by presenting hypocritical, self-indulgent, self-righteous, sloganizing literary characters whose anger and political beliefs were rationalizations of personal hatreds and discontents. Such individuals, in her fiction as sometimes in real life, projected upon their society frustrations and hostilities originating in the depths of their psyche, often in some emotional deprivation or personal conflict. Their personalities combined self-centeredness with communitarian longings, self-indulgence with a fiercely judgmental disposition, a proclaimed striving for authenticity with highly standardized demeanor, down to the details of hair and conversational style and the stereotyped badges of sartorial nonconformity. Creating these characters did not please critics such as Louis Menand, who was more sympathetic toward these types of people and their traits of character. Menand disapproved of her coldness toward "the ideals and illusions of other people" and her mocking "the belief that people can remake themselves by catching up with the times"[28]—a curiously vague formulation that leaves a lot to the imagination concerning the nature of the praiseworthy attributes to be incorporated into one's behavior. Presenting such literary characters, Lessing conveyed that the gulf between appearance and reality was as relevant for a better understanding of the vaunted idealism of the sixties as for the more common exposés of bourgeois morality.

Lessing has been among the handful of chastened supporters of Communist and other left-wing causes who concluded that people were attracted to them in the West (and especially in the 1960s and after) not so much because of moral indignation aroused by specific social injustices but rather due to disappointment with a wide range of unmet and unrealistic personal expectations. To be sure, these two sources of moral indignation are connected, since the frustration of high expectations (of personal fulfillment) makes specific social realities or arrangements seem more intolerable and unjust and intensifies moral outrage. Lessing sensed and pinpointed the connection between high expectations and the bitterly critical, alienated disposition:

> It [the alienation] can come only out of some belief, one so deep it is well out of sight, that a promise of some kind has been made and betrayed. Perhaps it was the French Revolution? Or the American Revolution which made the pursuit of happiness a right with the implication that . . . [it] is to be had as easily as taking cakes off a supermarket counter? Millions of people in our times behave as if they have been made a promise . . . that life must get freer, more honest, more comfortable, always better. . . . Yet nothing in history suggests that we may expect anything but wars, tyrants, sickness, bad times, calamities. . . .[29]

Lessing's evolving conception of human nature made it difficult to remain a supporter of causes and movements that relied on an unrealistically optimistic conception of human nature (in the long run) while in the present they treated actual human beings with a truly elitist contempt and condescension. Her skepticism about human nature became incompatible with the support of Communist systems and ideologies, especially as she came to believe that "every mass political movement unleashes the worst in human behavior."[30] In the same spirit she also reached the conclusion—most iconoclastic from the current perspectives of political correctness—that the experience of victimization does not provide immunity against mistreating others.

Lessing's political disenchantment suggests that the process requires several conditions, but none by itself makes it certain that it will occur. There must be experiences that prompt skepticism or critical sentiments, and these experiences must be faced and digested rather than dismissed as incidental or morally inconsequential; independence from closely knit groups or subcultures that provide emotional support for shared political attitudes; a sense of identity that does not depend on political participation; reliance on nonpolitical relationships, activities, and individual resources (in Lessing's case, being a successful creative writer); the influence and example of other individuals who made the break (of little importance in her case). Last but not least, as always, personality matters: a genuinely critical, anti-authoritarian, and independent disposition helps avoid, or liberate oneself from, engulfing political loyalties and beliefs. Lessing was, from an early age, of an inquisitive, anti-authoritarian disposition, reluctant to submit for long to any rigid organization, ideology, or mind-set.

MAURICE HALPERIN (1907–1995). The late Maurice Halperin is not widely known partly because much of his life was spent abroad: in France (1929–1931), Mexico (1953–1958), the Soviet Union (1959–1962), Cuba (1962–1968), and finally in Canada (between 1968 and his death in 1995).[31] He was a man of the left, a fellow traveler and allegedly a spy for the Soviet Union.[32] Unlike other Western leftists, he became closely acquainted with the political systems that many of his fellow intellectuals idealized from a distance. He may be the only notable Western intellectual who spent years in both the Soviet Union and Cuba, working in both countries. He is among the handful of American supporters of the Cuban regime who became critical of it and gave public expression to his disillusionment.

Fluent in Spanish, Halperin had wide-ranging interests in Latin American affairs. Preceded by an interest in Mexico, Cuba under Castro became his major academic field; he published three scholarly volumes on Castro's Cuba which increasingly conveyed his critical sentiments.[33] He also taught a course on the Cuban Revolution for many years at Simon Fraser University in British Columbia, Canada.

Halperin's slowly changing political convictions can be traced in his books on Cuba (especially the third volume) and have also been chronicled in Don Kirschner's biography.[34] None of his writings I am familiar with address explicitly or in any detail the process or the stages of his disillusionment.

Halperin came from a first-generation American Jewish family who owned a cigar store in Boston. He went to the famous Boston Latin School and then to Harvard, where he majored in Romance languages and took only three years to graduate in 1926. He married at age twenty and found his first job in Ranger, Texas, teaching French and Spanish in the local high school and junior college. A year later he enrolled in the graduate school at the University of Oklahoma in Norman. He continued his graduate studies in Paris in 1929 at the Sorbonne, where in 1931 he earned a doctorate in comparative literature. He returned to teach at the University of Oklahoma for ten years. Subsequently he taught at Boston University (where he established the Latin American Regional Studies Department), the National University of Mexico, the University of Havana, and finally at Simon Fraser University.

During World War II he worked in the U.S. Office of Strategic Services in Washington and was head of its Latin American Division. It was during that period that he provided information to the Soviet Union, including "highly sensitive material . . . from the State Department . . . and its importance is reflected in the material the KGB credits him with in the Venona messages."[35] There is no information as to how he was recruited and decided to work for the Soviet Union, and when he terminated these activities. He never admitted his spying to his biographer, who extensively discusses the evidence against him. He lost his jobs both at the University of Oklahoma and at Boston University for political reasons (not spying), the latter during the McCarthy era.

Halperin's family was well read, liberal, and left-leaning. He wrote: "I had been conditioned by my parents and the ideals of the French Renaissance of the sixteenth century and the Enlightenment of the eighteenth. . . ."[36] His leftist beliefs developed in the early 1930s, "during the years in Oklahoma that Maurice first turned his attention to Latin America; at the same time he began to drift leftward politically. . . . By 1936 [he] was moving more consciously toward the orbit of the Communist Party and by 1937 was, by his own description, a fellow traveler, . . ." his biographer wrote.[37] His political attitudes were influenced by the Great Depression, the migration of impoverished farmers in Oklahoma, his visits to Mexico, exposure to Southern racism, and by an academic friend who "steered" him to the writings of Marx, whose critique of capitalism impressed him. He came to share the belief widespread among left-leaning intellectuals in the 1930s that the Soviet Union was the only determined and steadfast opponent of Nazism. He inclined to accept the Soviet version of the purge trials largely because "he was above all bent on seeing that the trials did not divert attention from the single towering issue of the day, the threat of fascist expansionism."[38]

Halperin's thinking was, in general, nurtured by a secular, humanistic Jewish sensibility and "a strong commitment to the rational tradition" of the Enlightenment. As a result he was also sympathetic to the apparent egalitarian aspirations of the Soviet system: ". . . to their avowed goal of eliminating social inequality and economic insecurity. . . ."

The first blow to his beliefs was Khrushchev's revelations in 1956, when he still lived in Mexico. Although, according to his biographer, the purge trials of the 1930s troubled him, "he had long since put these doubts 'on the back burner' and left them there, almost forgotten. He continued to believe that the Soviet Union offered a path to the future, if only to a very remote future." But Khrushchev's disclosures forced him "to address the purge trials and worse. . . . Halperin conceded that he had been wrong about Stalin's Russia, but perhaps there was still hope that Soviet socialism would transcend the errant ways of the dictator." Or, as his biographer observed,

> For years the Soviet Union had been an ambiguous symbol for Halperin. He had reservations about its political excesses since the 1930s but he was always able to see the glowing ideals through the dark realities. He differed from the true believer by conceding those dark realities. . . . But he could not fully resist the promise of ideals that had been dear to him since he was a young man. . . .

He shared the hopes of other Western sympathizers that the Soviet Union after Stalin's death might yet become a more humane society and realize its original, authentic revolutionary aspirations.

It appears that his prolonged stay in the Soviet Union, even as a privileged visitor, compelled the first reassessment of his beliefs. Living and working there for three years (as a researcher in the Institute of World Economics and International Affairs of the Soviet Academy of Sciences) forced him to confront particulars, daily realities which could not be concealed or dismissed as insignificant by abstract theoretical generalizations. The severe underdevelopment of the Soviet Union was visible from his Moscow apartment: "From our bedroom window we looked down on an ancient rural scene: several dozen log cabins along winding lanes (muddy in springtime), with a couple of communal outhouses. We could see people lined up on a winter morning with the temperature at forty below zero."[39]

On another occasion while traveling he had the opportunity to see a rural town "in a deplorable state of disrepair, with muddy streets and mainly empty stores." In the center was "a large brick communal outhouse [which] dominated one of the main squares. The stench was unbearable. A large red banner over the entrance bore the customary legend: 'Hail to Our Glorious Communist Party.'" Many years later in Cuba, he found the deficiencies of socialist hygiene again evident: "A particularly depressing demonstration of austerity in socialist Cuba took place in the men's washroom. A third of the urinals were out of order on any given day. Meanwhile, sitting just inside the entrance to the facility was an attendant handing out single sheets of toilet paper to patrons in need."

Experiences of this kind wore down Halperin's idealistic hopes, preconceptions, and theoretical generalizations. He could not dismiss the pervasive shoddiness, bleakness, and endemic material scarcities as trivial or insignificant. The privileged housing he and his wife were given "was the smallest place he had ever lived in. . . . [He said,] I couldn't imagine a new building like this, the workmanship so shoddy . . . some of the bricks were crumbling already and it had just been put up. . . ."

The Institute where he worked was in a similar state of disrepair. "He was beginning to feel that anything old was shabby and anything new shoddy. . . . The cafeteria stood in about the same relationship to Western cafeterias as the toilet did to Western toilets." A hernia operation acquainted him with a Soviet teaching hospital where "the tap water was not potable" and "a local anesthetic [was] improperly administered," resulting in pain he had never felt before. In the communal toilet the windows were kept open due to the stench. Halperin turned down the option of the so-called Kremlin hospital which had superior facilities for the elite, intent as he was on learning about Soviet realities. When his wife was hospitalized in the brand-new hospital built for the personnel of the Academy of Sciences, its excellent facilities "brought home to the Halperins once again the inequities of life in this nation that was supposed to have abolished inequities."

The only decent food in Moscow Halperin found at a Hungarian, Georgian, or Chinese restaurant, but one had to wait in line for hours to get in, unless the captain was bribed. "In most restaurants the food ranged from bad to inedible, and the service was worse." He was not impressed by the chandeliers and marble in a section of the Moscow subway "when there was hunger in the land."

His rationalistic mind-set and keen awareness of the endemic inefficiencies of the system led him to observe that "The Soviet Union was an experience that one could not possibly anticipate in any way. You could be an intellectual giant and have read everything and you would not have anticipated the details, and the details are so important. You live the details." This was the Khrushchev era of greatly diminished repression, yet "it was difficult to hold a candid conversation with a Muscovite and impossible to exchange house visits, except with former gulag inmates. They . . . felt they were immune from further punishment. From them we got firsthand reports of the horrors of the Stalin era." His Russian relatives were unwilling to meet him; people "were afraid to be seen with an American."

Halperin concluded "that all aspects of life were hobbled by a system that simply did not work. . . . The cause was not external to the system: it was the system itself." He told his biographer: "My feeling was that there was something basic missing here. . . . Apathy, that's another word for it . . . there is something wrong here, something is not working. . . ." After three years, he left convinced that "in the motherland of socialism, socialism did not work."

It was in Moscow that Halperin read the classic indictment of communism, *The New Class* by Milovan Djilas: ". . . the book was a revelation. . . . [Halperin] was aware of all the details it spoke of, but Djilas was the first person in a Communist nation to put those details together and explain them to his satisfaction."

Despite these experiences, Halperin's rejection of the "Soviet model" was dispassionate and low key, more technocratic and pragmatic than theoretical or moralistic; there is little apparent moral indignation in his critiques. He diligently catalogued the inefficiencies, scarcities, and symptoms of backwardness but said little about official mendacity; the huge and persistent gap between theory and practice, propaganda and reality; and the psychological damage inflicted on human beings by a system that institutionalized mistrust and intimidation. He did not offer an analysis as to why the system did not work. Later in Cuba he recognized that lack of incentives and lack of access to consumer goods eroded workers' motivation and retarded productivity, but still he offered no broader theoretical reflections. As he ends his sojourn in the USSR, there is no indication of a rethinking of Marxism and its contribution to the conditions he so accurately perceived in the Soviet Union.

Thanks to an invitation extended to him by Che Guevara, whom he met in Moscow, he was ready to abandon his "Soviet experiment" and learn about the one in Cuba. "Maybe in the hands of these Cuban idealists, Halperin thought, the system would finally be made to work the way it was supposed to." Cuba made it possible, at least initially, to entertain the idea that the failure of socialism in the Soviet Union was due to historical and cultural factors. Perhaps under the "proper conditions" the system might work elsewhere.

In 1962 Cuba, and Havana in particular, was a welcome contrast to the Soviet Union and Moscow: "My first impression was that of a cosmopolitan 'first world' capital. The streets were lined with graceful, colorful façades, suffused with tropical light and teeming with neatly dressed, gesticulating people." The people did not smell, even on crowded buses; there were no drunks sprawled on the sidewalks (as in

Moscow); "coffee bars were ubiquitous. . . . Restaurants were plentiful, the food was always tasty, and service prompt." The Halperins' accommodations were also superior, "a nicely furnished, roomy, three-bedroom Havana beachfront apartment." Cuban toilets worked, the tap water was potable, the weather was pleasant and the people cheerful, unlike the Russians. "Havana was dazzling and the future seemed bright." It became clear only much later that "Cuba's infant socialism was living off the fat accumulated by Cuban capitalism." A senior economist of the Cuban Central Planning Commission told him: ". . . if only the Revolution could have been delayed ten years! We were making great progress in building tunnels, bridges, highways and factories and increasing manufacturing and food production."

In Cuba he was given a job at the Central Planning Commission, and later as an adviser to the minister of foreign trade; he also obtained a teaching position at the University of Havana. The school, however, provided new grounds for skepticism toward the system; standards of admission were low, and a large portion of the students were "illiterate 'riff-raff,'" as he put it. He was expected to pass every student. In his various positions he learned increasingly about the mismanagement that prevailed in many walks of life: "The arbitrariness, the unpredictability, the fickleness with which things were done in Cuba were a constant source of anguish to Halperin." Much of this had to do with Castro's unlimited power and belief in his own omnipotence and genius. The Cuban economy was run according to his rapidly changing convictions:

> It is difficult to measure the direct impact of Fidel Castro's personality on the day-to-day functioning of the Cuban economy except to say that it was constant and enormously disruptive. . . . There was no area affecting the economy . . . that was immune to the sudden intervention of the Maximum Leader, or to the near paralysis when his attention veered to another project. . . . The commander-in-chief would have a brainstorm. . . . This would trigger a crash program, with the total mobilization of all available resources. If it came to nothing, the failure was never acknowledged. If it succeeded . . . it was hailed as an example of the superiority of socialism over capitalism. In neither case were the costs taken into account.[40]

For example, "his [Castro's] disastrous project to produce a ten-million-ton sugar harvest in 1970 . . . was a personal decision made without paying any attention to his sugar experts, who knew it could not be done." For the first time in Cuban history, sugar had to be rationed.

Another example was Castro's impulsive decision a decade later to abolish, "without consultation," free markets (he had allowed them earlier, and they substantially improved food supplies) as he "became alarmed by 'millionaire garlic growers' (his words). . . . Capitalism, he declared, was rearing its ugly head, threatening the destruction of socialism. More likely, Castro was primarily concerned about a sector of the economy slipping from state control, that is, his personal control." Halperin also took a dim view of "voluntary work," which extracted free labor from the population and forced large numbers of people unfamiliar with agricultural and other work to perform such labor.

As in the Soviet Union, a fundamental problem in Cuba was the lack of incentives, notwithstanding Che Guevara's obsessive attempts to substitute "moral" for material incentives. Halperin quotes Jacobo Timmerman's observation that "In Cuba everybody has a job but nobody works." A physician he knew "was in a trap similar to that of most other workers in the socialist system. The state gave him a job but removed the incentive to do more than the minimum required."

Castro's power, personality, and impact on Cuba were clearly a major source of Halperin's disenchantment with the Cuban political system. He held the leader responsible both for the prevailing political repression and economic malfunctioning and for the resulting decline in Cuba's standard of living. He was just as critical of Castro's foreign policies, including his costly military campaigns in Africa, undertaken to prop up various leftist dictatorships, and his hostility toward Israel. Halperin came to consider Castro a megalomaniac suffering from a "personality disorder . . . [he] displayed as a child and throughout the rest of his life. He has had an uncontrollable compulsion to lead and to dominate—the results of an innate conviction of his superiority and of his destiny to make history." In the type of political system Castro built and maintained with Soviet help, there was no institutional mechanism to restrain such an individual or to mitigate the consequences of his impulsive and ruthless exercise of power.

In the end, Halperin discovered in Cuba virtually everything he had found alienating and disillusioning in the Soviet Union, including the new system of inequalities and politically determined privileges. He recalled:

> My wife and I were once invited to a dinner party at the home of a cabinet minister. We found an elaborate spread of vintage wines and gourmet delicacies unobtainable in any public market. Noting my surprise . . . my host took me aside and told me with an impish twinkle in his eye: "As we all know, when Cuba reaches the stage of commu-

> nism, there will be a great abundance of everything. What we have here is an experiment in adapting to the joys of communism. We are getting prepared for the future."

It was an experience reminiscent of Boris Yeltsin's critique of the privileges of the Soviet nomenklatura:

> A few dozen people live in the ideal conditions that are predicted as universal when we have reached the stage of "full communism," while the population as a whole lives in conditions that are barely tolerable. . . . If you have climbed all the way up to the top . . . then it is full communism![41]

In the course of living in Cuba for six years, one after another the alleged accomplishments of the system became hollow to Halperin, bought at the expense of deprivations of various kinds. He learned about the defects of the vaunted health-care system from a confidential public opinion poll made by the party in 1987 in Holguin province: "The poll revealed an astonishing figure. From a total of 10,756 opinions . . . 87.6% are unfavorable. . . . Most of the complaints . . . concerned 'the lack of attention, negligence and abuse of patients.' . . . In addition there were many complaints about the chronic absenteeism of both doctors and nurses and about favoritism in the treatment of well-connected patients."

Another incident that soured Halperin was the treatment of Oscar Lewis, the American anthropologist and a friend of his. Lewis, who had already conducted studies in Mexico and Puerto Rico on "the culture of poverty," was interested in finding out how ten years of socialism in Cuba had changed the lives of the poor. He and his wife were "longtime leftists and enthusiastic supporters of Castro's revolution." He was initially (in 1969) given freedom by Castro himself to conduct his study. After one year of research, "the authorities terminated the project and confiscated its files in 1970. . . . Two years later Raul Castro explained that the government acted because Lewis was engaging in deceit and espionage."

By the end of his stay in Cuba, Halperin "noticed a new mood of . . . doctrinaire conformism in the press, the ministry, and the university. . . ." The 1989 show trial of high-ranking military officers accused of drug trafficking, corruption, and treason was another sordid episode which reflected unfavorably on the judicial system, "the pervasive corruption in the Cuban armed forces," and Castro's personal vindictiveness. An important objective of the trial was to demonstrate "that neither Fidel nor Raul had any knowledge of the drug trafficking."

The prosecutor declared that Castro is "a symbol, an historic example of honesty never clouded by a lie. . . . Fidel is our representative to whom we turn in difficult times." Halperin had serious doubts about Castro's ignorance of the high-level drug trafficking and believed that "the need for the trial was to demonstrate that Fidel Castro had been deceived by his subordinates, that he was utterly opposed to the immorality of drug trafficking."

While (as in his Soviet experience) Halperin writes mostly about the economic failures of the system, he was also well aware of its police-state character. In his third book on Cuba he quoted the Americas Watch Committee's finding that "Cuba held more political prisoners as a percentage of population than any other country in the world. . . ." Halperin noted "the urgency and ferocity with which he [Castro] turned against the anti-Communist Huber Matos, an able and loyal commandante in the Sierra. In the trumped-up trial Castro personally charged him with treason and dictated a sentence of twenty years."

In the end, Halperin, with heavy heart, concluded that Cuban socialism had failed to escape "the structural characteristics" that eventually led to the collapse of the Soviet system and its East European dependencies. The state control over the economy was "the main obstacle to progress, and in Cuba Castro is the state." While in the sixties he still held out hope, on his last visit to Cuba in 1989 he found "the popular mood one of deep discouragement, perhaps born of suppressed anger after decades of seemingly unending and increasing austerity. I could see the toll being paid in the weary and cheerless faces I passed on the street."

His biographer wrote: "Maurice had come to Cuba in 1962 in part to answer a question. Was the failure of socialism in Eastern Europe the fault of socialism or of Eastern Europe? Might it take root and flourish in more fertile soil, or was it doomed everywhere? By the time he left in 1968, he had his answer. Socialism was not likely to work anywhere." He also concluded that Cuba "had an economic system that did not work and a political system that did not permit anyone to say that it did not work."

He decided to leave Cuba, increasingly unhappy about the contrast between his privileged living conditions and the way most people lived. He was also increasingly unhappy with the political system, its repressiveness, economic irrationality, and the part played by Castro in its operation. As the authorities became aware of Halperin's critical disposition, he was fired from his job in the ministry of foreign trade. He was hoping for an academic position in the United States but was offered one at the new Simon Fraser University of British Columbia in Vancouver. On the plane from Cuba to Madrid (there were no direct flights at the time), he had a memorable experience:

> . . . on the plane . . . these Cubans were poker faced . . . even the children, subdued, quiet faces. Then at one point we reached the point of no return. If something happens you go on to Madrid, not back . . . you are surely not going back to Cuba whatever happens. So the crew—this was a Spanish plane, Iberia—told the Cubans, "We have now reached the point of no return." Bedlam broke loose. These people started dancing in the isles and it was very touching.

Halperin's final disillusionment with his leftist ideals was brought to fruition by his six long years in Cuba. During that time he learned that the political regimentation and repression he saw was not just a reasonable price to be paid for better material circumstances, since the latter failed to improve and in some respects declined. He also learned that the planning system was no substitute for the free market and was compatible with chronic, systemic mismanagement; that a highly authoritarian and mendacious government could not provide credible "moral" incentives for work in place of the material ones; that Cuban socialism was dominated and deformed by the one-person dictatorship of a man whose hunger for power was insatiable and whose sense of mission gave him a limitless sense of entitlement.

If any factor can be singled out as particularly alienating, in the Soviet case it was chronic bleakness and endemic scarcity, in the Cuban case chronic mismanagement and personalized, arbitrary rule by Castro.

Having experienced firsthand and over extended periods of time the failures of both Soviet and Cuban socialism, Halperin—unlike many leftists in the West—could no longer suggest that nothing was wrong with Marxism, only with the people who tried to implement it and the settings where the attempts were made. He ceased to believe in "any variant of socialism." He was not sympathetic to the fulminations against consumer societies common in Western academic settings: "He says that when he first went to the Soviet Union he carried the usual left-wing bias against consumer society. . . . 'Well, let me tell you,' he says now, 'there is nothing like living in a society where there is nothing to consume to make you appreciate the consumer society.'"

At Simon Fraser University he met more Marxists than he had ever encountered either in the Soviet Union or in Cuba. He greatly disappointed those who—because of his years in Cuba—expected him to confirm their wishful fantasies about heroic Cuban socialism and the corruptions of the West.

Halperin's disillusionment was restrained and empirically based, lacking in agonized soul searching and pain. Both his involvement with and abandonment of the cause of socialism, and the political systems that claimed to be its incarnation, were measured and dispassionate.

Susan Sontag (1933–2004) fits into this study on several apparently conflicting grounds.[42] Earlier in her career she was one of many well-known contemporary Western intellectuals whose political misjudgments about the Communist systems of the 1960s and '70s were as stunning as those of her predecessors about the Soviet Union in the 1930s. Her formidable intellect, erudition, and capacity for critical thinking did not save her from extraordinarily naive and misguided assessments of Communist Cuba and Vietnam.[43]

The case of Sontag also proves (if more proof is needed) that a profound alienation from one's society has little if anything to do with powerlessness, poverty, marginality, or any other deprivation or disadvantage. Sontag enjoyed a splendid career as writer, culture critic, freelance academic, and occasional producer of films and plays. She received both critical acclaim and popular success as the author of best-selling books; she has been a beneficiary of numerous awards, grants, and fellowships (including the so-called "genius award" of the MacArthur Foundation). She received much favorable publicity and public attention and wielded a great deal of influence in cultural and literary matters. None of this prevented her from feeling profoundly estranged from her country and from considering its social-political order worthless.

More important for present purposes, Sontag came to recognize the folly of her unfounded enthusiasm for the political systems noted above; she was among a handful of leftists in recent times—former admirers of Communist systems in the Third World—who made a public break with her earlier political beliefs, or at any rate some of them.

A further reason for including her in this study is that while she ceased to idealize Communist states such as Cuba and Vietnam, she retained a high degree of hostility toward American society and its political system. Doubtless it was this profound and enduring estrangement from American society that predisposed her earlier to sympathy for Castro's Cuba and Communist Vietnam. (Ironically, one of the things she appreciated most about the North Vietnamese was their total lack of alienation.) After these sympathies were long gone, the estrangement nurturing them survived.

During the 1960s and '70s, when Sontag took her political stands, she was among numerous politically engaged "public intellectuals" as criticism of Western societies became widespread and standardized among intellectuals, both academic and nonacademic.[44] In the United States, the Vietnam War and racial discrimination provided the background for such public stands, especially among academics. Many were led not merely to the rejection of U.S. policies abroad but to fantasies of an imminent, major revolutionary transformation at home. In February 1966, according to her biographers Carl Rollyson and Lisa Paddock,

> [Sontag] emerged alongside Norman Mailer, Bernard Malamud, William Styron, Robert Lowell and other figures of the arts, as a political activist, adding her voice to a "Read-in for Peace in Vietnam" at Manhattan Town Hall. She spoke of writers who were "choking with shame and anger" because "a small nation of handsome people" were being "brutally and self-righteously slaughtered" by a "grotesquely overarmed" super-power. . . .[45]

In contrast to the fluctuations of her political views about Communist systems, Sontag's stance toward American society displayed a marked continuity: a profound and visceral alienation from American culture and condemnation of U.S. foreign policy. These attitudes persisted well beyond (and in spite of) the remarkable renunciation of her pro-Communist beliefs and resurfaced in her remarks following 9/11:

> This was not a "cowardly" attack on "civilization" or "liberty" or "humanity" or "the free world" but an attack on the world's self-proclaimed superpower, undertaken as a consequence of specific American alliances and actions. . . . The unanimity of the sanctimonious, reality-concealing rhetoric spouted by American officials and media commentators . . . seems unworthy of a mature democracy.

Sontag gave every indication of being far more outraged by the White House, including its "robotic president" and public figures who supported him, than by the terrorists.[46] A year later, writing on the anniversary of the attacks, she expressed the same suspicion of and hostility toward the federal authorities (the Bush administration), appearing to object far more strenuously to what she called "the jihad language of the American government" than to the actual jihad and its human cost.[47]

There are several questions to ponder as one tries to understand Sontag's uneven political transformation and her anti-communism preceded by her public involvement with the left. Most puzzling, what exactly prompted her dramatic, public rejection of her own leftist beliefs in 1982 and the rebuke she administered to the left? How can her rejection of numerous defining beliefs of the left be reconciled with an apparently lifelong and heartfelt animosity toward American society? Why this lifelong rejection of America in the first place?

It is likely that Sontag's anti-Americanism was initially largely cultural and "elitist"—an outgrowth of a contempt for philistinism, ignorance, ordinariness, mass culture, uneducated people, lack of taste, lack of refinement, lack of style. These are attributes easy to pin on "middle America" or mainstream America. This was a visceral anti-Americanism linked to the pursuit of a distinctive identity, and a cultural elite status also reflected in her admiration of France and French intellectual currents and customs. Probably her rejection of America had much to do with a quest for a unique identity and authenticity. Peter Berger's observation applies here: "In the ideology of many New Left intellectuals, authenticity and insurrection have been equated. The 'true self' creates itself in the act of violent rebellion against the bourgeois order."[48] Sontag's disposition conformed to Lionel Trilling's definition of the adversary culture and the adversarial mind-set, especially the belief that "a primary function of art and thought is to liberate the individual from the tyranny of his culture . . . and to permit him to stand beyond it in an autonomy of perception and judgment."[49] Sontag was certainly concerned with the "true self" and seemed convinced that its assertion and cultivation was incompatible with the acceptance of the dominant characteristics of American society. This form of self-assertion began at an early age. She "recalled that her main project at fourteen was to protect herself from the drivel of contemporary society threatening to drown her."[50] The political contours of this deep and broad rebellion emerged during the 1960s when intellectual elite status required taking certain political stands (anti-war, anti-racist, anti-capitalist, feminist, etc).

Even before her widely publicized 1982 break with the left, in a 1978 interview for a French publication she expressed misgivings very similar to her far better known statement four years later:

> . . . there is in the West a tendency to "excuse" what is happening in the East. To want to believe the *best* about everything that happens under the flag of communism or Marxism. One hears disagreeable things about the camps, the prisons, the psychiatric hospitals. Right away one tries to find an interpretation that will excuse that—their situation

> is difficult, they are surrounded, besieged, they started out from a "backward" situation. . . . I think that there is a long history . . . of this tendency to "find excuses." We are pitiless about situations . . . described as fascist, and very indulgent about anything that calls itself "socialist" or "communist." . . . To be anti-fascist means to be pro-communist. This is the logic that has influenced people's minds for the last fifty years. . . .

Sontag explained her own change of mind by referring to some of her readings: ". . . the shock came first, before Solzhenitsyn, from the book *Hope Against Hope* by Nadezhda Mandelstam. . . ." On the other hand she used to be reluctant to believe Solzhenitsyn and credited her friend Joseph Brodsky with convincing her that what he described was true. She also admitted her profound political ignorance, not having heard of Trotsky until the early fifties and having "undergone a real Stalinist 'brainwashing.' There was a formidably efficient censorship." As to her later ideological sympathies, she notes (in the same interview) that "In the sixties, at the time of the Cuban Revolution, I had started the classic journey for many intellectuals which consisted of transfering our political hopes to the 'Third World.'"

The Soviet invasion of Czechoslovakia in 1968 was "a shock," but by then she was preoccupied with Vietnam and abstained from a public condemnation of the Soviet Union. She freely admits that her gullibility did not end with her abandonment of the Soviet model. In Cuba, in Hanoi, in China she believed that those systems were far superior to that of the Soviet Union and that they thoroughly rejected Soviet practices: "We believed things coming from the East [the non-Soviet East, in this case] that we would not have believed for a second in our own countries." Sontag provides a partial explanation of these attitudes—the gullibility, the double standards, the wish to believe—in the "shame at being a bourgeois intellectual."

She came to realize that Communist states became so oppressive because of their commitment to sweeping change: "When you want to change everything you're forced to oppress. . . . If you want 'total' change you are asking for totalitarianism. You have to refuse to believe the myth of the 'new man.'" But of course it was precisely this commitment to sweeping change, to what Raymond Aron a long time ago called "the myth of the revolution," that made these systems appealing to Western intellectuals bored with the tinkering gradualism and the absence of drama and excitement in their own society.

At the end of the interview Sontag reaffirmed her desire "to remain a Marxist in a certain sense," as well as her aversion to "consumer society," and warned against the risk of "a total renunciation of politics" by intellectuals.[51] In short, the adversarial position continued to attract her even when she took a good measure of the available alternatives. The interview reflected political and intellectual currents in France in the mid-seventies, which she knew and which probably influenced her. The French anti-Soviet "new philosophers" made Sontag's anti-communism respectable and may well have inspired hers.

The famous and controversial Town Hall speech in New York in February 1982 was the apparent major milestone in Sontag's political evolution. The meeting was called to protest the suppression of Solidarity in Poland but was also used to criticize the Reagan administration for its policy in El Salvador. Sontag—presumably to everyone's surprise—used the occasion to launch an attack on the American and Western left and its long-standing reluctance to take a stand against the repression prevailing in Communist states. She expressed basically the same views she had already entertained in her interview with the French publication cited above, but in stronger language. Once more she concentrated on the double standards of Western intellectuals, their willful ignorance of Communist societies and their inexcusable gullibility. More important and inflammatory—as far as her audience and erstwhile political bedfellows were concerned—was her equation of Communist and fascist repression, and her unwillingness to entertain fine distinctions between the degree of evil represented by different Communist states. She had violated the taboo on the left that required abstaining from sweeping, unqualified anti-communist statements; that is, she repudiated the anti-anti-communism that had prevailed on much of the left ever since McCarthyism.

She began by noting:

> . . . much of what is said about politics by people on the so-called democratic left . . . has been governed by the wish not to give comfort to "reactionary" forces. With this consideration in mind, people on the left have willingly or unwittingly told a lot of lies. We were unwilling to identify ourselves as anti-Communists because that was the slogan of the right, the ideology of the cold war. . . .

She proceeded to examine what she considered the lessons of the events in Poland: ". . . the principal lesson to be learned is the lesson of the failure of Communism, the utter villainy of the Communist system." She recalled that Milosz's *The Captive Mind*, when it first appeared in 1953, "troubled" her, but she had regarded it "as an instrument of cold war propaganda giving aid and comfort to Mc-

Carthyism." In 1980 she took the book with her to Poland and on that visit learned that "Milosz had, if anything, underestimated the disgrace of the Communist regime. . . ." She chastised herself for her past reluctance to believe what Milosz and other exiles from Communist countries had to say. It all boiled down to the question of who were the political friends or enemies of the left: it was widely considered disgraceful to be on the same side as the contemptible right, "the professional anti-Communists." It would have been easier to learn the truth about Communist countries from the *Reader's Digest* (which no self-respecting left-liberal intellectual would touch) than from *The Nation* or *The New Statesman*, because the *Digest* published the revelations of emigrés from Communist countries—a remark her audience found particularly galling.

Similarly iconoclastic was her observation that

> many of us . . . did not try to understand the nature of Communist tyranny. We tried to distinguish *among* Communisms—for example treating "Stalinism" which we disavowed, as if it were an aberration, and praising other regimes, outside of Europe, which had and have essentially the same character.

In effect Sontag embraced the theory of totalitarianism and the moral equivalence it implied between fascist (or Nazi) and Communist systems. She added:

> . . . We should have understood a very long time ago: that Communism is fascism—successful fascism . . . Communism is . . . the most successful variant of fascism. Fascism with a human face . . . like many people on the democratic left I did not understand the *essentially* despotic nature of the Communist system. . . .[52]

Sontag presented her audience with an eloquent summary of her newfound convictions but said little about how she had come to them. In particular she never explained why she came to accept the testimony of exiles, why she "had to believe" what they said about Communist countries. Plenty of people, including other distinguished intellectuals, had no trouble *disbelieving* them or paying little attention to them. She had been one of them. By the time Joseph Brodsky came along, she was more receptive to information contradicting her earlier convictions and predisposition. This newfound receptivity was the key to her political attitude change; most likely it was created by the new anti-Soviet intellectual currents in France.

Sontag qualified her Town Hall remarks by rejecting Diana Trilling's welcome into the ranks of anti-Communists (in her response to comments also published in *The Nation*) and ended her *Nation* reply by expressing her support for the "democratic movement in El Salvador, whose struggle to overthrow the tyranny backed by the American government I passionately support."[53]

Sontag reiterated the main contentions of the Town Hall speech on other occasions. In an interview later that year she said,

> What I am saying is so obvious but it's never too late to say the truth. . . . I think that a very large portion of the left has underestimated the wickedness of the Communists. It's a mistake I shared from the early 60's, when I went to Cuba and was terrifically impressed with the Cuban revolution . . . through the invasion of Czechoslovakia in '68.

She noted that the period of liberalization in the Soviet Union ended with the invasion of Czechoslovakia, which was the starting point of her changing political views. In the same interview she revealed that she was working on "a long essay on intellectuals and communism."[54] The essay—completed or not—was never published.[55]

In a 1984 interview she was asked if, in light of her views expressed in the Town Hall speech, she was led to reevaluate her own work. She responded:

> . . . I was not expressing new ideas but rather feelings I'd had since the mid 70s when I started to meet a lot of people, like Joseph Brodsky, who were in exile from Communist countries. I had to believe what they said about how terrible conditions were in these countries. The 60s (when I visited many of these countries) had been a great time of hope. . . . All this ended in 1968 with the invasion of Czechoslovakia.
>
> I had a very discouraging experience with an essay in which I was to discuss the relationship between intellectuals and the idea of revolution. . . . I abandoned it. It's quicksand![56]

Further explaining why she abandoned this essay, Sontag said that if she had written about "the romance of Communism" her audience would have been broader (than it was at Town Hall), and she was "not interested in giving aid and comfort to the neo-Conservatives. It's a crucifying dilemma. I was finally defeated by it. I spent a year and a half writing hundreds of pages and gave up."[57]

Abandoning this essay, and her reasons for doing so, seem to mark the limits of Sontag's political soul searching. She was apparently torn between a desire to rebut the author of *Political Pilgrims* (and in doing so to defend her views on Cuba and North Vietnam) and the rather different and daunting undertaking of a broader, critical exploration of the political follies of her fellow intellectuals, which might have given "aid and comfort" to the neo-conservatives—something she could not bear to do. The solution was a partial retreat from politics. Her own ambivalence about the iconoclastic political stance she once took is indicated by the fact that the *Susan Sontag Reader*—supposedly tracing the author's intellectual evolution—excluded the Town Hall speech, as if it had been an embarrassment to be forgotten.

The interviews and statements quoted above were not the only indications of Sontag's fluctuating political views. Two years after the article in which she expressed her love for the Cuban Revolution, in the spring of 1971 she was among the signatories of a public letter protesting the imprisonment of the Cuban writer Heberto Padilla.

Until the Yugoslav civil war and the siege of Sarajevo in the early 1990s, Sontag turned her back on politics. The conflict in Bosnia, and the fate of Sarajevo in particular, once more mobilized her capacity for moral indignation and political involvement. The explanation may be found in her identification of Sarajevo with the Spanish Civil War, which provided great opportunities for Western intellectuals to take untarnished public stands; once more an opportunity presented itself to show solidarity with fighters for freedom and social justice and thus exemplify the proper role of the committed intellectual, "whose vocation is to take up the best causes." This conflict also provided another opportunity to castigate her fellow intellectuals who failed to rally to the side of the people of Sarajevo: "Most intellectuals are as conformist, as willing to support the prosecution of unjust wars as most other people exercising educated professions. The number of people who have given intellectuals a good or (depending on your point of view) bad name—as troublemakers, voices of conscience—has always been very small. . . . Why so little response to what happened in Bosnia?"[58]

One explanation of Sontag's changing political positions may be found in her abiding apprehension about becoming inadvertently associated with the enemies of the left, "the professional anti-communists" of the right abhorred by liberal intellectuals in good standing. How was one to distinguish between acceptable and unacceptable anti-communism? One major distinction could be found in the "respectable" anti-Communists' insistence that Marxist theory remained a beautiful ideal that should not be blamed for what had been done in its name. Another important distinction was that respectable anti-Communists persevered in the belief that capitalism remained the overarching source of evil in the world. Third, and partly flowing from the former, this respectable anti-communism was not supposed to provide any license for taking a more charitable view of American (or Western) society.

In all probability Sontag would have also agreed with her son, David Rieff, on the difference between the two kinds of anti-communism: "The decent feeling of mourning for a great human hope is what is missing from neo-conservativism; though its anti-communism is correct, its way with ideas is coarse and vulgar when compared to the tradition it criticizes."[59]

In the final analysis it is easier to understand why Sontag admired Communist Cuba and Vietnam than to comprehend her retreat from these attitudes. Her admiration of these political systems coincided with the intensification of the anti–Vietnam War movement that became associated with a far-reaching rejection of the social and institutional order of her own country. As I have discussed elsewhere, Cuba and Vietnam were the apparent alternatives to everything Sontag and her fellow radicals detested in their own society.[60] Probably the most important factor in Sontag's case was an unease, a sense of estrangement she harbored from an early age: "she had never been comfortable in America."[61]

The transformation of her politics could be most directly linked to the influence of Joseph Brodsky, her close friend from the mid-seventies who "reoriented" her politics, as her biographers put it. He was a great poet and an authentic witness to the inhumanities of the Soviet system; learning the political facts of life from a human being one respects and trusts carries far more weight than information extracted from books. Besides their shared Jewishness, reverence for literature, and high culture, Sontag also had in common with Brodsky "a sense of displacement," of "being internal exiles."[62]

The 1968 Soviet invasion of Czechoslovakia that figures in her retrospective political reassessment was not a major source of attitude change when it happened, just as *The Captive Mind* failed to make much of an impact when she first read it. In 1968 she was not yet receptive to information casting doubt on the virtues of Communist systems.

Her biographers offer a further conjecture as to why she changed her political worldview: "Illness had driven Sontag to reexamine the sources of her own thinking. . . . During her illness she had also begun to reappraise her politics"—a reappraisal that found first expression in the 1978 interview in the French journal.[63]

Finally, one may entertain the possibility that Sontag's changing political beliefs and attitudes reflect a devaluation both of the importance of politics and of durable convictions in general. As her biographers put it, "Sontag dislikes the idea of being tied to her opinions, and they often trail after her like orphans she would rather not acknowledge."[64] This observation is supported by her preoccupation with novelty and by seeing herself as a superbly sophisticated trendsetter. If so, her "openness to change" and preoccupation with reinventing herself suggest that in some respects she was more thoroughly and solidly American than she would have liked to think.

CHRISTOPHER HITCHENS (1949–). The abandonment of radical leftist beliefs and political activities of Christopher Hitchens, the prolific writer and journalist, has been among the most noteworthy of such changes of heart in recent times. His change of attitude is all the more remarkable since he used to have little sympathy for such political converts.

On the occasion of a conference dedicated to "second thoughts" about past support for New Left positions and worldview, he asked, "Who needs yet another set of breast-beating recusants, this time accusing themselves of a past mired in terrorism, crime and family maladjustments?"[65] He noted that he has "never been a Stalinist, a Weatherman enthusiast or a Black Panther groupie,"[66] unlike some of the conference participants—a circumstance that probably moderated his own, much later soul searching discussed below.

In fact, the "second thoughts" displayed at this conference were quite dissimilar from those he came to entertain some fifteen years later. Hitchens indicated (in a personal communication) that the piece quoted above was a good indication of his thinking at the time, but if he were to reprint it now he would make some changes; he also noted that he later became friends with some of the conference participants.[67]

A self-declared Trotskyite and a columnist for twenty years for the flagship publication of the radical left in the United States, *The Nation*, author of books denouncing Henry Kissinger as a war criminal, Mother Teresa as a fake, and former President Clinton as an all-round sellout and opportunist, Hitchens's debunking impulses also found expression in inveighing against Winston Churchill, John F. Kennedy, and the Dalai Lama; he compared Paul Johnson, the well-known British author, to a "carrion bird" and characterized him as a "would-be informer and stool pigeon." On the same occasion he referred to Norman Podhoretz, the American conservative author and editor, as "another moral and intellectual hooligan who wishes he had the balls to be a real-life rat fink."[68] Hitchens does not aspire to nuanced judgments. On one occasion he expressed undisguised contempt for "former and actual radicals [who] intone piously against 'the politics of confrontation . . .,'" and averred that "if this collection has a point, it is the desire of one individual to see the idea of confrontation kept alive."[69]

Hitchens resigned from *The Nation* in late 2002 and was thereafter "excommunicated from the left,"[70] ceasing to be part of the subculture and political community to which he belonged for much of his adult life. In 2004 he told an interviewer, "I don't really consider myself to have any political or party allegiance any more."[71] Nonetheless his break with his political past has not been complete. Even after his own "second thoughts," he still considered himself "a man of the left" or a "Marxist libertarian." He did not distance himself from his past even as he admitted errors of judgment.[72]

Hitchens's break with the radical left seems to have been prompted more by the attitudes and positions of his former political friends and allies than by disappointment with any particular Communist system or Marxist ideology. What offended him most were the obfuscations, double standards, and moral evasions he encountered in the radical left subculture, especially its unwillingness to rally to the defense of Western ideals and institutions when they came under attack from Islamic extremists.

While personality always plays an important role in the formation and revision of political attitudes, it looms especially large in Hitchens's case. He is a self-described "contrarian," a highly individualistic, polemical, and "judgmental" person congenitally incapable of submitting to authority and obeying rules. He thinks of himself as a loner; he does not prize "the solidarity of belonging" which, he rightly feels, has "too many suffocating qualities."[73]

An unusual attribute of Hitchens is an awareness of his personal privileges, considering himself among the most fortunate 1 percent of humanity and yet "wake[ing] up every day to a sensation of pervading disgust and annoyance"[74] with much of the world. Notwithstanding such a professed disposition, he comes across, both in his writings and in personal contact, as a cheerful, sociable, outgoing, and curious individual capable of warmth; an optimistic rationalist who believes that

> the instinct for justice and for liberty is just as much "innate" . . . as are the promptings of tribalism and sexual xenophobia and superstition. People know when they are being lied to . . . they do not love their chains. . . . The crucial organ is the mind, not the gut.[75]

An extreme and freely expressed anti-religious outlook is another of Hitchens's hallmarks. He regards religion as "the most base and contemptible of the forms assumed by human egotism and stupidity."[76] Not only does he regard all religions as "versions of the same untruth," he holds "that the influence of churches and the effect of religious belief, is positively harmful"; religion is "a sinister fairy tale."[77] This impassioned rejection of religion helps explain both his attraction to classical Marxism (given its powerful demysification of religion) and his recent disenchantment with elements of the Western left for failing to reject decisively Islamic religious fundamentalism and fanaticism. Revulsion from religion played a part both in his becoming a Marxist social critic and more recently in his rejection of the secular pieties and hypocrisy of his erstwhile comrades. His aversion to religion eventually carried over to a broader antipathy to all belief systems demanding unconditional respect and submission, including secular religions such as Marxism-Leninism.

Unlike most Western intellectuals and especially those here discussed, Hitchens did not remain in the society where he grew up: he moved from Britain to the United States at a time when, given his politics, there was no apparent reason to prefer the United States.[78] How he balanced what he called his "love of America . . . only an immigrant is capable of"[79] against his New Leftist critiques of American imperialism, capitalism, and mass culture is a matter that needs better understanding. Most likely he regarded American society as more egalitarian and open than the British, and offering more opportunity in every sense of the word. He wrote: "I have found the patch of soil on which I will take my own stand. . . . It's the only place in history where patriotism can be divorced from its evil twins of chauvinism and xenophobia." He added, "The United States of America has been very kind and hospitable to this immigrant. . . . My adopted country has found a defender in me."[80] By contrast he shows a striking lack of warmth in his writings about his native country.

Arguably Hitchens's attraction to America was largely apolitical; he found appealing things here that had little direct political relevance or resonance, such as the character and manners of the people, especially the "common people," and the spaciousness and geographical variety. His admiration of the "common people" is reminiscent of Orwell's. In the wake of 9/11 he wrote of "the burly, uncomplaining, stoic proletarian defenders, busting their sinews in the . . . wreckage and carnage of downtown."[81]

For a restless, peripatetic nonconformist, the United States offered a more hospitable and tolerant environment than any other country could, even if Hitchens harbored serious critiques of its social, economic, and political arrangements and institutions.

Hitchens was never a supporter of the Soviet Union, but he briefly shared the soft spot his political generation had for Third World Communist systems, seen as more authentic and revolutionary than the Soviet. Even at a time when his older political loyalties were firmly in place, he did not abandon his critical faculties, though occasionally he succumbed to wishful thinking and projection regarding these systems. Thus in 1980 he discerned similarities between the atmosphere of Communist Angola and revolutionary Petrograd of 1917 and Barcelona of the Spanish Civil War.[82] He dismissed the notion of "the revolution betrayed" as applied to Sandinista Nicaragua, but he also noted "symptoms of encroaching orthodoxy" and the indisputable existence of a "one-party state" as well as the censorship of opposition newspapers. On the other hand he considered the regime's "achievements in social welfare and education . . . spectacular and moving."[83] In 1968 he went to Cuba "with the express purpose" of raising questions about the Cuban government's support of the Soviet invasion of Czechoslovakia that same year (as he told me in a letter). On the other hand, as of 1983 he believed that the success of the Bay of Pigs invasion "would have been much more disastrous" than its failure.[84] Over the passing years he ceased to have illusions about Cuba and showed a sharp awareness of the prevailing repression there and the chronic, high-handed mismanagement of the country. Unlike so many of his fellow former leftists, he did not find excuses for Cuba's repression and economic failures in American policies. In 1989 he wrote: "Spare me letters that remind us all that Cuba has a good health-care system and abolished literacy. A healthy, literate people do not need to be told that they can read. . . ."[85] More recently, following a visit, he concluded that Cuba, permitting capitalism and profiteering but not free expression, might be called "the worst of both worlds." He also wrote:

> The only leader in Latin America who always wears a military uniform and who steadfastly and on principle refuses elections, is Fidel Castro. Cuban citizens are forbidden . . . to use hotels reserved for the rich and may not even enter many stores and pharmacies which trade only in dollars. After forty years, there are few senior black faces in

the supposed "leadership." Many doctors have been trained but they are paid less than the hotel doormen or policemen in the segregated tourist districts. . . .[86]

Hitchens also took a good measure of the North Korean regime during a visit in 2001. This was hardly an occasion for disillusionment since North Korea, a truly Stalinist state, never enjoyed the revolutionary mystique of Third World communist systems (such as Cuba, Mao's China, and wartime North Vietnam) bestowed upon them by Western sympathizers. In the course of his visit he was shown the "International Friendship Exhibition," where presents from foreign admirers of the regime were displayed and where he came upon "a silver box, with CNN logo, from Ted Turner and Jane Fonda. An English version of Kim Il Sung's essays with a foreword by Eldridge Cleaver, from Harrison Salisbury of the *New York Times*. A white crane sculpture, listed as given by 'The Religious Leader of the United States,'" who turned out to be Billy Graham.[87] While in North Korea he realized that "the whole place is for show. . . . Newspapers . . . contain no news. Restaurants produce menus of nonexistent dishes. At the airport . . . barely any planes. In the national art gallery . . . almost all the paintings are of the same two people." North Korea was a "famine state" and "a garrison state, a society organized for war," deformed by the historically unprecedented "fervor and single-mindedness of . . . deification" of the father-son dynasty.[88]

In examining Hitchens's political transformation, three matters require careful consideration: What exactly were the beliefs he abandoned? What were the precipitating events or circumstances? What remains of his old beliefs which survived the break with the radical left? As one observer put it, ". . . What is far less clear . . . is whether Hitchens has ever been, like Orwell, an anti-Communist (as opposed to merely an anti-Stalinist). . . ."[89]

We need some background for trying to understand these matters. Hitchens, in his own words, came from "a longish line of naval and military types" on his father's side and was "brought up on and around bases."[90] Whether or not this had any tangible effect on his political beliefs is not clear. His Jewish mother was a liberal, and his father did not seek to influence his political outlook (so he told me). He has, however, been estranged from his brother (also a journalist and writer) who became a "fundamentalist Anglican" and attacked him in the British journal *The Spectator*.[91]

Hitchens once summarized his political evolution to an interviewer:

> At the time and place when I came to political awareness, which was the early mid-1960s in England, the governing Establishment was that of the Labor party in its most corrupt and opportunist form. . . . The charm and appeal of the "social democratic" project was thus very slight. And coming from a generation which had read *Darkness at Noon* and *Nineteen Eighty Four* . . . the option of illusion in orthodox Communism did not seriously exist. I think it is this formative background that meant that, in Western Europe at least, the radical and insurgent spirit was attracted to one form or another of "Trotskyism."[92]

Mark Falcoff in 2003 characterized Hitchens's political attitude formation somewhat differently: "Originally a Trotskyist, at some point in the 1980s Hitchens drifted toward a kind of pink-tinged Euroneutralism cum knee-jerk anti-Americanism. There he seems to have stayed mired until only a year or so ago." Falcoff also noted that Hitchens has been "steadily in the forefront of the hard Left's crusade against Zionism and the state of Israel"[93]—an attitude that found expression in his co-editing with Edward Said in 1988 the pro-Palestinian volume entitled *Blaming the Victim*. His long-standing friendship with Said ended when he criticized Said's new introduction to his book *Orientalism* as well as some of the main themes of the book itself. Hitchens was specifically critical of Said's suggestion that "the American forces in Baghdad set themselves to annihilate Iraq's cultural patrimony" by looting and destroying museums and libraries.[94] When I wondered how he had managed earlier to overlook Said's intense hostility to the United States, Hitchens thought this was a mistaken impression; Said, while emotional, was not "a hating type," he said.[95] In any event, Hitchens said he preferred to discuss literary matters with Said rather than politics, but there is little doubt that a shared pro-Palestinian disposition was an important political bond between them. Hitchens, responding to my question, stands by the views expressed in the book he co-edited with Said and feels strongly about the injustices Palestinians suffered at the hands of Israel. To what degree these sentiments are part of a residual "third worldism" is not clear, nor is it easy to locate the source of the special concern with the fate of Palestinians, given the large number of other oppressed groups around the world which did not stimulate similar expressions of concern on his part.

Understanding Hitchens's political transformation, genuine and far-reaching as it has been, is complicated by remnants of the radical left worldview. He is not embarrassed about his political past. In 2001 (but before 9/11) he wrote: "I have not . . . abandoned all the tenets of the left. . . . I still think that there are opposing class interests: I still think that monopoly capitalism can and should be distinguished from the free market and that it has certain fatal tendencies. . . ."[96] In 2003 he declared that he still uses "the method of historical materialism (not yet surpassed by any rival)."[97] Elsewhere Hitchens has suggested that "the essential element of historical materialism as applied to ethical and social matters" is its capacity to demonstrate "how much unhappiness and injustice and irrationality was man-made"[98]—an insight not peculiar to historical materialism.

Among the old articles of faith Hitchens has retained are scaled-down utopian longings, or at any rate a respectful attitude toward them. He wrote:

> My old mentor and friend Robert Conquest . . . is still I think mistaken when he suggests that most of our woes derive from idealists, social engineers and Utopians. He is correct in his way, and we shall never again be able to look indulgently on the sort of radical who claims to act like a pitiless surgeon or a ruthless engineer. However . . . the worst crimes are still committed in the name of old traditional rubbish: of loyalty to nation or "order" or leadership or tribe or faith. . . .
>
> . . . We are somehow so constituted as to feel the permanent lash of discontent. It is not possible to immunize people against the hope of extraordinary change.[99]

There is also some nostalgia for the 1960s apparent in his revelations:

> I of course like to think of myself as having been a "Sixty Eighter" . . . rather than being merely a "Sixties person"—there seemed the chance not only of contesting the atrocious imperial war in Vietnam but of ending the dictatorial regimes of De Gaulle, Franco, Salazar and Papadopoulos, and of extending this movement across the Berlin Wall. . . . To have been involved in street-arguments in Havana [he doesn't say with whom] while Chicago was erupting and Prague was being subjugated was to feel oneself part of a revolutionary movement. What I didn't understand then was that this was the very end of something—the revolutionary Marxist tradition—rather than a new beginning of it. But it had its aspect of honor and glory. Its greatest culmination turned out to be in 1989 when the delayed or postponed effects of 1968 helped to bring down the Berlin Wall. . . .[100]

The conflation of the fall of the Berlin Wall in 1989 with the radical left movements of 1968 invites questions. None of those movements showed much interest in or had much knowledge of what went on behind the Iron Curtain, and even if they had had such concerns it would have made little difference to developments within the Soviet Bloc. The New Left was rooted almost entirely in and impelled by Western social-cultural processes and discontents, and its critique of the Soviet Union had much more to do with perceiving it as another industrial-bureaucratic superpower (a somewhat preferable counterpart to the United States) than with repression behind the Iron Curtain. There was also considerable ignorance of the nature of such repression; the New Left was in the forefront of obscuring its dimensions by its belief in the moral equivalence of the superpowers. This is not to deny that the crushing of the Hungarian Revolution of 1956 and that of the "Prague Spring" in 1968 hastened and sometimes precipitated Western disillusionment with Soviet communism; but such disillusionment did not readily (if at all) translate into pressures undermining the Soviet Union and its control over Eastern Europe.

The fusion of the 1968 Soviet invasion of Czechoslovakia with Western student movements of the same period is equally (or even more) questionable. Especially dubious is the claim that the "delayed effects" of the events of 1968 in the West helped bring down the Wall or, more generally, hastened the collapse of Soviet communism. It may be that it is sixties nostalgia that finds expression in the effort to recast the period and its Western student movements as some sort of a universal liberation campaign, overlooking or forgetting that these movements were weighed down with and compromised by their support of highly repressive Third World communist dictatorships (Cuba, China, Vietnam) and by their embrace of some of the most radical Leninist ideas; these were also movements that displayed an aggressive intolerance of free expression and moderate political positions and groups, including a vocal contempt for liberals.

Touching on these matters in personal conversation, Hitchens argued that specific leftist groups in the West, in particular the International Socialists to which he used to belong, were deeply concerned with events and conditions in Eastern Europe. "The potential symbiosis" between "Sixty-Eighters and Eighty-Niners"[101] has remained one of his preoccupations.

Hitchens's durable reverence for Trotsky is another indication that it is not easy to part with an identity determined to some degree by a sense of belonging to the vanguard of a revolutionary movement. Trotsky appealed to him because he represented "the fusion of the man of ideas with the man of action" and because he became "the lonely outcast"[102] and finally the victim of brutal assassination. "Even today," Hitchens writes, "a faint, saintly penumbra emanates from the Old Man."[103] Clearly Hitchens retains a soft spot for Trotsky, appearing unconcerned with the ruthlessness he showed in 1921, among other occasions, when in charge of suppressing the Kronstadt rebellion.

Reverence for Trotsky is paralleled by Hitchens's sentiments toward another romantic and martyred figure of the left, Che Guevara. As in the case of Trotsky, Hitchens was impressed by Guevara's authenticity, by the blend of idealism and action, and by Guevara's willingness to make harsh demands on himself, culminating in the doomed effort to organize a guerrilla war in Bolivia that led to his death. Important to note here is that the propensity to idealize Che Guevara did not prevent "the realization that Guevara's Cromwellian, ascetic demands on people bordered on the impossible, even the inhuman." Moreover "the very element that gave him his certainty and courage—his revolutionary communism—was also the element that condemned him to historical eclipse."[104] These remarks come close to acknowledging that Guevara's idealism and commitment to utopian social engineering were inseparable from the intolerance and ruthlessness that found expression in the institutionalized and durable repression in Cuba.

The reluctance to break all emotional and ideological bonds with the past also appears in Hitchens's appraisal of Noam Chomsky. In 1985, Hitchens sought to exonerate Chomsky of the (wholly justified) charges that he sought to minimize the massacres of Pol Pot and had given moral support to the Holocaust revisionist Robert Faurisson.[105] More recently in the context of Kosovo and 9/11, he sharply disagreed with Chomsky but retained favorable views of his past political positions. In 2004, Hitchens said that Chomsky "was one of the great figures of conscience during the crisis of the 1960s. . . . [He] has [also] been a useful opponent of the postmodern relativist tendency in the academy and has always believed in verifiable truth and standards of evidence."[106] To be sure, Chomsky is no relativist in his denunciations of the United States, Israel, and capitalism. On the other hand his supposed belief "in verifiable truth and standards of evidence" is rather questionable in light of his comments about U.S. responses to 9/11 (which included the alleged preparation of a "silent genocide in Afghanistan") and his repeated dismissals of the massacres of Pol Pot in the late 1970s.

Notwithstanding his positive assessments of Chomsky's past pronouncements, Hitchens has recently observed that Chomsky's "regard for the underdog mutated into support for mad dogs."[107] Hitchens has also pointed out that Chomsky "has lost or is losing the qualities that made him a great moral and political tutor in the years of the Indochina war." The persisting perception of Chomsky as "a great moral tutor" and "great figure of conscience" is rather problematic, to say the least.

On the other hand, Hitchens was duly appalled by Chomsky's denunciation of Vaclav Havel for preferring the United States to the Soviet Union and by his insistence that "by addressing a joint session of Congress in the fall of 1989 [Havel] was complicit in the murder of Jesuits in El Salvador."[108] Hitchens seems to resist the realization that Chomsky's more recent irrational and hate-filled pronouncements are not exceptional and do not follow from a decline of mind and judgment sometimes associated with aging; they have been present throughout his public career, testifying to a seriously impaired capacity for "moral tutoring."

Hitchens's decisive break with the American left was prompted by the events of 9/11, more specifically by the left's response to the attacks. Perceptions of dishonesty, hypocrisy, and bad faith always ranked high among the stimulants of his moral indignation and passion. These events led him to break ranks publicly not only with *The Nation* and Chomsky but also with Ramsey Clark and the journalist Alexander Cockburn; he also aimed a withering critique at Michael Moore, at the time basking in the fame and popularity of his movie *Fahrenheit 9/11*.

It may well be that the deepest source of Hitchens's conflict with the left is his belief that in the struggle against Islamic terrorism "the very first step we must take . . . is the acquisition of enough self-respect and self-confidence to say that we have met the enemy and that he is not us but someone else."[109] It was a proposition that flew in the face of the entrenched conventional leftist wisdom that endlessly accused the United States of creating the "root causes" of terror and, more generally, the leftist conviction that American society had no grounds whatsoever for self-respect or self-confidence. Hitchens could not subscribe to the belief that "John Ashcroft is a greater menace than Osama bin Laden."[110]

Hitchens was among the few to point out that "to the extent that the United States underwrote Saddam in the past, this redoubles our responsibility to cancel the moral debt by removing him." Unlike many on the left, he was incapable of thinking of "Milosevic and Saddam as victims"[111] and of persisting in the belief that "American imperialism is the main enemy."[112]

Hitchens's passionate and unqualified condemnation of terrorism has been conditioned by factors peculiar to his life and personality. They include his strong, sentimental identification with American society as an immigrant and his affection for and attachment to the city of New York. Of further, possibly greater importance is his lifelong aversion to religion and the kind of religious fanaticism that nurtures and motivates the terrorists.

A year after 9/11 he wrote:

> The most depressing thing, for me . . . has been to see so much of the Left so determined to hamper this process [taking action against Milosevic and the Taliban], which is why, after 20 years, I have given up my column in the *Nation* magazine. The left has . . . maintained that any resistance to ethnic cleansing in Bosnia and Kosovo would lead to a wider war. . . . It forecast massive quagmires and intolerable civilian casualties. If this sounds familiar it may be because you are hearing it now . . . from those who thought the Taliban–al Qaeda base in Afghanistan was not worth fighting about.[113]

Hitchens suggests that 9/11 is not the initial and singular cause of his "turning point": "The realization that we were in a cultural and political war with Islamic theocracy came to me . . . not on 11 September 2001 but on 14 February 1989, when the Ayatollah Khomeini offered money in his own name to suborn the murder of my friend Salman Rushdie."[114] Whether or not it was the plot to assassinate Rushdie, the events of 9/11, or the reign of terror in Iraq under Saddam,[115] Hitchens arrived at a new appreciation of Western political systems and values and came to reject the familiar attributions of moral equivalence favored by his former ideological allies. Even more important, he came to "the realization [in Sarajevo] that American power could and should be used for the defense of pluralism and as a punishment for fascism. . . ." It was the first time he found himself "in the same trench as people like Paul Wolfowitz and Jeane Kirkpatrick: a shock I had to learn to get over."[116]

In this statement, as in his coinage of "Islamic fascism," Hitchens betrays another link to his political past: a fixation on "fascism" as a singular and self-evident metaphor or yardstick for designating and discrediting indisputable evil. Susan Sontag did the same in her critiques of Communist systems when she called communism "the most successful variant of fascism."[117]

Hitchens's political learning experiences and evolution culminated in the durable insight that "the search for Nirvana, like the search for Utopia, or the end of history, or the classless society, is ultimately a futile and dangerous one. . . . There is no escape from anxiety and struggle."[118] This insight, needless to say, represents a decisive refutation of the utopian impulses he had earlier entertained.

SEVEN

Disaffection and Resisting It: The Rank and File in the West

In late 1994 and early 1995 I placed the following advertisement in *The Nation*, *The New York Review of Books*, and *Dissent*:

> For a study of political attitudes and commitments I would like to hear from people who at any time in their lives felt drawn to either the Soviet Union, Mao's China, Castro's Cuba, Vietnam, Sandinista Nicaragua or other similar systems. I am interested in both the sources of the original attraction and in the reassessments of such attitudes in recent times. If a more substantial investment of time were to be made (in writing such an account) I could offer modest compensation. For further information contact . . . [my name and office address followed]

The purpose of these advertisements was to learn about disillusionment with Communist systems and beliefs in the late twentieth century (and especially in the wake of the collapse of the Soviet Union) as experienced by less prominent, more anonymous individuals. More specifically I placed the notices, because, as noted earlier, there is little information about such attitude changes in recent times, and few written accounts have been published by those who have undergone them. The information I hoped to obtain also promised an opportunity to compare the path to disillusionment of a handful of well-known individuals (who had published substantial accounts of their experiences) with the corresponding experiences of the presumably more numerous unknown or lesser-known individuals.

Of course, there was no way to know how the people who might respond to such notices differed from the far larger number of otherwise similar individuals who did not, even if both groups shared a changed attitude toward communist systems and beliefs.

As it turned out, and somewhat unexpectedly, the communications I received revealed far more about resistance to political disenchantment and the retention of long-held beliefs than about disenchantment. Most respondents were more interested in discussing the circumstances and sources of their political involvements and attractions than in their reassessments, insofar as they had occurred. I learned more about the varied circumstances which led to left-wing political convictions and affiliations than about the processes that undermined these beliefs. But that too was of interest since one cannot be understood without the other.

I should explain why these materials I received more than a decade ago were not used earlier. In late 1994 and early 1995 when the ads were placed, I had contemplated writing a book about the collapse of Soviet communism that was to combine an analysis of its apparent causes with an examination of Western disillusionment with all existing varieties of communism, including those still in existence. I intended to compare the loss of faith both within and outside the Soviet Bloc with special emphasis on the impact of the collapse on Western sympathizers.

I came to realize that such an undertaking would have required more than a single volume to accomplish. The book I actually wrote[1] ended up as an effort to explain the decline and fall of Soviet communism (no small undertaking in itself) by focusing on the loss of political will and conviction among Soviet leaders and functionaries (mostly the Gorbachev-Yeltsin generation) and some of their Czech and Hungarian counterparts. The examination of Western disaffection with Communist systems in more recent times was deferred.

I received approximately fifty responses to my ads. The responses varied greatly in length and in the amount of useful information provided, ranging from a handwritten note to an essay of twenty-nine typed pages. Besides those written by Americans, I had responses from Australia, Canada, England, and India. To all those who responded, I wrote back asking if they would be willing to complete a questionnaire, that is, to write a personal account addressing specific questions I was to provide. In addition to the written responses to my questions, I obtained supplementary information from interviews with a handful of respondents who lived nearby or were better known and expressed interest in being interviewed.

It is difficult to provide comprehensive information about the respondents in terms of the standard sociological data (age, education, occupation, ethnicity, religious affiliation, etc.) since not all of them disclosed this information. Many of them were academics in the humanities and social sciences; there were also scientists, physicians, lawyers, schoolteachers, social workers, freelance writers, a few businessmen as well as dropouts and people with problematic careers. Most were well educated, with college or postgraduate degrees; they were predominantly middle-aged and usually older, many of them retired.

The respondents generally welcomed the opportunity to write or talk about their attitudes and experiences. Many of them had visited a Communist country: the older ones the Soviet Union, others China, Cuba, or Nicaragua, especially the last two. Several wrote at great length, sometimes enclosing materials they considered important, such as family correspondence, excerpts from unpublished autobiographies, articles which had some bearing on the issues explored, in a few instances articles or pamphlets they had written. Several of them used the opportunity to embark on broader soul searching and self-reflection aimed at a better understanding of the meaning of their entire lives, well beyond a reconsideration of their political positions.

On the whole this was an articulate and thoughtful collection of individuals who continued to reflect upon, or agonize over, their political beliefs and decisions and their revisions. Most of them struck me as decent, serious, and idealistic.

The respondents could be placed into three groups. First was a handful who had no second thoughts, no reservations about their earlier beliefs, and offered no reassessments. Second was a similarly small group who had completely rejected earlier beliefs. Third, and by far the largest, was a majority who sought *some* modification of their beliefs but not a wrenching and far-reaching rejection or reassessment. What follows is a sampling of the responses I received, beginning with those in the first group.

The Unwavering

E.H., a retired Jewish professor in the New York city college system (in a department of education) comes from what she describes as "a left liberal family"; her father was involved in the campaign of Henry Wallace; she read *The Nation* in high school. She writes: "I was a part of a family which criticized American society for its racial, ethnic and class injustices . . . [and] carried on this tradition. . . . I have always been a left-winger and plan to be one till I die." She came of age in the 1930s "when it was respectable to be a leftist." In college she was one of a "small group of leftist intellectuals." She has remained politically active locally and has been contributing money to "lots of left wing, feminist, environmentalist groups." She visited the Soviet Union in 1971, China in 1976 and 1979, Cuba in 1979. In both Cuba and the USSR she was "impressed by the healthy population," in China by attempts to solve disputes "in the community rather than in courts." She saw Cuba "as a country . . . being done in by the U.S. . . . trying to bring that small island back into the capitalist orbit by starving its occupants."

She declares that she "never went through any crisis of belief because I never thought Stalin or Mao were gods" and did not consider their systems "wonderful." Nonetheless she also writes that "I feel more disillusioned than ever with capitalism in my declining years, not with socialism. As I see our country becoming a society with ever-increasing numbers of poor people . . . I am discouraged. It is not easy to fight the enormous power of the conglomerates. . . . I was always a left-liberal and still am—I am a democratic socialist."

She doesn't consider the question whether or not a democratic socialist can or should be sympathetic to Castro's Cuba or Mao's China. She is not entirely unaware of the shortcomings of the Chinese system but treats them as minor blemishes, whereas the shortcomings of the U.S. loom large and determine its entire moral character. Thus she writes: "I was sympathetic to many of the goals of the Soviet Union, Mao's China, Castro's Cuba . . . and I still am. And I certainly supported the Sandinistas in Nicaragua. . . . I believe . . . that health care should be available to everyone . . . that university education should be free. I do not believe that multinational corporations should be in charge, as is pretty much true in our own country. . . ."

She recognizes that she has "a high quotient of moral indignation which invades my personal life. I have always . . . had great compassion for animals and small children." She has always been a person "who takes action" when she sees injustice; she interferes in fights on the street, rescues lost animals, approaches women in the supermarket who mistreat their children. Her unchanging political disposition seems rooted in loyalty to parents and an idealistic liberal-Jewish political tradition; her beliefs were supported throughout her life in congenial academic settings. She looks back on her personal and professional life with satisfaction. She sees little reason for a political reassessment since the defects of her society persist and the defects of Communist systems (past or current) are minor in comparison (this is implied) and, in any case, irrelevant to the abundant injustices she confronts in the United States. Her visits to Communist countries confirmed rather than invalidated her political attitudes; on those visits she was not in a position to learn about matters which would have stimulated her moral indignation.

D.S. is a physician, author of many articles (including at least one in the "theoretical journal" of the American Communist party) and co-author of one book. He writes: "If I had to single out a single influence on my political interest and spectrum it would be easy—my father." He came from a Jewish family. In his youth he marched on picket lines and helped his father sell (or give away) the *Daily Worker* to migrant farm workers; as a college student he distributed leaflets at union rallies and on May lst marched with William Z. Foster, Gus Hall, and Ben Davis, leaders of the American Communist party.

From an early age he was "uneasy with the plight of the world's people," and *Das Kapital* "solidified" his thinking on such matters. He came to the realization that capitalism was responsible for the ills of the world. For more than twenty years he made many trips to Cuba, "always in the official capacity of a teacher." He knew of "no more Machiavellian foreign policy . . . than that [of the United States] toward Cuba. . . . Cuba's survival . . . is a marvel and a tribute to the quality of its system and its people. It is rivaled only by the stamina . . . [of] the people of the USSR who were finally done in by the CIA and the cabal . . . that left them too fragile to resist" [referring to the collapse of the Soviet Union in 1991].

Of Marxism he writes: "Marxism is not difficult to implement at all. . . . That myth is one of many that is extolled by the enemies of the working people. . . . Marxism is . . . pragmatic and viable. It is in trouble, not because Marx was wrong. . . . It is because it is surrounded by its enemies." The collapse of the Soviet Union, besides the long-standing intrigues of "the forces of the right," was the result of "the final betrayals of Mikhail Gorbachev and Boris Yeltsin. . . ." He is convinced that "time is on the side of socialism. Today, over one-fifth of the world's people live under Marx. Its future is secure." (Presumably this refers to China but overlooks the compromises its rulers have made with capitalism.)

He credits the CIA and the "U.S. multinational complex" with the violent defense of the status quo, including the murders of Lumumba, Allende, Mossadegh, and "maybe JFK." He also believes that the United States invaded Korea.

Nothing could be farther from his mind than a reevaluation of his political beliefs:

> Disillusionment? With what? Success? The people of China are now literate, schooled and opium and syphilis free. The people of Cuba, despite their harsh way of life due to the American embargo, are ed-

> ucated, with full health care and 99% literate. . . . In the USA, children die of measles. In Cuba, there is not a child without immunization. Not one. In Cuba today there are . . . billboards screaming out . . . Socialismo o Muerte! Fidel has no trouble selling that idea to his people. . . .

In the last sentence of his statement he writes: "Suffice it to say that I am quite comfortable with my political agenda. As I go on in life, I thank whomever for what I was blessed with—part of which was a sense of social justice that has not wavered but gets stronger and stronger every day." The views of capitalism here entertained (which include responsibility for the Holocaust) resemble those expressed in the *Protocols of the Elders of Zion* recalling the relentless and ubiquitous Jewish striving for the domination of the world.

His comments shed little light on political disillusionment but confirm the patterns associated with the persistence of old beliefs. These beliefs have been central to his sense of identity and a favorable self-conception. They are deeply and firmly rooted in his youth and were nurtured by his father. Equally clear, his sympathy for Cuba, China, and other Communist states is largely due to his belief that these systems righted the shocking wrongs which—he believes—abound in his own society. He has succeeded in shielding himself from all disconfirming information about these political systems, their economic and human failures. His understanding of Marx and of the relevance of his ideas to our times is strikingly limited and apparently conditioned by the wish to believe.

Short of interviews and intimate knowledge of his life, we will never know the circumstances that shaped this true believer who gives every indication of complete satisfaction with his convictions. As in other, better-known instances, his attitudes confirm that a scientific education provides no defense against grotesque political beliefs and wishful thinking.

M.D., an Englishwoman, wrote the longest account of her political beliefs and activities. She comes from what she calls an "upper middle class, conservative family"; her father was a navy doctor. She went to private schools and became a socialist ("of the Communist variety") at age fourteen.

> This early conversion—so inconsistent with my background!—was, I think, the result of my being at a formative stage during . . . the war years, when the Soviet Union was our ally, praised at the highest, most

> official level, and admired by ordinary people . . . and when literature from the Soviet Union was readily available . . . and when my enthusiasm for that country and its ideology did not arouse in my teachers and relations . . . shock and horror. . . .

Russia also fascinated her as a country "different from all other countries, and 'wicked' into the bargain." The latter, apparently, was her parents' view. She was "attracted by all things Russian. . . . Socialism was something specifically Russian like samovars and balalaikas." At roughly the age of fourteen, having read *Challenge* (the journal of the British Young Communist League), she "discovered in one blinding flash of revelation that Socialism was for all countries. . . ." As a result of this reading material she joined the League.

It was her interest in Russia that led to her interest in socialism, and she became convinced of its "greater morality and fairness," i.e., "the common ownership of all sources of wealth, sharing the benefits among all . . . chance to realize their full potential, and regarding all races as one's brothers. . . ."

While attending Oxford University and studying Russian, she joined the Communist party and was chairman of the university's Socialist Club. In the summer of 1947 she went to Yugoslavia to work on the "Youth Railway." In the same year she attended the Soviet-sponsored "World Youth Festival" in Prague. She recalls that "all I heard and saw on these expeditions strengthened my belief in socialism," to which she was strongly predisposed. In Yugoslavia "the atmosphere was like that depicted on Soviet posters of the Five Year Plan period, or portrayed in idealistic, romantic films . . . red flags, stars, slogans, singing, dancing, fraternization between brigades from different countries, unbounded enthusiasm, and a shared belief that we were building not only a railway but a whole new world of peace and brotherhood."

Her case is one of many in whose lives youthful beliefs and idealism became the foundation and proof of lifelong commitment. While in Yugoslavia she met and was deeply impressed by the Bulgarian brigade, and in 1948 went to Bulgaria to work on a dam. As all these activities suggest, her commitment was all-embracing and cumulative. After the break between Tito and Stalin, which pained her, she loyally rejected Yugoslavia and decided to switch her attention to Bulgaria, leading her to study Bulgarian language and history at London University. She married a fellow brigade member, but the marriage did not last; they had one daughter who shares her political views.

Our correspondent was active in the British Communist party and the Society for Friendship with Bulgaria, which she chaired from 1958 to 1973. In 1963–1964 she taught at the English Language School in Sofia. In the early 1970s she applied for a job as a lecturer in Bulgarian history at the School for Slavonic Studies at the University of London; she had already published two books on Bulgarian history but did not get the job for reasons, she suspected, that were political. Between 1973 and 1979 she again taught English in Sofia and in 1979 received a doctorate from Sofia University for a book she wrote about a Bulgarian historical figure. She was also given the position of "guest lecturer" at Sofia University, where she remained until her retirement in 1989, when she returned to England and continued to write books "on Bulgarian themes."

During the 1960s and '70s she made four visits to the Soviet Union and was impressed by "the magnificence of the public buildings" and the imposing city centers "undisfigured by advertisements and commercialization . . . the absence of tawdriness [and] squalor, and anything remotely suggesting pornography." What she saw measured up to her expectations. She "found the Soviet Union a refreshingly wholesome and high-minded society, more cultured and less corrupt than ours and I always felt better for going there. I enjoyed the emphasis on peace and brotherhood."

Her admiration for Bulgaria was based on living and working there for seventeen years. Due to her biography of a famous Bulgarian historical figure and its publication in Bulgaria, she was "treated like a visiting princess . . . loaded with flowers and presents." She admitted that her "position in Bulgaria was unusual and privileged." While acknowledging shortcomings, including "irritating bureaucracy" and "very erratic supplies in shops,"

> by and large, life was serene, secure and constantly improving. There was no striking difference between rich and poor, no real poverty, and little anxiety about the future, because there was full employment . . . prices were stable . . . and the necessities of life were cheap and often state-subsidized. Education . . . was . . . totally free. . . . Medical and dental care was free. . . . Culture was subsidized so that everybody could afford to go to the cinema, theater, opera, concerts. . . . Most enterprises, trade unions had their own holiday hotels. . . . Rents were low. . . . It was a safe, non-violent society. . . .

Only after 1985, in her view, did conditions in Bulgaria begin to deteriorate. Following the first free elections in 1990, "people now have the worst of both worlds: the positive achievements of Socialism are being systematically destroyed and the worst aspects of the Western way of life are being imported."

This long autobiographical account gives every indication that its author found a safe haven in Bulgaria, where she made a new life for herself and basked in the warmth directed at the rare English devotee of the country and its political system. Except for a brief reference early on, she makes no further mention of the failed marriage (or another new one), or of any other long-term relationship and no further reference to her daughter; nor is anything else said about her parents or friends either in England or Bulgaria. This apparent personal isolation was probably compensated for by living in a society that closely approximated her political ideals and aspirations. Thus it is hardly surprising that

> The collapse of the Soviet Union and other socialist countries was very traumatic for me—a kind of bereavement. . . . There had, of course, been other earlier traumatic moments, such as the original attack on Stalin by Khrushchev, and the events in Czechoslovakia and Hungary. I had great hopes that Gorbachev would succeed in setting in motion reforms which would strengthen Socialism by correcting the distortions. . . . As things got worse, I felt as though someone dear to me had taken to prostitution and drug abuse and ended in the gutter! It was very galling to discover that the critics of the Soviet system had, in some respects, been right . . . and I felt shame, and sometimes horror, that I had tried to deny or defend things which were like cancer in the body politic of the Socialist world. . . .

Even in the wake of the collapse of Soviet (and Bulgarian) communism she wrote:

> . . . I must declare that I am still a Socialist. I still want the kind of society that I believed the Soviet Union to be. . . . I want to find a way of achieving all the good features without the negative ones. Nothing that has happened in Eastern Europe, or the world at large . . . has shaken my belief in Marxism and Socialism. Indeed it has confirmed it. It was deviation from Marxist principles, rather than adherence to them which led to the collapse of Communism in Eastern Europe. Even in its imperfect East European form Socialism has shown itself to be capable of sharing wealth more or less equally and of providing every citizen with the essentials for a decent life. . . . Capitalism is incapable of doing this. . . .

This brings her to the observation that socialist society, unlike all previous societies, must be "consciously desired and created. . . . It is a public garden . . . it constantly needs the attention of skilled gardeners who genuinely care for the individual plants and the whole, and it is very susceptible to weeds, pests and weather." Numerous enemies made it difficult for socialist countries to prosper. Many of the repressive aspects of Soviet communism must be blamed on those who were intent on "strangling" it. But the fundamental problem was the fallibility of human beings: "many of those in positions of power in the Socialist countries were not Communists at all." The nomenklatura came to include many who were "radishes": red on the outside and white inside. The Communist parties in power came to attract "careerists." Yeltsin was one such "chameleon" who pretended to be a true Communist.

She also concluded that "a one-party system should come about only when, and if, everybody is agreed on a single course." The careerist bureaucrat is one of the greatest dangers to implementing socialism. It was also a mistake to impose travel restrictions since, in her view, the Bulgarians who went to the West returned with a greater appreciation of socialism.

A major influence on her political thinking was wartime Soviet literature which offered "a vision of a new and fairer society" and Russian literature in general with its "civic ideal." Among the Soviet writings that influenced her she singled out Ostrovsky's *How the Steel Was Tempered*, a classic of socialist realism which was required reading under Stalin throughout the "Socialist Commonwealth"—a novel that portrays a highly implausible, endlessly self-sacrificing positive hero.[2]

Falling back on a culinary metaphor, she argues that "in itself the recipe was not faulty," but some wrong ingredients were used. By contrast, nothing good can be said about capitalism: "the very nature and purpose of capitalism prevent it from seeking or achieving an equitable distribution of wealth and benefits, and from protecting the weak, the disadvantaged and the losers." She believes that "the purpose of society should be to care for all its members . . . i.e., act as a good family does. Therefore I still choose Socialism, and hope that in time we shall get it right and build the kind of society that the pioneers of Socialism will recognize and applaud." She still believes that the socialist experiment, as tried in Eastern Europe, is "worth repeating."

She ceased being "a cardholding member of the (British) CP, not because I have changed my views" but because she lost touch while in

Bulgaria and because of the splits in the party and the absence of local organizations where she has been living.

It is not difficult to understand why this idealistic and puritanical woman could not abandon her youthful and lifelong beliefs. These beliefs, her work, and the way of life built around them were the foundation of her life and sense of identity. A cumulative buildup of commitments and actions supported one another: her studies, memberships in the appropriate organizations, volunteer work in the idealized countries, professional involvement and success that was rewarded and appreciated by those who mattered. Neither her family nor her country offered much satisfaction whereas her somewhat fortuitous involvement with Bulgaria became a source of solid gratification and provided a sense of community. Too much was invested in her idealized beliefs to abandon them, even when she came to see some of the flaws of the cause and its political embodiments. But the flaws of Communist systems remained largely abstract; it is unlikely that she ever spoke to a former political prisoner or that she read accounts of Gulag inmates or stood in a line at a socialist food store. In her privileged position in Bulgaria, she was shielded from the worst and most telling flaws of the regime, though she learned of some of its "imperfections." Her likening the good society to a family (as quoted above) suggests a great thirst for community ungratified in her personal life, and one that is not easily satisfied in modern, secular, capitalist democracies.

J.V. is another of those not disillusioned; his account reaffirms and seeks to explain his political beliefs. He was born into a family of Italian immigrants, attended college in New York City, and worked his way up to chairman and CEO of an advertising agency from which he retired. Nowadays he "play[s] golf at a country club and tennis at a downtown club and go[es] to Florida in the winter." And yet, he writes, "I have always found myself on the left side of virtually any political issue." He believes this was due to parental influences: his mother and father were garment workers in New York City and members of the ILGWU. He often heard stories about their difficult working conditions and of the improvements following unionization.

While in high school (run by Jesuits) he discovered "that the real story of America bore little resemblance to what the [school] textbooks said." He claims to have been "radicalized" by "this dichotomy between the text and reality," including "the genocide of the Indians, slavery, the labor wars, the expansion of the West, the Mexican and Spanish Wars and other aspects of American imperialism." But millions of high school students who read similar texts were not radicalized; there had to be a predisposition to discern these "dichotomies" and to become indignant about them.

His views "hardened" during the Alger Hiss case; even before it he was "already upset by Nixon's red baiting." He found it "impossible to believe that Nixon and Chambers could be right and Hiss wrong." In later years he felt that "the left always had the better side of any issue," and it required little reflection "to decide which side to be on." Not surprisingly, the Vietnam War solidified his convictions, as did Reagan's support of the Contras in Nicaragua.

He was "ardently" opposed to the Vietnam War and participated in protest marches. "Of course" he was "for the Sandinistas against the Contras"—after all, Reagan and Dan Quayle were for the contras. He also wrote:

> As I look back over 50 years of leaning left, how do I reassess my point of view?
>
> I think the left was right about FDR; about the unions . . . about civil rights, about the damage McCarthyism and Nixonism caused to reasoned political discourse.
>
> Where did the left go wrong?
>
> It romanticized Russia in the 30s. . . . It ran out of intellectual energy. It ran into Jimmy Carter and was smothered by 12 years of Reagan and Bush.

Curiously, he makes no reference to the revival of the left during the 1960s. He looks forward to being on the left in the coming years.

This short account—like others of a similar nature—does not help us better understand the sources of political attitude change since there has been none to speak of. The perfunctory acknowledgment that Stalinist Russia was totalitarian does not constitute a reassessment of political attitudes. The points of interest in this account include the compatibility of the way of life of the well-to-do advertising executive with left-wing convictions and the rejection of American society, and the apparently effortless maintenance of such beliefs over a lifetime. Apart from parental influence, the origin of these beliefs remains unclear.

As is so often the case, the discovery of the divergence (real or imaginary) between the way things are and the way they are supposed to be (theory and practice, ideals versus realities) was the enduring source of moral indignation and adversarial disposition toward his own society. (It is also the major ingredient of disillusionment with Communist movements and states on the part of other individuals.)

B.T., a biologist at a major university, was reading Edward Said's *Culture and Imperialism* when she responded to my advertisement. Her two-page letter revealed attitudes deeply critical of the United States in general and specifically of its policies in Central America. She used to be active in the civil rights movement in California, read widely about issues of race, and "lost many of the illusions planted in my school days about the great American state and the wisdom of its people." She was attracted to Castro's Cuba and Sandinista Nicaragua because she perceived them as societies "which feed and vaccinate and treat their children better than other societies with comparable resources." She was also attracted to them because of their accomplishments in furthering literacy and the status of women. She read widely about these countries and found "the statistics about the quality of life [in Cuba] stunning." She felt no need to pay attention to the "downside" of the Cuban system since in her opinion "99%" of "American culture" was far more negative. She also expressed interest in Kerala, a state in India where the Communist party was in power. Her view of Nicaragua was very similar to that of Chomsky: she was convinced that it was the victim of a "criminal and heartless war" conducted by the United States to make sure that its idealistic government would not succeed: "It had a chance of working, so they had to be stopped."

The brief communication provides no hint as to the origins of her worldview rooted in a rejection of American society and U.S. foreign policy.

The Disillusioned

Only a handful of respondents fit unambiguously into this category. A.E., a lawyer in California, is one of them. He is married and of a working-class background, "presently in the struggling middle." He grew up in the Presbyterian church and held many unskilled jobs before (and during) college and becoming a lawyer. His account is striking in its lack of rancor or bitterness and the sense of moderation it reflects. He writes that his "formative experiences would include good elementary school education, great parents, good health and good friends." Presumably for all these reasons he comes across as a reasonable, decent, and thoughtful person. He has a broad range of interests: social, political, historical. At one point in his life he wanted to teach. His past sympathy with the Soviet Union "had more to do with some leaders' ideals than with the system that resulted from Lenin's anti-democratic action." His familiarity with the writings of

Rosa Luxemburg and Trotsky provided further immunity against an uncritical admiration of the Soviet system.

While critical of the United States during the Vietnam War, he was "never under the illusion that Ho Chi Minh was a democrat," and he even knew about the purges Ho had carried out. Sympathy toward Cuba was dispelled by the writings of K. S. Karol (which made him realize that "The Marxism that the Castroites imported was of a strictly Stalinist variety") and further eroded by "some of the prison literature from that country."

This unusually well-read lawyer not only availed himself of books that challenged some of his early beliefs and enthusiasm about these systems; even more unusually, he did not brush aside the criticisms these readings conveyed. While he never sympathized with Mao's China, its American ally, the Progressive Labor party ("representing all that was wrong with sectarian politics"), further discredited the system with its misplaced admiration. He felt that these American supporters of Mao's China "were so authoritarian and rigid. . . ."

Like many others drawn to Communist systems, he too believed that capitalism was defective in catering to "basic human needs." Influenced by the writings of Michael Harrington, he considered socialism "a more moral system." He traveled widely, including to the countries that used to be called "the Socialist Commonwealth" as well as China. Evidently his experiences and impressions of these countries did little to deepen his sympathy toward them.

He does not consider himself disillusioned since he was never enamored with these systems. He thinks of his past political attitudes as "basically social democratic" and the current ones "closer to libertarian socialist." He has never been "revolutionary in perspective." Although he sympathized, up to a point, with Communist systems, these sympathies were conditioned and restrained by what seems to be an ingrained moderation, a willingness to learn from new information, and a critical curiosity.

In this group S.W. was the most decisively estranged from the left-wing worldview on which he was raised by his parents. He sent both highly personal letters and reprints of some pamphlets and newsletters he has produced. In one of them, entitled "Occasional Papers in Social Democracy," he writes:

> Does Being a Leftist Mean Never Having to Say You're Sorry? . . . Since the collapse of communism we have heard the deafening roar of

> many political silences. How many of my peers, those who have consistently opposed American foreign policy . . . have stood up in public and said, "Maybe we were just downright wrong about these issues, maybe communism WAS so evil it deserved opposition and containment. Maybe snickering about 'anti-communist hysteria' was unjustified." . . . A personal note: I was born into a Communist Party family, although my parents quit in the late 1950s. My father became more anti-left . . . my mother remained a fellow-traveler. . . .

His father was wounded in the Spanish Civil War (he served in the Lincoln Brigade) and in World War II. He estimates that his parents spent a half- to one million dollars on foreign travel, mostly to Communist countries. They also contributed to "CP-orbit, anti-American organizations, publications, etc." He describes his mother as a "big-time political pilgrim." Both he and his sister felt much resentment toward their parents, whom they considered deeply hypocritical. Apparently these parents neglected their children while focusing their altruistic impulses on large, impersonal causes, making "loyalty to Marxism and communist regimes a substitute for generosity in their own lives. . . ." His father, even after breaking with the party, "defended Stalin's conduct in Spain against POUM, anarchists, Orwell etc."

S.W. came to believe that he could "understand how the ordinary citizens/victims of communism felt; egalitarian rhetoric, privileges for the party elite . . . disgusting and more hypocritical than capitalist greed. . . ." It seems plausible that such sensitivity to hypocrisy evolved against a background of parental hypocrisy. He recalls his father confessing that he was well aware of the guilt of the Rosenbergs while "he ran around proclaiming their innocence." He considers his mother a real "dupe."

Given his rejection of "the greed and unnecessary brutality of capitalism we saw around us," he became "a Harrington/Howe democratic socialist." He feels that it is "my job to help repair the damage that my parents' Stalinism did (while recognizing the limited good)—and I somehow feel like modern adult German or Italian children of fascists. . . ."

Even these somewhat disjointed communications make clear that ambivalence toward, if not outright rejection of, his parents and their political beliefs are inextricably intertwined. The emotional tone of his rejection of leftist beliefs (except the mild variants represented by Harrington and Irving Howe) suggest that a closer relationship with his parents might have resulted in quite a different political outlook.

N.C., a Chinese historian and retired professor at a distinguished New England college, responded to my notice with misgivings since he was never ardently sympathetic to Mao's China: "Though I was never by any means an academic Maoist, and like to think I maintained at least a degree of healthy scepticism, I had . . . a conventionally favorable view of many aspects of the P.R.C. through the later sixties and into the early seventies." Like many reputable China scholars, he was even willing to overlook "some of the absurdities" of the Cultural Revolution, given its anti-bureaucratic thrust.

His views changed as a result of "more knowledge." The fall of Lin Biao in 1971 showed "that nothing coming out of Peking could be trusted; here was a man elevated to be Mao's successor . . . hailed as Mao's revolutionary comrade, now denounced as traitor." This was similar to the fantastic accusations made in the Soviet purges, which also required a suspension of disbelief that some were capable of but not others. N.C. was further influenced by the writings of Simon Leys and those of Ivan and Miriam London reporting the famine that followed the "Great Leap Forward." True believers such as William Hinton denounced the 1989 massacre as "fascist" to avoid implicating the Communist system, he recalled. Our correspondent reached the conclusion without much difficulty that "leftists in the 60s and 70s needed an idealized society to criticize the shortcomings of their own country, and China filled the bill."

The seemingly effortless shifting of ideological gears in this case seems to rest on a sound critical disposition and the absence of an emotional investment in the rejection of American society.

Somewhat unexpectedly a homosexual activist/journalist in Australia also responded to the notice in the *New York Review of Books*. His short letter summarized his political journey from intense involvement with radical causes and organizations in the early 1970s (including the "youth arm" of the Marxist-Leninist Communist party of Australia, "a splinter party from the Communist Party of Australia . . . a militant and ultra sectarian group which took part in a number of acts of violence against perceived 'class enemies' . . .") to his final and complete break after the Tiananmen Square massacre in 1989. His political attitudes evolved from "a vague leftism" to Maoism, influenced by numerous "highly visible" Maoists at Monash University in Melbourne, which he attended. What makes his case unusual is that at the time of his involvement with Maoism he was a homosexual and yet "gravitated to the left which retained the old Stalinist view of homosexuality as 'bourgeois decadence.'" He doesn't mention, though must have known, that under Mao homosexuals in China were severely persecuted. Another conflicting attitude he recognizes is that while in his "personal dealings . . . [he] had a horror of violence," he nonetheless joined a group that "engaged in violent intimidation of its opponents." He notes that there were "good psychological explanations for these strange loyalties" but does not specify what they were.

In addition to the Tiananmen Square massacre, the collapse of Soviet communism in Eastern Europe and the Soviet Union enabled him "to make a complete emotional break with the 'revolutionary mystique' of communism and specifically Maoism." At the time of his writing he saw himself "somewhere between a social democrat and a libertarian." He thinks his homosexuality has given him "insights on the links between sexual repression and political extremism," but once more he does not spell out what they are.

This case, like many others, raises the question of the relative importance of personal factors, psychological forces as opposed to external events, in the process of both involvement and disenchantment. We don't know what first induced him to gravitate to radical groups other than a general sense of marginality associated with his sexual preferences. One may respond to such marginality without aligning oneself with a movement that despises the very source of the marginality. Presumably his political commitment was problematic from the beginning, given the Maoist hostility toward homosexuality. Nevertheless this tenuous association and alignment could only be terminated by a major external event such as the televised 1989 massacres.

F.L. is a highly articulate, cosmopolitan, widely read (aspiring) filmmaker, media consultant, and occasional speechwriter for "progressive politicians" as well as controller of a "private investment conglomerate" in California. He is "of the educated WASP bourgeoisie . . . largely Southern . . . family nominally Episcopalian." He grew up in "a liberal household where such figures as Norman Thomas were respected. . . . The idea that American society was vulnerable to criticism came naturally."

He believes that having spent several months in Mexico in his childhood and adolescence contributed to his questioning of American society and U.S. foreign policy. But evidently Vietnam was the major radicalizing influence:

> . . . I discovered that there are non-Communists in the world . . . who are so brutal and obtuse and corrupt that they make all Communists admirable and that some of these people . . . identify themselves as lib-

> erals. When Scoop Jackson died I threw a party. . . . Those people were the purest shit. . . . I developed more benevolent feelings toward Communism; I'd long admired the Viet Cong and the Hanoi regime for their steadfastness; I now forgave Fidel the soccer-field executions that had once soured me on his regime; and of course there has never ever been anybody cooler than Che. The Cultural Revolution made a certain sense too. . . .

Sandinista Nicaragua also evoked "a deep resonance." He recognized, unlike many respondents, that his "sympathy and charitable hopes for the regimes in question was/has been largely on the basis of Know Them By Their Enemies rather than because of any significant perceived merits of their own." By the time of his writing, however, he had come to understand that "all that Marxism-Leninism accomplished was to replace an older class system with the Party-underwritten nomenklatura." He saw China "hopeless" and "Fascist at the top." Such hard-nosed disillusionment appears in a strange combination with a residual and somewhat naive idealism, in his belief that "the only political ideal ultimately worth pursuing remains the Classless Society." It is not easy to understand how he manages to consider this ideal realizable, and if not, why he felt it was worth pursuing in view of the well-documented costs of this failed pursuit by the regimes he came to reject?

The political ideal of the classless society may be at the root of his durable self-conception as a leftist: "Today I'm as far 'left" as I've ever been," he writes. Such self-identification combines with contempt for American liberals and with an awareness that he himself belongs to some degree to the ranks of "affluent, sybaritic liberal[s] with . . . [their] refined attitudes and predilection for the exotic. . . ." He finds the "PC . . . of the Left oppressive, but the bloody-mindedness of the Right . . . more offensive." This would seem to be an important distinction suggesting that his distancing from the left is of a more rational and restrained character, while the revulsion from the right taps into a rich emotional vein.

F.L. comes across as a sophisticated cynic except for his ringing affirmation of the ideal of a classless society. His alienation from American society is uneasily complemented by his evidently lucrative involvement with the private investment business. He notes at one point that he "had no particular problem with capitalism per se." It must be somewhat problematic to balance an upper-middle-class way of life that depends on taking advantage of the capitalist system, with the role of the moralistic social critic.

R.S. is a historian at a state college in upstate New York. His life and beliefs, as summed up in a tightly organized, thoughtful statement of fourteen pages, reflect stability, coherence, and contentment. Here, as in some other accounts, there seems to be an inverse relationship between a sense of personal contentment and radical social criticism; to say the least, they are not easy to reconcile.

The defining influence on the political thinking of R.S. was his parents, radical Jewish immigrants who, rather unusually for Jews, became farmers: "My father impressed upon me very early the importance of citizenship, the need for courage in political speaking and analysis, and the importance of reason, science and vision. The strength he and my mother demonstrated have always been an inspiration. They were always outgoing and tolerant. My father's ideas [were] shaped by left-wing and socialist experiences . . . he espoused egalitarian democracy and often socialist policies." Besides his father, his other role models included Eugene Debs, Paul Robeson, Franklin and Eleanor Roosevelt, and I. F. Stone.

Earlier in life he followed his parents' farming career and expected to remain a farmer: "the occupation was healthy, socially productive." Yet he also became aware of the problems of family farming in a capitalist economy, found farm work exhausting and draining, and developed a desire for higher education. He enrolled in Cortland College in New York and later attended graduate school at Cornell, earning a Ph.D. in history in 1972. He obtained a full-time teaching position at Empire State College, an experience he found "wonderful."

Later in life his political beliefs diverged somewhat from those of his father, especially in regard to the conflict between espousals of egalitarian democracy and elitism widespread among leftists convinced of their moral-political righteousness. While in college and graduate school he participated in the Vietnam War protests; he also became interested in U.S.-Latin American relations and wrote his dissertation on the subject. But as the years went by, his interests in and tolerance for thinkers broadened to include Machiavelli, Hobbes, and Burke. Among contemporary authors who influenced him he mentions Hannah Arendt, Robert Bellah, Peter Berger, Jean Bethke Elshtain, Mary Ann Glendon, Christopher Lasch, Jürgen Habermas, amd Barrington Moore. While a student at Cortland he became friends with a Cuban refugee who taught Spanish and helped him understand "that revolutions were complex and multi-faceted"—that is, this Cuban helped him to resist the idealization of the Castro regime prevalent in academic circles at the time.

He certainly has few illusions about the redeeming qualities of Marxism and doesn't claim that it has never really been tried:

> Marxism is difficult to implement . . . as an ideological system . . . [it is] extremely appealing. Its success however requires levels of political organization and discipline, technical competence and industrial development and affluence that are very hard to achieve. Moreover these levels do not automatically yield situations in which people are willing, without coercion, to accept communism. . . .

He also notes the association of Marxism, especially as an official ideology in the USSR, with human rights "disasters," environmental failures (Chernobyl), and imperial adventures such as Afghanistan. But Marxist regimes also failed in Nicaragua, Cuba, and Mozambique, he points out.

He is not sure what label best fits him but leans to "left-liberal" or "left-liberal with communitarian tendencies." He notes, however, that such identification "won't work if a left-liberal must be a knee-jerk defender e.g. of affirmative action in all instances and against all criticism."

While involved in communal affairs and volunteer work in the city of Rochester where he has lived for a long time, he continues to "ruminate about the problems of liberalism relating to individualism and freedom vs. social obligations."

He also writes: "What I had been learning about the world . . . made me no less radical in belief. However it had convinced me to be more realistic about politics and more thoughtful about the uses of power and the need for moral justification for political ideas and public acts." He seeks to balance reason against "the necessary roles of emotion and faith." He appears to be a lifelong idealist who has avoided the pitfalls of fanaticism and dogmatic commitment.

Modified Commitment

Since these responses were the most numerous, the following is only a small sampling of them.

C.C. grew up in New York City and got a degree from the Juilliard School of Music and an M.A. in musicology from Brooklyn College. She then changed careers and went to medical school, graduating in 1976. She also taught music before a teaching career in medical schools. She was raised as an atheist by highly educated parents who were the major "formative influences" on her political thinking: "both active left-wingers; father briefly member of CPUSA . . . mother more of an anarchist. . . ." The community she grew up in (on the Upper West Side) "was mostly left-wing (Trotskyites were the conservatives)." She was "raised as a critic of American society and capitalism."

She traveled extensively but not to Communist countries. She had Cuban friends who enlightened her about the unappealing aspects of the Communist system. Her mother visited the Soviet Union several times in the sixties and seventies and was "predisposed to miss evidence of repression"; she did not accept her reports having read Medvedev's *Let History Judge* and Theodore Draper's history of the American Communist party; she also read Orwell on the Spanish Civil War. In her youth she read *Das Kapital* and an early Lenin book on the first Five Year Plan which favorably impressed her, especially the idea of worker ownership of the means of production, which she still thinks is "crucial to economic justice."

She is among those who believe that "Communism (Marxism) was not really tried in the USSR, China, Albania, etc." A more serious attempt was made in Cuba "but derailed by totalitarianism." She still believes that socialism can succeed if it incorporates free expression. Some of its failures had to do with the size of the countries that tried it as well as their lack of democratic tradition. She was greatly disappointed by the electoral defeat of the Sandinistas. She is strongly anti-Castro but hopes "when Castro dies socialism doesn't die with him because of his excesses."

Her disillusionment was also a product of reports by friends who had lived in the Soviet Union "and told stories of fear, arrests and repression"; and stories by friends about China and speeches of Vaclav Havel that she read in the *New York Review of Books*.

She concludes with this summary of her political evolution:

> . . . in childhood I followed my parents' ideas, more dogmatically than they. We were registered Democrats who voted in every election, hoping for non-violent substantive change leading to economic justice, more equal distribution of wealth and real democracy.

At present she thinks "Socialist libertarian" would define her best; she would like to see "worker ownership . . . jobs for all; government spending to reduce inequities and remedy infrastructure, education, ill health—but would like no interference at all in morals, private lives, beliefs, religion, sex life, guns, motorcycle helmets, etc."

Evidently she was never a "true believer." Her beliefs were always moderated by information, reason, and a sense of personal and professional security; nor did she abandon wholesale her youthful social-political ideals.

M.M., born in a World War II Japanese internment camp, is the daughter of "liberal to radical parents." Her father had "a great aversion to doctrinaire politics of any kind." She was a Peace Corps volunteer in Latin America, upon her return an "organizer in East Harlem" (she doesn't say what she organized) and also worked for the New York City government; later she worked for Pacifica Radio. She is author of one novel. As these activities indicate, she has been intent on improving society.

Of her politics she writes:

> Though conflicted about the tactics of the New Left in the 60's I was supportive of North Vietnam. Perhaps it is better to say that I was against our intervention in the region. The same is true of my stand on Central America. I went further there than I did during the Vietnam war. I actively worked on the Sandinistas' behalf by helping to build a hospital in Managua. . . . I have also always supported Cuba's right to remain communist.

In spite of these commitments, she still considers herself "informed" by her father's "populism and anti-doctrinaire leanings." But being a "practical person," she writes, it has been difficult for her "to go completely over when it comes to supporting communist states." She means, I suppose, going over to the other, anti-Communist side. On the other hand, she writes, "a revelatory visit to Nicaragua fed the more skeptical side of my conflict. . . ." This is a sincere and intelligent idealist who, despite the tug of appealing rhetoric from the Communist systems, has retained sufficient critical capabilities to maintain a more nuanced and conflicted political position.

A.A., born in 1906, is probably the oldest among those who responded to my notice and the only one who fought in the Spanish Civil War in the Lincoln Brigade against Franco. He sent extensive autobiographical notes; I also met him once in his home in a small town in northeastern Massachusetts. He was a high school dropout who joined the navy at age seventeen in 1923, "in rebellion against [his] father" who was "a respectable bookkeeper." His family was middle class until his father lost his money in the 1920s. His "folks" were Republicans. After three years of navy service, he returned to Massachusetts to look for work; he also began writing short stories, selling only one. At a church supper he met an MIT-trained engineer who was a Communist and who drew his attention to prevailing inequities (it was the time of the Great Depression). The engineer made him realize that capitalism was responsible for the ills of society: "Suddenly it hit me. . . . The whole thing was a gyp. Competition made us all slaves to the meanest, cheapest sons-a-bitches of all." He began reading voraciously—Marx, Engels, Stalin, and the *Daily Worker*. His beliefs were supported "by other Party members in the small local [organization], by my reading and by my experiences as one hopelessly unemployed." In 1937 he volunteered to fight in Spain and became a section leader. He was in Spain for a year and was wounded. He liked Spain and would have stayed "if we had won."

His "moral concerns" predated the depression and emerged while in the navy, on a stop in Shanghai where he saw abject poverty. He joined the Communist party in 1938 after his return from Spain and stayed in it until 1943 when he was "too busy" to attend meetings. But he "remained a radical ever since." In 1934 he met a local girl and married her in 1941; he worked in a New Hampshire textile mill as a carpenter, then in a local paper mill as a millwright; she ran a private kindergarten of her own. He also became a reader of the classics: Shakespeare (his favorite), Zola, Balzac, Conrad, Hemingway, Dostoevsky, Turgenev, Tolstoy. He always wanted to become a writer.

After World War II his political aspirations found expression in active support of the presidential campaign of Henry Wallace. When Wallace won only one million votes, A.A. said to himself, "Democracy is dead in this country." Nonetheless, he wrote, "I never became disillusioned, because I'm still as much radical in my beliefs as ever, but I've certainly had some shocking disappointments." The defeat of Wallace was not the only one:

> My next big shock was in 1956 with the news about Khrushchev's speech revealing that Stalin was a maniac. For years I'd wondered why Stalin seemed to do some crazy things, but always made excuses, and figured, in the end he had to be right. And of course I never believed the bourgeois papers. . . . But I had to believe Khrushchev. . . . So I still had faith in the USSR, right up until the Berlin Wall came down. Then I had to believe that the whole thing had to have been a great big tragedy of errors . . . and monstrous crimes. And that both Mao and Stalin had been maniacs.

At the same time he was also "sickened" by "the idiots around the world flocking to embrace free enterprise, free markets and capitalism.

I still hate and despite the whole bunch. I am convinced, socialism is the only decent way to organize society." He concludes: "I am not really disillusioned because I don't think that socialism has had a fair chance yet to show what it can do. And no matter what, I despise and hate capitalism, which inexorably leads to wars." He also wrote: ". . . when the Soviets broke up and people began cursing socialism I became bewildered. But now that phase is over I believe in socialism just as strongly as ever. (Capitalism is such a mean, miserable, petty, stingy system to depend on!) And I think now, there is a good chance that the Communists will come back into power in Russia, some day." He is still a Communist at heart but not a party member.

In the end our correspondent confronts an insoluble dilemma: capitalism remains intolerable and vile, but socialist states ended up ruled by "maniacs" and did not get much accomplished. He cannot abandon the notion that socialist ideals are superior and under unspecified conditions might bring about the just and good society he has always dreamed of. At the end of a long life, his sanguine rejection of capitalism gained the upper hand over the realization that the systems which sought to replace it were also deeply flawed.

E.F. (aged sixty-nine at the time of her writing) grew up in Kansas and later moved with her family to Salt Lake City. She graduated from the University of Utah as an English major. Among those influencing her political thinking was a liberal grandfather, an eighth-grade social science teacher, a fellow journalist at her first job in Oakland, California, and her second husband. After acquiring teaching credentials, she taught in a "very poor" area of Richmond, California. She also obtained master's degrees in international relations and library science. Later in life she worked for seventeen years in the Sacramento County Office of Education. Her second husband, a political science professor at Chico State University, was also a leftist. She wrote: "We went through the Vietnam and Civil Rights Marches. One stepson was very much into Mao; he later went to Nicaragua. We went to the Soviet Union in 1985, when things were just beginning to change . . . on a small group tour sponsored by Educators for Social Responsibility. . . . We both had mixed feelings about what we saw but more of them were positive than negative." In 1992 she traveled in Eastern Europe and later to Cuba. "Both above trips were informative, left me reassessing, but still not convinced that the cooperative premise was wrong. I was very touched by the tenacity of many of the Cuban people. . . ."

She has been a supporter of the Democratic party and for a shorter period of the Peace and Freedom party. She has also been associated with the One World/Philadelphia II, the World Federalist Association, Educators for Social Responsibility, UNA/USA, Peace Child International, and Solar Cookers International [sic] as well as a supporter of Global Exchange, which helped her visit Cuba whose people "haven't given up their dreams yet." She was also an officer of the AAUW and the League of Women Voters. She considers herself "a Liberal and an idealist." She tried hard to understand the reasons for the collapse of the socialist/Communist experiment in the Soviet Union and Eastern Europe. She has retained "a strong identification with the poor of our country and the world."

Concluding, she writes: "I believe my major concern is that we help all young people feel a moral commitment toward their fellow citizens—both in their own country and around the world." An idealist-activist, she has been preoccupied with the deficiencies of her society which have led her to a sympathetic but not totally uncritical interest in the Communist states she has visited. Their collapse made an impression, but not a major one.

T.K. considers himself a "non-dogmatic ultra-leftist" or a "Marxist Relativist." He is not disillusioned: "I never subscribed to the notion that Soviet and Chinese Marxists were more humane or egalitarian. . . . Socialist and Communist organizations never impressed me as being genuinely leftist-humanitarian . . . hence I always supported or opposed them in an ad hoc fashion." At the time of his writing he was teaching political science at San Francisco State University.

Both of his parents ended their education in eighth grade and were poor. His father was "a rather brutal man . . . and became what psychologists would label a sociopath." He did terrible things to his family and barely escaped imprisonment. The writer of these reminiscences headed in the opposite direction and "seem[s] to have been born a bleeding heart liberal," as he puts it. He wanted his father "To become gentle and compassionate and love me along with all other creatures. I suspect my political radicalism as an adult is a full-blown version of such attitudes and inclinations." Presumably he means that his compassionate radicalism evolved in opposition to his father's brutality.

R.W. responded to my ad because it gave him "a chance to unload some of [his] gushy nostalgia." He described himself as "a fresh faced, blonde, blue-eyed teenager who had nothing to revolt against. A son of that Republican middle-class aristocracy that never had to use a racially designated restroom . . . never had to fight the system for a job. . . ." In 1958, on his sixteenth birthday, he quit school and went to work on the railroad; later he enlisted in the army. He spent six years in the military, then went to college on the GI Bill. The Cuban Revolution made a great impression on him. He also had a religious conversion experience of the "Protestant fundamentalist variety," which nonetheless somehow "opened the door for more liberal views." He spent several years in Europe while in the army and was briefly married to an educated German woman who introduced him to "true liberalism with the more militant Marxist trappings." After discharge from the army he returned to the Midwest to a variety of sales jobs, but then he reenlisted again and was sent to Europe once more. After his second discharge from the army he was doing "his Kerouac thing," moving around a lot.

Louis Fischer's biography of Gandhi was a turning point that prompted him to become politically engaged. He fiercely protested the first Iraq War and was deeply disappointed by his "fellow liberals" who did not because "they did not have the courage of their convictions." He compared the United States of 1989–1990 to Germany in 1933. He lost faith in his country. He concluded that "money now controls everything." In the early sixties he "began to see all the B.S. [he] had been taught starting to unravel." He also felt that, aside from the injustices of racism and war, we have also become subject to control and manipulation by television and the computer.

He was attracted to all Communist systems but visited none of them and admired Ho Chi Minh. But he was critical of Marxism for "not figuring the human factor, human nature." He saw Mao as a "tyrant" and had nothing positive to say about the USSR and Eastern European Communist states. He considers himself "left of center." It is not clear what his occupation was at the time he responded to my notice.

B.Z., in her sketchy response, comes across as a highly intelligent, articulate idealist who used to be an "activist in college" in the later sixties but "never shared" the "infatuation" of people she knew with Mao's China, Castro's Cuba, or North Vietnam. Nonetheless, she writes, "their experiments in social engineering provided me with a vision of an alternative society and a way to challenge my own country to alter itself for the good of us all." Her interest in these alternatives was also spurred by her "familiarity with the kibbutz movement"—her mother was a child of Zionists and "a big booster of kibbutzim."

B.Z. was "searching for different ways for people to live" and had an especially strong interest in improving the lives of women and in utopian communities.

She returned to school to study clinical psychology and had numerous experiences with what she called "visionary projects" involving global peace and nuclear disarmament. Her many idealistic activities included being director of a peace center at a church in California, education/issues director of Medical Aid for El Salvador, seminar coordinator at a Nicaraguan Film Institute, monitor of human rights violations in El Salvador, etc. As of her writing she was a licensed therapist with an M.A. in clinical psychology.

She appears to be idealistic but not angry, deeply committed to various altruistic undertakings, her approach therapeutic rather than political.

H.D. is a Canadian academic, a "post-secondary educator" with an uncompleted Ph.D. Very articulate and well read, he responded thoroughly and informatively to every question I had in the questionnaire. He has several M.A.s and an A.B.D. in "history and philosophy of education." Has written high school history and social studies texts. His parents were deeply affected by the Great Depression. As a young man he was shocked by the execution of Caryl Chessman and "stridently opposed" capital punishment. At about the same time (while still in high school) he became an organizer of the Canadian Student Committee for Nuclear Disarmament. He was distressed by the U.S. invasion of the Dominican Republic and participated in a sit-in outside the U.S. consulate in Toronto "as a token supporter of the Selma march." Later, at the University of Hawaii, he met Stokely Carmichael, Harvey Cox, Paul Goodman, Jules Feiffer, and other exciting figures, and while there he worked for the campaign of Eugene McCarthy. After returning to Canada he was influenced by the writings of E. P. Thompson, Christopher Hill, Eric Hobsbawm, and Ralph Miliband. His political involvements have focused on his trade union, the Ontario Public Service Employees Union, in which he has served in many positions.

He offers as his current self-definition "a sort of postmodern cynic." He does not "subscribe to, nor expect to see a comprehensive and progressive alternative to liberal democratic governance nor a pragmatic replacement for a mixed capitalist economy. . . . My anger is directed toward specific and . . . reducible evils within a society that will remain fundamentally flawed. This anger . . . may have psychological roots of which I am only partly aware. . . ."

He is well read in Marxist-Leninist literature and provided a long list of books he was familiar with; he is also a regular reader of the *Monthly Review*, *New Left Review*, and *Socialist Register*. He was never attracted to the Communist states mentioned in my notice, though he did see them as victims. Given their economic underdevelopment, he did not expect much of either Russian or Chinese socialism. He never considered the USSR "the worker's paradise that Marx had envisioned," but he did not think the dismantling of the Berlin Wall was all good for he anticipated the rise of nationalism and ethnic conflicts in the former Soviet empire. He expressed hope that the demise of the USSR "does not mean . . . the utter repudiation of the Marxian critique [presumably of capitalism]." As to China, he no more "bought into the notion of happy peasants than that of happy workers [in the USSR]." He deplored both the Cultural Revolution and the 1989 massacres. Concerning Nicaragua he "was unhappy at Ortega's defeat" but pleased with the end of the civil war. He had visited Cuba but was "no fan of Castro," and the firing squads "did not warm [his] still slightly Christian heart." He was in Cuba during celebrations of the fifteenth anniversary of the revolution and was favorably impressed by "the sincerity and stoicism" of ordinary Cubans he met. But he experienced "a bit of chill when some members of the Committee for the Defense of the Revolution began to suspect that I was the kind of creative Stalinist with whom they should be amiably chatting about . . . baseball." He does nonetheless "continue to admire many things done there and . . . [is] appalled by others. . . ."

His major disillusionment remains with "western society, its insubstantial commitment to democracy, its self-serving invitation to economic prosperity, its hollow call for human rights. This is a deep disillusionment." Despite entering middle age and attaining "some of the material trappings of the bourgeoisie, I have not mellowed."

This is a thoughtful person with nuanced judgments and few illusions about Communist systems, yet he is deeply estranged from the Western world.

There is, finally, the late Herbert Aptheker (1915–2003), who also responded to my notice and subsequently agreed to be interviewed.[3] He was a Marxist historian; a member of the Communist Party of the United States between 1939 and 1991 (when he and many others left it due to disagreements with Gus Hall, its leader); served on the Central Committee of the party between 1957 and 1991; and was the founder and director of the American Institute for Marxist Studies and editor of the party's theoretical monthly, *Political Affairs*, between 1952 and 1963. In 1976 he ran for the Senate on a Communist party ticket in New York against Daniel Patrick Moynihan and received 25,000 votes.[4]

While best known for his many books on slavery and black history in the United States, Aptheker is also the author of *The Truth About Hungary* (1957) and *Czechoslovakia and the Counter-Revolution: Why the Socialist Countries Intervened* (1969), both wholeheartedly supporting and justifying Soviet armed intervention in these countries. He also traveled to Hanoi with Tom Hayden and Staughton Lynd and in 1956 published *Mission to Hanoi.*

I learned in our conversation that he became a Communist as a result of his personal and professional preoccupation with racism in the United States at a time when, in his opinion, the party was the only political force genuinely opposed to racism and included the "best people" fighting it. The concern with racism was rooted in his childhood in a wealthy Brooklyn family, where he was largely raised by a nurturing black woman; an experience of segregation and abject black poverty in the South at age thirteen made another indelible impression and laid a foundation of enduring moral indignation and compassion.

His views of the Soviet Union appear to be a by-product of his allegiance to the American Communist party. He considered the Soviet Union "a bulwark of resistance against reaction in Washington." He fully approved of the Nazi-Soviet pact in 1939 as reasonable self-defense on the part of the USSR. In response to my question, I learned that he did not follow closely events in the Soviet Union during the 1930s such as the purges and the Moscow Trials; he had no particular interest in Soviet affairs as his primary concern was American society and its racial and social injustices.

His major beliefs remained intact regarding capitalism as the source of most of the evil in the world (greed, exploitation, inequality) and racism (directed at blacks) in particular. He held capitalism responsible for racism since it benefited from exploiting the putatively inferior group. He vigorously disputed my suggestion that anti-Semitism too was a form of racism; he considered it rather a species of nationalism. Earlier in his career he had difficulties finding regular academic employment because of his involvement with the Communist party but after the 1960s this was no longer the case; he also became the recipient of many honors in the academic world and a popular campus speaker; his books were widely published and used in colleges.[5]

He was shocked and dismayed by Khrushchev's revelations in 1956 ("a tremendous blow") but felt they were irrelevant to his concerns and did not invalidate the good works and idealistic efforts of American Communists. After the collapse of the Soviet Union he left the party, repelled by its policies, leadership, and historic subservience to the Soviet Union. He was dismayed to learn that it had been financed by the Soviet authorities. He still considered himself a Marxist because it offered, in his view, the best grasp of history. He did not think the Soviet Union was truly Marxist but a system seeking to establish a socialist society. He had no regrets about his political positions and activities, though he admitted he could or should have been more critical of (the American) party policies. He was proud of what he considered his work for peace, including a trip to Vietnam that he organized during the war and other travels in different parts of the world in the 1960s when he was head of the World Peace Council, a Soviet-dominated organization. He also visited Castro's Cuba on two occasions, on one of them when he was invited to lecture party leaders about African-American history. He found the new Cuban society a "humane civilization" and its leadership free of corruption; he was also impressed by free medical care and education. He thought at the time that "human beings were changed" for the better in Cuba.

At my prodding we talked about Soviet-dominated Eastern Europe and the Hungarian Revolution of 1956. He believed that after World War II there was no alternative in Eastern Europe but to move to socialism, to Soviet domination. The Hungarian Revolution, in his opinion, was on the one hand a response to genuine evils, but on the other an event fomented and influenced by the United States, which did not wish to see a truly democratic Hungary emerge from the revolution but simply hoped to detach the country from the Soviet Bloc.

As of 1998 his views of American society remained highly negative and defined by his long-standing beliefs, including "the class-based and race-based nature of higher education" and the grip of the ruling class on the teaching of history:

> That hasn't changed [these characteristics of higher education]. And it will not change short of a revolution here. . . . The fundamental reins of power remain in their hands [the ruling class, that is]. . . . We will not really win because we are living in a bourgeois society controlled by the bourgeoisie and history is very important to it. The teaching of history is decisive ideologically and so the ruling class . . . is not going to give that up.[6]

Aptheker succeeded in resisting any major reassessment of his beliefs partly because he devoted all his life to them and suffered for them, and because he could dissociate the pro-Communist (and pro-Soviet) attitudes and activities from his idealistic commitment to black Americans. Concluding our conversation, he reaffirmed his belief in the possibility of alleviating or eliminating major social injustices in the world.

One of the conclusions to emerge from the comments of these respondents is that in many if not most instances, initial political attitudes and beliefs were deeply embedded in the families they came from. (This was not the case with Aptheker, whose father was a well-to-do manufacturer with no political interests or sense of guilt over his wealth.) In most cases the leftism, or leftist radicalism, was not something born out of some kind of rebellion but was part of a family heritage or ethos. Men in particular were greatly influenced by their fathers and did not hesitate to say so. Many used to be members of, or children of members of, the American Communist party, one respondent of the British Communist party. Many were active in the various protest movements of the 1960s and '70s.

Few of these respondents sought to end all their political involvement and activity after various degrees of disappointment with leftist causes or systems; instead they attempted to find more moderate but still leftist political positions, often social democratic or "democratic socialist" or "libertarian leftist." Some rejected any political label. A minority refrained from registering *any* disappointment or reassessment, convinced of the fundamental righteousness of their original commitment, unaffected either by the collapse of Soviet communism or by available information about the profound moral, political, or economic flaws of the remaining Communist states.

Few expressed bitterness on account of their political disappointments; rather they sought some continuity with their youthful commitments and beliefs. There was no indication that disaffection, such as there was, led to a newfound appreciation of any aspect of the American political system, Western democracy, or capitalism. A hesitant recognition of the absence of obvious alternatives to American social arrangements did not make their defects more acceptable.

Although these correspondents responded to a notice seeking information about political attitude change, most of them remained deeply engaged in efforts to save, salvage, or preserve in some form their old attitudes and commitments. Old political convictions were cherished, it seemed, because they were felt to be authentic and idealistic, often associated with their youth; their wholesale abandonment would have been a major blow to a sense of identity, to a positive self-conception of which a secular political idealism was an integral part.

One common thread ran through the diverse accounts: the principal political positions or attitudes held resulted less from the attraction of specific ideals of socialism (and the countries or political systems that claimed to pursue or realize them), but rather from a highly critical disposition toward their *own* society. Virtually every respondent harbored deep disaffection from American society and an acute awareness of its shortcomings and injustices, its unrealized ideals.

Many respondents insisted, in virtually uniform language, that they were not disillusioned because they had never had illusions. This assertion rested largely on a somewhat critical view of the Soviet Union. Some respondents claimed they had become more "realistic" or "pragmatic" due to certain readings and political experiences.

Unlike some of the authors of the autobiographical accounts examined earlier, none of these respondents cited personal friction or disagreement (other than the familial) with those with whom they had earlier shared their political beliefs. No one recalled or reminisced about conflict with rigid party officials or Weathermen fanatics or corrupt Black Panthers. No one recalled a stark, traumatic experience leading to a reexamination of beliefs. Those who reported visits to various socialist states did not return with their eyes opened, though in a few instances such visits led to modifications of belief and diminished enthusiasm. In other cases the visits vindicated existing convictions.

Sometimes modifications of belief appeared to result from readings, from meeting specific individuals, from historical events such as the collapse of Soviet communism, or from a more general and gradual process of maturation.

A wounded idealism seeking an outlet in leftist social or political activism appeared to be the most widely shared trait, indeed the defining characteristic of these respondents. The responses reinforced the observation (supported by an abundance of historical and cultural data) that American culture, far more than most others, has a unique capacity to stimulate idealism and high expectations.[7]

EIGHT

Patterns of Disillusionment

Even the small number of cases examined on the preceding pages allows, indeed prompts, certain generalizations and conclusions. Let me recall that this study sought to increase and update our understanding of the roots and circumstances of disillusionment with Communist systems and their supporting ideologies in the twentieth century, especially its last decades. I was interested in the disillusionment of both those who had lived under such systems and those who sympathized with them from a distance in the West, chiefly the United States. In doing so I was also hoping to shed further light on the change and persistence of political attitudes and beliefs in general.

I begin with the most clear-cut and least disputable findings. The political disillusionment dealt with in this study was well founded; the disillusioned did not attribute traits or failings to these systems that were imaginary or maliciously exaggerated. The written accounts of defectors, exiles, and dissidents were supported implicitly by the millions who escaped under dangerous conditions, "voting with their feet" without making public statements about their reasons for departing these countries. Those who lived under these systems had good reasons to become disillusioned since they were familiar from personal experience with the wrongs perpetuated; what required explanation is why it took some of them such a long time. Equally thought-provoking remains the question why in the West only a handful were willing to express similar disenchantment publicly in recent times.

The political disillusionment here examined, rather than experienced as a bracing release from misplaced loyalties and delusions, was a painful experience, as painful as other kinds of deeply personal disappointments, comparable to the failure of romantic attachments and the loss of romantic illusions. Political disaffection also resembled the collapse of religious faith, which is similarly wrenching and distressing. As Geoffrey Wheatcroft has observed: "A century and a half ago you could witness the agonized writhings of those whose intellectual belief in traditional revealed religion was shaken, but who could not shed its thrall emotionally. It must have been a painful, disturbing and often a moving spectacle. It still is."[1] In the West the political disenchantment discussed here was a particularly difficult process because there was less social, subcultural support for it.

A "red-diaper baby" of recent times offers this example and summary of the residues and difficulties of the struggle with the loss of political faith:

> As a teenager I was secretly disdainful of my peers because they were oblivious to the suffering of others. My family and I were part of a morally superior secret society that cared more about the fate of the world than did our bourgeois, materialistic neighbors. . . . My grandparents were socialists who escaped the ghettos of Russia. . . . My parents were Communists who fought for social justice in the 1930s. As the third generation of this proud leftist family, I wanted to make good. . . .
>
> In 1968, I went to Cuba and signed up for the Venceremos Brigade. . . . That experience was my reality check.
>
> I'd spent my life on the ideological left . . . with utopian dreams of participatory democracy. I discovered that an actual Communist dictatorship bore no resemblance to my fantasy. . . . I realized I'd rather be ruled by Richard Nixon than by the kids in the Weather tent. . . . When I got back I traded in my politics and went into therapy. . . .
>
> The Weatherpeople were clearly delusional. . . . My parents passionately believed that the Soviet Union was the promised land, another treacherous fantasy . . . anarchism was a utopian crock. What was left? . . . I became a cynic. . . .
>
> I still long though, for a political movement I could wholeheartedly embrace. . . .[2]

The political disillusionment examined on the preceding pages was a lengthy, difficult, halting, and gradual process ranging from years to decades. I did not come across cases of abrupt, dramatic conversions precipitated by a single, transformative experience. The disillusionment rarely came about as the result of some particularly shocking and traumatic experience, such as Orwell had during the Spanish Civil War. For him there was a "transcendent or crystallizing moment" when he "suffered the premonitory pangs of a man living under a police regime: a police regime ruling in the name of socialism and the people. For a Westerner . . . this epiphany was a relatively novel thing."[3] Orwell's political trauma, a sense of betrayal, resulted from discovering the Soviet-inspired persecution of anarchists and other groups disinclined to submit to Soviet Communist control during the course of the civil war.

It was no particular experience or type of information that was decisive. In most cases there was no lack of information about the morally discrediting features of these systems or movements; illusions or ignorance were not major impediments to the reassessment of the political faith, certainly not on the part of those who had lived in Communist states.

This was not the case in the West. With modest effort, Western sympathizers could insulate themselves from information about Communist states that might call their beliefs into question. This is not to suggest that such information was not available; it was both available and avoidable. Most important was that sympathizers in the West did not and could not experience daily life in Communist societies; if they learned about their depriving and morally delegitimating features, it had to be secondhand, from books, specialized journals, or the mass media, rarely through personal contact with former citizens. Occasional visits to Communist countries were a poor substitute for experiencing life as the natives did, and only rarely did such visits contribute significantly to the loss of illusions.[4]

Still, it was not impossible for Westerners to learn about the unappealing attributes of Communist systems from a distance, and many did. But even when they did, they too, like their countertparts inside Communist states, were able to fall back on a capacity to rationalize, neutralize, and compartmentalize discrediting information and experience. This capacity was more important for maintaining commitment (up to a point) than ignorance or illusion. More precisely, the attitudes of Western believers combined ignorance, illusions, the wish to believe, and the capacity to dismiss dissonant information in order to resist or postpone disenchantment.

Individuals in both East and West displayed remarkable resilience and resourcefulness in the face of potentially disillusioning and devastating experiences, and successfully employed various techniques to ward off disillusionment over long periods of time. The most important among them was the single-minded fixation on—and an exceedingly favorable evaluation of—the long-term goals pursued by these systems. This focus made it possible to greatly reduce the moral-ethical significance of various transgressions committed in the pursuit of these goals. The overwhelming importance and perceived desirability of the ends made it possible to overlook the moral quality and degradation of the means, the human costs exacted in the course of striving for the long-term goals.

Another summarizing proposition easily arrived at that the personalities of these individuals—as distinct from their experiences, the social-historical settings, or short-lived situations in which they found themselves—made a great difference to their political evolution and choices, and especially to their disillusionment. As Henry Kissinger once said: "As a professor, I tended to think of history as run by impersonal forces. But when you see it in practice, you see the difference personalities make."[5]

The most obvious indication of the importance of personality is found in the fact that people respond differently to similar, even identical experiences. To be sure, identical facts or situations are not experienced in the same way. As has often been said, one person's terrorist is another's freedom fighter; the bodies of civilians killed by terrorists may be seen as innocent victims, individuals complicit with the enemy, or the enemy itself. Selective perception and projection color the quality and interpretation of experience, even shared experience. This is not a denial of objective realities but an affirmation that they are perceived and experienced differently. Differences in personality and personal needs determine how identical experiences (objective realities) are processed and responded to.

Personality differences that had an obvious impact on political disaffection included a questioning, nonconformist, contrarian, or anti-authoritarian disposition leading to a reduced tolerance for the shortcomings and failures of any political system, and to a greater likelihood of conflicts with it and its representatives. But even such personality types function differently in different settings: many Western intellectuals who displayed a highly critical and skeptical disposition in their own society proved capable of being credulous and uncritical in the societies they approved of.[6]

The social-political environment circumscribes and molds these personal impulses and their expression in other ways too. Prudential considerations for personal safety obviously make a difference for a rebellious individual who lives in a highly authoritarian, repressive society. Personality traits played a smaller part in the disillusionment of those living in Communist states than for those in the West since their environment discouraged political self-expression, and especially any indication of nonconformity.

Although this study indicates that personal motives and needs were often at work both when individuals were drawn to political beliefs and systems and when they discarded them, these influences were not the same in the two settings. The disaffected in Communist states were products of societies which, notwithstanding their sweeping revolutionary transformations, retained elements of a traditional society in which individualism was less developed; these were also societies which as a rule did not generate high expectations. Political participation in such societies, even when entirely voluntary, was not intimately connected to the more intangible or obscure needs of personal fulfillment, self-realization, or the pursuit of community and new meaning in life, as has often been the case in the West.

Virtually all those individuals discussed in this book who became supporters of Communist movements or governments in Russia, Eastern Europe, or the Third World did so when these systems were in their early, revolutionary stages and full of promise; most of them participated in some ways in their initial efforts to realize this promise. Except for those in Eastern Europe, these systems were initially capable of authenticating themselves by their revolutionary credentials. Under these circumstances the pursuit of identity (or a new, improved sense of identity) rarely or barely entered into the support of these systems. That is, personal needs and motives were less important than objective conditions, both in the process of being attracted to these systems and in rejecting them. For all these reasons it was easier to explain and understand the disenchantment of the believers who had lived in Communist states than the abandonment of faith among similarly disposed Westerners. Given the far greater external pressures and constraints on the attitudes and behavior of those who lived in Communist systems, variations in personality mattered much less.

An attribute of personality especially important in the shaping of political attitudes is what I call the moral threshold (or breaking point), the internalized moral norms that define in a compelling way what kinds of behavior, policies, or events are morally acceptable or unacceptable. Our daily experiences make clear that individuals differ greatly from one another in this dimension; the higher the moral threshold, the more difficult it is to tolerate, rationalize, or compromise with unsavory conduct or policies, with the subordination of means to ends, with mendaciousness and deception. But this moral threshold is, in turn, influenced by another important attribute: the wish and the capacity to believe. The stronger this wish, the more expedient and compelling it becomes to ignore morally disturbing matters that undermine belief. There is an apparent relationship between selective perception—which made it easier to ignore or minimize the repellent features of Communist systems or movements—and the hopeful determination to find these systems and movements praiseworthy and promising. Many of the disillusioned recognized this in retrospect.

It is more difficult to decide what part idealism (the selfless desire to do good for a larger cause) played in the erosion of political belief and commitment. On the one hand it would seem that the more idealistic an individual, the more difficult it is to accept tarnished means (used in the attempted transformation of society) and the human costs of these supposedly beneficial social transformations. On the other hand, idealism converted into a lasting investment of emotional and intellectual resources into a semi-sacred cause makes it more difficult to disengage and renounce the "investment" and confront the mistaken judgments made earlier. Such an investment exerts pressure to persist in the conviction that the efforts were not in vain, and to find vindication for the original commitment. The length of time invested in the devotion and service to the cause is obviously an important determinant of the attitudes. More specifically, idealism, or the pressure exerted by idealism, can lead to an overwhelming emphasis on the ends and a ruthless indifference to the means used in attaining them.

In the writings examined we can find both outcomes of idealism: pained disenchantment as opposed to dogged persistence, the stubborn clinging to the emotional investment.

Personality also plays a part in the attachment to power, when achieved. As David Horowitz observed, ". . . individuals who rose to the fore in revolutions were likely to be fanatics with an aptitude for violence. . . . In volatile situations the momentum was always seized by those most certain of their conviction, least impressed by ambiguity. . . ."[7]

The contribution of political commitment to a person's sense of identity was also instrumental in preserving or discarding commitment. An individual with strong family ties and/or a strong sense of professional identity—that is, a sense of identity less dependent on political roles, beliefs, commitments, and associations—could more easily reevaluate and shed these beliefs and ties than those without such sources of strength and sense of identity. (Doris Lessing was a good example of this.) Conversely, unmet needs for community and social affiliation in some cases (as for instance those of Belli, Gimes,

Rittenberg, etc.)[8] played a part in drawing individuals to these causes and political communities and made it more difficult, though not impossible, for them to extricate themselves.

Two variables external to the individual played an important part in the process of disaffection, the first applicable only to those who lived in Communist states. One was the way the system treated (or was expected to treat) the individual. When a person felt rejected by the system, or came under suspicion, when his (and his family's) safety was endangered, it was no longer possible to remain loyal to the system. A number of the individuals discussed had decided to defect under such circumstances. In other instances, unquestioning loyalty was undermined by demotion or some sign of official disfavor not necessarily culminating in defection. The disillusioned in the West were not threatened by such prospects, but often the expectation of ostracism in their social circle or political community was a deterrent, delaying the decision to break with the movement or the cause.

A second important external variable, especially in Communist states, was the rise and existence of social-political movements that also questioned these systems. When such a widely shared rejection of the system emerged, individuals felt free to express long-suppressed feelings. These were the times when many former supporters became capable of soul-searching self-criticism. Two Hungarian writers captured the ethos of such a period, which in this case led up to the revolution of 1956:

> When they looked back on the past years and at themselves during those years, they were horrified to see that they were . . . helpers, spokesmen, propagandists of the system. . . . Suddenly they hated themselves, as shame and guilt blended. . . . It was hard to say which one was stronger: shame for their blindness over the years or guilt for trying to misguide those who saw things without their blinders. Their faith might have been excusable . . . it originated in the conviction that they were duty-bound to build a new world—the trouble was that it was a blind faith. . . .[9]

In these times the isolated critic or doubter ceased to be one; social support encouraged him or her to express critiques or even to break openly with the system. This was the case in much of Eastern Europe and the USSR after Stalin's death and especially during the "thaw" under Khrushchev, and much later under Gorbachev when *glasnost* and *perestroika* legitimated questioning; likewise in China after the death of Mao. In these periods not only did the disaffected find support among other critics but the risk of public expression of dissent itself diminished. Such ferment in Communist states also had some effect on Western sympathizers, but *their* commitments depended far more on the social movements and subcultures within their own societies which, by and large, resisted and retarded the reassessment of political beliefs and commitments in recent times.

While certain stimulants to and patterns of disenchantment may be identified, internal and external, most difficult to pinpoint is the kind of specific event or experience that will trigger disaffection, except an imminent threat to individual safety. Aside from such a threat, the supporters generally succeeded, for varying periods of time, in neutralizing potentially traumatic and disillusioning experiences and preventing them from triggering emotional responses leading to drastic reassessment.

A recurring problem in this study has been to determine *when* doubts and objections first emerged, and when their causes were identified. The disillusioned wrote about these processes years after they began; it was difficult to separate how they felt at the time of writing from recalling when the original feelings first emerged.

It was equally difficult to ascertain when these individuals become willing and able *to generalize from particular incidents and experiences*—a crucial stage in the process of disillusionment. When the person becomes capable of such generalization, he can no longer regard these incidents and experiences as isolated, atypical, or insignificant. At that point the foundations of belief become seriously undermined, and the path opens to the rejection not merely of the means but of the ends.

A summary of the most apparent sources of disillusionment applicable to both settings (East and West) should begin with the sense of betrayal, of having been deceived, and the realization that the accomplishments of the system sharply, even fraudulently diverged from expectations. That is, objective conditions or facts, discouraging as they were, often seemed to matter less than the feeling of betrayal. It is of course a highly subjective matter what stimulates these feelings, but most of the disaffected—both former citizens of Communist states and Western sympathizers—referred to them while attributing these sentiments to different reasons.

The disillusioned came to feel that what was promised by the leaders of the regimes and their foundational doctrines remained unrealized.

I called this the discrepancy between theory and practice, promise and reality, the ideal and the actual. While such a divergence is a preeminent feature of all social systems and a key human experience (that is, realities not measuring up to ideals, neither in the social-political nor personal realm), Communist systems excelled in aggravating this gap by their insistent, pervasive, and self-righteous ideological claims and ceaseless barrage of propaganda. It was an experience available to all those who lived under these systems, and it was the major source of the contempt, cynicism, and hostility they inspired. Many examples of this mendaciousness were cited in memoirs and recalled on the preceding pages. It was a peculiarly delegitimating feature of all Communist systems and compelled comparisons of experienced reality with its routine, official representation and misrepresentation. Alexander Wat, the Polish author, summed up this phenomenon memorably: "The loss of freedom, tyranny, abuse, hunger would all have been easier to bear if not for the compulsion to call them freedom, justice, the good of the people."[10]

The persistent official denial of this divergence, and the pressure on the population to acquiesce in the official make-believe and pretend that the misrepresentations of reality were truthful, led to the simulation of conformity and loyalty, to the necessary, vigilant, and sharp distinction between private and public, between personal and political realms and communications.

Numerous influences and circumstances led to these conclusions and feelings, far more readily acquired by those living in Communist states than others contemplating them from afar.

The most obvious was the experience of deprivation and mistreatment, though the interpretation and moral meaning of such deprivation varied. Moral revulsion did not invariably and necessarily follow from experiences that should have provoked it. Sometimes those subjected to such deprivations (including imprisonment) managed to retain their original commitment by considering their own fate a minor matter in the larger scheme of things, a mistake or misunderstanding that had no bearing on the overall character of the system, its goals and accomplishments. Some of those innocently victimized convinced themselves that the supreme leaders were unaware of such errors and injustices.[11]

Another major stimulant to rejecting the system was the influence of an important, credible individual—parents, friends, co-workers. Sometimes specific readings helped undermine commitment, though people usually turned to such "subversive" sources in search of confirmation or clarification, after their beliefs were already wavering for other reasons.

For citizens of Communist states, a posting or even a tourist trip abroad was sometimes an important eye-opening experience, providing refutation of the official misrepresentations of life in Western countries. Visiting rural areas of their own countries sometimes had a similar impact.

Numerous other substantive experiences were also central to disillusionment, especially of those who lived in Communist states. They include:

1. The experience or knowledge of the policies or specific acts of political violence, repression, or intimidation.

2. Elite privilege; politically determined inequality.

3. Material scarcity, deprivations associated with misplaced priorities, economic mismanagement, ideological rigidity or corruption.

4. Unequal distribution of power, strikingly manifest in the cult of particular leaders, their arbitrary policies, and the mandated unquestioning obedience to them; the human qualities of these leaders (insofar as known)—their brutality, ruthlessness, and duplicitousness (spectacularly contrasting with their official image).

5. Major policy changes or official admission of serious errors, for example the Nazi-Soviet pact in 1939 or Khrushchev's revelations in 1956.

6. Historical events such as the Soviet crushing of uprisings in Eastern Europe or the Chinese invasion of Tibet.

7. The theoretical foundations of these systems were also subject to criticism and held responsible for the deformities of institutions and wrongheaded policies. Three aspects of Marxism were singled out for criticism: a) the doctrine of class struggle, which came to justify political violence; b) belief in the redeeming consequences of abolishing private property; and c) a fixation on the future, which helped to justify indifference to the means used to achieve the distant ends.

It is important to note that the sources and stimulants of disaffection closely resembled one another in different Communist states, regardless of their location, history, size, and level of economic development. The reasons for moral revulsion and the ultimate rejection of these systems were virtually identical whether the setting was Eastern Europe, the Soviet Union, China, Cuba, Vietnam, or Ethiopia. Communist systems shared virtually all the traits, defects, and policies that led to the disaffection of the formerly committed as well as to the aversion of masses of ordinary people who sought to escape the hardships these systems created.

This is not to say that these systems were uniform. For example, Cuba has had no Soviet-style purges and far fewer show trials; the kind of political violence associated with the Cultural Revolution was peculiar to China; Communist systems in the Third World came to be established by indigenous revolution, not by an occupying army as was the case in Eastern Europe at the end of World War II. Not every Communist state mismanaged its economy in the same way or to the same degree; for instance, the backyard furnace campaign was a Chinese specialty (though not the policy of rapid industrialization it was supposed to promote). Not every Communist country experienced famines such as the Soviet Union, China, and Ethiopia, resulting, for the most part, from wrongheaded official policies. There was also variation in the level of repression, substantially diminished in post-Stalin Eastern Europe as it was in post-Mao China. Despite such differences, the attempted implementation of shared doctrines created conditions and hardships that were quite similar as experienced by those who lived in these countries.

It was for different and sometimes more personal reasons and under different circumstances that Western sympathizers broke off their support for Communist systems and movements. Their disenchantment had more diverse and less direct stimulants, and firsthand experience of Communist systems was not one of them. Visits to Communist countries rarely produced disillusionment; the exceptions include Gide and Koestler, and more recently Doris Lessing and Ronald Radosh. For Eric Hobsbawm, a visit to the Soviet Union was a dispiriting experience but in the final analysis had little impact on his ultimate values and beliefs. Maurice Halperin's experiences were unusual for he lived for several years in two different Communist states and thereby became well acquainted with their failings.

A small contingent of American radicals of the sixties generation (Peter Collier, David Horowitz, and Radosh) became disillusioned less with any particular Communist system or ideology than with their fellow activists and the New Left subculture; the same applies to Christopher Hitchens, whose disenchantment proceeded from the revulsion over Islamic terror and fanaticism to anger at those on the left making excuses for them. Eugene Genovese, from a distance, took a good measure of the late Soviet system and found it wanting; he was never drawn to other Communist systems in the Third World and found the cultural radicalism of the New Left thoroughly unappealing. Unlike others here discussed, he was aided in his political reawakening by his revitalized Catholic faith. Occasionally former citizens, witnessess to the misdeeds of these systems, exerted influence on Western sympathizers, such as Joseph Brodsky on Susan Sontag. Doris Lessing gradually grew out of her leftism, having encountered many unattractive human beings on the left.

All disillusioned Westerners were eventually influenced by certain historical events and conditions testifying to the moral or economic failure of Communist systems: the uprisings, the outflow of refugees, the show trials, the purges, the massacres, the endemic scarcities, the obligatory worship of megalomaniacal leaders. One historical event that undermined faith and was mentioned with great frequency in both East and West: Khrushchev's speech at the 20th Party Congress in 1956, which authoritatively revealed the horrors and falsehoods of the Soviet system and the repellent personality of its hitherto deified leader.

Unlike in the Communist states, disenchantment in the West did not benefit from or was not encouraged by indigenous social movements or political currents; it was more typically an isolated and isolating individual experience. On the contrary, social-cultural movements and subcultures in the West, in the 1960s and after, helped perpetuate left-wing beliefs and attachments, especially in the United States.

Another important difference between the two groups of the disillusioned is that many Westerners continued to nourish a residual attachment to Marxism and were reluctant to recognize a connection between Marxist theory and the character of the Communist states. Many vehemently disputed that such a relationship ever existed while those who lived in these states had little doubt about a connection. The latter believed, for example, that the Marxist idea of class struggle made political violence more acceptable for the rulers by legitimating it as historically ordained; likewise the theoretically determined belief in the value of abolishing private ownership of the means of production undermined incentives, reduced productivity, and contributed to endemic scarcities.

The disillusioned in Communist countries risked the dangers and uncertainties of escape or exile (or persecution); Westerners who publicly expressed such disaffection faced only the derision or contempt of their former comrades. In the West there was far greater latitude for political choice and commitment. Taking a political stand (even a controversial one) was more a matter of choice than a response to social-political forces and pressures, and this choice had more to do with intangibles of personality and accidents of personal experience.

In the final analysis, the rejection of Communist systems and their supporting ideologies was, in both settings, as much rooted in idealistic motives as was their initial embrace. No single or dominant pattern of political disillusionment emerged that would make prediction of such an event possible; a variety of patterns was found, some more common than others. Broad generalizations about political disaffection are as difficult to make as about any other important aspect of human behavior and attitude formation.

NINE

Resisting Disillusionment

Although this is a study of disillusionment with communism, resistance to such disillusionment among Western intellectuals has been a phenomenon important enough to merit attention. Comparable resistance in the former or still surviving Communist states has not been notable, hence it need not detain us here.[1]

I am not suggesting that specific Communist states, extinct or surviving, remain widely admired in the West; it is certain ideas and hopes associated with these systems that continue to exercise attraction in conjunction with the critiques and rejections of Western capitalist democracies and the United States in particular. As Kenneth Minogue has written: "When regimes collapse, as they have collapsed all over the communist world in 1989, the principles and ideals which animated them can be glimpsed creeping stealthily away from the rubble, unscathed. Communism 'never failed'—its exponents can be heard muttering—it was 'never tried.'"[2] This is especially the case when "celebrity utopians need a new address for their fantasies"[3] and no such "address" is available, that is, when no new political systems or movements exist upon which wishful fantasies may be projected. What remain are the good intentions, ideals, and hopes that proved impossible to realize. This is why Cornell West could write that "Marxist thought becomes even more relevant after the collapse of Communism in the Soviet Union and Eastern Europe than it was before."[4]

What is retained is a loyalty to ideals that promise to transcend the sordidness of existing social-political realities, especially those for which capitalism is blamed. These ideas constitute a "romantic dream of the healing of all contradictions and the . . . wholeness of nature and history, man and spirit."[5] There is resistance to the notion that the human condition cannot be radically altered and that attempts to do so require large amounts of coercion and violence—as the history of "actually existing" Communist states has shown. Leszek Kolakowski's observation about the influence of Marxism, made in 1978, remains largely valid at the beginning of the twenty-first century:

> The influence that Marxism has achieved, far from being the result of its scientific character, is almost entirely due to its prophetic, fantastic and irrational elements. Marxism is a doctrine of blind confidence that a paradise of universal satisfaction is awaiting us. . . . Almost all the prophecies of Marx . . . have already proved false, but this does not disturb the spiritual certainty of the faithful . . . for it is a certainty not based on any empirical premises or supposed "historical laws," but simply on the psychological need for certainty. In this sense Marxism performs the function of religion, and its efficacy is of religious character.[6]

The resistance to disillusionment involves more of a clinging to these imaginary alternatives (unspecific as they may be), or a residual utopianism strong enough to inspire a rejection of the status quo (and a low-grade alienation), than a specific attachment or loyalty to any existing political system or movement (an orientation exemplified in the book *Empire*, discussed below).

A better understanding of the resistance to disillusionment is likely to shed some light on disillusionment as well. By learning something about those who successfully resist it we may also learn something about the disillusioned. Limitations of space preclude a lengthy examination of this phenomenon, but even a handful of characteristic cases may offer some insights about both the transformation and the persistence of identity-giving political beliefs and commitments.

The late **E. P. Thompson** (1924–1993), the famous British social historian and anti-nuclear activist, is an excellent example of the deep attachment to ends and ideals that may persist in the face of disillusioning experiences. The experiences in question were Khrushchev's revelations in 1956 and the uprisings in Eastern Europe; more generally it was the experience of half a century of Soviet communism.

In a hundred-page "letter" to Kolakowski, Thompson reaffirmed his faith in the form of a polemic. Kolakowski had ceased to venerate not only the Soviet Union but, to Thompson's chagrin, Marxism as well. In his "letter," Thompson reasserts, in a variety of ways, that

Marxism remains untainted by the depredations of Stalinism or by the flaws of "actually existing" socialist states.

His other main theme is that the undiminished menace of capitalism demands continued vigilance and ought to modify attitudes toward the existing socialist states, their deficiencies notwithstanding. Thompson rebukes Kolakowski for his critiques of Marxism and for perceiving a relationship between it and the "actually existing" Soviet-style systems. In particular he reproaches Kolakowski for implying that "from the past fifty years in Russia and Eastern Europe it is legitimate to deduce conclusions about 'real communism.' . . . Fifty years is too short a time in which to judge a new social system."[7]

Above all, Thompson is anxious to reemphasize the utopian potentials of Marxism and the desirable political arrangements it may still create. "We both sought to rehabilitate the utopian energies within the socialist tradition," he writes somewhat plaintively, though by the time of his writing Kolakowski had clearly abandoned that undertaking. Thompson further declares that "our solidarity was given not to Communist states in their existence but in their potential—not for what they were but for what . . . they might become." For good measure he makes clear that "I and several of my comrades affirmed our general allegiance, not to the Communist Party as an institution or as ideology, but to the Communist movement in its humanist potential." It was an allegiance to an agreeable and sustaining fantasy, to potentials, hopes, and wishes.

Thompson also argues that "the hostility of Western social-democrats and liberals towards communism has not been always . . . informed by principled opposition to its 'deformities'; it has as often . . . been directed against its achievements or promise." Thompson remains beholden to this promise.

He is particularly disturbed by Kolakowski's critiques of the left because it might be interpreted by the enemies of the left to suggest "that all the Left has failed . . . all Marxism is incoherent." Like Deutscher who proposed that the disillusioned who contributed to *The God That Failed* were in the grip of irrational impulses, Thompson suggests that "you write like a man in a state of shock whose subjective despair has engulfed . . . his workman's morale."

Kolakowski is further criticized for not being sufficiently appalled by capitalism, for not finding it as menacing as Thompson does, for his "failure to give full weight to the concept of capitalism as a system," and for underestimating the "hegemony" of "capitalist ideology" and its entrenched, concealed, and assumed character. Presumably if

Kolakowski would grasp "the concept of capitalism as a system" he would be properly repulsed by it and less harsh on the flawed alternatives of the "actually existing" Communist states.

Thompson recalls experiences that gave him a glimpse of the kind of utopian possibilities he still believes in—during his participation as a volunteer after World War II in a Yugoslav railway construction project:

> I was a participating witness, in 1947, in the euphoric aftermath of a revolutionary transition, of . . . a transformation of attitudes. Young Yugoslav peasants, students and workers, constructing with high morale their own railway . . . had this new affirmative concept of *nasha* ("our"). . . . The fact that this moment of euphoria proved to be evanescent . . . does not disallow the validity of the experience.

While indeed the evanescence does not invalidate the experience, it could or should raise questions about the likely durability of such experiences and how far one may generalize from such short-lived moments of euphoric solidarity and good cheer to the way social and political institutions operate over the long haul, and how personal versus collective interests (if the latter can be clearly identified) mesh or conflict.

Thompson doesn't shy away from sketching his own conceptions of utopia, somewhat reminiscent of Marx's musings about life in Communist utopia offered in *The German Ideology*:

> My own utopia . . . would be a world (as D. H. Lawrence would have it) where "money values" give way before "life values.". . . With sources of power easily available, some men and women might choose to live in unified communities, sited . . . in centers of great natural beauty, where agricultural, industrial and intellectual pursuits might be combined. Others might prefer the variety and pace of an urban life which rediscovers some of the qualities of the city-state. Others will prefer a life of seclusion and many will pass between all three. Scholars would follow disputes of different schools in Paris, Jakarta or Bogota.

Finally, Thompson warns that "disenchantment in revolutionary aspirations leads on . . . to ultimate reconciliation with the pre-existent status quo—or even to zealous ideological partisanship on behalf of the status quo—. . . And it [the disenchantment] has, within capitalist ideology today, a very important confirmatory and legitimating function." If capitalism is the ultimate and universal evil (as Thompson clearly believed), the disenchanted are in grave danger of wittingly or unwittingly supporting the greater, indeed the greatest evil, which has no redeeming utopian promises or potentials.

Thompson comes across as the prototypical true believer who cannot let go of the promise and hope associated with certain ideas—in this case, Marxism. He also personifies the connection between seeing capitalism as the unchanging source of all evil and the complementary view of Marxism as the correspondingly unchanging source of all good.

ERIC HOBSBAWM (1917–). One of the reviewers of Hobsbawm's work raised an important and interesting question, relevant not only to Hobsbawm but to other figures discussed in this book: "How could such a celebrated and accomplished historian have remained so oblivious of the lessons of recent history?"[8]

Eric Hobsbawm has been a "man of the left" throughout his long life and has enjoyed an extraordinary global reputation in the academic world, foremost among left-leaning intellectuals and liberals. He has been a champion honorary doctorate recipient, conference invitee, and subsidized world traveler. He has also been a regular on the mass media of several countries. (A photograph in his autobiography[9] shows him on Dutch television in the apparently congenial company of Markus Wolf, former head of the East German intelligence service, with whom he shares a distaste for expressing regrets about long-standing political commitments and convictions.)

Hobsbawm's global acclaim is not merely a reflection of his excellence as a historian. His fame and reputation rest in large measure on successfully personifying a particular political position and mind-set: the unrepentant leftist and unwavering believer in Marxism who has held on to his convictions in face of the vast accumulation of historical evidence that should have undermined them. As Tony Judt has observed, "Unlike almost every other intellectual to fall under Communist spell, Hobsbawm evinces no regrets. . . . [He] refuses to stare evil in the face and call it by its name; he never engages the moral as well as the political heritage of Stalin and his works."[10] As of 1994 Hobsbawm still insisted that even if he had known in 1934 that "millions of people were dying in the Soviet experiment" he would not have renounced it, because "the chance of a new world being born in great suffering would still have been worth backing."[11] As such a remark suggests, Hobsbawm has not been the common garden-variety leftist academic so abundant in our times but an unrepentant member of the British Communist party, a "card-carrying Communist"—therein may lie the secret of his acclaim.

All those who seek to retain their leftist beliefs have found encouragement in Hobsbawm's steadfast loyalty to and successful preservation of what strike them as noble and idealistic impulses and commitments—ingeniously divorced from their human costs, from the political catastrophes they created or contributed to.[12] Hobsbawm has shown how one may admit that all existing Communist systems were deeply flawed ("it must now be obvious that failure was built into this enterprise from the start"), concede that the original good intentions of their creators had horrific unintended consequences, *and yet* continue to regard these intentions and the ideas underpinning them as admirable and inspiring. Or again, as Neil McInnes put it, for him "communism [was] the tragic hero of the century."[13] Hobsbawm thus personifies idealism in the face of adversity, a high-minded refusal to give in to discouragement or yield to disillusionment. His loyalty to the party was, in all probability, intended to be, and came to be seen as, an emblem of pride and quixotic courage.

Hobsbawm contrasted the seriousness of his youthful commitments with the more frivolous political playacting of the sixties radicals: "Unlike the 1968 generation, few interwar communists went into the revolution as into a political Club Med. . . ." He also makes clear that he has not been a sixties-style radical "cultural dissident." And unlike the radicals of the sixties, his loyalties were firmly anchored in the party: "The Party was what our life was about. We gave it all we had. In return we got from it the certainty of our victory and the experience of fraternity. . . . It represented the ideal of transcending selfishness." Another special bond linked him to the October Revolution: ". . . I belonged to the generation tied by an almost unbreakable umbilical cord to hope of the world revolution and its original home, the October Revolution." In an earlier work (*The Age of Extremism*) he averred that "it was the only political cause, which even in retrospect, appears as pure and appealing as it did in 1936."[14]

In search of a more pragmatic basis for his support of the party and Western Communist movements, he also argued that "the Communist intellectual, in opting for the USSR and his communist party did so because on balance the good on his side seemed to outweigh the bad." For these intellectuals (himself, of course, included), the axiomatic, overriding "badness" was capitalism. He also wrote, rather self-servingly, that "modern political choice is not a constant process of selecting men or measures, but a single or infrequent choice between packages, in which we buy the disagreeable [sic] part of the contents because there is no other way to be politically effective."[15] What this seems to mean is that once commitment is made to the lesser evil, it is no longer necessary to adjust one's political loyalties in light of new information that may call into question the original commitment.

Hobsbawm insists in his autobiography that "people like myself did not remain in the Party because we had many illusions about the USSR, although undoubtedly we had some. For instance, we clearly underestimated the horrors of what had gone on . . . under Stalin until it was denounced by Khrushchev in 1956." Elsewhere he pleads ignorance of the worst Soviet atrocities: "Of course we did not, and could not, envisage the sheer scale of what was being imposed on the Soviet people under Stalin at the time when we identified ourselves with him and the Comintern, and were reluctant to believe the few who told us what they knew or suspected." Nonetheless a few lines later he observes that "it is anachronistic to suppose that only genuine or willful ignorance stood between us and denouncing the inhumanities perpetrated on our side. . . . In the total war we were engaged in, one did not ask oneself whether there should be a limit to the sacrifices imposed on others any more than on ourselves." Such a "total war" is the time-honored excuse every modern dictatorship has offered for its repressive policies, (and the Soviets for their campaigns of terror in the 1930s) here invoked by Hobsbawm. He clearly had little idea of the actual nature of the Soviet system while imagining that it held the great promise of comprehensive human liberation. The abstract quality of his youthful affections for the Soviet Union is also revealed in his negative reactions to Soviet realities during his visit in 1954–1955, from which he returned "depressed and without any desire to go there again."

Even the partially chastened, mature Hobsbawm has retained blind spots of impressive proportions, which for example enabled him to believe that East Germany (he insists on calling it the German Democratic Republic) "was not a bad society: work and careers for all, universal education . . . social security and pensions, holidays in a firmly structured community of good people doing an honest day's work . . . open-air leisure and sports, no class distinctions."

Hobsbawm's worldview required a perception of the Soviet Union as relatively weak and lacking in the "global ambitions and aggressiveness of the USA." At the same time he praised the USSR for being able to provide worldwide support for "national liberation movements" and assorted revolutionary systems. He wrote:

> . . . Communists [i.e., himself] saw the USA and its allies threatening the total destruction of a still besieged and vulnerable USSR, in order to

> bring to a halt the global advance of the forces of the revolution. . . . To us it was obvious that the USSR was not in a position to conquer the world for communism. . . . It was . . . a system with severe defects, but with titanic [!] achievements and still with the unlimited potential of socialism[!]. . . . Supporting and defending the Soviet Union was still the essential international priority.
>
> So we swallowed our doubts and mental reservations and defended it.

These remarks highlight the degree to which Hobsbawm's alignments and beliefs were predicated on the appeal of good intentions, potentialities, and a future superior to the present. It was the attribution of these great hopes to the USSR that prevented him from a proper appreciation of its "severe defects" and allowed them little weight in his moral-political accounting.

Hobsbawm has been a student of modern European history and well acquainted with Communist systems and movements in the twentieth century, hence his ignorance of their failures could not have played a substantial role in cementing his early loyalties, largely unrevised, to ripe old age; nor is he an unreflective individual, as this autobiography indicates. Yet neither knowledge nor a degree of self-reflection has prevented him from effortlessly subordinating intellect to emotion[16]—a condition far from unknown among politically committed intellectuals. Consider how this passage illustrates the durable emotional determination of his beliefs:

> The months in Berlin [he was in his teens at the time] made me a lifelong communist, or at least a man whose life would lose its nature and its significance without the political project to which he committed himself as a schoolboy, even though that project has demonstrably failed, and, as I now know, was bound to fail. The dream of the October Revolution is still there somewhere inside me. . . . To this day I notice myself treating the memory and tradition of the USSR with an indulgence and tenderness. . . . I belong to a generation for whom the October Revolution represented the hope of the world.

Such affirmations and reaffirmations are scattered throughout Hobsbawm's autobiography, which is permeated by a Marxist view of the world that is taken for granted. But he does not discuss how and why Marxism influenced the failed policies of Communist states, and why, if it lent itself to such chronic misuse, it should still be revered. He seems to equate Marxism with truth-seeking and the endemic struggle against injustice—that is, poverty and inequality. But like many leftist Western intellectuals, he manages to be at once egalitarian and elitist. On the one hand he believes that his work has considerable historical importance and sees himself belonging to an international fraternity of enlightened elite intellectuals. On the other hand he is a champion and brother of the downtrodden. He writes, "The enormous advantage of communism, especially when reinforced by friendship, is that one could simply not treat a comrade other than as an equal." It is not easy to imagine how this feeling translated into reality during encounters with representatives of the Latin American or Mediterranean peasants he admired and wrote about, or other members of the working classes.

A considerable amount of name-dropping supports the imputation of these elitist inclinations. Hobsbawm seems to take great pleasure in referring to his innumerable distinguished "friends" who achieved high office, renown, or distinguished intellectual status. He relishes recollections of his own high-flying career, when the Rockefeller Foundation flew him first-class to various exotic destinations. He comes across as a tireless networker affably cultivating his global connections and heartily enjoying the status he achieved after overcoming earlier difficulties in his career caused by his obstinate attachment to the British Communist party. After the 1960s the attachment ceased to matter and in fact became an asset.

Hobsbawm's early life offers clues for understanding the development and persistence of his political commitments. His childhood and adolescence were shadowed by the threat of Nazism, a disorganized family life, and the downward social mobility of his parents. His father was a highly unsuccessful breadwinner. His early life was marked by social, economic, and emotional instability, years of "tragedy, trauma, loss and insecurity." It was also the time of the Great Depression.

From an early age Hobsbawm was one of many Jews (and liberal gentiles) who believed that only the Communist movements and the Soviet Union were steadfast opponents of Nazism. Even sixty years later, in an autobiography filled with historical facts, he could not bring himself to make any reference to the 1939 Nazi-Soviet pact.

His father died when he was twelve, his mother when he was fourteen. He was raised in different places by relatives and attended seven different "educational establishments" in Austria, Germany, and England before landing at Cambridge University. His political beliefs and affiliations apparently became the essential foundation of a sense of identity and provided him with lifelong emotional support, coherence, and focus. He recalls with great warmth the mass demonstrations he took part in as a young man:

> Next to sex, the activity combining bodily experience and intense emotion to the highest degree is the participation in a mass demonstration at a time of great public exaltation. . . . It implies some physical action—marching, chanting slogans, singing—through which the merger of the individual in the mass . . . finds expression. The occasion has remained unforgettable. . . .

Later in life he still found satisfaction in such activities as shown in the photographs of him protesting nuclear weapons in Trafalgar Square. Among the five components of his Communist disposition he includes this "sense of 'mass ecstasy'" in addition to "pity for the exploited, the aesthetic appeal of a perfect and comprehensive intellectual system, 'dialectical materialism,' a little bit of the Blakean vision of the new Jerusalem and a good deal of intellectual anti-philistinism." Elsewhere he writes that "what made Marxism so irresistible was its comprehensiveness."

Upon arrival at Cambridge University he was in a position to join, or overlap with, what he called "the reddest and most radical generation in the history of the university," which included some of the notorious spies of the period such as Blunt, Burgess, Maclean, and Philby. He writes:

> I knew those of my contemporaries who became Soviet agents as militant members of the student Party. . . . We knew such work was going on, we knew we were not supposed to ask questions about it, we respected those who did it, and most of us—certainly I—would have taken it on ourselves, if asked.

In light of these sentiments it should not surprise the reader that in 1950, while still associated with King's College, he made a special point of inviting Alan Nunn May, "just released from jail for nuclear espionage, to a King's feast." Hobsbawm evidently did not disapprove of spying for the Soviet Union. In a similar spirit in later years he supported leftist guerrillas in various parts of the world "where successful guerrilla conquest was realistically on the agenda"—that is, when they had a chance to win. He did make an exception for the Shining Path guerrillas of Peru, "a left-wing revolutionary movement I did not want to win." On the other hand he appeared favorably disposed toward the similarly murderous FARC of Colombia.

Besides the weight of youthful commitments and the rewards he reaped later in life, Hobsbawm also persisted in his beliefs because he disliked those who opposed them and would have found their company distasteful: ". . . I was strongly repelled by the idea of being in the company of those ex-communists who turned into fanatical anti-communists." He was also "repelled" by "Cold War rhetoric and free market liberalism" during the 1980s and disapproved of François Furet's belief that communism was "a dangerous dream." He further explains that "what made it easier . . . to maintain the old faith, more than anything else, [was] the crusading global anti-communism of the West in the Cold War."

Hobsbawm remains convinced that no matter what Communist systems have done or failed to accomplish, the corruptions of capitalism are worse and continue to demand undiminished critical attention: "capitalism is still rapacious and exploitative and socialism is still good," he wrote. Such avowals, notwithstanding his conceptions of the socialist consummation, are remarkably vague (not unlike those of Marx): "But what would such a [socialist] society be like? Socialism is an instrument, not a program, and all we can say about . . . the eventual future of socialism . . . [is that] like Karl Marx, we do not know." This vagueness is hardly dispelled by his pronouncement that "today socialism is the only political force in civilized society . . . that recognizes the need for a society in which all men and women can live as human beings and which is more than the sum of its individual members."[17]

Hobsbawm's abiding and profound loathing of capitalism and his conviction that it is the root of all evil appears to rest (in part) on a conflation or confusion of capitalism with the afflictions of modernity, perhaps even more important, with those of the human condition. It is an attitude he shares with numerous notable critics of capitalism discussed in these pages (as well as many others not discussed) who resist modification of their political positions and beliefs, and especially their virtuous anti-capitalism.

Hobsbawm's contempt for Israel equals and possibly exceeds that toward capitalism. He characterizes it as "the small, militarist, culturally disappointing and politically aggressive nation-state" that asks, in vain, for his solidarity on racial grounds. He had no difficulty extending such solidarity to the Palestinians during his visits to occupied Palestine.[18]

Hobsbawm has shown few deviations from the loyalties sketched above. The crushing of the Hungarian Revolution of 1956 moved him to challenge the party line in a letter published in the non-party press. In his autobiography he muses about "living in a land of the blessed: a region [Western Europe] without war, without the prospect of fear of social upheaval, in which most people enjoyed a life of wealth, a range of choices in life and leisure, and a degree of social security beyond the reach of all but the very rich in our parents' generations. . . ." This would seem to be an admission that there is, after all, such a thing as capitalism with a human face. And at the end of his book Hobsbawm unexpectedly suggests that "in some ways the United States represents the best of the twentieth century . . . [and] promises greater openness to talent, to energy and novelty than other worlds." Tributes are also paid to American economic, technological, and scientific achievements followed "on the other hand" by listing some of the human costs of the system, including the "unspeakable" prisons and huge prison population.

As an old leftist and old-style Marxist, Hobsbawm is properly critical of identity politics and intellectual undertakings such as black, queer, or women's studies. Commendably enough, he advocates moving "beyond one's roots. . . . History needs distance not only from the passions, emotions, ideologies and fears of our own wars of religion but from the even more dangerous temptations of 'identity.'"

In the end Hobsbawm sees himself as one who "recycled" himself "from militant to sympathizer or fellow traveller, or . . . from effective membership of the British Communist Party to something like spiritual membership of the Italian CP, which fitted my ideas of communism rather better." But this progression understates his commitments and obscures the bases of his sizable self-esteem. Besides pride in his wordly successes, he sees himself as a man of the best possible intentions, a fighter for a better world who tries to make sure that humanity will not "live without the ideals of freedom and justice" and one still possessed of an unquenchable thirst for "a fundamental reconstruction of society."[19] In the final analysis it is "the desire to find at least some residual meaning in the whole Communist experience"[20] that best explains his unusually durable political attachments.

Noam Chomsky (1928–). It would be hard to find a better illustration of the persistence of political attitudes and beliefs than those of Noam Chomsky. Even among those who have not changed their mind (despite outlandish and discredited political positions), Chomsky stands out, towering above all other prominent critics of the United States. Not only has he persisted in his beliefs and convictions for several decades, but they appear to have become hardened, indeed ossified with the passage of time. He remains energized by a peculiar, one-sided, burning moral indignation and radiates a matter-of-fact self-righteousness. He displays a missionary zeal and unwavering certainty in his ceaseless efforts to enlighten his audiences about the evil the United States represents and spreads throughout the world—the only message he sends time and again. His belief in the importance of his political ideas finds expression in their tireless propagation in books, articles, speeches, and interviews.

Chomsky is deeply convinced that the misdeeds of the United States (and those of Israel) have a uniquely evil quality, and it is his bedrock conviction that no moral outrage can surpass those actions he ascribes to the United States. He habitually compares the United States to Nazi Germany and on at least one occasion has suggested (in a speech at a national convention of philosophers) that it is actually worse than Nazi Germany.[21]

Chomsky's impregnable moral certainty has few rivals among contemporary secular political thinkers, whatever their worldview. Only among the most orthodox Muslims or some fundamentalist Christians could one find voices capable of comparable levels of self-assurance and moral certainty.

Chomsky's main rhetorical posture is that of the fearless social critic who separates fact from fiction, myth from reality, right from wrong. As a reverential student of his ideas put it, "he regards most of what he has to say as being self-evident."[22] He seeks to convey, in his inimitable rhetorical-polemical style, that there is simply no reasonable or honest alternative to his views of the world and often expresses pained surprise that people of goodwill or "minimal intelligence" (one of his favored expressions) may not share these views. "No one with even a shred of honesty would disagree" is a characteristic bit of Chomskyan throat-clearing. In the same spirit Chomsky has observed that ". . . if we are not moral hypocrites we would agree that Sudan was the morally worse crime than the World Trade Center. . . ."[23]

Like most social critics, Chomsky is eager to unmask, demystify, replace falsehoods with truth, and tell his audiences how things really are. He spends much effort in seeking to expose what he considers the endemic misrepresentations of reality and the deceitfulness of those he criticizes: American policymakers and political elites, the media and intellectuals insufficiently outraged by what he regards as outrageous. He believes that educational institutions are inculcating false consciousness into the masses: ". . . it is a fair guess that as the level of ducation increases, the level of understanding of these social realities will decline. We see evidence for this conclusion in that these topics can be barely discussed within the ideological institutions managed by the educated classes: the media, the schools, the universities, the journals of opinion."[24]

Chomsky expressed these beliefs in 1987, at a time when the adversarial worldview of the 1960s had already been fully integrated into these institutions. It was difficult to find a college course in the social sciences that did not reflect in some measure Chomsky's views about American political and economic institutions.

What sets Chomsky apart from other social critics is that his enraged denunciations are embedded in an elaborate pretense of reasonableness. He lubricates his writings and speeches with recurring language that seeks to create an impression of objectivity, detachment, and self-evident rectitude. These recurring expressions include "it is surely not in doubt," "assuming that facts matter," "it is an obvious truism that," "for those who care to consider the factual record," "the available facts lead to one clear conclusion," "evidence from sources that seem to deserve a hearing," "observers of evident bias and low credibility" (i.e., people he seeks to discredit) as opposed to those "with [unspecified] excellent credentials." Views he dismisses are never "subject to possible verification," never possess a "shred of credibility." He may sententiously observe that an author he dismisses "might have troubled to inquire into the source of his allegations." As to the massacres of Pol Pot, for instance, "evidence is slight and informed opinion [!] ranges over quite a wide spectrum."[25]

Such terminology is intended to conjure an aura of rationality; readers are to be impressed by the repeated appeals to evidence, facts, reason, verification, informed opinion, sources that deserve a hearing, and the rest of the polemical paraphernalia. But the appeals to reason compete with expressions of consuming rage which impel Chomsky to resort to invective and ad hominem arguments. Sidney Hook reported that "Chomsky's response to my criticism . . . was an unbridled attack against my mind, character and whole life/career as a thinker on social and political issues."[26] Even in the classroom he cannot tolerate disagreement. In a seminar discussion he was observed "to berate for a long time" a student who disagreed with him and ignored the student's attempts to speak. "People cried out 'Let him talk!' but to no avail. Another student stood up . . . but Chomsky ignored him. People made loud, disgruntled noises in protest of his treatment but Chomsky ignored those too."[27]

The soothing appeals to reason and facts thus coexist with a remarkable level of rage and verbal violence: "he uses certain words over and over, atrocity, murder, genocide, massacre, genocide . . . until through repetition the words lose their meaning."[28] They also lose their meaning because they are used without discrimination to deepen the moral degradation of his adversaries and especially U.S. policymakers by, for example, labeling their every alleged misdeed "genocidal."

The same self-righteous fury appeared in the personal letter I received from Chomsky a quarter-century ago (dated December 27, 1978), occasioned by a letter I had written to the local newspaper (the *Daily Hampshire Gazette* of Northampton, Massachusetts, published November 28, 1978). My letter was prompted by a talk he gave at the Unitarian Church in Northampton, reported in the same paper, which dealt with American media coverage of Cambodia. In my letter I described him as "the best-known apologist" for the Pol Pot regime and one who sought to minimize the atrocities it had committed. My assertion was based, among other things, on an article Chomsky had published in *The Nation*, entitled "Distortions at Fourth Hand," written with Edward Herman, in which they referred to the massacres of the Pol Pot regime as "tales of Communist atrocities." He and Herman concluded—with the help of unnamed "highly qualified specialists . . . who have studied the full range of evidence"—that "executions numbered at most in the thousands" and even those were to be blamed on "peasant discontent . . . aggravated by the threat of starvation resulting from American destruction and killing."[29] Notwithstanding these propositions, he characterized my letter as "false and slanderous (technically libellous)" and demanded that I send a written apology to the same newspaper in order to meet "minimal standards of honesty."

In their book published two years later the authors continued to blame the United States for the violence in Cambodia and even suggested that further studies might discover that the killings were "an understandable response to [the] . . . extreme savagery of a U.S. assault that may in part have been designed to evoke this response."[30]

In the *Nation* article Chomsky and Herman also criticized François Ponchaud for relying on refugee accounts in his discussion of these massacres, arguing that "They [the refugees] naturally tend to report what they believe their interlocutors wish to hear . . . refugees questioned by Westerners or Thais have a vested interest in reporting atrocities on the part of Cambodian revolutionaries, an obvious fact no serious reporter will fail to take into account."

In startling contrast to their skepticism about the credibility of refugees, they accepted without reservations the official explanation of a food shortage for the evacuation of Phnom Penh and dismissed Ponchaud who argued that it was prompted by political-ideological considerations.[31]

In the 1979 book Chomsky elaborated on the views expressed earlier in *The Nation*, arguing that those who gave credence to the testimony of refugees wished "to defame the regime," and that it was unfair to blame the regime for deaths due to "malnutrition and disease." He quoted with approval Richard Dudman ("an experienced foreign correspondent with excellent credentials") who "did not find the grim picture painted by thousands of refugees who couldn't take the new order." Among the signs of popular satisfaction with the regime, Dudman observed, we learn from Chomsky, that farm workers "appeared to be reasonably relaxed at the height of the busy harvest season. They sometimes leaned on their hoes like farm workers everywhere. And they often . . . wave. . . . There were no signs of government cadres giving orders or armed guards enforcing the working hours, although individuals seemed to know what was expected."

Thus, aided by Dudman's report, Chomsky concluded that

> the peasant population probably didn't regard "the austere standard of hard manual labor" . . . as an onerous imposition of the regime. . . . One might reach the conclusion that much of the population may well have supported the regime, particularly, if it is true, as Dudman was informed [no skepticism here] . . . that "decisions were taken collectively" in the cooperatives and even the army.

As to the massacres

> there has been extensive fabrication of evidence. . . .
>
> It is surely not in doubt that it was U.S. intervention that inflamed civil struggle. . . .
>
> It is a truism, obvious to anyone who dealt with refugees . . . or simply uses common sense that "accounts of refugees are indeed to be used with great care" . . .
>
> It is quite evident that to understand the aftermath of the war it is necessary to pay attention to the historical background of the peasant revolution which was further inflamed and deeply embittered by the U.S. attack culminating in the bombing of 1973.
>
> . . . While many questions remain open about Cambodia during the 1975–78 period . . . on another question . . . we feel the facts are

> clear and overwhelming. . . . It is a fair generalization that the more extreme the condemnation of Cambodia, the more confident the claim that "Communism" lies at the root of the present travail. . . .
>
> . . . Where evidence [of the massacres] is subject to some independent check, it repeatedly and with remarkable consistency turns out to be fabricated. . . .[32]

It is easy to understand why Chomsky sympathized with the Pol Pot regime; it was a reflexive response toward a political system with radical revolutionary credentials, one strongly opposed by the United States. His later denial that he ever tried to minimize the atrocities of the Khmer Rouge was an attempt to salvage his reputation after these atrocities became widely known and recognized, even by those on the left.

Steven Lukes, the British social philosopher, in an article entitled "Chomsky's Betrayal of Truths," suggested "that Chomsky has become so obsessed by his opposition to the United States' role in Indochina that he has lost all sense of perspective" regarding the atrocities committed by the Pol Pot regime.[33]

Chomsky's comments on Cambodia are rooted in a persistent and quite literal incapacity to feel morally repelled by outrages which cannot be ascribed to or associated with the United States. He seems unable to contemplate any non-American outrage without comparing it to some greater and far more repellent U.S. or Israeli alleged misdeed. Mention 9/11 and he will compare it to the American bombing of a pharmaceutical factory in Sudan (which killed one person), or to the American mistreatment of native Americans.[34] While "He takes pride in noting that he has always described the attacks on the World Trade Center as an atrocity . . . he always adds that such attacks pale next to the West's 'deep-seated culture of terrorism.'" [35] Already in 1987 he was convinced that the United States was a "global terrorist" state.[36]

To say that Chomsky demonizes the United States is an understatement. As a leftist author put it, "His only hesitancy concerns whether the United States is 'totalitarian' or 'fascist.'"[37] He is never at a loss to detect the conspiratorial designs of American elites and those serving their interests. Although not a professed Marxist, he perceives economic interests at the root of all American policies, the "greed and desire to maximize personal gain at the expenses of others."[38] It is axiomatic for him that American foreign policy is based on the determination to preserve "the freedom to rob and exploit" other nations, an impulse "rooted in the unchanging institutional structure of military-based state capitalism."[39]

He attributes an exceptional ruthlessness and cynicism to American elites and policymakers:

> If peasants starving to death in Honduras can look across the borders [to Sandinista Nicaragua, that is] and see health clinics, land reform, literacy programs, improvements in subsistence agriculture . . . in a country no better endowed than their own, the rot may spread; and it may spread still farther, perhaps even to the United States where many people suffering from malnutrition or the homeless in the streets of the world's richest country may begin to ask some questions. It is necessary to destroy the rotten apple before the rot spreads through the barrel.[40]

Chomsky the skeptic had no doubts about the good intentions or the actual accomplishments of the Sandinistas and believed that their policies could have had a domino effect, sparking welcome social unrest in neighboring countries such as Honduras. Even the poor and homeless in the United States might be inspired and made restive by the Nicaraguan example.

Concerning the U.S. role in Nicaragua, he wrote: "Even if the harshest charges with a shred of credibility are accepted, the Sandinista leadership is positively saintly in comparison with the gangsters the U.S. supported throughout Central America and beyond, not to speak of Washington itself."[41] In a letter to a kindred soul, Alexander Cockburn, Chomsky wrote: "In comparison to the conditions imposed by U.S. tyranny and violence, East Europe under Russian rule was practically a paradise." In the same place he denounced Vaclav Havel because in a speech to the U.S. Congress Havel contrasted the United States favorably to the former Soviet Union. Chomsky characterized the favorable congressional response to Havel's speech as "one of the most illuminating examples of the total and complete intellectual and moral corruption of Western culture."[42]

Chomsky's belief in the uniquely evil U.S. character is linked to a vast exaggeration of its power. As Richard Wolin has noted, Chomsky "present[s] a portrait of U.S. power at home and abroad so monolithic and impregnable that despair or inaction become the only possible responses."[43] The exaggeration of American power helps portray the United States as exceptionally dangerous and threatening, and further justifies its ceaseless vilification.

According to a sympathetic writer, "Chomsky's views have not changed significantly since he was ten,"[44] though it was not until the Vietnam War that he became a full-time social critic. The depth and finality of his rejection of American society was already apparent in 1966 when he wrote:

> [American] schools are the first training ground for troops that will enforce the muted, unending terror of the status quo in the coming years of a projected American century; for the technicians who will be developing the means for extension of American power; for the intellectuals who can be counted on . . . to provide the ideological justification for this particular form of barbarism. . . .[45]

Chomsky has also been sympathetic to all those willing to take violent action against domestic political authorities and the existing social order. He was among the signers of a letter supporting and sympathetic toward Kathy Boudin, convicted to twenty years to life for her participation in the 1981 Brinks holdup and murders. The signers of the letter lauded her idealism, deplored the sentence as unduly harsh, and criticized the legal system as a whole for its repressive character and violations of human rights.[46]

Chomsky's critiques of American society follow conventional Marxist lines, though he prefers to think of himself as an anarchist (or "anarchosyndicalist") or a "libertarian socialist."[47] Such self-styled anarchism did not prevent him from supporting highly regimented authoritarian Communist regimes in the Third World.

His attraction to Communist systems has been episodic and largely a result of their being the enemies of his archenemy. He was sympathetic to the Vietcong and North Vietnam during the Vietnam War and to Pol Pot's regime in Cambodia; he was warmly supportive of Sandinista Nicaragua. He called Mao's China "an important example of a new society in which very interesting and positive things happened . . . in which a good deal of collectivization and communization was really based on mass participation and took place after a level of understanding had been reached in the peasantry."[48] As to Cuba, he wrote:

> . . . the real crime of Cuba was never the repression, which . . . doesn't even come close to the kind of repression we have traditionally supported, and in fact implemented, in nearby countries. . . . The real crime of Cuba was the *successes* . . . like health care and feeding people and the general threat of a "demonstration effect" that follows from that—that is, that people in other countries might try to do the same things.[49]

Chomsky's critiques of American society are far from original; they are anchored in the familiar leftist designation of capitalism as the source of most evil in the world. He has consistently argued that business interests are the unshakable foundation of U.S. foreign policy:

> The first principle of U.S. foreign policy is designed to create and maintain an international order in which U.S.-based business can prosper, a world of "open societies," meaning societies that are open to profitable investment . . . and to exploitation of material and human resources on the part of U.S. corporations. . . .
>
> What all this means for much of the Third World . . . is that the primary concern of U.S. foreign policy is to guarantee the freedom to rob and exploit. . . .
>
> The major enemy . . . is always the indigenous population, which has an unfortunate tendency to succumb to strange and unacceptable ideas about using their resources for their own purposes. . . .
>
> A second and related principle is that an ideological system must be constructed to ensure that the population remains passive, ignorant and apathetic, and that none of these matters are understood among the educated. . . .

As to matters domestic:

> In a capitalist democracy [such as the United States] everything tends to become a commodity, including freedom: you can have as much of it as you can buy.
>
> In a capitalist democracy the primary concern of everyone must be to ensure that the wealthy are satisfied; all else is secondary. . . . State policy is determined by those groups that command resources. . . .

Chomsky also firmly believes that the American mass media show a "systematic deference" to business interests and that "journalists and columnists have the choice of conforming or being excluded."

As these propositions indicate, Chomsky subscribes to a highly conspiratorial conception of American society, where nothing is left to chance and everything is relentlessly manipulated by exceedingly cunning and unscrupulous elites. He has also adopted Herbert Marcuse's notion of "repressive tolerance" (though Chomsky does not credit him with the idea in his writings). Chomsky too believes that since the rulers use less violence domestically than abroad, it is all the more important and "necessary to control what people think"[50] at home. In American society the very narrow margin of free expression is tolerated to create illusions of freedom, as a tactical concession.

Chomsky believes that American intellectuals have sold out and now assist the dark forces in power, lulling the masses into acquiescence: "the intelligentsia—particularly the dominant liberal intelligentsia—have, in my view, tended to be state propagandists";[51] they are "purveyors of the ideology of the state . . . subordinat[ing] their responsibility to the truth to satisfying the demands of the state."[52]

It is difficult to understand how Chomsky reached these conclusions in light of the adversarial positions adopted by huge numbers of American intellectuals since the late 1960s, now virtually institutionalized in academic settings and various cultural institutions. His conclusion may be explained by the fact that while the great majority of liberal intellectuals have been critical of American society and U.S. foreign policy, they have not been as fiercely critical as Chomsky, and as he thinks they should have been. Moreover, some liberal intellectuals have not been sufficiently respectful of Chomsky's political ideas.

Can we learn anything from Chomsky's certitudes and his chronic if one-sided moral indignation about conditions that affect the change and persistence of political beliefs and attitudes? About intellectuals' commitment to truth and the exercise of critical sensibilities? About the connection between personality and political disposition?

Chomsky's celebrity status helps explain the persistence (but not the origins) of his political beliefs, which are reinforced by the favorable response of his audiences. Unlike many other detractors of the United States, Chomsky has become a political celebrity, influential and popular among all those who, for whatever reason, detest U.S. foreign policy, American culture, capitalism, and the West. Rock groups like Bad Religion and Pearl Jam proudly quote his writings in interviews and their music.[53] He ranks eighth among the ten most frequently cited sources of all times, including the Bible.[54]

Not only has Chomsky published abundantly, he is endlessly on the lecture circuit and generously gives interviews (mostly to interviewers receptive to his ideas), spreading his message energetically around the world even at an advanced age (he was born in 1928). Every indication is that Chomsky enjoys the political role he has played for much of his life—that of the righteous, defiant social critic (a defiance that has been risk-free and well rewarded). He has no reason to abandon this role given the admiration he receives from people sharing and thriving on his outlook.

Given the extreme and immoderate character of his beliefs, their revision or reassessment is not an option. Chomsky's personality seems to have become so absorbed and dominated by his political utterances and attitudes that it is hard to imagine how he could extricate himself from them. In a recent interview he was asked if he ever doubted his ideas. Amazingly enough, he said: "All the time. You should read what happens in linguistics. I keep changing what I said. Any person who is intellectually alive changes his ideas. If anyone at a university is teaching the same thing they were teaching five years ago, either the field is dead or they haven't been thinking."[55] It may be noted that the interviewer was not inquiring about the persistence of Chomsky's views on linguistics but on politics.

It is always easier to understand the persistence of long-held, identity-giving beliefs than their radical revision or abandonment. In Chomsky's case the most pressing question is not why he has preserved his beliefs intact over his entire life but how he acquired them in the first place and why they became such rigidly held certainties. What is to be explained is not the liberal or left-leaning mind-set, common enough among academics, but the exceptional intensity and unwavering character of these convictions.

The self-confessed anarchist-libertarian impulses provide some explanation. Apparently Chomsky is among the countless angry romantic critics of modern society—and especially of contemporary American society—who believe that human nature is benign and abounds in cooperative and communitarian impulses but is thwarted by reprehensible social-political systems imposed on laudable dispositions.[56] Chomsky seems to regard greed (key to his condemnation of capitalism) as the most contemptible human trait and finds it deeply and uniquely embedded in American culture and society. By the same token, social-political systems that appear to encourage cooperation and communitarian dispositions—as Communist systems claimed and appeared to—win his approval.

It is more difficult to assess the influences exerted by his Jewish background, a part of his identity he is reluctant to express. The virulence of his anti-Israeli sentiments (as intense as his anti-Americanism) suggest a problematic Jewish identity, unless one accepts the dubious claim that one may hate Israel and still love the Jews. It is hard to know how important his father's strong Jewish identity was in stimulating a problematic and conflicted Jewish identity in the son.

Chomsky's beliefs and behavior certainly confirm the far from novel proposition that learning and excellence in a particular field (linguistics in his case) provide no protection against questionable and extreme beliefs held hostage to strong emotions.

Chomsky's fulminations also stimulate reflection about the part played by hatred in political attitude formation and the making of political judgments. The popularity of his utterances brings a renewed realization that a posture of consuming hatred can be an enduring foundation of political attitudes, and that such hatred and its impassioned expression is attractive and enjoyable to people who share similar sentiments but are less adept at their expression.

Despite the impregnable self-righteousness and the endless repetition of his messages, Chomsky is not a true believer in the sense of possessing some transformative, redeeming social-political vision. He offers no alternative to the corrosive corruption that (in his view) dominates American life; he tells us endlessly what is wrong with the world but not how things should be made right. This sets him apart from many other radical thinkers and social critics whose hatred of existing social arrangements is complemented by a vision of alternatives.

A convincing and thorough explanation of what really motivates Chomsky, of the roots of his political beliefs and the sources of his hatreds, must await a probing psychological examination by a researcher familiar with the history of his personal life.

WILLIAM KUNSTLER (1919–1995) is the only lawyer discussed in this book. He "use[d] the law politically" but didn't really believe in it; he recognized that "it has certain exploitable factors."[57] His major objective was "to obtain the release of political activist defendants so that they might continue their organizing and revolutionary activities. . . ." Legal proceedings on behalf of such defendants were also used "to generate a loss of public confidence in the judicial system, and by extension, the entire government apparatus."[58]

Kunstler exemplifies the committed radical activist whose beliefs and zeal never wavered and who never even came close to reassessing his political beliefs, let alone to political disillusionment. Truthfully he wrote ". . . I worked toward a single goal and followed a single vision."[59] As his biographer put it, he "never wavered or bent with the wind: he held on to his convictions."[60] He achieved his steadfastness by resolutely focusing on the ills and evils of his own society and by his association with a supportive, influential subculture of like-minded radical social critics. A deep longing for approval and community bolstered his political positions. In the 1960s and '70s the most potent source of such communal support and approbation was to be found in the radical subcultures, in the protest movements.

The collapse of Soviet communism, the electoral defeat of the Sandinistas in Nicaragua, the adoption of free-market policies in China—such historical events and trends had little effect on Kunstler's outlook.

He was never preoccupied with or interested in ideology, Marxism, or Communist societies abroad, though he was certainly sympathetic to them. While consumed by an awareness of the defects of his own society, he was, as his biographer pointed out, "weak in an agenda for a replacement of the system. . . . [He] told a reporter that he had 'come to the conclusion that capitalism . . . is destructive of human beings and must be replaced, but by what I don't know.'"[61] Moreover he was a person not inclined to introspection, reflection, or retrospection. His law partner, Ronald Cuby, called him "one of the least introspective people in the world."[62] For that reason too, the action-oriented ethos of the 1960s was especially congenial for him.

In 1979, Kunstler refused to sign a letter circulated among liberals that criticized North Vietnam for its mistreatment of political prisoners. He explained, "I do not believe in public attacks on socialist countries, even where violations of human rights may occur."[63] It was a perfect illustration of an impressive capacity to dissociate ends and means. Human rights violations were not something he favored, but being "socialist" was far more important than such transgressions, and he had no problem overlooking or excusing such violations when committed by supposedly socialist states. What mattered was not what was done but by whom and for what purpose.

Kunstler could overlook and excuse not only human rights violations in socialist states but also violence in American society—when committed on behalf of causes he supported, when he sympathized with the aggressor and not the victim, and when the ends vindicated the means. For instance, he admired

> the Weathermen's dedication to a world without racism and oppression and their willingness to jeopardize themselves to attain it . . . enjoyed the cloak-and-dagger aspects of meeting clandestinely with people the government was eager to find and prosecute. The danger also appealed to me because I was always a little uncomfortable with the fact that the lawyers took no risks while our clients took many. Meeting with the Weather Underground gave me a chance to demonstrate that I was ready, willing and able to take some chances; it increased the camaraderie we felt with each other.[64]

He told a crowd at a rally in Oakland, California that, "the cop [John Gleason of Plainfield, New Jersey] was justifiably executed . . . stomped to death by an enraged crowd of blacks. . . ." These recollections were followed in the next paragraph by the statement that

"While I think the violence is wrong, sometimes it is the most effective method of dramatizing grievances."[65] He was particularly indulgent of black violence. When Larry Davis (his defendant) wounded six New York policemen, he said, "Any black guy that shoots six cops and puts the fear of God in police officers I think is great."[66] Presumably he entertained the notion that given the vast amount of violence policemen commit, the actions of his defendant were morally insignificant or actually meritorious, serving to intimidate the police.

Of the probable murderer[67] of Meir Kahane, he wrote: "Do I think Nosair was guilty? Who knows? . . . I am not inside his head, and I was not at the scene of the murder. But I deeply believe in Nosair's right to defense. . . . I think it's ethically correct to defend someone who I believe is guilty. . . . Defending an individual accused of killing a man such as Kahane can be viewed as a positive act because Kahane's racism and fundamentalism had the potential for interfering with peace negotiations between Arabs and Jews."[68] He also said: "If Nosair killed Kahane, it was a political assassination. And political assassination of the right person is not something I would always describe as wrong."[69]

His response to the assassinations of John and Robert Kennedy is a further illustration of these attitudes: "The world was a better place without the Kennedys. . . . They were two of the most dangerous men America ever produced."[70] In 1990 Kunstler participated in the twentieth-anniversary celebration of the violence in Santa Barbara, California, that included the burning of a Bank of America office. His presence on the occasion was particularly appropriate since the violence commemorated had followed directly a fiery oration he delivered to the students who engaged in it.[71]

Kunstler's career and political evolution was an integral part of the 1960s, its causes and protest movements. His popularity in these circles was a major anchor of his commitments: being well-liked was an extremely important lifelong goal, a project ardently pursued, as was a sense of belonging to a group, a community. Given his prominent and durable position in the adversary culture, it would have been inconceivable for Kunstler to abandon the radical causes and beliefs that made his life meaningful and earned so much approval. His lifelong "craving for recognition, admiration and a sense of belonging" was gratified by his prominent place in the radical political subculture and the attention it lavished on him. His first wife believed that he "had a low sense of self-esteem, that he needed to be pumped up by praise . . . and it was a bad day if he received none." This attitude presumably also contributed to what his biographer calls his "compulsive womanizing,"[72] much of it during his first marriage.

He liked the sixties for cultural-social reasons as well: "Drugs opened our minds. Rock, jazz and soul music gave us our rhythm and freedom. . . . The sixties seduced me, and I felt as if my entire life had led me to this time and place, to this work."[73] In the same period he engaged in considerable sexual activity, including one-night stands and affairs with the political groupies who clamored for his attention. In short, he "discovered in middle age the joys of freedom from convention."[74]

His day-to-day legal activities and their frenetic pace also secured his commitment; he did what he believed in, enjoyed his legal battles and the associated publicity, and chose to represent the most notorious and violent political activists he regarded as the most "politically unacceptable outcasts . . . a long line of those who are hated by society" and who in turn harbored an even deeper, sometimes murderous hatred against the same society. He regarded most of his clients' political cases, people who "opposed the government in one way or another, . . . [as] members of an oppressed class . . . society's outcasts." Initially most of his clients were black; he believed that "any time a black person is charged with a crime against a white law enforcement officer I consider it political."[75]

Kunstler's core belief was that racism was the great and ineradicable stigma of American society, "that our society is always racist" and "incapable of genuine change."[76] Later in life he also became drawn to Arab terrorists and their supporters and associates. Anyone with a violent hatred of the United States or American society qualified for his legal, political, and moral support and sympathy. They included the so-called Chicago Seven; a large number of prominent Black Panther activists such as H. Rap Brown; the participants in the Attica prison uprising; members of an armed underground Puerto Rican group called Los Macheteros; Joanne Chesimard, convicted in the murder of a state trooper (she escaped from jail and to Cuba, where Kunstler visited her in 1992 and they had "a wonderful reunion"[77]); Karl Armstrong, the bomber of a research center at the University of Wisconsin (which resulted in a fatality); and violent militants of the American Indian movement. He assisted the defense in the Brinks robbery case. More recently his clients included flag burners; a member of the Central Park rapist gang; Colin Ferguson, the multiple murderer on the Long Island railroad ("whose defense he based on 'black rage' caused by 'years of exposure to white racism'"[78]); and Sheik Omar Abdel-

Rahman, convicted in the first attack on the World Trade Center. He also assisted in the defense of notorious nonpolitical criminals such as Mafioso John Gotti, whom he regarded as less of a threat and an embodiment of evil than white-collar criminals or government officials:

> I cannot regard someone like John Gotti more evil than someone in George Bush's position. This doesn't mean John is a Sunday school principal; he engaged in very rough business, much of it illegal, violent, deadly. . . . But on the other hand he didn't commit the many indecencies that some officials get away with . . . Oliver North and Caspar Weinberger, for example. . . . What's worse—organized crime or corporate crime?[79]

He had little doubt about the answer.

Kunstler took great pride in doing battle with sinister adversaries (the government, its various agents and institutions) that he perceived as far more powerful than himself—David versus Goliath, he thought.[80] Feeling besieged and confronted with overwhelmingly powerful adversaries doubtless provided him with a sense of entitlement to the methods he chose in this putatively unequal struggle.

To the end of his life he retained the core belief that the United States was the most repressive, corrupt, and unjust society in the world, possibly in history, and saw himself as a participant in an enormous struggle against evil.[81] He declared that the "law in the United States . . . [is] a charade and a buttress to the system . . . just a terroristic device . . . a method of control created by a socio-economic system determined, at all costs, to perpetuate itself by all and any means necessary, for as long as possible. . . ." In 1969 he confidently anticipated the rise of fascism in the United States under the guise of law and order.[82] At the end of his autobiography he wrote, "I oppose our current system of government which I view as a tool utilized by the powerful few to control the powerless many. While I have not found a better system, I cannot approve of ours."[83] As such remarks suggest, Kunstler was not a deep political thinker. The only impulse that guided him was a sense of outrage against the establishment and sympathy for the underdog, as he and other sixties radicals defined it. He was not particularly interested in the poor as such, only in blacks and later Muslims who detested the United States.

According to Kunstler's biographer, three circumstances in his life and experience best explain his political convictions. First was a preoccupation with racism, nurtured by early experiences of black servants in the prosperous household where he grew up (his father was a physician). Second, he had a markedly poor relationship with his father, which prompts speculation that such negativity might have been transferred to other authority figures and society at large. Third, he displayed a rebellious disposition from an early age. He wrote: ". . . I cannot remember a time when I did not feel within me the desire to resist authority, oppose convention and champion the underdog."[84]

According to his biographer, "As a youngster Billy misbehaved continuously."[85] At the age of thirteen he joined "an interracial gang otherwise comprised of blacks and Hispanics. . . . We broke windows, stole from penny gum machines, busted in warehouses, and attacked other kids. I rebelled against hanging out with the middle-class Jewish kids in the fancy high-rise apartment house where my family lived and reveled in my gang." In the home where he grew up, "the housework was done by maids and the children were overseen by governesses." Evidently there was something to rebel against in his early youth, including the "stereotypical racist ideas" of his parents. Or, as he put it, "Coming from a family that had provided me with a childhood of comfort and security, I felt that in order to validate my life, my time on earth had to count for something. I felt a need to justify the air I breathed, the food I ate and the water I drank."[86] A large dose of white guilt, and especially white Jewish upper-middle-class guilt, lay at the root of these sentiments.

His biographer observed that Kunstler actually wanted to be black; the Jewish identity was gradually abandoned.[87] He was the sixties radical par excellence, though of an older generation which thrived on and gave its benediction to the young rebels.

Kunstler typifies what is probably the most widespread characteristic of political convictions acquired early in life: they change little over time unless some powerful external or internal influence appears. It is far more convenient and reassuring to hold on to old, familiar beliefs—especially when they are also upheld by one's own group or community, by people who matter—than to painfully disengage from them, with all the soul searching and self-reproach this process entails. The adversary culture that supported Kunstler survived; his family and friends shared his convictions; his legal battles and successes appeared to vindicate the stands he had taken; he suffered no personal trauma that would have created incentives for self-reflection, leading to a reassessment of the beliefs that were so central to his life. Unlike some other radicals, he did not mellow with age; he had no second thoughts or reservations, he preserved not only his core beliefs but their entirety. It is hard to imagine what conditions or events could have changed his worldview.

EDWARD W. SAID (1935–2004). There is no evidence to suggest that Edward Said was an admirer or supporter of any Communist state or movement, but he did consider himself to the end of his life "a man of the left."[88] Aside from his literary scholarship, he is better known as a fierce critic of American foreign policy and Western attitudes toward the non-Western world, especially the Orient, and an advocate for the Palestinians. He was also a critic of capitalism and globalization. While his consuming preoccupation was the fate of the Palestinians, it was also said of him that he "taught a whole generation of English professors to search for racism in writers (like Jane Austen) who did not think as the professors do."[89]

Said came from a wealthy Christian-Arab family. His father grew up in Jerusalem but emigrated in 1911 to the United States. He returned to the Middle East as a U.S. citizen after World War I and founded "the largest office equipment and stationery business in the Middle East."[90] A self-made, successful businessman, he apparently had a limited appreciation of his son's interests and personality; Said notes in his memoirs that he was "hectored and bullied" by his father.[91]

Although completely Westernized, Edward Said was deeply estranged from American society where he lived from age fifteen (or sixteen, depending on different recollections)[92] and which provided him with an elite education, professional recognition, honors, security, opportunity for free expression, and material prosperity. He came to the United States by himself, having been sent by his parents to a boarding school. He eventually rose to the distinguished and privileged position of "university professor" at Columbia University, where he taught all his life. He was also president of the Modern Language Association, received numerous honorary degrees, served on the executive board of the PEN Club, and was a member of the Council on Foreign Relations and a fellow of the American Academy of Arts and Sciences and of the Royal Society of Literature in England. He was a regular on major TV programs, talk shows, and panel discussions, often interviewed in the electronic media and the press. He was hardly the marginalized, besieged, lonely dissenter he sometimes thought himself. His case is one of many fine illustrations of the contemporary compatibility of a deep sense of alienation and bitterness (harbored by many prominent intellectuals) with a secure, prosperous, and successful way of life rich in accomplishments.[93]

Whatever the correct date of Said's arrival to the United States, there is little doubt that his sense of homelessness was acute and genuine, especially in his youth when he "resolved to live as if I were a simple transparent soul and not to speak about my family or origins except as required and then very sparingly." While at an expensive boarding school in Mt. Hermon, Massachusetts, he experienced "utter loneliness" and considered it a "dreadful, godforsaken place." Later, as an undergraduate at Princeton University, he found the social atmosphere "poisonous." Also at Princeton, he was advised by a rabbi at the university to return to Egypt and attend to the "misery, ignorance and illness among the Arabs . . . your people need you."[94] He did not take the advice but much later became a passionate advocate of the Palestinian-Arab cause in a manner that suggests a compensatory aspect since he stayed in the West and become totally Westernized (he even managed to speak American English without an accent). While at Princeton he was drawn to the political issues that preoccupied him for the rest of his life. His "politial awakening in the late 1960s"[95] led eventually to a firm and lifelong embrace of a radical political identity that was, in all probability, a welcome change from the uncertain sense of one he experienced while at Princeton and earlier, that is, "unaccomplished, floundering, split in different parts (Arab, musician, young intellectual, solitary eccentric, dutiful student, political misfit)."[96] This transformation was also described by an observer of his career:

> The sixties changed all that [the sense of homelessness, etc.]. Said found solidarity and a home of sorts among the crowds of antiwar protesters. After the Six Day War, the rise of Palestinian nationalism provided him with a link to the homeland from which he had otherwise been estranged. By opposing America's alleged imperialism in the Middle East, Said was able to reconnect himself to a Palestinian identity that he had never really consolidated.[97]

Said's estrangement from American society (though not from the academic adversary subculture that embraced him) had several sources. One was his deeply held and frequently expressed conviction that being "out of place," metaphorically as well as geographically and culturally, was the only desirable way of life for the true intellectual. He told an interviewer: ". . . I never really lived in any place where I felt completely at home. . . . Wherever I was, I felt that I didn't really belong."[98] But he also wrote that he *preferred* "not ever to feel too much at home anywhere,"[99] as if such emotional comfort were incompatible with the vigilant critical identity of the true intellectual. He believed that keeping a distance from one's society was a precondition of being a productive and ethical intellectual. This was hardly an original idea, but Said held it with uncommon conviction, and it did have connections with the circumstances of his life, his upbringing, and the rootlessness he experienced and embraced. He also valued commitment as such and considered it an obligation of the intellectual, or the public intellectual he aspired to be: "I have been unable to live an uncommitted or suspended life. I have not hesitated to declare my affiliation with an extremely unpopular cause."[100]

Whether or not the cause he supported was really "extremely unpopular" may be questioned in light of the acclaim he received in the settings where he lived and moved and where his cause was in fact both popular and politically respectable. Said appeared to overlook the fact that alienation from society at large was (and remains) compatible with belonging to a sustaining, tightly knit subculture (as he did), one that had its own pressures, enticements, and influences which were also capable of contributing to the loss of intellectual autonomy. In this subculture—the left-liberal, academic subculture—upholding the Palestinian-Arab cause hardly required uncommon determination, defiance, or courage.

The second pillar of Said's lifelong adversarial position was his vocal and bitter rejection of the United States as the major supporter of Israel. Said's pro-Palestinian beliefs and activities in turn were inextricably linked with his self-conscious and somewhat implausible embrace of a Palestinian-Arab identity. It was implausible because while he was indisputably born in Jerusalem, he spent very little of his life in the territories considered to be Palestine.[101] He visited Palestine for the first time in 1992 after an absence of forty-five years.[102] What is not in dispute is that before permanently moving to the United States he spent most of his childhood and adolescence in Egypt and Lebanon, not Palestine. Nor did his Christian-cosmopolitan family have a pronounced Arab-Palestinian identity. His education was thoroughly Western, encompassing the elite Cairo School for American Children, the American elite private boarding school in the United States, followed by Princeton University for undergraduate studies and Harvard for his Ph.D. He spent the rest of his life as a professor at Columbia University occupying a named chair in comparative literature. His academic work was also thoroughly Westernized, focusing on Western literary classics and classical music; he was also an accomplished player of classical music. Notwithstanding his literary interests and work, it is likely that, as one of his admirers pointed out, his "intellectual legacy will be primarily political."[103]

The ambivalence about his own Westernized identity found first and major expression in *Orientalism* (1978), widely and correctly seen as a major anti-Western "text" and a lasting source of Said's fame and influence in the Western academic world. It has sold more than a quarter-million copies and has been translated into more than thirty languages.[104] *Orientalism* is an impassioned attack on Western scholarship about the non-Western world (especially the Arab-Islamic world), combined with a critique of Western imperialism and colonialism. Said argues that not only are Western scholars and intellectuals inherently incapable of understanding the Islamic world (and, by extension, the entire non-Western world), but their analysis and interpretation are purposefully subordinated to the colonial policies of their countries and their ruling elites. As was pointed out by one critic, "the upshot of his theory is that no Westerner, at any time or place, is capable of attaining a fair or truthful knowledge of a non-Western culture."[105] As his sometime friend, Christopher Hitchens, put it, "Said characterized Western scholarship about the East as a conscious handmaiden of power and subordination. Explorers, missionaries, archeologists, linguists—all had been part of the colonial enterprise."[106]

Said would not concede that non-Westerners, trying to understand or interpret the West, would face similar or corresponding difficulties.[107] He would not suggest that all cultures, and their human representatives, have trouble understanding one another; or that all incline to project on the other imaginary or poorly understood attributes; or that it is difficult, in general, to identify with groups different from one's own. What Said believed was that the malevolent misperceptions and distortions he described were peculiar to Western observers and specialists on the non-Western world, the East in particular. In the same spirit, Said appeared to be unable or unwilling to concede, or even to note, the historical manifestations of non-Western imperialism, Muslim or Turkish or other. Images of victim and aggressor dominating his writing and thinking were frozen and immutable.

While Said's critiques of American society and capitalism were less voluminous and subsidiary to his preoccupation with Arab-Israeli matters, they partook of the familiar pattern of critiques and denunciations widespread since the late 1960s. Said shared Noam Chomsky's view of the world and the U.S. role in it, called him his "great hero,"[108] and admired his "uncompromising . . . opposition to oppressive socio-political forces." Said also shared Chomsky's view of the United States as the singular global imperialist superpower, "responsive neither to the citizenry nor to the natural environment, but to a vast structure of global corporations . . .," and one with "an unparalleled global military reach."[109] He further shared with Chomsky a view of the United States as the Great Satan, a genocidal power with "a history of reducing whole peoples, countries and even continents to ruin by nothing short of holocaust." With a stroke of moral equivalence, he suggested that "when it comes to war crimes, in comparison to Bill Clinton, Madeleine Albright or Sandy Berger, Slobodan Milosevic is 'a rank amateur.'" [110]

With Herbert Marcuse and C. Wright Mills, Said shares a perception of America as a brainwashed nation in the grip of "repressive tolerance," a society characterized by "deprivation and repression that compel people to follow along meekly."[111] He also wrote,

> . . . if one is endlessly lectured by certified experts who explain that the freedom we all want demands deregulation and privatization or war . . . there is very little inclination to address this order with anything like individual or even collective demands. Chomsky has relentlessly addressed this paralyzing syndrome for several years.[112]

As Said saw it, not only were the American masses sadly unprotesting but "a new period of Leftist quietism may have set in" in England as well. As to the United States, "public discourse is saturated with interests, authorities and powers whose extent in the aggregate is literally unimaginable in scope and variety. . . ." All these forces press for "the acceptance of a neoliberal postwelfare state."[113] Elsewhere he concluded that the "analytical powers [of the American people] are dulled and anesthetized."[114] A figure on the far left whom Said admired was Ralph Nader, "a genuine adversarial intellectual" whose presidential campaign rose above familiar appeals to "greed or simple assent."[115]

Said was among the resolute opponents of globalization, which he held responsible for "widening the gap between rich and poor," especially in the Middle East.[116] He shared the conventional leftist wisdom about capitalist weapons manufacturers intent on keeping the Middle East (and other parts of the world) "in a state of turmoil and conflict in order to sell more and more weaponry" (as his interviewer put it).[117] He believed in the importance of the continued criticism of capitalism, which he held culpable for a wide range of "ideological, economical and political problems" around the world.[118]

After 9/11 Said argued with a new virulence and bitterness, and with increasing frequency, that the terror (sometimes in quotation marks) had been used to discredit justified critiques of U.S. foreign policies and the conduct of Israel. In 2003 he said:

> . . . this relentless pursuit of terrorism is in my opinion almost a kind of criminal thing. It allows the United States to do what it wishes anywhere in the world. . . . Terrorism has become a sort of screen created since the end of the Cold War by policymakers in Washington . . . who have their meal ticket in that pursuit. It is fabricated to keep the population afraid, insecure and to justify what the United States wishes to do globally . . . [acts of terrorism] are . . . blown up to insensate proportions that have nothing to do with their . . . real threat. . . . This focus obscures the enormous damage done by the United States . . . militarily or environmentally or economically, on a world scale that far dwarfs anything that terrorism might do.[119]

Terrorism, he suggested, was also used to stifle domestic dissent and free expression: "'Terrorism' has become synonymous with anti-Americanism which in turn has become synonymous with being critical of the United States . . . with being unpatriotic."[120]

In a familiar recourse to moral equivalence, Said also proposed that "The West's almost obsessive emphasis on terrorism and fanaticism in the Arab World is a form of exorcism. They see it in Islam so they won't have to recognize that the same elements exist in their own societies, and in alarming levels."[121]

Elsewhere he complained about the huge amounts of sympathetic attention drawn by victims of suicide bombings in Israel while Palestinian victims of Israel were ignored: "It is worth noting that victims of 'terrorism' like Netanyahu and Leon Klinghoffer get institutions and foundations named after them, to say nothing of enormous press attention, whereas Arabs, Moslems and other nonwhites who die 'collaterally' just die, uncounted, unmourned, unacknowledged by 'us.'"[122] Here Said, in his zeal to champion the Arab victims of Israeli violence, appears to question—by putting quotation marks around terrorism—that the word was appropriately applied to Klinghoffer's murder. Klinghoffer, it may be recalled, was the aged, disabled, wheelchair-bound man who was shot and then pushed into the sea by PLO terrorists in October 1985 when they hijacked the *Achille Lauro* cruise ship in the Mediterranean.

Occasionally Said was capable of more nuanced and judicious statements about terrorism. He was, for example, willing to point out that the 9/11 suicide pilots were not poor, deprived, and desperate "but obviously middle class." He also said (as did many other critics of terror) that ". . . out of this sense of desperation and pathological religion, there develops an all-encompassing drive to harm and hurt . . . as was the case in New York. . . . These are people appointed, obviously by themselves, who feel within themselves . . . the confidence of a people bearing in a kind of twisted way the burden of a great civilization responding to the attacks of barbarians."[123]

More typically he was fiercely critical of those who did not share his point of view. He ceaselessly castigated the "Israeli Lobby" and the "Holocaust industry" and all those allegedly beholden to it. Martin Kramer, author of ten scholarly studies on Islam and the Middle East (some published by Columbia University Press that also published Said), was dismissed as "an outrageous Israeli."

Said blamed Israel for "90%" of the "overpopulation, poverty, ignorance, hunger" in the Gaza Strip. He was contemptuous of "former leftists like Christopher Hitchens, Michael Ignatieff and Michael Walzer, who have come aboard in this extraordinary campaign to show that Islamic terrorism is a free-standing thing . . . lodged at the very heart of Islam." Daniel Pipes, a well-known scholar of the Middle East and critic of Arab extremism, became "someone named Daniel Pipes, who is basically a second rate, unemployed scholar."[124] Other traitors to the Arab cause included Fouad Ajami and Kanan Makiya, who also took "outrageous" positions and sold out to the neo-conservatives. Ignatieff, Max Boot, and George Will "are the apologists of empire." The *Wall Street Journal*, *New Republic*, and *Commentary* were nothing but "propagandists who have a racist hatred of Palestinians."[125]

Said's angry embrace of the Palestinian cause culminated in the famous incident in July 2000 when he was photographed hurling a rock toward an Israeli guardhouse from the Lebanese border. He dismissed the incident as "a symbolic expression of joy" over the end of Israel's occupation of Southern Lebanon. But elsewhere "he has given several different explanations for it. In an interview with the Israeli newspaper *Haaretz*, he said it was merely a competition with his son to see who could throw farther."[126] Most likely it was both an expression of joy, as he averred, and a symbolic embrace of liberating violence, a gesture perhaps prompted by the desire to demonstrate, however fleetingly, that he was not just a bookish intellectual but a man of action, a potential warrior.

Consumed by righteous anger, Said developed a besieged mentality and convinced himself that Israel and its supporters dominated the field of public debate, "that dissent and rational discussion have been virtually banned,"[127] by which he meant points of view sympathetic to the

Palestinian cause. This allegedly dominant view included the belief that "Israel is a peace-loving state. Therefore, the Arabs are delinquent and this is part of the world we ought to nuke. . . . After 9/11, the media suggests that, yes, that is in fact what should be done." Also characteristic of this mind-set was the claim that "television in the United States considers itself to be an arm of the government as it mobilizes for war."[128]

From the time of his "political awakening" Said became increasingly politicized and convinced that the only honorable role for him to play was that of the engaged, aggrieved intellectual fighting for the rights of his people. Emblematic of this orientation is that "ultimately Said turned away from a theoretician like Foucault to the work of Franz Fanon . . . who worked with the Algerian liberation movement. . . ."[129] Fanon advocated righteous, liberating violence in the anti-colonial struggle. Although Said disdained the postmodernists, wittingly or not he strengthened their case by arguing (in *Orientalism*, among other places) that there is no such thing as disinterested knowledge and understanding untainted by considerations of interest and power.

Said's problematic and conflicted sense of identity was at the root of the persistence of his political beliefs and commitments and his rejection of the West.

BILL AYERS (1944–). Among the recent generation of unbending revolutionaries, the case of Bill Ayers may be the most noteworthy. The perplexity expressed by Norman Podhoretz about the anger and alienation of the young radicals of the 1960s perfectly fits the case of Ayers, who held to his beliefs with remarkable consistency:

> Among the many puzzles thrown up by the . . . 1960s in the United States, none seemed more perplexing than the virulent hostility toward their own country . . . felt by some of the most privileged elements of American society. . . .
>
> . . . Why should young people from prosperous families . . . who were enjoying what to all outward appearances was a life of luxury, indulgence and ease, and who could look forward . . . to positions of comparable status and reward in the years ahead, characterize themselves as "nigger"?[130]

The questions raised by Alan Wolfe about the activities of Kathy Boudin and David Gilbert (convicted members of the Weather Underground) are also relevant to the beliefs and behavior of Bill Ayers, though he did not participate in the murderous Brinks holdup that Wolfe alludes to:

> How did a group of high-achieving kids find themselves in the midst of such violence? By what processes of reasoning could intelligent people conclude that criminals were revolutionaries? How could individuals who claimed to be on the side of the working class participate in the murder of a local policeman? In what ways is the search for racial equality advanced by removing the only African-American policeman in town from his job, let alone from his life?[131]

An incomplete answer to these questions can be gleaned from Bill Ayers's self-vindicating memoir.[132] The pressure for such self-justification is particularly strong when much of one's life has been dedicated to dubious or—as many would see it—destructive and irrational goals. The first task of the self-vindicating memoir is to persuade the reader that the objectives pursued by its author were neither foolish nor destructive but noble and high-minded, whatever the outcome. Second, the author must show that these goals were at least in some measure achieved. And third, he must defend the methods used to achieve the objectives if they appear questionable or unethical. Bill Ayers attempted to accomplish all this to the satisfaction of some of the elated reviewers of his memoir: "Edward Said . . . blurbed the book for 'its marvelous human coherence and integrity.' Studs Terkel called it a 'deeply moving' elegy to all those young dreamers who tried to live decently in an indecent world.' . . ."[133] By contrast, Brent Staples described Ayers as one of "a group of affluent white kids [who] played at being revolutionaries"; John Patrick Diggins judged him to be "arrested in his convictions" and possessed of "a pathetic delusion." Ronald Radosh saw him as "a man in love with his years of violence."[134] David Horowitz found him, like the other Weathermen he interviewed, "to be little more than political delinquents with only the shallowest understanding of themselves or what they had done. . . . After recounting to me his life as a political terrorist and celebrity, Ayers summed up his career in an epigram: 'Guilty as hell, free as a bird—America is a great country.'"[135]

Ayers also reminds this author of a fictional character of Philip Roth's: "full of fantasies of the 'working class' [blacks for Ayers] . . . [displaying] angry, infantile egoism thinly disguised as identification with the oppressed . . . [embarked] on a reckless adventure. . . ."[136]

Whatever were the author's intentions, this memoir is a comprehensive (and mostly uncritical) record of the beliefs of a true believer of the sixties generation. As such it offers valuable insight into the mind-set of people who were the charter members of the adversary culture. The book helps but doesn't fully explain why Ayers has retained his beliefs largely unmodified. To be sure, it is always easier to understand the persistence of strongly held beliefs than their discarding or dramatic reversal. Still, the massive accumulation or dramatic surfacing of disconfirming evidence can make it difficult to persevere in old attitudes and beliefs. The collapse of Soviet communism and the embrace of a market economy in Communist China and other state socialist societies have created problems for Ayers's generation. Stressing their attachment to ideals unrelated to the policies of any existing political system (including those earlier idealized and considered socialist), these developments may be neutralized to a degree.[137]

Ayers differs from many former radicals who, with the passage of time, retreated—at least in their public statements—to the notion that back then, in the 1960s or '70s, they were idealistic young people who did things they would not do today; they no longer approve of blowing up buildings or shooting policemen, but back then there was nothing wrong with what they sought to accomplish with somewhat questionable means.[138] If they failed to achieve all they aspired to, it was due to the inertia, indifference, and obtuseness of their fellow citizens (unaware of their real interests) and the cunning and power of the rulers and manipulators of American society.

Ayers believed, as most committed revolutionaries do, that the majority of his fellow citizens had a low level of political consciousness and insufficient awareness of the iniquities surrounding them:

> I think back to my childhood, to the houses in trim rows and the identical lawns and the neat fences; I remember everyone sleeping the deep American sleep, the sleep that still engulfs us. . . . We are living our isolated lives in our shattered communities. . . . The world roils in agony and despair, the catastrophe deepens, and our ears are covered, our eyes are closed. Perhaps only the bark of bombs at our doors will shake us up after all.

Ayers sought to contribute to such an awakening by providing a modest share of "the bark of bombs."

A great deal of evasion and equivocation permeates these reflections and recollections. The first line of defense is a repeated hedging about the accuracy of his recollections, the warning that memory is not to be trusted, though obviously he wishes to be taken at his word. In particular, his participation in acts of violence is subject to recurring equivocation and modification. At the end of the book he writes, "I can't quite imagine putting a bomb in a building today. . . . But I can't imagine entirely dismissing the possibility either." In a *New York Times* interview he went further: "I don't regret setting bombs. . . . I feel we didn't do enough. Alliances with violent groups such as the Black Liberation Army is relegated to 'insurgent mischief.'"[139] The bombing of the Pentagon is recalled with outright nostalgia: "Everything was absolutely ideal on the day I bombed the Pentagon. The sky was blue. The birds were singing. And the bastards were finally going to get what was coming to them." But in the next line he tries to wiggle out of the admission: "I did not actually bomb the Pentagon—WE bombed it in the sense that the Weathermen organized and claimed it. . . . The government was dead wrong, and we were right. In our conflict we don't talk, we don't tell. We never confess."

They were not terrorists because "terrorists destroy randomly, while our actions bore, we hoped, the precise stamp of a cut diamond." They were "freedom fighters" who engaged in "armed propaganda." But elsewhere he admits that "We had devolved from freedom fighters into criminals, from political radicals to minor technicians of illicit crafts." But he also insists that a memorial is overdue for his late friends who blew themselves up in the Greenwich Village townhouse while assembling a huge bomb that was designed to kill large numbers of military personnel[140]—not exactly a nonviolent gesture designed merely to win attention for a good cause.

The crux of the position Ayers and his fellow radicals adopted was that compared to the enormity of the evils around them—foremost the Vietnam War and racism—their violent actions were minor lapses undeserving of self-reproach. In the *New York Times* interview, Ayers said, "I don't think you can understand a single thing we did without understanding the violence of the Vietnam War."[141] Correspondingly, a good deal of his book is devoted to detailing the evils of American society and history that are supposed to explain and justify all his questionable beliefs and behavior.

Most important for his generation has been the affirmation of youthful idealism and the sense of identity linked to it. He shares with his erstwhile comrades the belief in belonging to an enlightened elite who knew precisely what was wrong with their society and were willing to do something about it. They were imbued with "a brimming sense of our specialness, the exceptional good luck at being young and eager to take on the waiting world—so much was in such desperate need of repair. . . ." He was dedicated to the wholesale remaking of America, its somnolent citizens and corrupt institutions, and ultimately the whole world:

> Everything was on the agenda now: justice and peace, education and culture and spirituality, work, sexuality, gender, art. . . . I wanted to

> become a new man and to dance or march . . . with others toward a brighter future, an expanding sense of humanity. . . . It fell to us . . . to save the world. . . .
>
> I wanted to be a Weatherman forever, a revolutionary outlaw, and I loved the symbol of peace and reconciliation balanced by the hot bolt of justice. I eventually tattooed the rainbow on my skin. . . .

To understand the persistence of political beliefs and commitments we must turn to their apparent roots as well as to the strength and quality of group (or subcultural) support for them. Most important is the connection between these commitments and the individual's sense of identity. Thus we come once more to the vexing connections between "the personal and the political," that is, the part played by political convictions in the formation of personal identity. When political beliefs and actions satisfy important emotional needs, they are likely to endure. This was certainly the case with Bill Ayers. He writes: "The personal is political, we said, and we meant that . . . everything was part of a grand experiment in liberation." He describes revealingly his initial involvement with the anti-war movement:

> I felt suddenly transported. . . . I felt swept along . . . by the dream of peace, and the captivating idea of social change as a calling, perhaps as the calling of all callings. . . .
>
> I felt now at the epicenter of resistance. . . . It had already shaken us lucky ones from the scripted [!] lives we were expected to lead. . . .
>
> Our watchword was action. . . . Push the limits. . . .
>
> The movement swept us away completely because it demanded everything of us and because it offered everything . . . high purpose, real work to do, love, dreams, hope. . . . It required harmony between . . . words and deeds. It said the personal was political. . . .

Brent Staples believes that "class guilt" is the key to Ayers's attitudes. Todd Gitlin, a former radical who distanced himself from many of the beliefs that sustain Ayers to this day, holds a similar view: "They [the Weathermen] had permuted class guilt into a theory that permitted them to abase themselves before a stereotyped, united Third World and yet retain for themselves a special mission."[142]

Michael Walzer's reflections about "the radical failure of the left's response" to 9/11 are also relevant to Ayers's attitudes: "Maybe the guilt produced by living in such a country and enjoying its privileges makes it impossible to sustain a decent (intelligent, responsible, morally nuanced) politics" as opposed to "the politics of guilt and resentment."[143] These remarks echo the musings of a fictional character of Philip Roth in *The Dying Animal*:

> Living in a country like ours, whose key documents are all about emancipation, all directed at guaranteeing individual liberty, living in a free system that is basically indifferent to how you behave as long as the behavior is lawful, the misery that comes your way is most likely to be self-generated. It would be another matter if you were living in Nazi-occupied Europe, or in Mao Zedong's China. There they manufacture misery for you. . . . But here, free of totalitarianism, a man like you has to provide himself his own misery. . . .[144]

From the very beginning of his memoir, Ayers comes across as volatile, impulsive, and impressionable. He was endlessly "ecstatic." His involvement with the causes of his time had an aspect of falling in love. He "long[ed] to give himself to a cause" and was

> fueled by a shimmering vision of a democracy that would be participatory, a society free of racism, a planet at peace and full of justice—a state of affairs I thought we would achieve through love, mainly, through goodwill, sacrifice and applied activism. . . .

Living in the nuclear age was also invoked as further explanation of his political attitudes: "I don't remember America dropping the Bomb . . . because I was just a baby. . . . But I've lived my whole life in its thick and sticky shadow, and I grew up on the noble story of this most excellent and worthy A-bomb. . . ." These were sentiments often voiced by his generation growing up in "the shadow" of the atomic bomb—a condition that supposedly lent a tragic dimension to their life and justified their misbehavior. Ayers was convinced that using the atomic bomb against Japan was unjustified, immoral, and inhumane. He imagined Truman "drooling" over, "fetishizing," and "eroticizing" the Bomb; his "love[ing] this bomb."

Ayers's beliefs changed little over time. Already in prep school he felt that "It's not difficult . . . to see how America achieved such fabulous wealth: free labor on stolen land, conquest and slavery and an attempted genocide." In an interview directly following the publication of these memoirs, he declared: ". . . our worst paranoid fantasies about what the government is capable of in the mid-60's turned out to be mild in comparison to what it did. . . . You can't live in a society like this . . . and not sell your soul."[145]

As he was growing up "from the ordinariness of my life, war was a vivid and welcomed event. . . . I was swallowed by war at the movies,

I played war with my friends. . . . I was powerful in war, just like the heroes in those movies. . . ." He had an unusual hobby as a child: "a love affair with explosives"—a remark that casts some doubt on his alleged, unadulterated love of peace when protesting the Vietnam War. These confessions also bring to mind those of Richard Hyland, another lesser-known radical, writing in the *Harvard Crimson* in 1969:

> We have an irreconcilable tension in our existence, all the way from breakfast to bedtime. Blowing up a bad thing will relieve much of that tension. So that the preceding sentence doesn't become evidence for any of the rampant psychological reductionist theories about radicals, it should be pointed out that the psychological problems most of us have are very directly capitalism's fault.[146]

Why and how did Ayers reach the conclusion that this was a profoundly unjust and corrupt society that made it difficult if not impossible to lead a decent and meaningful life, and justified the use of explosives to change it? In the first place he was predisposed to rebel against what he calls "mindless conventionality," the prospect of a "scripted life," suburban consumerism and inauthenticity, "the childlike fifties in the padded and privileged suburbs of America . . . and a kind of willed blindness [that] had afflicted people." There were also likely to be some ill feelings toward a father who "was once considered for Secretary of the Army"—an organization that his son regarded as "ground zero for war and conquest, organizing headquarters of a gang of murdering thieves, a colossal stain on the planet. . . ."

The felt inauthenticity of suburban upper-class or upper-middle-class life seemed to have created a thirst for a more adventurous existence, more fulfilling, intense relationships, and especially a sense of community. These longings were aptly expressed in the way various activist groups called themselves "tribes."

Explaining the beginnings of his career as a radical political activist, Ayers writes: "Every story of rebellion begins as a story of oppression. And every story of oppression starts with the cries and groans of unjustified suffering . . . stories of human beings in chains or under the boot." These were precisely the experiences he and his fellow protesters did *not* have. They knew little of pain, suffering, oppression, of "being in chains and under the boot"—such conditions could not account for their moral indignation and discontent. Instead Ayers was one of a huge number of young people coming of age in the 1960s who found middle- or upper-middle-class life stultifying and repellent; such feelings had little in common with any genuine experience of oppression.

Ayers wrote of his background:

> The place I grew up was straight off the cover of the *Saturday Evening Post*—my oak-lined street, the volunteer fire department, the Busy Bee Barber Shop. . . .
>
> Where we lived . . . the grass was always green, the moms were always smiling. . . . Our kitchen was sparkling: white cabinets and countertops, gleaming linoleum and Formica, white-bread sandwiches[147] with Velveeta cheese and lunch meat. Our house was all electric . . . electric garage door and stove, electric waterheater and garbage disposal . . . we had the earliest electric knife. . . . We always looked nice, and we tried to always sound nice, too. Nice was crucially important.

It may be noted that Ayers's father was president of Commonwealth Edison in Chicago, which provided electricity for the gadgets he held in contempt. Ayers intimates that all this cleanliness, comfort, and gadgetry was inauthentic, alienating, impersonal, and dehumanizing. Smiling and trying to be nice were especially galling, suggestive of the hollowness and phoniness of middle-class attitudes and relationships. Such inauthenticity was the most widely and strongly detested attribute of middle-class life for sixties radicals. Even at ripe middle age Ayers is anxious to defy middle-class conventions by the repeated use of "shit" and "motherfucker" on the pages of his memoir.

The private school Ayers attended was another odious and oppressive embodiment of inauthenticity:

> I hated school—everyone walking around in a rut with white smiles pasted on our dead heads. I looked at my fellow students with anguish at first, then disgust. We were mostly conformist bores, unadventurous . . . acting out scripts already written, destined for conventional lives of canned happiness just as dull as our parents.

Schools in general were not to his liking:

> I believed that most schools tried to break and control kids, enacting some cleaned-up kind of Calvinism, beating the hell out of them for their own good. I wholeheartedly embraced a contrary idea: kids are naturally good and will blossom beautifully if raised in freedom.

For Ayers and his like-minded contemporaries, the unsatisfactory nature of their private and family lives converged with the discovery of large social-political injustices and issues such as racism and Vietnam. The urgency and intensity of their involvement in these causes and their fiery moral indignation is not easy to understand without some reference to this convergence. Apparently these injustices vindicated a smoldering alienation from their suburban life that preceded the Vietnam War and the discovery of racial inequalities. Ayers's anti-war sentiments had less to do with his love of peace than with his hatred of the United States. ("I am not so much against the war as I am for a Vietnamese victory. I'm not so much for peace as for a U.S. defeat.") He also writes:

> I knew the war was illegal. . . . I felt its dead, dehumanizing grip. . . . What kind of a system is it that disenfranchises Black people in the South, leaves millions upon millions impoverished and excluded . . . creates faceless and terrible dehumanizing bureaucracies and puts material values before human values . . .?

Ayers and his peers were deeply concerned with impersonality and the insufficiency of pure, good feelings. For that reason the communal, communitarian aspects of their political activities were especially cherished:

> The rally was vibrant and sparkling . . . the crowd reaching out to welcome me. Soon I was embraced by chanting, singing sisters and brothers, and I felt myself a charter member of a just-made society, fresh and crisp, our own beloved community. . . .

Coincidentally he became involved with an "alternative school" and community organizing in Cleveland, in the course of which his moral indignation over poverty greatly increased while his romanticizing of the poor, and especially poor blacks, knew no bounds. The poor he met were pure and happy (in a fashion), radiating class and racial solidarity and the righteousness of shared victimhood. For someone who chose to live in the slums (but not forever), it was an exhilarating adventure:

> The mood was festive one minute, like a giant community picnic, everyone laughing and sharing and handing things around—although the things being handed around weren't hamburgers but stolen goods . . . and the next minute there was the sound of shots fired from somewhere.
>
> . . . I so loved the unity of those times. . . . I mostly loved everything I was seeing, and especially all that I was learning. I thought Stokely [Carmichael] made perfect sense. But by that time I also thought that I was black.

As the memoir progresses it provides a widening panorama of irrationality and a frenzied activism. Even the author admits in hindsight that he and his comrades were gripped by delusions of grandeur, an arrogant elitism (". . . white people are mostly brainwashed. We lucky few will wake them up. I could imagine the tall towers in downtown Chicago shaking"), and a delusional commitment ("our ambitions stretched around the globe"). Moreover,

> we felt . . . the full weight of catastrophe unfolding before us. The world was in flames. . . . Human existence itself seemed in grave doubt . . . it was up to us to rescue everyone. We imagined that the survival of humanity depended on the kids alone. . . . We wanted to break from the habitual and the mediocre, to step into history as subjects not objects. We would combat the culture of compromise . . . our watchword was simple: Action! Action! Action!

Ayers harbored a similarly deluded belief in a brotherhood with all the oppressed peoples around the world, a solidarity between angry, alienated white youth from privileged backgrounds (such as his own) and those an American sociologist called (in a different context) "the truly disadvantaged." Repeatedly he invokes the sufferings of the poor blacks at home and the downtrodden masses in the Third World in order to legitimate his own anger, discontent, and hatred of "the system." What Ayers says about his comrades—that "each was fueled by some deep interior anger"—applies to him as well.

Distaste for suburban inauthenticity and cheerfully impersonal parents was not enough to justify Ayers's revolutionary posturing, his feelings of "rage." These feelings (whatever their real source) provided the sense of entitlement for the increasingly aggressive and destructive behavior and rhetoric. Ayers claims that it was police brutality during the 1968 Democratic Convention that gave rise to these aggressive and violent attitudes among the protesters. But his own recollections suggest that violence and aggression had their own appeal and fascination. He and his comrades were anxious

> to develop an armed unit, a brigade, or legion or a division . . . to build a force of clandestine militants. . . . We meant to learn to fight through fighting . . . growing in strength and power through the practice of the revolution. We set out to found an American Red Army.

The book contains many references to "getting high" on political action and expressions of pride in being a good street fighter:

> We shrieked and screamed as we ran, ululating in imitation of the fighters of *The Battle of Algiers*. I saw us become what I thought was a real battalion in a guerrilla army . . . I felt a warrior rising up inside me—audacity and courage, righteousness . . . and more audacity.

He also writes: "I was on a freedom high, and all I needed to feed my habit was one more hit of the action. . . ."

There is a striking similarity between such sentiments and those expressed and cherished by radical leftist terrorists in Europe during the same period, suggesting that these attitudes were not peculiar to a handful of young and privileged Americans. Bommi Baumann, a young German terrorist active in Germany, recalled his feelings after throwing a Molotov cocktail at a newspaper delivery truck: "Standing there in front of the flames, I realized that this is how you can get somewhere. Then we went around the corner . . . to one of the Junta [Greek government] offices and smashed that up too. A lot of crazy shit happened that night; you got energy from it, a real high."[148] Baumann also enjoyed slashing the tires of parked cars and "got a lot of aggression released in a totally irrational action"—though he later insisted that he "slashed tires to protest against society."[149]

The group Baumann was affiliated with proclaimed: "It is time to destroy. . . . Shit on the society of middle age and taboos. Become wild and do beautiful things. . . . Whatever you see that you don't like, destroy. Dare to struggle, dare to win." Baumann shared with Ayers and his fellow radicals a great admiration of the Black Panthers and was impressed by their violent methods. They were role models while "Mao provided our theoretical basis."[150]

Although he came from a vastly different social background (lower class) and was far more inarticulate, Baumann shared with Ayers an alienated sensibility that he acquired under very different circumstances: "As long as you fit in, you don't get hassled. You have felt this instinctive pressure . . . against the pressure to achieve. . . ." He resolved that he did not "want to participate in this mindless activity [regular work] just to get your old age pension or social security." He eventually reached the theoretical sophistication that found expression in this statement:

> This bestial society has succeeded in arranging everything in such a way that everyone is forced to participate or to die in the gutter. . . . As long as the economic conditions are not changed, a humane life is not possible. There is only one way out of our situation . . . social world revolution, world civil war. We have to put our proletarian solidarity in the place of competition. . . . Instead of alienated capitalist labor . . . we will build a means of work based on the satisfaction of people's needs. . . . It's a matter of creating the man of the 21st century, like Che says in his legacy. . . . We will fulfill this legacy, cost what

> it will! Like Eldridge Cleaver says: "We will be human beings . . . or the world will be flattened in our attempt to become so."[151]

Like Ayers, Baumann too lived in communes and later went underground, but here the similarities end. As far as I know he did not become a tenured professor of education at a state university, as Ayers did later in life.

After the Weathermen's "days of rage" in Chicago in 1968 (which largely involved a few hundred protesters breaking shop and car windows) Ayers recalled that

> even though we'd been routed, everyone felt triumphant. We had fought like madmen and been beaten down, but we had also upped the stakes. . . . We exhaled energy. . . . It was a time of transgression and I was of a generation guided by the precept, Break as many rules as you can . . . defiance and insubordination was life itself. . . .
>
> We have a responsibility as mother country radicals to attack this monster at its heart and . . . to disable it. . . . We must open up another front against U.S. imperialism. . . . I spoke and people chanted and pumped their fists. . . . It filled me with an intoxicating sense of strength. . . .

During the 1968 Democratic Convention in Chicago, the radicals fantasized that "we would be Vietcong guerrillas attacking an American outpost. . . ." In the same spirit, Ayers writes elsewhere: "We would . . . retaliate for racist attacks, and fight alongside our Black revolutionary comrades." These recollections of the rioting in Chicago, with their frequent references to "feverish revelry" and "chanting frenzy," bring to mind Le Bon's classic work on crowd behavior.

Ayers and his fellow radicals "were captivated by the autobiographies of revolutionaries, encouraged by stories of lives lived in struggle. . . . We rummaged through them . . . for inspiration. . . ." He was particularly inspired by Ho Chi Minh, who "had become like an adopted grandfather to me—I thought of him as saintly but very tough . . . [a] warrior and sage, fighter and poet—the loving activist. . . ." Another role model was "the eternal internationalist, Che Guevara, [who] spoke to us every morning from a huge poster above our bed: 'In revolution one wins or dies.'"

There was also endless talk and fantasizing about "smashing the state" followed by "smashing monogamy"—the latter providing ideological justification for multiple revolutionary copulations.

Ayers and his fellow revolutionaries alternated between seeing the United States "as an ultimately doomed and helpless but temporarily deeply destructive giant" and the most coldly efficient machine of repression ever known to history. Their self-assessments too fluctuated between despair and vulnerability and an intoxicated sense of invincibility. Nothing seemed impossible; revolution was imminent, and with it the transformation of everything:

> Our job is to drive a stake into the heart of the monster . . . opening up a front behind enemy lines and fighting . . . side by side with Black people and with the people of the world. It was an exhilarating and exhausting politics. The city was full of fervor and fire and we intended to stoke it with anything at hand. . . .

They egged on the authorities to provoke more violence, and when set upon by the police they felt still more righteous and victimized; police brutality was to a some degree a self-fulfilling prophecy. As Tom Hayden said, exhorting the troops in Chicago at the time of the Democratic Convention,

> This demonstration has the potential like nothing we've done before to expose the face of the enemy . . . to force him to reveal himself as violent, brutal, totalitarian and evil. It will be difficult—and dangerous—taunting the monster, stabbing him in his most exposed and vulnerable places, but it's got to be done. . . . We can reduce this demon to a pitiful, helpless giant.

It would be unfair to say that Ayers learned *nothing* from his life as a violent radical activist. Rather it seems that what he learned is neutralized, time and again, by the impulse of self-vindication and fidelity to youthful idealism and the hardships of his underground years. He does express occasional reservations about life in the underground collective of the Weathermen and about the triumph of the political over the personal. It was particularly difficult to reconcile a flamboyant individualism with the avid pursuit of community:

> We jogged. We marched. We drilled. More criticism. Organize, fight, practice, criticize. Criticism and self-criticism. . . .
>
> It was fanatical obedience, we militant nonconformists suddenly tripping over one another to be exactly alike. . . . I cannot reproduce the stifling atmosphere that overpowered us. . . .
>
> Criticism/self-criticism became a regular practice in the collectives, but was harder and harder to manage because any particular honest

> sense of self was disappearing and the collective assumed the stance of an eagerly policing superego.
>
> . . . We began to speak mostly in proverbs from Che or Ho. . . .
>
> We were becoming prisoners of our schemes, intoxicated on theory.

He reflects at the end of the book about a movie (*Underground*) that was made about him and his fellow underground activists by a sympathetic Italian filmmaker:

> I was embarrassed by the arrogance . . . the absolute certainty that we and we alone knew the way. . . . I saw again how the impulse toward community too can betray us. . . . We want a solution to every problem . . . clear and definitive answers. . . .
>
> We see ourselves [in retrospect] . . . in the posture of the faithful . . . all marching for a just cause. And the cause is always just.

These self-reflective comments are contradicted by Ayers's remarks in the *New York Times* interview.

His "pilgrimage" to Vietnam twenty-five years after the American defeat (with his fellow radical spouse Bernardine Dohrn) is further indication of a clinging to old beliefs: "We went to remember, to recover some parts of our lives. . . ." Like other political pilgrims, they were greatly impressed by everything they saw (or could see): "We were exhilarated in Viet Nam, breathing in the whole experience in big gulps. . . . Everyone greeted us with enthusiasm. . . ." He was well prepared for the friendly reception, distributing copies of the couple's old wanted posters he took with him. He was one of many sixties radicals whose "alienation allowed the possibility of imagining that a genuinely egalitarian Communism was taking shape in the third world . . . [and he too] had trouble distinguishing dictators from democrats, so long as the dictators were on the left."[152]

The persistence of old commitments is confirmed in the acknowledgments to Ayers's book, in which he proclaims that "his heart and hope is with every freedom fighter, who is even now imprisoned for speaking out fearlessly, for acting on a passionate conviction that we might work toward a future of peace and justice." These heroes and heroines of Ayers allegedly seeking a peaceful world went far beyond "speaking out fearlessly"; they were, for the most part, convicted murderers such as Jamil Al-Amin (H. Rap Brown), Kathy Boudin, David Gilbert, Mumia Abu Jamal, Anthony Ortiz, Leonard Peltier, and others. Ayers enthusiastically embraced the late I. F. Stone's helpful rationalization that "a guerrilla movement is a political and not a criminal phenomenon, however many crimes it may commit."

Ayers was by no means the only unrepentant Weatherman. Occasioned by the parole of Kathy Boudin in 2003 (imprisoned for her participation in the Brinks murder/robbery), a *New York Times* reporter looked up other old Weathermen and found that "Many former Weathermen have taken up careers that they see as extension of their political commitment: teaching, social work and advocating causes like environmental protection, care for AIDS patients and prisoners' rights. Today they proclaim the same ideals they held four decades ago, and sharply condemn American policies at home and abroad." One of the former Weathermen interviewed, Brian Flanagan (a participant in the "Days of Rage" in Chicago), told the reporter: "I was regretful over about 5% of what we did. . . . I think 95% of what we did was great and we'd do it again."[153]

Another well-known unrepentant voice of the sixties was the late Stokely Carmichael, who changed his name to Kwame Ture to signal his newfound African identity. "Asked about his mistakes or regrets, Mr. Ture is hard pressed to find any." He used to answer his phone "with his customary greeting, 'Ready for the revolution.'"[154]

Ayers is no longer quite as thrilled by political violence as he used to be, though he was jubilant about the "wonderful activism"[155] of the protests against globalism in Seattle and Genoa, which were accompanied by a good deal of violence. Age and family obligations probably best explain a greater reticence in such matters. Since his emergence from the underground, Ayers has obtained a tenured position at the University of Illinois in Chicago, which provides him with both a secure and materially comfortable life and a forum from which to express his beliefs about the evils of American society and capitalism. He is married to his comrade-in-arms and has several children. To some degree existence (including age) does determine consciousness, and Ayers's current way of life is not compatible with setting off bombs or hurling rocks at policemen or shop windows. Nonetheless his old beliefs and commitments remain cherished and a source of an enduring sense of moral identity.[156]

Antonio Negri (1933–) and **Michael Hardt** (1960–), authors of *Empire*, published in 2000 by Harvard University Press, are (or used to be) academic celebrities. Not only are they exemplars of resistance to the political attitude change discussed in this book, they seek a revitalization of radical political beliefs and values rooted in the 1960s. Negri is no mere theorist but a former radical activist, leader of the

Red Brigades which in the 1970s committed numerous high-profile terrorist acts in Italy. He was charged with armed insurrection and given a prison sentence (which, however, required him to spend only nights in jail). In the late 1970s he identified with the terrorists who wore ski masks, and wrote:

> I live the life of the sniper, the deviant, and the worker who doesn't show up at his job. Every time I put on my ski mask, I feel the warmth of the proletarian, worker community around me. . . .
>
> Every action of destruction and sabotage seems to me a manifestation of class solidarity. Nor does the eventual risk bother me: rather it fills me with feverish excitement as one waiting for his lover. Nor does the pain of my adversary affect me. . . .[157]

It is hard to think of a better example of false consciousness than the sentiments here quoted: the university professor's wishful fantasy of his bonds with the Italian working classes, who were no more supportive of the Red Brigades than American workers were of the Weathermen.

Empire is particularly noteworthy since it "has come as close to becoming an international best-seller as a university press book . . . is likely to get." It made Negri an intellectual-political celebrity in numerous Western countries, though not in Italy. The book has gone through ten printings and been translated into many languages. It has also received "eye-popping reviews" including the blessings of Frederic Jameson of Duke University who called it "prophetic" and "the first great theoretical synthesis of the new millennium." Such acclaim is all the more remarkable since the book is permeated by impenetrable postmodern jargon, written in "prose that insults language," as a dissenting reviewer put it.[158] Evidently, as has often been the case, such ponderous obscurity has been mistaken for profundity and allowed congenial readers to project upon it a variety of adversarial impulses and sentiments. Sentences such as these abound in the volume:

> The great industrial and financial powers . . . produce not only commodities but also subjectivities. They produce agentic subjectivities within the biopolitical context. . . . In the biopolitical sphere, life is made to work for production and production is made to work for life. . . . The deeper the analysis goes, the more it finds at increasing levels of intensity the interlinking assemblages of interactive relationships.

Elsewhere the authors write:

> Certainly there must be a moment when reappropriation and self-organization reach a threshold and configure a real event. This is when

> the political is really affirmed—when the genesis is complete and self-valorization, the cooperative convergence of subjects, and the proletarian management of production become a constituent power.[159]

The reception of *Empire* makes clear that there remains a substantial reservoir of support among leftist intellectuals and those influenced by them for the attitudes and beliefs the book represents, especially Negri's effort to unite "theory and practice" by involvement with the Red Brigades and the associated transgressions of bourgeois morality.

The major message of the book, insofar as it can be deciphered, is summed up in its title. "The empire" conjured by the authors is a new entity, much different from and far more sinister and insidious than either old-fashioned imperialism or capitalism; it is more to be feared and hated, something invisible yet uniquely powerful and overwhelming. Described variously as "both system and hierarchy, centralized construction of norms and far-reaching production of legitimacy, spread out over world space . . . a dynamic and flexible systemic structure . . . 'governance without government' . . . at times imperceptible but always and increasingly effective. . . . The systemic totality has a dominant position in the global order, breaking resolutely with every previous dialectic and developing an integration of actors that seems linear and spontaneous." It is also described as "a new paradigm of power, a postmodern sovereignty [that] has come to replace the modern paradigm and rule through differential hierarchies of the hybrid and fragmentary subjectivities." To clarify the matter further, "Empire takes form when language and communication, or really, immaterial labor and communication, become the dominant productive force." Most important, "In Empire corruption is everywhere. It is the cornerstone and keystone of domination. It resides in different forms in the supreme government of Empire and its vassal administration, the most refined and the most rotten administrative police forces. . . . Through corruption, imperial power extends a smokescreen across the world and command over the multitude is exercised in this putrid cloud, in the absence of light and truth."[160] There are echoes here of *The Communist Manifesto*—the idea of "false consciousness"—and Marcuse's concept of "repressive tolerance," repression cunningly concealed hence superbly effective.

In addition to the dubious concept of "empire," the reader is also introduced to the related notion of "biopower":

> Empire not only manages a territory and a population but also creates the very world it inhabits. It not only regulates human interactions but

> also seeks directly to rule over human nature. The object of its rule is social life in its entirety, and thus Empire presents the paradigmatic form of biopower.

We learn of biopower that it "is a form of power that regulates social life from its interior, following it, interpreting it, absorbing it, and rearticulating it. . . . Biopower thus refers to a situation in which what is directly at stake in power is the production and reproduction of life itself."[161]

These conceptual-theoretical innovations are part of what the authors intended to accomplish: "What we hope to have contributed in this book is a general theoretical framework and a toolbox of concepts for theorizing and acting in and against the Empire."[162] Like many other radical leftist intellectuals, Negri and Hardt remain enthralled by the fantasy of uniting theory and practice.

The major themes animating *Empire* are an impassioned reaffirmation of the evils of capitalism (seen as reinvigorated by globalism) and a reaffirmation and romanticization of violence, sanctified by the evil it is designed to combat. The latter is particularly appealing to the more radical elements of the sixties generation who used to argue that given the "essential" or "inherent" violence of capitalism, violent actions against it were morally unproblematic and wholly defensible.

None of these is an original idea; it is the authors' unreflective, enthusiastic reaffirmation of them, in connection with the new evil of globalization, which explains the appeal of the message at a time when such ringing reaffirmations are hard to come by. Negri's status as a convicted felon doubtless adds to the attraction of the book; in the eyes of his admirers he is the fearless man of ideas *and* action who suffered for his convictions.

As Alan Wolfe sees it, "*Empire* is best understood as an attempt, using Marxist jargon, to bring back to life the political urge Marx spent so much of his life opposing: anarchism and particularly the more destructive forms of anarchism. . . ." Hence the "celebrat[ion] of rap groups or window-smashing anarchists." On the other hand, Marx would not have disputed the message of these authors that "redemption will come from the multitude, who, despite their oppression . . . remain pure in heart."[163]

Not only does *Empire* reaffirm an entrenched and deeply felt anticapitalism (combined with apprehensions of modernity), it also offers an optimistic perspective about its coming demise and provides support for adversarial actions and postures. The book validates the sense of diffuse, often apolitical alienation for which capitalism has been plausibly blamed. This alienation has many sources, chief among them the decline of a sense of community, identity, and meaning as a consequence of modernization and secularization—not peculiar to the evils of capitalism.

The appeal of the book is also related to its apparent linking of the cultural and political radicalism derived from the 1960s and '70s. Cultural radicalism was more self-indulgent, political radicalism more fanatical and disciplined.

Finally, *Empire* displays an inchoate utopianism that promises "a revolution no power will control—because bio-power and communism, cooperation and revolution remain together, in love, simplicity and also innocence. This is the irrepressible lightness and joy of being communist."[164] Notwithstanding the insidious power (or biopower) of the Empire the authors offer further hope:

> Today after so many capitalist victories, after socialist hopes withered in disillusionment . . . why is it that instances of militancy still arise, why has resistance deepened, and why does struggle continually reemerge with new vigor? . . . Militancy today is a positive, constructive, and innovative activity. . . . Militants resist imperial command in a creative way. . . . Resistance is linked immediately with a constitutive investment in the biopolitical realm and to the formation of cooperative apparatuses of production and community. Here is the strong novelty of militancy today: it repeats the virtues of insurrectional action of two hundred years of subversive experience, but at the same time it is linked to a new world. . . . This militancy makes resistance into counterpower and makes rebellion into a project of love.[165]

As one reviewer put it, "Negri has managed to summon a new radical vision in the global age. Its confident . . . rhetoric at a time when most of the left has retreated from revolution is a big part of its appeal. . . . It is a vision based on little more than the mystique of protest. . . ."[166]

In the final analysis, the attachment to the muddled illusions and beliefs presented in this book rests both on the authors' deep conviction that they have perceptively identified a new, unique, and exceptionally threatening entity and on the paradoxical confidence that they, and their followers, can overcome this engulfing evil.

LYNNE STEWART (1940–), the elderly radical lawyer, would likely have found the themes and messages of *Empire* congenial. She was also well acquainted with and tolerant of political violence employed in the service of ends and ideals she approved of, and to which she dedicated her professional life. She remarked that "I don't have any problem with Mao or Stalin or the Vietnamese leaders or certainly Fidel locking up people they see as dangerous."[167]

Like William Kunstler, Stewart was a "movement lawyer" who "didn't just defend the legal rights of her clients; she also advocated their politics." She was "always drawn in the most personal way to the outcast." Her clients included "violent members of the splinter groups that were all that remained of the revolutionary dreams of the 60s—the Weather Underground, the Ohio 7, the Black Liberation Army." Later she took on "drug dealers, cop killers, mobsters, mentally ill assassins . . . Colin Ferguson, the Long Island Rail Road shooter . . ."[168] Like Kunstler, she sympathized with anyone who was an outlaw and could be considered either an opponent or a victim of the "system" she abhorred. Most famously, she defended (unsuccessfully) Sheik Omar Abdel Rahman, the spiritual leader of the global jihad, sentenced to life in 1996 for "conspiring to wage a terrorist war against the United States." She became the sheik's lawyer at the urging of Ramsey Clark,[169] who also deserves our attention in this chapter on similar grounds.

Subsequently Stewart was convicted in February 2005 for helping the sheik communicate from prison with his followers and violating the highly specific rules that governed her legal relationship and contacts with him in prison.[170]

In Stewart's eyes the sheik was "a fighter for national liberation on behalf of people oppressed by dictatorship and American imperialism. She came to admire him personally too. . . ." As with others she defended, it was first and foremost a case of being drawn to the enemy of her enemies. It was an attraction complemented by her "true goal . . . always to be on the right side of history," as she put it.[171] Being on the right side meant an implacable hatred of capitalism, which she described as "a consummate evil that unleashes its dogs of war on the helpless; an enemy motivated by insatiable greed. . . . In this enemy there is no love of the land or the creatures that live there, no compassion for the people."[172] She made these remarks as keynote speaker at the 2003 convention of the National Lawyers Guild, a venerable radical left organization.

Stewart exemplifies the unity of the personal and political, having been radicalized during the sixties, according to one account, by a black man, still her companion after forty years. "Together they became New York revolutionaries . . . and so they remain long after the radical years have ended and others have moved on."[173]

Her radical sympathies and legal as well as emotional support for convicted terrorists, domestic and foreign, have not made her an outcast in the legal or academic world. In 2002 she was invited to be a "visiting mentor" at the Stanford University Law School and was scheduled to speak on Veterans Day and to be introduced by Deborah Rhode, a professor at the same law school and a former president of the American Association of University Professors. The invitation was later rescinded by the dean of the law school.[174] Still, Professor Rhode expressed deep apprehension about the prosecution of Stewart for passing messages from her client to jihadist groups abroad.[175]

Ramsey Clark (1927–), attorney general under Lyndon Johnson, was described by John Judis, a liberal journalist, as "inhabit[ing] the furthest reaches of the fevered swamps of American politics. He has become not simply a critic of American administrations, but the best hope of their foreign adversaries, from the Libyans to the Iraqis."[176] Clark has in common with Lynne Stewart an avid interest in defending the adversaries of the United States, domestic and foreign, but the evolution of his political attitudes is more puzzling.[177] After his career as attorney general he joined William Kunstler to represent two of the so-called Attica Brothers accused of killing a prison guard during the prison uprising in upstate New York. He also represented Radovan Karadzic, the Bosnian Serb general indicted for war crimes, and gave legal advice to Slobodan Milosevic.[178] Moreover, as Judis wrote in 1991, "in the last two years Clark has plummeted to new lows. . . . He has become the lead counsel and leading apologist for Lyndon LaRouche [the prominent right-wing extremist]. . . . [Clark] accepted the leadership of an 'anti-war' coalition, run by the Workers World Party, a pro-Saddam sect. Clark's coalition was against sanctions as well as war."[179] (This was the first Gulf War in 1991.) Clark's eccentric support of LaRouche is reminiscent of Chomsky's support of Faurisson, the French Holocaust denier.

More recently Clark joined the legal team to defend Saddam Hussein, about whom he made warm remarks while he was still in power: "I've met with him four times, probably averaged two to three hours at a time. . . . He is reserved, quiet, thoughtful, dignified you might say, in the old-fashioned sense." Clark strongly opposed demonizing Saddam. Beth Stevens, an attorney who represented Bosnian Muslim women who sued Karadzic in 1993, observed that Clark "think[s] that any enemy of the United States is a friend of his."[180]

It is not clear why Clark became an embittered critic of the United States. As Judis wondered, "How could a distinguished former attorney general become an ally of neo-Stalinists and Third World autocrats and the defender of LaRouche?"[181] There are some, partial explanations. During the Vietnam era Clark prosecuted prominent opponents of the war such as Dr. Benjamin Spock, William Sloane Coffin, and Muhammad Ali, and might have come to regret it, given his emerging political convictions. In another thought-provoking incident in his legal career, "one of his first steps (as attorney general) was to drop the case against Judith Coplon . . . charged with passing secrets to her Soviet lover." It was none other than Clark's father Tom who initially brought the case against Coplon when *he* was attorney general.[182] Judis called this "anti-Papa politics," and it may have played a part in Clark's political evolution. His last years in office under Johnson were "a personal disaster," and Johnson came to be highly critical of his performance. In turn, Nixon during his election campaign accused Clark of serious derelictions. In light of these developments, it is likely that Clark left his high federal position embittered and disillusioned with "the establishment." His defeat in the primary for a Democratic Senate seat in New York in 1976 presumably deepened his estrangement:

> Clark's defeat, a former associate says, "dispirited him in a profound . . . way." As Clark resigned himself to being an outsider, he became more contemptuous of the insiders. [Subsequently] he threw himself at every exotic cause and became a mark for every domestic and foreign liberator and liberation movement. He became the lawyer for . . . Philip Berrigan; headed a commission to investigate the killings of Black Panthers Fred Hampton and Mark Clark; went to North Vietnam to condemn U.S. bombing over the "Voice of Vietnam." [In a "Face the Nation" interview] he refused to describe Saddam as an evil force. . . . "I don't judge people as good or evil."[183]

Clark displayed no such reticence in his own judgments of U.S. policies and politicians; like other deeply committed partisans of various causes, Clark had a highly selective nonjudgmental disposition. As he approaches eighty years of age, it is safe to predict that he will persevere in his beliefs.

Alexander Cockburn (1941–) has been notable not merely for persevering in his radical beliefs but for doing so with an uncompromising ferocity (though without setting off bombs), earning rebuke even from some of his comrades on the left.[184] In Cockburn's judgment, even Oliver Stone—not exactly a man who minces his words about the corruptions of American society—is soft on America. According to Stone, Cockburn is "convinced that a democratic society cannot be good, and could not elect a leader who wasn't merely another link in the inherently evil system."[185]

A journalist and columnist for *The Nation*, Cockburn is a transplant from England and a close personal friend and admirer of such radical American social critics as Noam Chomsky and Andrew Kopkind. His reverential view of Chomsky is a good measure of the depth of his rejection of American society. Cockburn wrote:

> People will go to a talk by Chomsky partly just to reassure themselves that they haven't gone mad; that they are right when they disbelieve what they read in the papers or watch on TV. For hundreds of thousands of people over the years . . . Chomsky has offered the assurance . . . that there is another way of looking at things. . . . [His] greatest virtue is that his fundamental message is a simple one.[186]

It is not clear why the young Cockburn left England (where he grew up and was educated) for the United States, given his boundless disdain for American society. Presumably he was looking for opportunity, or perhaps he felt that prospects for radical activism were better here than on the other side of the Atlantic. Neither is it clear, given his British background, how he developed the consuming preoccupation with the evil he believes the United States represents. He easily rivals Chomsky in the conviction that the United States is the single, dominant embodiment and source of all social injustice and political repression in the world today, and has been for some time. But it is harder to tell if the primary culprit is capitalism (which finds its most powerful embodiment in the United States) or if the evil entity is the United States or American culture, independent of its association with capitalism, and if so, what is so uniquely odious about it.

The intensity of Cockburn's rage directed at the United States suggests that it is not only an unworthy political and economic system, or an overbearing superpower, but the symbol and root cause of all that is wrong with societies and human beings. This uncommon outrage and fierce indignation cannot be explained satisfactorily as merely a response to the specifics of exploitation or inequality. Capitalism and the United States appear also to be held responsible for whatever is inauthentic, false, or duplicitous in life—for the loss of meaning, the coarsening of human relationships, the destruction of primeval innocence and the essential goodness in human beings.

In the rhetoric of critics like Cockburn, one finds echoes of Marx's bitter complaint about capitalism putting an end "to all feudal, patriarchal relations," its sundering of "motley . . . ties" found in traditional societies, its "drown[ing] the most heavenly ecstasies of religious fervor," its "stripp[ing] of its halo every occupation hitherto honored," and, above all, its profaning "all that is holy."[187]

Cockburn shares with Chomsky not only the sweeping indictment of the United States and American-dominated global capitalism for their crimes against humanity (poverty, inequality, and political repression) but an elevated, permanent revulsion toward what he sees as the hypocrisy, the pretense, the deceptiveness inherent in these systems. As in Marx, the romantic roots of the criticism and indignation directed at capitalism and bourgeois values are discernible. The sentiments rest on an exceedingly positive conception of human nature (along the lines of the noble savage), seen as befouled by the greed, ruthlessness, and unworthy aspirations nurtured by capitalism.

Alexander is the son of Claud Cockburn (discussed below), and there is little doubt that the filial ties go a long way to explain Alexander's political beliefs and activities. Every indication is that the father succeeded in passing his political disposition on to his son, that without the affectionate ties between father and son, Alexander's worldview might have been different.

The case of David Horowitz is an instructive counterexample: his estrangement from his Communist father is a notable aspect of his disillusionment, making it easier to reject the entire ideological heritage the father represented and which found new expression in the radicalism of the New Left. I am not suggesting that Horowitz's difficult relationship with his father was responsible for his political disillusionment, only that it helped him develop a critical attitude toward the Movement and its various causes. Being a critic of his father as a human being (as well as a representative of leftist beliefs) made it easier for Horowitz to move to criticism and eventual rejection of the sixties radical beliefs. Alexander Cockburn's political loyalties, on the other hand, were not only nurtured by his relationship to and admiration of his father (who used to be a Communist and a correspondent for the *Daily Worker*, the publication of the British Communist party) but probably also benefited from the unity of both his parents' beliefs. Mrs. Cockburn, an unconventional woman who came from a prominent aristocratic family, shared and supported her husband's politics and subsequently those of her sons. Alexander's journal also reflects a close relationship with his mother. He certainly does not fit the stereotype of the bitter, alienated rebel estranged from his family who, at some unconscious level, conflates the experience of parental neglect with bearing witness to monstrous and monumental social injustice. Alexander did not have to become "radicalized"; it would seem that he imbibed, from an early age, the familial radical left worldview. Moreover he came of age in the 1960s when such views were common among university students and faculties and among intellectuals generally.

The most telling manifestation of the depth of Cockburn's rejection of the Western world and the United States in particular is that not even the collapse of Soviet communism made a dent in his convictions and outlook. Even in 1989 he argued indignantly that enemies of the Soviet system grossly exaggerated the number of its victims. He considered the Brezhnev years "the golden age for the Soviet working class" on account of "an egalitarian wage structure, guaranteed employment and basic food prices."[188] He believed that it was the great historic service of the Soviet Union to aid and protect Third World revolutionary countries such as Cuba, Vietnam, Nicaragua, and Angola, taking for granted the superior virtue of these systems and the desirability of their survival. The Korean War was an expression of the determination of the United States "to crush indigenous revolution"[189]—a peculiarly bewildering idea considering that the war began with the North Korean invasion of the South with huge conventional forces.

In a television program devoted to the collapse of the Soviet Union, Ted Koppel noted that Cockburn chose to talk instead about the evils of capitalism. Cockburn argued on the occasion that "in order to understand why millions of people around the world are still fired with radical ideals you have to understand that if actually existing communism was and is abhorrent to some, actually existing capitalism is abhorrent to others."[190] Cockburn has also harbored an abiding dislike of Orwell: "When I grew up, if you ever, at school tried to come up with the slightest radical statement or exhibited radical hopes, some idiot would always bring up *Animal Farm*."[191] He shared Chomsky's vitriolic contempt for Vaclav Havel on account of Havel's praising the United States as "the defender of freedom."[192] He wrote of the late Irving Howe, the democratic socialist, that his "prime function, politically speaking, in the last thirty years of his life was policing the left on behalf of the powers-that-be. . . . Howe was a foot soldier in the ideological Cointelpro campaign to divert political currents electrifying America and supporting liberation movements in the Third World. . . ."[193] He found particularly reprehensible Howe's critiques of the violence and authoritarian tendencies of the

New Left and his rejection of the New Left cults of Castro, Ho Chi Minh, and Mao.

Several circumstances further help explain the persistence of Cockburn's political beliefs. Being an expatriate who joined the radical political subculture in the United States may have strengthened Cockburn's political beliefs: distancing himself from his political causes and commitments could have resulted in greater personal isolation in the new country he came to live in. He made his living as a radical journalist and occasional speaker, and there was no obvious alternative to this calling. Equally important is that he moved among people who by and large shared his beliefs. There was little if any incentive to undertake a painful political soul searching.

Claud Cockburn (1904–1981), unlike his son Alexander, presents a more complex picture, which often includes an apparent, cheerful ambivalence about his own beliefs. Although he ceased to support the Soviet Union and the British Communist party in the late 1950s, he did so with so many reservations and qualifications that his attitudes are more informative of the process of resisting disillusionment than of disaffection. In his recollections he touches or invokes virtually every important psychological factor that bolsters resistance to the repudiation of strongly held political beliefs and commitments. At one point he asks: "If a man was fool enough to be fooled by a lot of fools and furthermore fooled for years on end, should any intelligent person pay much attention to his testimony?"[194] It is not clear in what measure he thought this applied to his own case.

The older Cockburn was quite self-conscious about the unusual circumstances of his withdrawal from his political alignments. He wrote:

> People have asked me repeatedly . . . how precisely I came to move into the Communist Party and how precisely I came to move out of it. . . . People . . . expect something abrupt, sensational and Pauline in the way of a conversion—some explosion on the road to Damascus capable of explaining so drastic a decision. . . . In my case nothing of that sort occurred. . . .
>
> It was a gradual process involving countless factors which were by no means all "political" in the strict sense of the word.

Being horrified about the policies of Stalin's regime in the Soviet Union was not a major factor:

> The fact was that like innumerable non-Russian Communists . . . I was sheathed, so to speak, against indignation and disgust regarding

> many atrocious events in Russia, by two suits of protective clothing. The first was that . . . during a great part of my life I had listened to anti-Communists telling the wildest lies about Communism. . . . The result was that even when they told the truth one almost instinctively rejected it. . . .
>
> The other protective suit was . . . woven of two beliefs. One was the belief that after all, on balance, the Soviet regime was, so to speak, on the side of angels—that is to say, that despite many deviations and shortcomings its mere existence was an asset to the oppressed of the earth, a challenge and a threat to the oppressors. . . . But out of this belief grew a second article of faith which was more dangerous—the conviction that actions which would be violently condemned if performed by any other regime must be quite differently assessed when performed by the Government of the USSR.

These were precisely the conclusions and insights Koestler and Leonhard arrived at in the course of their far less ambiguous rejection of the cause.

Cockburn emphasized that once the disaffected former supporter "accuses the Russian Communists of some hideous malpractice, he finds himself, to his horror, in the approving company of half the leading ruffians of the western world." This was a sentiment widely shared among those who hesitated to express their disenchantment or resisted it altogether, as for example Eric Hobsbawm. Not to give aid and comfort to the enemy was and remains a powerful emotional imperative, more compelling than any need for public reassessment and admission of error.

Other subjective, emotional factors that made Cockburn's break difficult included a certain pride. He wrote: ". . . quite apart from the high political rights and wrongs of the matter . . . I was dominated by the feeling that I had, of my free will, joined, so to speak, a regiment and that I had better soldier along with it, particularly at a moment when it was . . . going to come under pretty heavy fire." He also succeeded in convincing himself that the means did not matter a great deal as long as the ends were glorious: ". . . what I feel . . . is that what matters is not whether the weapon is good but whether the cause is."

But he also hung on to his beliefs as long as he could persuade himself that he was doing something useful and honorable. He was inclined to activism and had an adventurous streak and a "propensity . . . for treating action as an end in itself; for acting . . . without asking ultimate questions; for taking hasty decisions. . . ." Conversely his growing awareness of the minimal impact of the British Communist party and his own propagandizing on the larger scheme of things contributed to his withdrawal.

A major disillusioning experience was the Hungarian Revolution of 1956, which shocked him not so much because of its brutal repression but by revealing that people were willing to take up arms against a system that clearly did not work. After many conversations with people in Soviet-controlled Eastern Europe, he found himself "afflicted with a painful uncertainty as to whether the classic Communist formula for ultimately solving the difficulties was really calculated to bring home, as they say, the bacon."

At least one experience indicates that it was not exclusively pragmatic considerations that tilted the balance for Cockburn. It was the treatment of Earl Browder, the American Communist party leader, by Moscow that exemplified the lack of principles all too apparent in Soviet political practice:

> Without a word of warning, he [Browder] had been served notice that his entire policy, a policy imposed with almost ferocious rigidity upon all members of the American Communist organization, a policy which . . . had been proclaimed to constitute . . . the map which was going to show the path to the heights, was not only ill-considered . . . but was . . . a blatant and disgusting betrayal of the interests of the working people of the entire world, a piece of sabotage and sell-out.

On the whole, Claud Cockburn's disillusionment was pragmatic and restrained, incorporating every defense mechanism employed with different degrees of success both by those who prolonged disillusionment as well as those who succeeded in averting it altogether.

A lesser-known case adds further variety to this brief survey of the persistence of political faith and commitment. The individual discussed below sought to unite, in her own way, theory and practice, or certain ideals with actions promoting them.

MELITA NORWOOD (1912–2005), an Englishwoman, was eighty-seven years old in 1999 when she decided to reveal her lengthy record of spying for the NKVD. Her work for the Soviet authorities had begun in 1937. "On her retirement in 1972 the KGB files complimented her as 'a committed, reliable and disciplined agent, striving to be of the utmost assistance.' When she visited Moscow with her husband in 1979 she was given . . . the Order of the Red Banner" in recognition of her services.[195] She spied while working as a secretary for a research organization involved with Britain's nuclear research program. She "regularly removed files from a safe after hours, copied them and turned them over to Soviet agents."

She told the reporters assembled in her suburban garden that "I did what I did not to make money but to help prevent the defeat of a new system which had, at great cost, given ordinary people food and fares which they could afford, a good education and a health service." It was a matter of unsullied idealism.

In an interview with the London *Times*, Norwood made clear that she was not tempted by second thoughts about her beliefs and activities: "In the same circumstances, I know I would do the same thing again." In her "unrepentant confession" she explained that "in addition to sympathizing with the social gains that the Soviet experiment promised, she thought that in the postwar era the Soviet Union represented the only counterbalance to capitalism and that the West should not be allowed . . . sole possession of nuclear bombs."[196]

Reportedly "people in the neighborhood said they were aware that Mrs. Norwood, locally famed for the quality of her homemade chutney, held radical views for their largely Conservative voting area. Along with the geraniums in her windows there are anti-war and nuclear disarmament stickers, and on a cupboard shelf visible through the kitchen window is a mug with Che Guevara's bearded face on it."[197] She was also in the habit of buying thirty-two copies of the Communist daily newspaper the *Morning Star* and placing them in the mailboxes of friends and neighbors.[198]

Norwood's mother was "active in leftist causes," her father was a follower of Tolstoy. Her husband "shared her Communist ideology but disapproved of her actively aiding the Russians." Norwood joined the British Communist party in 1932 as a "secret member." Her husband was also a member. We do not know how precisely she acquired her strong pro-Soviet convictions, but her parents' attitudes must have played a part; nor do we know if her mother approved of or helped inspire her spying. (Her father died when she was six.) According to the *Guardian* obituary, "she had seen the victims of the depression begging for food as well as a job." Presumably that too had an impact on the evolution of her political attitudes. Doubtless at some point she became convinced that English society was unjust and undeserving of sympathy or support; her quoted remarks make clear that she did not think well of capitalism and favored a counterforce to it, such as the Soviet Union. Nonetheless it is a large and consequential leap from attitude, belief, and sympathy to action such as devoted, meticulous, and routinized spying.

As her remarks suggest, Norwood was totally innocent of any knowledge of the nature of the Soviet system and conditions of life in the Soviet Union. For reasons not quite clear (but most likely under parental influence), she developed a charitable and strongly protective disposition toward the USSR and held it unflinchingly throughout her life.

Spying became for her a combination of ideologically motivated duty and a hobby. Apparently her age saved her from prosecution. I failed to discover what motivated her to make a public revelation of these activities at a ripe old age.

Several conditions may be identified that influence the preservation of political commitment and help resist disillusionment.

It must be repeated that it is almost always easier to retain well-established, internalized, familiar beliefs than to change them radically. Most of us, under most conditions, prefer continuity to change in such matters. The greater the length of time invested in a political cause, movement, or ideology, the more difficult it is to abandon it. Many of the well-known representatives of such enduring, unchanging commitments are of advanced age or deceased. They include Noam Chomsky, Ramsey Clark, William Kunstler, Edward Said, Lynne Stewart, and others discussed above. Many others in this category (not here discussed) are also aged, aging, or deceased, such as Johnetta Cole, Angela Davis, Andrea Dworkin, Frederic Jameson, Jonathan Kozol, Norman Mailer, Ralph Nader, Victor Navasky, Michael Parenti, Theodore Roszak, William Sloane Coffin, Gore Vidal, Howard Zinn, and many others.

Gus Hall (1919–2000), the general secretary of the U.S. Communist party for several decades (and a member of the party from 1927), is another remarkable example of a virtually lifelong, unwavering commitment to the Soviet system and the Soviet-controlled American Communist party. As the *New York Times* obituary put it, Hall "never apologized for or wavered from the increasingly marginalized ideology he championed." From Khrushchev to Gorbachev, "he enjoyed the patronage of every Soviet head of state and was received as a dignitary on his yearly pilgrimages to Moscow." He also received $40 million in assistance from the Soviet Union between 1971 and 1990. In 1991, when the Soviet Union was collapsing, he was asked at a news conference if he had plans for future visits, and he demurred. Instead he told the reporters: "The world should see what North Korea has done . . . it's a miracle. If you want to take a nice vacation, take it in North Korea."[199] He was not joking.

What these individuals have in common are certain durable core convictions about the corruptions and injustices that, in their view, *define* American society and much of the Western world. Some of them also harbored fleeting or more enduring sympathy toward particular Communist states. Those discussed in the chapter about the "rank and file" (mostly aged) also sought to hold on to or salvage similar commitments and beliefs.

Aside from the time invested, the other major factor in the durability of these beliefs (and associated activities) is their centrality to the individual's sense of identity. Resisting disillusionment was more important for Western intellectuals since their sense of identity was deeply involved with their beliefs and with their self-conception as critics of the societies they lived in—a role that complemented a favorable disposition toward Communist systems, movements, and ideologies. While such a favorable disposition often did not endure, the aversion toward their own society did.

Political (or other) beliefs are also more likely to be retained if they are shared with a group, a sustaining community, or a subculture to which the individual belongs. Breaking with the beliefs would result in the loss of important human bonds, social connections, and friendships, perhaps leading to social isolation, ostracism, or contempt on the part of those who had earlier played an important part in the individual's life.

Western intellectuals resisting a reappraisal of their political commitments benefited from being spared the personal experiences readily available to those who had lived in Communist societies. For those in the West, the unappealing attributes of Communist systems remained abstract and far less affecting than direct personal encounter would have been.

In almost every single case of those who refused to reexamine their beliefs it appears that the objects of dislike or hatred were far more important than what they liked or admired. That is, preoccupation with and relentless hatred of the Enemy led to solidarity with enemies of the Enemy, who were warmly embraced and all their sins forgiven. They might be Communist dictators, Third World autocrats, Islamic fanatics, or domestic terrorists; what mattered was the shared, profound animating hostility to the archenemy. Todd Gitlin recalled: "You can hate your country in such a way that the hatred becomes fundamental. A hatred so clear and intense came to feel like a cleansing flame. By the late 60s, this is what became of much of the New Left."[200]

Such sentiments are also found in the motivation of the type of person Eric Hoffer designated as the "true believer": "Passionate hatred can give meaning and purpose to an empty life. Thus people haunted by the purposelessness of their lives try to find a new content not only by dedicating themselves to a holy cause but also by nursing a fanatical grievance."[201]

The single most important factor that enables the individual to retain his or her beliefs in any set of ideals (and the political entities supposedly devoted to their realization) is the resilient capacity to dissociate ends from means, theory from practice, ideals from realities. It may simply be called the capacity or need for belief, or contextual thinking in which the context defines the judgment. Several times in the preceding discussion this capacity for dissociation has been referred to, following Koestler's formulation, as "the doctrine of unshaken foundations." This capacity for dissociation rests on the superior moral importance attributed to the ends, which allow one to overlook or altogether dismiss the human costs of their pursuit.

TEN

Conclusions: "Regions Where No Persuasion Can Penetrate": The Personal and the Political

Much of this book has been written in the shadow of Islamic terrorism, a preeminent fact of life in the early twenty-first century, and proof, if more is needed, of how closely behavior can be determined by ideas—illustrating "the darker connections between ideas and behavior." It is a paradox that although modernization and secularization continues apace around the world, in seeming association with scientific rationality, the number of those who qualify for the designation of true believer[1] appears to grow by leaps and bounds, especially among those professing Islamic religious beliefs.

The ideas discussed in this book rarely provided motivation for dramatic acts of political violence such as suicide bombings; they were nonetheless central to the lives of the protagonists while they were held, and often even after they were discarded. All those individuals discussed here believed that acting on one's beliefs is desirable and a hallmark of authenticity.

This study suggests another similarity between Islamic fanatics and the true believers in some kind of Communist utopia or revolutionary social transformation. The latter share a religious mentality with the former, though of course the substance of these beliefs was very different. The most ardently committed secular political activists displayed what Irving Howe called "unacknowledged religious appetites," which found expression in the nonrational qualities of their beliefs, the suspension of disbelief, the orientation to the future, and the conviction that serving the system and seeking to live up to its commands would solve all personal problems and make life fully meaningful.

This mentality also found expression in the ready acceptance of inflicting great suffering on behalf of glorious ends, in the untroubled subordination of means to ends. Neither secular nor religious true believers were, as Pankaj Mishra has written,

> worried about the terror and violence . . . the demonizing of entire sections of the population. . . . Like other high-minded revolutionaries—Jacobins, Bolsheviks, Khmer Rouge—they too spoke casually about the necessary elimination of "decadent" Brahmins, "kulak" landlords, "reactionary" government officials and the "comparador" class of shopkeepers. . . .
>
> . . . Armed with the idea of the enemy they had begun to dream the old western dream of revolution: the swift and complete transformation of society in all its aspects . . . the making from scratch a pure state and society which alone could guarantee human happiness and virtue. . . .[2]

The mentality discussed here also entails the acceptance of policies leading to untold suffering as if divinely ordained, on the tacit assumption that the infallible leaders know best. As Eric Hoffer noted, "Though ours is a godless age, it is the very opposite of irreligous."[3]

The autobiographical writings consulted for this book vividly reaffirm the reality of the concept of "secular religion," including the strong influence of highly polarized conceptions of good and evil on ostensibly nonreligious individuals, among them supposedly skeptical intellectuals. The preoccupation with ends, the expressions of nonrational devotion, a compulsion and capacity to believe (in matters not subject to empirical determination) strongly suggest that a desire for self-transcendence underlay these attitudes and commitments which were comparable to conventional religious beliefs and attitudes. Like religious believers, the political devotees willingly and demonstratively suspended disbelief, assigned virtually supernatural powers to particular political leaders, organizations, and doctrines, and were openly intolerant of nonbelievers. Repeatedly they acknowledged how painful and difficult it was to repudiate these sustaining beliefs and left no doubt about their centrality to their lives. Gerda Lerner, an American feminist historian, nicely summed it up: "Like all true believers, I believed as I did because I needed to believe: in a utopian vision of the future, in the possibility of human perfectibility, in idealism and heroism.

And I still need that belief, even if the particular vision I had embraced has turned to ashes."

Tzvetan Todorov, the French-Bulgarian philosopher, observed of a similar case: "It is striking how the reasons for joining the Communisty Party given by Buber-Neuman resemble religious conversion, which provides many of the same benefits: . . . a creed with elevated ideals, the sense of belonging to a community, and the reassurance of dogma—with loyalty to the party taking the place of blind submission to the church."[4]

The religious frame of mind of many Communist revolutionaries, functionaries, and Western sympathizers suggests that religious impulses are difficult to suppress—they seek and find unexpected expression. Several of the disillusioned recognized in retrospect the religious qualities of their former beliefs.

Religious and secular religious believers also have in common a capacity, or at least a desire, to subordinate personal morality to larger causes and ideals—the personal to the political. While the commitment is in place, personal morality becomes replaced by some superpersonal ideology or theory. While it lasts, this state of mind can be a highly satisfactory form of self-transcendence.

Not surprisingly, this study vindicates the notion that political beliefs have deep emotional roots, as indeed all strong beliefs do. Centuries ago Spinoza, among others, observed that "men are led by blind impulse rather than by reasons," and that "experience supplies more than enough evidence that it is no more in our power to maintain a sound mind than a sound body."[5] Not all political beliefs have deep-rooted emotional determinants, but the more radical ones do, especially when they are an integral part of an individual's sense of identity. These emotional impulses were more apparent in the attitudes of Western sympathizers, for whom political beliefs were an important source of identity. It was an important circumstance that for those in the West, their beliefs had little or no connection to the exercise of power and thus could not be tarnished by it.

The influence of ideas and beliefs on political attitudes and behavior was less pronounced and distinctive in Communist states, where political commitment and conviction had other, existential determinants. In these societies the committed not only believed in these systems and their legitimating ideas but also worked for them; commitment became routinized and often hard to separate from conformity, work satisfaction, career, material interest, and the need to survive. This was not the case in the West where, for better or worse, the ideas were embraced in a more willed, disinterested, and benighted fashion. Self-interest as generally understood played little part in political involvement, and those involved had little if any opportunity to witness the difficulties and unintended consequences that followed the attempted realization of these ideals. It is hardly surprising that it was easier to retain commitment when it was nurtured by illusions unchallenged by experience, by a distant reality.

These reflections lead to the vexed issue of the relationship between the personal and the political and the problems of identity formation, especially in highly modernized Western societies. Problems of individual identity barely existed in the former or surviving Communist states, which retained, despite their sweeping and coercive policies of modernization, numerous traits of traditional societies. Until the time of their disintegration in the late 1980s and early 1990s, none of the Communist states came close to the level of modernity achieved in the West, especially in regard to the rise of individualism, one of the more intangible and problematic products of modernity. This is also true of the remaining Communist systems, except perhaps those segments of Chinese society undergoing rapid but still politically controlled modernization.

While in Communist societies people experienced a wide range of difficulties and deprivations, the problems of a sense of identity, let alone identity crises, were not among them. Identity concerns are intimately tied to individualism, the conviction of the uniqueness of the self and his or her needs, to the multiplicity of options, opportunities, and choices, to the plurality of socializing influences, the decline of community, and high standards of living—all of which are the mixed blessing of modern Western societies.

The historian David Potter wrote of contemporary American society that it "produced a much increased number of people who were confused as to their identity and who disliked authority. . . . Society was losing its capacity to assign roles, by which people can achieve identities."[6] Potter made these observations well before it became conventional wisdom among American intellectuals that everything, including one's sexual identity, was "socially constructed." This belief, thought to be helpful for self-realization, did not make life easier, though undoubtedly it contributed to the growing number of sex-change operations.

Problems of identity are pronounced in a culture (such as America's) that places great value on the uniqueness of individuals and encourages them to reinvent themselves in order to achieve a sense of self that will be most gratifying.[7] The stronger the belief in the uniqueness of the individual, the greater the hostility to authority that might make demands not to his liking, disregarding his special needs and qualities. This individualism explains the complaints about depersonalization that were a hallmark of the sixties generation and of their descendants. (Ayers's memoirs, among other sources, strikingly document these observations.)

David Potter further pointed out that "the process of identity formation is closely related to the problem of the rejection of society; for it appears that traditional processes of developing social identity have tended to produce a high proportion of men and women who attained their independence by adopting, quite readily, the roles which society expected of them. The adoption of such roles was, itself, a way of accepting society."[8] This has obviously *not* been the case in recent times. All those enamored with the idea of their unique selves do not take kindly to the notion of being shoved into social roles.

The matter of identity formation has a twofold relevance to the political disposition of many Western intellectuals and those under their influence. In the first place, the difficulty of achieving a satisfactory sense of self—that is, identity—is conducive to difficulties in personal relationships and to some degree of social isolation, which may turn into a generalized discontent and the rejection of the society held responsible for these difficulties. As Hoffer noted, "all the advantages brought by the West are ineffectual substitutes for the sheltering and soothing anonymity of communal existence."[9] The quest for community, as Robert Nisbet argued, may lead to embracing extremist movements and the admiration of totalitarian systems that offer new, substitute communities.[10]

Second, when the traditional ways of identity formation fail, many individuals (intellectuals in particular) may turn to political roles and activities and to social criticism as major sources of a new identity. Potter wrote: ". . . when identification with a person fails, a great psychological void remains, and to fill this void people incapable of genuine interpersonal relationships will identify with an abstraction. . . ."[11] Such an abstraction may be a social movement, a political cause, a social ideal. Potter somewhat overstates the case: people who have problems with their sense of identity need not be *incapable* of forming "genuine interpersonal relationships," rather they have difficulties in forming and maintaining them.

The part played by political commitment in identity formation (and maintenance) seems especially important for Western intellectuals whose self-conception as righteous social critics (of their own society) was often a key component of their sense of identity. *Their* career or personal security did not hinge on loyalty to the authorities and conformity to official doctrines. In the West, unlike in the Communist states, people drawn to Communist systems and ideologies were not motivated by the blend of idealism, opportunism, and concern for personal safety that prevailed in Communist states, where advancement in most occupations required a demonstration of political loyalty.[12]

Potter also introduced the idea of "negative identification" associated with the rejection of traditional role models, conventional social norms, and the social system as a whole: "In the impulses of the present day to identify with the wretched of the earth, there may be altruistic compassion but . . . also a component of negative identification."[13] That is, the victims (usually an abstraction rather than individuals personally known) are embraced because by doing so one exposes and rejects the victimizer. Discontent and the rejection of society become legitimized by conspicuous compassion for its victims. Such altruistic concerns also further a positive self-conception. More recently, three American sociologists have observed that "protesters are not so much *for* the downtrodden as *against* the powers that be. . . . Identification with the downtrodden . . . issued less from a desire to elevate the disadvantaged than from disrespect for the well-off and established."[14]

Potter explicitly links personal discontent to the rejection of society, to political estrangement:

> Discontent has many sources. One of these is social injustice, which might be called a public source. . . . But there are many others, some of which may be called private: an individual may be discontented because of emotional friction with members of his family, because he has not attained some desired goal . . . because of an awareness of some personal inadequacy or defect, or because of random disasters that may have befallen him. . . .[15]

These reflections go to the heart of the relationship between the private and the public, the personal and the political:

> . . . in any society a certain portion of discontent will be rationally derived from . . . conditions which are wrong in the sense that they cause . . . suffering which is not necessary in terms of the capacities of society. . . . But in any society another portion of discontent will arise from problems of a personal, less public nature. . . . This kind of discontent is emotionally generated; it does not recognize its own source . . . [it]

> is a free-floating discontent, ready to be discharged . . . against any object . . . not protected by . . . inviolable psychological sanctions. . . . It follows . . . that the degree of discontent in any society is not necessarily correlated to the degree of injustice or evil in the institutions of the society. . . . The degree to which men reject society does not necessarily depend upon the degree to which something is wrong with society.[16]

These sociologists likewise observed that "personal estrangement/alienation from the world is projectively recast as the essential corruption of the world."[17]

Blaming the social environment for personal problems has been encouraged in American society by the increasingly popular acceptance of the idea that the social environment overwhelmingly determines personal lives.[18] This takes us back once more to the relationship between the personal and the political with which this book began.

In Communist states this relationship was simplified, despite or because of the enormous pressures brought upon the citizen to curtail or politicize the private realm; there was little inclination to confuse or conflate the two, let alone to claim priority for the public-political over the private-personal domain. People in Communist societies were well aware of official policies aimed at expanding the political over the personal; they were encouraged or pressured to elevate public over private concerns, and they sought to resist these pressures with varying degrees of success.

It is in Western pluralistic societies that some radical groups have lately insisted on the subordination of the personal to political considerations, claiming that power relations are inescapable.[19] These radicals declare that even the most intimate personal realms and relationships are penetrated and determined by political criteria and considerations. They believe that personal unhappiness has ultimately political explanations, rooted in social injustice and political repression.

In another rendering, the relationship between these realms is exactly the opposite: it is the personal that trumps the political. This is the psychological perspective, still under the influence of Freud. In this perspective the deeply alienated, angry critics of society are consumed by a deep personal discontent that need have no political source or content. They project personal feelings—anger, frustration, and a sense of enduring grievance—upon the broader social environment; they may or may not be aware of the connection between their personal grievances and their social-critical disposition.

It is difficult to tell what makes a person truly angry and indignant: social injustice, such as racial, ethnic, or sexual discrimination; extreme inequalities of wealth; an unjust war; *or* a personal history of being neglected by parents, deprived of love and affection, poor health, or being ridiculed in school for some bodily deformity or personal peculiarity. One may wonder if it is possible for an individual to become deeply and genuinely enraged or indignant about social ills or political injustices of which he or she has had no personal experience and is unlikely ever to experience. This is not to say that such injustices cannot create strong disapproval of a less impulsive and emotional kind. The degree and kind of indignation hinges on the capacity to identify with the victim.

I do not contend here that there is no connection between the personal and the political. The question is how the two realms relate to one another. Instead of trying to designate one or the other as unambiguously determinant, it is more fruitful to ask in what manner and under what circumstances people connect individual, personal grievances with the grievances of others, with those of total strangers, anonymous masses, and groups, or with larger social causes and social injustices.

An obvious example may be a rape victim who becomes an ardent feminist. The victim of such deeply humiliating violence makes common cause with other women who were or could be similarly victimized. She seeks broader and deeper causes of her personal misfortune because it is easier to come to terms with personal suffering if it can be seen as part of a broader pattern of injustice—in other words, if it is shared.

The Vietnam War protest illustrates a more ambiguous fusion of personal and political. Many of the young male critics of the war might have been drafted (unless they had college deferments), hence they faced an element of personal risk that enhanced or colored their indignation over the destructiveness and pointlessness of the war that harmed millions of others.

On the other hand, the white radicals of the 1960s and '70s had no personal experience of racism and no risk of becoming its victim, yet they appeared to be genuinely outraged by it and vigorously protested it. Since the 1960s, every indictment of American society put forward by white social critics has focused on its racist character and the injustices and inequalities associated with it. Such protests against racism are not inauthentic, rather they are, or might be, part of a broader and deeper disposition linked to the "obscure personal rage" alluded to earlier in Horowitz's recollections of some of his fellow radicals.

There was little obscure in the personal rage of Jean Genet, the famous French writer with a criminal background, who offers another striking example of the tight connection between the personal and the political. An admirer of Genet wrote: "As early as 1974 Genet had said in the Paris newspaper *Le Monde*, 'It was completely natural for me to be attracted to the people who are not only the most unfortunate but also crystallize to the highest degree the hatred of the West. . . . I am drawn to people in revolt. And this is very natural for me, because I myself have the need to call the whole of society in question.'" The groups he was drawn to, indeed admired, were the Black Panthers in the United States, the Red Army Faction (urban terrorists) in Germany, and especially the Palestine Liberation Organization.

It was also observed of Genet that "he admits that political action filled the void left in his life when he was awakened from his reverie as an artist—a frank acknowledgment of his creative and personal despair." He felt "rage at his real mother for having abandoned him. Even when Genet was in his sixties he told someone that if he knew where his mother was buried he'd spit on the grave." This mother, an impoverished, unmarried servant girl, handed him to public welfare authorities when he was seven months old. In addition to such sources of bitterness, his homosexuality placed him into another minority despised at the time.

The elusive connections between the personal and the political are further illustrated in the case of Robert Scheer, one of David Horowitz's radical contemporaries. Horowitz observed that "he 'projected onto the socialist future the human connections he had failed to achieve in his own life.'" Horowitz knew other radicals too who "were disconnected from family and real community."[20] He seems to suggest that such personal isolation was a source of bitterness and resentfulness which found expression in radical political beliefs and attitudes, and especially in a search for community in the radical movements.

White radicals such as Bill Ayers detested the world and values of their parents. Their preoccupation with hypocrisy, later transformed into wide-ranging social criticism, were stimulated by what they observed at home—thus did the personal and political converge.

The difficulties of attaining a satisfactory sexual identity may be another example of the connections between the personal and political. Minority status and past discrimination against homosexuals and lesbians may be transformed into a resentment against the entire social system. This has clearly been the case of some well-known homosexual and lesbian activists and authors.

This emphasis on the connections between the personal and the political may be misused to reject well-founded social criticism. Thus if a case can be made that a protester or social critic is a chronic malcontent, unable or disinclined to separate his or her personal difficulties from larger social causes, his critiques of social injustice may be more easily dismissed. But there may be sound bases for social criticism, even if arrived at by an indirect route of personal grievances or experiences, by themselves irrelevant to political judgment or attitude. The fact that Herbert Aptheker had a black woman taking care of him as a child, and who became his loving "second mother," had a decisive and lasting impact and created a capacity for deep moral indignation about racial discrimination. But this highly personal experience does not invalidate his later critiques of the phenomenon.[21] On the other hand, this early experience does not validate or help explain his later conviction that capitalism was the prime source of racism.

At the same time one may still question the accuracy of embittered social criticism that reflects or suggests a profound and diffuse personal discontent, and cannot persuasively be derived from external political or sociological causes or considerations.

This study suggests that personal needs and motives are more likely to shape political attitudes and behavior than the other way round, at any rate in Western pluralistic societies. It is a different matter in regimented, totalitarian systems where the political institutions and authorities determine to a far greater degree the personal realm.

I have argued earlier (see especially Chapter 1) that the politicized view of the personality and personal relationships which prevailed among the radicals of the 1960s (and before them among many groups of revolutionaries at various times) is empirically incorrect and morally wrong. Disputes between men and women about who takes out the garbage or does the dishes do not constitute a power struggle. Not every dispute between human beings is colored by disagreements over the distribution of power. The proposition that the personal is generally subordinated to the political is empirically questionable. In the normal course of events, the political realm rarely determines the personal; people infrequently act out in clear-cut fashion their supposed political, collective, or "class" interests; political practices rarely reflect political theories or beliefs, though this sometimes happens with disastrous results. More often, the political is subordinated to personal needs, impulses, longings, or resentments, which tend to take precedence over other—public, group, or political—considerations. Sometimes it is impossible to disentangle the personal from the social.

People often join a political movement not so much because they find its goals congenial and admirable but in order to overcome personal isolation and find a sense of community they failed to find elsewhere. Political power is often sought not to accomplish political objectives but because those holding it enjoy wielding power or using it to enrich themselves and their families, or improve their social status. Mary McCarthy wrote: "Most men had come to socialism by some all-too-human compulsion: they were out of work, or lonely. Or sexually unsatisfied or foreign born or queer in one of a hundred bitter, irremediable ways."[22] Presumably this view was based on her observations at a particular moment in American society.

Individuals also take political positions to conform to the expectations of those around them, to gain their approval and moral support. Many pathways may lead to political participation or the pursuit of political power that have little to do with substantive political goals or programs.

Endorsing the supremacy of the political over the personal rests on the certitude that certain political beliefs and values are morally superior to purely personal needs, likes, and dislikes. To say the least, such subordination results in the impoverishment of the personal realm. Philip Roth observed through one of his literary characters: ". . . When you decide to contribute your personal problems to an ideology's agenda, everything that is personal is squeezed out and discarded and all that remains is what is useful to the ideology."[23] The true radical (Communist, feminist, nationalist, Muslim, or any other kind) feels obligated to toss aside bonds of family and friendship if they interfere with his or her political values or objectives; he or she must not allow the luxury of being friends with or compassionate toward those of different political persuasions. Individual hobbies and preferences must be abandoned when they compete with political tasks and obligations. Lenin famously deplored listening to Beethoven's *Kreutzer Sonata* since he thought it made him "soft"; he also gave up playing chess at an early age since it diverted him from more important political work.[24]

The identification or definition of political (class or collective) interests raises further questions: how can they be properly determined, and who has the authority and competence to do so? Radical true believers have a solution: when people act in ways antithetical to their supposed "true interests"—as, for example, by following religious beliefs, or being content to be housewives, or working hard for a capitalist employer, or voting for certain political parties or candidates, etc., etc.—they are diagnosed as suffering from false consciousness.

Eric Hoffer's concept of the "true believer" is also relevant to the relationship between the personal and the political. His views are similar to those of David Potter but are more boldly and uncompromisingly put forward. Hoffer postulates the existence of a type of person endowed with certain traits, attributes, and needs who becomes a true believer and thereby a political actor, a highly motivated, fervent participant in political conflicts: the extremist, the radical, the fanatic. He may support a wide variety of causes, secular-political or religious. What distinguishes him (rarely her) is the unconditional, nonrational commitment that has compelling psychological sources. Hoffer's message is loud and clear: the personal (or personality type) determines the political, the private the public. He writes:

> There is a certain uniformity in all types of dedication, of faith, of pursuit of power. . . . All forms of dedication, devotion, loyalty and self-surrender are in essence a desperate clinging to something which might give worth and meaning to our futile, spoiled lives. . . .
>
> . . . [The true believer's] sense of security is derived from his passionate attachment and not from the excellence of the cause. He embraces a cause . . . because of his desperate need for something to hold on to. . . . What matters is not the contents of the cause but the total dedication and the communion with a congregation. . . .[25]

Hoffer added: "It is the true believer's ability to 'shut his eyes and stop his ears' to facts that do not deserve to be either seen or heard. . . . And it is the certitude of his infallible doctrine that renders the true believer impervious to the uncertainties, surprises and unpleasant realities of the world around him."[26]

For many of those discussed above, Marxism-Leninism was such an infallible doctrine while they were under the spell of their political commitment. Its infallibility was posited in the official history of the Soviet Communist party: "The power of Marxist-Leninist theory lies in the fact that it enables the Party to find the right orientation in any situation, to understand the inner connection of current events, to foresee their course, and to perceive not only how and in what direction they are developing in the present but how and in what direction they are bound to develop in the future."[27]

By no means were all those described in this volume true believers as Hoffer defined them, but many displayed some of their characteristics.

Two large questions were at the root of this study: Why had some individuals experienced political disillusionment and come to express it, while others exposed to similar experiences did not? Secondly, how did moral sensibilities (the moral threshold) affect such disillusionment or resistance to it?

The first question may be answered in part by pointing out that, as far as Communist systems were concerned, the opportunity to express disaffection was quite limited and available only to those who had the opportunity to defect, were exiled, or belonged to the small number of dissenters willing to risk serious consequences for such expression. Thus it is not so difficult to explain why only a small number in these states came to express what were in fact widely shared sentiments. In the Western settings it is harder to explain why only a small number were willing to give public expression to such disenchantment, given the freedom of expression, the availability of political choices, and, more recently, the accumulation of new information further discrediting these systems. The primary explanation of such reluctance was found in the influence of adversarial subcultures, which made it easier to preserve earlier beliefs, commitments, and core values.

As to the second question about moral sensibilities and their impact on political attitudes, it was impossible to specify why some people found it easier to dismiss or redefine moral considerations, except by reference to personality differences.

This study strongly suggests that the durability and depth of commitment and faith (political and other) rest on the wish and the capacity to believe—a capacity that is an integral part of human beings. These wishes and capacities determine the different moral thresholds of different individuals, i.e., what they can or cannot accept morally.[28] *When* this threshold is crossed is influenced by the volume and quality of experiences that may undermine faith and commitment, and by the unique personal circumstances of the individual in question. It is impossible to specify the conditions when this happens, or to locate a clear-cut "moral breaking point," that is, to specify what kinds of actions, forms of behavior, or policies would *invariably* bring about unconditional moral indignation or revulsion, regardless of who commits these acts and under what circumstances. The discovery of such a moral threshold (or breaking point) would be proof that there is some kind of invincible and universal moral-ethical instinct, conscience, or superego that many of us would like to believe exists and that is immune to and independent of various religious or political doctrines, propaganda, fanaticism, deception, upbringing, and self-interest. Such a discovery may yet be made in different studies by other authors.

Some readers may conclude that much of my discussion, and especially my conclusions in this book, lean toward what is called in the social sciences "psychological reductionism." This is the tendency to give undue weight to personality and mental states, emotional factors, the subjective realm at the expense of more tangible, objective variables and realities found in the physical, social, or cultural environment, in historical events and conditions. I am a firm believer in an objective reality that exists outside our individual consciousness and is independent of our needs, wishes, and imaginings. Nonetheless the source materials utilized in this book impressed upon me (once more) the power of the human psyche to mold the perception and impact of objective reality according to personal needs and preferences. The ultimate, though not singular, determinants of both political attitude change and its persistence appear to have roots in this personal, psychological domain.

The findings of this study also lend themselves to some reflections about human nature, gloomy or more cheerful depending on the disposition of the reader. The darker conclusion to be drawn is that human beings have an apparently limitless capacity for wishful thinking and self-deception in order to preserve mistaken commitments and beliefs, and tirelessly cling to noxious illusions. Further evidence has been provided of the human capacity to venerate destructive causes, irrational beliefs, and brutal, inhumane leaders, and that the highly committed may altogether obscure or efface reality by their longings and hopes.

On the other hand, the disillusioned, and especially those who learned their hard lessons from living in Communist states, also show us that human beings are capable of learning from experience and mistakes, that many have the courage to reject comforting but groundless beliefs and adapt to a world with fewer illusions and false hopes.

Notes

Chapter 1. Political Belief and Personal Morality

1. Peter Berger, "History as a Disappointment Machine," *New York Times Book Review*, April 18, 1992, p. 9.

2. Daniel Bell, "The Fight for the 20th Century: Raymond Aron Versus Jean Paul Sartre," *New York Times Book Review*, February 18, 1990, p. 1.

3. *Political Pilgrims* (1981) by this author is one inventory of the strongly held political misjudgments of Western intellectuals.

4. The phenomenon I am alluding to is often called "cognitive dissonance" and its handling by the individual experiencing it is highly relevant to the process of (or resistance to) political disaffection. (See Leon Festinger, *A Theory of Cognitive Dissonance*, Stanford, Calif., 1957.) For a discussion of the phenomenon in a recent, post-Soviet context, see Peter Kenez, "Dealing with Discredited Beliefs," *Kritika*, Spring 2003, pp. 369–377.

5. Grace Paley, the American writer, was among those taking pride in her unwavering loyalty to the leftist beliefs of her youth and what she saw as a stable configuration of right and wrong. Apparently she found, throughout her life, comfort in "view[ing] herself as a prophet railing against the injustices of the world around her." According to a reviewer, ". . . for Paley, the left of her lifetime is all of a piece. Since the left contains good ideas, and since it is populated by good people, it stretches in one unbroken line from the 1950s to the 1990s." By contrast, she is fully convinced that "everything America does is immoral." The latter conviction is among the important continuities between the old and New Left she represents. Alan Wolfe, "The Saint," *New Republic*, June 29, 1998, pp. 36, 38.

6. Claud Cockburn, *Crossing the Line*, London, 1958, p. 183.

7. Quoted in James Atlas, *Bellow: A Biography*, New York, 2000, p. 575.

8. Isaac Deutscher, *Heretics and Renegades*, Indianapolis and New York, 1969 [first published 1957], pp. 14–15, 15, 18, 16, 13, 20, 16, 11, 15, 13.

9. Elsewhere in the same volume Deutscher, revealingly, ascribed the following desirable attitudes to an imaginary political leader in Eastern Europe: "The real choice, as he sees it, is not between tyranny and freedom, but between Stalinist tyranny, which is in part redeemed by economic and social progress, and a reactionary tyranny which would not be redeemed by anything." Ibid., p. 33.

10. Michael Walzer, *The Company of Critics*, New York, 1988, p. 232.

11. Richard Posner, *Public Intellectuals: A Study of Decline*, Cambridge, Mass., 2001, pp. 75, 182.

12. Michael Andre Bernstein, *Bitter Carnival: Resentment and the Abject Hero*, Princeton, 1992, p. 183.

13. See also Irving Kristol, "The Adversary Culture of Intellectuals," *Encounter*, October 1979, esp. p. 9, and Paul Hollander, "The Pursuit of Identity, Community and Social Justice: The Cult of Victimhood Revisited," in *Discontents: Postmodern and Post-Communist*, New Brunswick, N.J., 2002.

14. Edward Shils, "An Age of Embarrassment," *Encounter*, October 1978, p. 84.

15. Paul Hollander, "The Left Looks Back," *Wall Street Journal*, May 25, 1988.

16. Martin Peretz points out some of the similarities between the attitudes of Western apologists (in the politically correct churches) for the Communist systems of the past and contemporary apologists for Islamic terror. "Anglicans and Israel," *New Republic*, July 11 and 18, 2005.

17. The long-standing nature of these interests is indicated by the recent discovery of a paper I wrote in the 1959–1960 academic year when I was a first-year graduate student at the University of Illinois, Urbana, about "commitment and defection" in Communist movements and systems.

18. Mark Lilla, "An Idea Whose Time Has Gone," *New York Times Book Review*, July 25, 1999, p. 12.

19. Quoted in Rudolf Tokes, *Hungary's Negotiated Revolution*, New York, 1996, p. 469.

20. Hobsbawm affirmed this retrospective loyalty to the "Soviet Experiment" because, as he saw it, despite all the mass murders and great sufferings it had created "the chance of a new world being born in great suffering would still have been worth backing." Quoted in Robert Conquest, *Reflections on a Ravaged Century*, New York, 2000, pp. 10–11.

21. Quoted in Mark Lilla, *The Reckless Mind*, New York, 2001, p. 185.

22. Ibid. p. xi.

23. Ibid., p. 198.

24. In Richard Crossman, ed., *The God That Failed*, New York, 1950, p. 87.

25. Norman Podhoretz, "Why the God That Failed," in *The Bloody Crossroads: Where Literature and Politics Meet*, New York, 1986, p. 21. William Pfaff ranked this volume with *Darkness at Noon* and *Animal Farm* "as the most important and influential anti-Communist texts" of the wartime and postwar period. *The Bullet's Song*, New York, 2004, p. 265. For an earlier attempt to apply some of the insights of *The God That Failed* to the period following the collapse of Soviet communism, see Paul Hollander: "Which God Has Failed?", *New Criterion*, Fall 2001.

26. Crossman, *Failed*, pp. 11–12.

27. Ibid., pp. 183, 185.

28. See Noam Chomsky and Edward Herman, "Distortions at Fourth Hand," *The Nation*, June 25, 1977. See also their *After the Cataclysm: Postwar Indochina and the Reconstruction of Imperial Ideology*, Boston, 1979. The latter includes this memorable sentence about the massacres: ". . . evidence is slight and unreliable and informed opinion [!] ranges over quite a wide spectrum"[p. 290].

29. "12 Americans Stage Protest Hussein Is Happy to Allow," *New York Times*, October 27, 2002, p. 8.

30. Ramsey Clark, et al.: *Challenge to Genocide, Let Iraq Live!* International Action Center, New York, 1998, pp. 21, 27.

31. *Collected Essays of George Orwell*, Vol. III, London 1968, p. 369.

32. Stanley Milgram, "The Compulsion to Do Evil," *Patterns of Prejudice*, November–December 1967, p. 6.

33. This dubious idea can be traced at least as far back as Marx's romantic abhorrence of specialization, his belief that the division of labor was a major source of all evil and had to be eradicated. An illuminating analysis of the subordination of the personal to the political—in the Soviet Communist context—may be found in Nathan Leites, *A Study of Communism*, Glencoe, Ill., 1953.

34. Irving Howe, "Some Romance!," *New York Review of Books*, April 6, 1978, p. 12. Gornick's book was entitled *The Romance of American Communism*.

35. Vivian Gornick, *The Romance of American Communism*, New York, 1977, p. 265. See also Paul Hollander's review of it in *Contemporary Sociology*, January 1979, pp. 125–127.

36. Christopher Hitchens, *Letters to a Young Contrarian*, New York, 2001, pp. 112–113.

37. Crossman, *Failed*, p. 53.

38. Tony Judt, "The New Old World," *New Republic*, November 4, 2002, p. 26.

39. Crossman, *Failed*, p. 102.

40. Ibid., p. 216.

41. Isaiah Berlin, *The First and the Last*, New York, 1999, pp. 54–55, 57.

42. For a sampling of these attitudes, see Paul Hollander, "The Resilience of the Adversary Culture," *National Interest*, Summer 2002.

43. Quoted in Alexander Stille, "Apocalypse Soon," *New York Review of Books*, November 7, 2002, p. 49.

44. The most famous case was Mailer's patronage of Jack Henry Abbott, the murderer with literary aspirations, foreshadowed by Mailer's 1957 article on "The White Negro" which glorified criminal violence. The widespread glorification of the Black Panthers among white radicals and even liberals during the 1960s and '70s reflected a similar fascination with the seeming combination of strength, authenticity, and impassioned defiance of conventions and authority further legitimated by the historic victimization of blacks.

45. Crossman, *Failed*, p. 90.

46. Ibid., p. 134.

47. Ibid., p. 161.

48. Ibid., pp. 161, 163, 171.

49. On the treatment of intellectuals (visiting and resident) in Communist states, see *Political Pilgrims*, pp. 173–176, 262–267, 331–335.

50. Crossman, *Failed*, p. 186.

51. Ibid., pp. 189–190, 194, 202.

52. Ibid., pp. 209, 225, 226, 227, 228, 231.

53. Christopher Hitchens, *Love, Poverty and War*, New York, 2004, p. 267.

54. Ibid., p. 265.

Chapter 2. Behind the Iron Curtain: The Soviet Union and Eastern Europe

1. Social-political systems may be assessed either by the intensity of the desire of their own citizens to leave them or, conversely, by their attraction to immigrants. Elaborate measures such as the "Iron Curtain" to prevent unauthorized departure are a revealing indicator of official determination to prevent citizens from "voting with their feet."

2. It is also the conclusion of the only study of Soviet defectors I am aware of that most of them were "ideological defectors" or "escapees of concience." Vladislav Krasnov, *Soviet Defectors: The KGB Wanted List*, Stanford, Calif., 1986, pp. 44, 162.

3. For the small literature on defectors, see Krasnov, *Soviet Defectors*, and Gordon Brook-Shepherd, *The Storm Petrels: The First Soviet Defectors, 1928–1938*, New York, 1977. See also Ch. 2, "Defectors and Exiles: Disillusionment Before the Fall," in my book *Political Will and Personal Belief: The Decline and Fall of Soviet Comunism*, New Haven, 1999.

4. In J. Arch Getty and Roberta T. Manning, eds., *Stalinist Terror: New Perspectives*, New York, 1993, pp. 40–41.

5. Mary McCarthy, "My Confession" [1954] in Stephen Spender, Irving Kristol, and Melvin J. Lasky, eds., *Encounters: An Anthology*, New York, n.d. [1953–1963], pp. 34, 40.

6. For example, the FBI did not realize until 1953 "that the greatest expert on Soviet subversion and espionage [Alexander Orlov] had been living quietly in their midst for the past fifteen years." Brook-Shepherd, *Petrels*, p. 225. See also ibid., pp. 215, 244. For a discussion of official unease in the United States about defectors in the period of detente, see C. Fenyvesi, "The Unwelcome Defector," *New Republic*, April 22, 1978.

7. Frederick Schuman, "Horrors of Bolshevism Inc.," *New Republic*, May 6, 1946, pp. 667–668.

8. "Rash U.S. Cheers for Soviet Defectors," Letter by Von Laue, *New York Times*, October 10, 1979.

9. Quoted in James William Crowl, *Angels in Paradise*, Washington, D.C., 1982, p. 143.

10. Ibid., pp. 145, 166.

11. Susan Sontag, "Communism and the Left," *The Nation*, February 27, 1982, p. 230.

12. See Alex Inkeles and Raymond Bauer, *The Soviet Citizen*, Cambridge, Mass., 1959, and by the same authors plus Clyde Kluckholn, *How the Soviet System Works*, Cambridge, Mass., 1956; see also James R. Millar, ed., *Politics, Work and Daily Life in the USSR: A Survey of Former Soviet Citizens*, Cambridge, England, 1987. These studies were based on information obtained from refugees.

13. Chomsky ridiculed the Cambodian refugee accounts and declared them untrustworthy. Chomsky and Edward Herman, "Distortions at Fourth Hand"; see also their *After the Cataclysm*, Boston, 1979. More recently the *New York Times* columnist Nicholas D. Kristof voiced doubts about the credibility of refugee reports about conditions in North Korean concentration camps. "Survivors Report Torture in North Korean Labor Camps," *New York Times*, July 14, 1996.

14. Alexander Orlov, *The Secret History of Stalin's Crimes*, New York, 1953, pp. ix–x.
15. Brook-Shepherd, *Petrels*, pp. 202–203.
16. Orlov, *Crimes*, p. 259. Quotations from Orlov that follow are from this book, pp. 7–342, passim.
17. David Kelly, "Introduction" to G. A. Tokaev, *Betrayal of an Ideal*, Bloomington, Ind., 1955, p. ix.
18. Ibid., p. 218. Quotations from Tokaev that follow, except as noted, are from this book, pp. 31–321, passim.
19. G. A. Tokaev, *Comrade X*, London, 1956, pp. 271, 282.
20. Tokaev, *Betrayal*, p. 172.
21. Ibid., pp. 203–204.
22. Tokaev, *Comrade X*, p. 82.
23. Ibid., pp. 233–235.
24. Tokaev, *Betrayal*, p. 195.
25. Tokaev, *Comrade X*, pp. 103–104. Further quotations from Tokaev are from this book, pp. 45–359, passim.
26. Peter Bond, "Obituary of Grigori Tokaty" (his name in his native Ossetian language), *The Independent* (London), November 23, 2003.
27. Lev Kopelev, *Ease My Sorrows: A Memoir*, New York, 1983, p. 218.
28. Lev Kopelev, *To Be Preserved Forever*, Philadelphia, 1977, p. 259.
29. Lev Kopelev, *The Education of a True Believer*, New York, 1980, p. 235.
30. Ibid., pp. 250–251.
31. Ibid., pp. 249–250.
32. Kopelev, *Preserved*, pp. 12–13.
33. Kopelev, *Education*, pp. 289–290.
34. Ibid., p. 267.
35. Kopelev, *Preserved*, p. 92.
36. Ibid., p. 93.
37. Kopelev, *Sorrows*, p. 246. Further quotations from Kopelev, except as noted, are from this book, pp. 11–244, passim.
38. Kopelev, *Education*, p. 197.
39. "Afterword" in Kopelev, *Preserved*, p. 266.
40. Kopelev, *Sorrows*, p. 245.
41. Ibid., p. 248.
42. I have also written about Kravchenko, Shevchenko, Yakovlev, Leonhard, Hegedus, and Mlynar in *Political Will and Personal Belief*.
43. Victor Kravchenko, *I Chose Freedom*, New York, 1946, p. 31. The quotations that follow are from pp. 3–452, passim.
44. Arkady N. Shevchenko, *Breaking with Moscow*, New York, 1985, p. 85. The quotations that follow are from pp. 18–445, passim.
45. Alexander N. Yakovlev, *The Fate of Marxism in Russia*, New Haven, Conn., 1993, and *A Century of Violence in Soviet Russia*, New Haven, Conn., 2002.
46. Yakovlev, *Century*, p. 4.
47. Ibid., p. 7.
48. Ibid., Foreword, p. xv.
49. Stephen F. Cohen and Katrina van den Heuvel, eds., *Voices of Glasnost*, New York, 1989, p. 42.
50. Ibid., p. 33.
51. Yakovlev, *Marxism*, p. 2.
52. Yakovlev, *Century*, pp. 8, 9.
53. Yakovlev, *Marxism*, pp. 130, 4, 130–131, 4, 59, 47, 44–45, 52, 58, 49.
54. Ibid., pp. 58, 49.
55. Ibid., pp. 9, 54, 15, 29, 17.
56. Wolfgang Leonhard, *Child of the Revolution*, Chicago, 1958, p. 4. Quotations to follow from this book are from pp. 4–508, passim.
57. Arthur Koestler, "Soviet Myth and Reality" in *The Yogi and the Commissar*, New York, 1961, pp. 123–124.
58. The discussion that follows is based on Hegedus's memoir, *Under the Spell of History and Power* (in Hungarian), Budapest, 1988, and on a conversation I had with him in

August 1992 in Budapest. Quotations from the memoir are from pages 127–342, passim. (All Hungarian sources quoted were translated by me unless otherwise indicated.)

59. In Hungary, members of the party's Politburo ". . . could obtain their daily necessities in secret, exclusive stores free of charge. . . . They were also provided with an open account from which they could draw any amount they wished without being required to account for their expenses. . . . They paid no rent, their clothing was also paid for by the party . . . as were their household employees, including gardener and chauffeur. . . . They lived not under socialism but communism where—according to the teachings of Marx, Engels, Lenin and Stalin—money had no longer any value and everybody could gratify his or her needs as deemed appropriate." Tamas Aczel and Tibor Meray, *Tisztito Vihar* (Cleansing Storm), Munich, 1978, pp. 268–269. Yeltsin made virtually identical remarks about the way of life of the Soviet party elite (nomenklatura) in his *Against the Grain*, New York, 1990, p. 70.

60. Zdenek Mlynar, *Night Frost in Prague*, London, 1980, p. 7. Quotations to follow were drawn from the same volume pp. 3–259, passim.

61. Julius Hay, *Born 1900*, La Salle, Ill., 1975, pp. 48–49. Quotations to follow from this book are from pp. 21–372, passim.

62. For good reasons, such as Brecht suggested, the show trials in Hungary were called "conceptual trials."

63. Serge Kirov was a high-ranking party official in Leningrad whose assassination in 1934 triggered the beginning of mass terror. There has been much speculation that he was killed on Stalin's order.

64. Sandor Revesz, *Egyetlen Elet: Gimes Miklos Tortenete* (A Single Life: The Story of Miklos Gimes), Budapest, 1999, pp. 221, 5. Preface by Gyorgy Litvak. The quotations from this book that follow are from pp. 37–425, passim.

65. Aczel and Meray, *Vihar*, p. 276.

Chapter 3. In the Third World: Vietnam and China

1. For a sampling of such accounts, see Paul Hollander, ed., *From the Gulag to the Killing Fields*, Wilmington, Del., 2006.

2. Bui Tin, *Following Ho Chi Minh: Memoirs of a North Vietnamese Colonel*, Honolulu, 1995, p. 6. The quotations to follow are from this book, pp. 6–191, passim.

3. Bui Tin, *From Enemy to Friend*, Annapolis, 2002, p. 121.

4. Truong Nhu Tang, *Vietcong Memoir: An Inside Account of the Vietnam War and Its Aftermath*, New York, 1985, p. 1. The quotations to follow are from pp. 4–289 of this book, passim.

5. Such scenes reminded this author of those he observed on the streets of Budapest in 1945, swarming with newly arrived Soviet troops who also appeared to be impressed by being in a country richer than their own and who were availing themselves of everything they could carry, from wristwatches to bathroom fixtures and furniture.

6. Merle Goldman, "Foreword" to Liu Binyan: *China's Crisis, China's Hope*, Cambridge, Mass., 1990, pp. vii–viii.

7. Liu Binyan, *A Higher Kind of Loyalty: A Memoir*, New York, 1990, p. 7. Other quotations to follow are from the same book, pp. 8–276, passim.

8. Simon Leys offered a striking description of these attitudes and practices: ". . . in China people have now at their disposal two levels of language: one, human and natural, which allows them to speak in their own voice and which they use to talk about their health, the weather, food . . . and so forth and another one, mechanical and shrill, to talk about politics. . . . During one conversation, the person . . . may well switch several times from his normal voice to a kind of ideologic ventriloquism, according to the topics." Simon Leys, *Chinese Shadows*, New York, 1977, p. 168.

9. Fang Lizhi, *Bringing Down the Great Wall*, New York, 1991, p. 317. Unless otherwise indicated, further quotations to follow are from the same book, pp. xviii–317, passim.

10. H. Lyman Miller, *Science and Dissent in Post-Mao China*, Seattle, Wash., 1996, pp. 18, 125.

11. Ibid., pp. 215–216, 234, 268, 19–20.

12. Wei Jingsheng, *The Courage to Stand Alone*, New York, 1997, p. 230. Unless otherwise indicated, further quotations from this book are from pp. 19–251, passim.

13. Sophia Woodman, "Wei Jingsheng's Lifelong Battle for Democracy," in ibid., p. 251.

14. Ibid., pp. 259–260.
15. Gary Rivlin, "A Long March from Maoism to Microsoft," *New York Times*, December 5, 2004.
16. Sidney Rittenberg and Amanda Bennett, *The Man Who Stayed Behind*, New York, 1993, p. 22. The quotations that follow are from the same book, pp. 31–453, passim.
17. In one remarkable case the staff from Rittenberg's office was taken to a model farm and shown a "phenomenal harvest" of wheat that was produced on a small plot of land by dense planting. But the density prevented sufficient air and light to reach the stalks of wheat. The problem was "solved" by "long boards that stretched across the field . . . every six feet or so. Village children at either side tugged on the ropes activating the boards that fanned the wheat from side to side. . . . Otherwise . . . the grain would die from lack of air and sunlight." Ibid., p. 227.

Chapter 4. In the Third World: Cuba, Nicaragua, and Ethiopia

1. Carlos Franqui, *Family Portrait with Fidel: A Memoir*, New York, 1984, p. 210. Unless otherwise indicated, other quotations from this book are from pp. 18–224, passim.
2. Heberto Padilla, *Self-Portrait of the Other*, New York, 1990, pp. 40, 41, 42.
3. Ibid., p. 39.
4. Raymond Aron, *The Opium of Intellectuals*, London, 1957, pp. 35, 43.
5. I am not suggesting that Castro's popularity was wholly artificial. He was certainly admired in the early years of his rule, but given the police state conditions that have prevailed in Cuba it is impossible to establish when his popularity began to wane or how widespread it was at different times, how his positive and negative perceptions competed among the population, and which groups were more or less susceptible to his charisma.
6. Padilla, p. 28. Further quotations are from the same book, pp. 49–244, passim.
7. Rafael del Pino, "Inside Castro's Bunker," manuscript, n.d., p. 1. The quotations that follow are from this manuscript, pp. 19–222, passim.
8. Gioconda Belli, *The Country Under My Skin: A Memoir of Love and War*, New York, 2002, p. 15. All citations from the book are from pp. ix–325, passim.
9. See "The Appeals of Revolutionary Violence: Latin American Guerillas and American Intellectuals," in Paul Hollander, *The Survival of the Adversary Culture*, New Brunswick, N.J., 1988, pp. 207–232.
10. Stephen Kinzer, "Love in a Time of Revolution," *New York Review of Books*, November 21, 2002, p. 13.
11. Davit Wolde Giorgis, *Red Tears*, Trenton, N.J., 1989, pp. 3–4. Further citations from this book are from pp. 1–365, passim.
12. The Ethiopian authorities, like those of other Communist states, were quite successful in misleading public opinion abroad about some of their most destructive policies, such as the forcible resettlement of peasants. Members of an American aid group called "USA for Africa," taken to resettlement sites, "saw only what was programmed by Party officials, who had carefully prepared places for foreign viewing and secretly assigned people they could talk to." Party activists were disguised as peasants to talk to the foreigners who consequently "found the 'peasants' cheerful, willing and in excellent health." The "USA for Africa" delegation was also led to believe that patients in the hospital they were shown were famine victims whereas they were casualties of the civil war. Ibid., pp. 217–218.
13. Giorgis does not say who financed his studies at Columbia—his family, the government of Ethiopia, or the university.
14. Clifford D. May, "Africa to Jersey: A Relief Worker Fights Poverty," *New York Times*, November 29, 1988.

Chapter 5. Disillusionment in the West: I

1. Howard Fast, *The Naked God: The Writer and the Communist Party*, New York, 1957, p. 38. The quotations that follow are from this book, pp. 19–136, passim.
2. In another, later memoir (*Being Red*, Boston, 1990, pp. 139–149), Fast describes the incident somewhat differently. First, he says that he and his comrades prevailed on the ambassador, who then asked the driver to join them for lunch. Second, he relates a subsequent conversation with his wife about the incident in which his wife argued, and convinced him, that his demand that the driver eat with them was an expression of an unrealistic romantic egalitarianism.

3. Fast, *Being Red*, pp. 86, 90. Further quotations are from this book, pp. 86–355, passim.

4. David Horowitz, *Radical Son*, New York, 1998, p. 2. Unless otherwise indicated, citations to follow are from his book, pp. 8–358, passim.

5. Michael Klare wrote: "There are a handful of former 60s radicals who have followed David Horowitz and Peter Collier in repudiating their militant New Leftism and in embracing the crass materialism of the Reagan epoch." Letter, *New York Times Magazine*, August 13, 1989. Alexander Cockburn called Horowitz a "renegade," "career opportunist," and "self-advertising turncoat." See his *The Golden Age Is Us*, London, 1995, pp. 9, 215–216.

6. Arthur Koestler, "The Complex Issue of Ex-Communists," in Patrick A. Swan, ed., *Alger Hiss, Whittaker Chambers and the Schism in the American Soul*, Wilmington, Del., 2002, p. 52.

7. Kingsley Amis in Swan, *Hiss*, p. 101.

8. Quoted in Edward Alexander, *Irving Howe: Socialist, Critic, Jew*, Bloomington, Ind., 1998, p. 114.

9. Email, September 12, 2002.

10. Some of the discussion to follow overlaps a review I wrote of Radosh's memoir in the Summer 2002 issue of *Academic Questions*.

11. See also John Bunzel, ed., *Political Passages*, New York, 1988.

12. Ronald Radosh, *Commies: A Journey Through the Old Left, the New Left and the Leftover Left*, San Francisco, 2001.

13. Ronald Radosh and Joyce Milton, *The Rosenberg File: A Search for the Truth*, New York, 1983.

14. Radosh, *Commies*, p. 160.

15. Ibid., p. 25.

16. Ibid., pp. 44–45.

17. John Corry, "California Coed Is Red Party's Foremost Ingenue," *New York Times*, November 21, 1965.

18. Radosh, *Commies*, p. 118.

19. Ibid., pp. 125, 127.

20. Malcolm Muggeridge wrote of these attitudes among favorably disposed visitors to the Soviet Union in the 1930s: "They were earnest advocates of the human killing of cattle who looked up at the massive headquarters of the OGPU [political police] with tears of gratitude in their eyes, earnest advocates of proportional representation who eagerly assented when the necessity of the Dictatorship of the Proletariat was explained to them, earnest clergymen who walked reverently through anti-God museums . . . earnest pacifists who watched delightedly tanks rattle across Red Square. . . . earnest town-planning specialists who stood outside overcrowded ramshackle tenements and muttered: 'If only we had something like this in England!'" *The Sun Never Sets*, New York, 1940, p. 79.

21. "The Intellectual in Politics: The Case of the Webbs," *Journal of Contemporary History*, No. 3, 1971, p. 11.

22. Quoted in Ronald Radosh, ed., *The New Cuba: Paradoxes and Potentials*, New York, 1976, pp. 64, 65.

23. Radosh, *Commies*, p. 128.

24. Ibid., pp. 139, 147, 152, 156, 157.

25. Ibid., p. 171.

26. Ibid., pp. 175, 182, 179, 184, 185.

27. See Eugene D. Genovese, "The Origins and Progress of the Historical Society—Presidential Address," pamphlet, Boston, 1999.

28. Genovese, "The Question," *Dissent*, Summer 1994, p. 374.

29. Quoted in Christopher Hitchens, "Radical Pique," *Vanity Fair*, February 1994, p. 32.

30. The incident was discussed in ibid., p. 32.

31. Genovese, "Critical Legal Studies as Radical Politics and Ideology," *Yale Journal of Law and the Humanities*, Vol. 3 (Winter 1991), pp. 131.

32. Ibid., p. 9.

33. Genovese, "The Question," p. 375.

34. Review of Frank E. Manuel, *A Requiem for Karl Marx, National Review*, January 29, 1966, p. 66.

35. Ibid., p. 66.

36. The conversation took place on April 16, 2003, in his home in Atlanta. The letters date from 2005.

37. Genovese, "The Collapse of Socialism: A View from the Left," presentation at the American Enterprise Institute in Washington, D.C., May 1992, p. 2.

38. Ibid., p. 4.

39. Ibid., p. 3.

40. Letter from Ronnie Dugger, *Dissent*, Winter 1995, p. 143; letter from Charles Bloomstein, ibid., pp. 141–142.

41. Genovese, AEI speech, p. 1.

Chapter 6. Disillusionment in the West: II

1. Lessing "vehemently denies that she is, or ever was, a feminist: 'I wasn't an active feminist in the sixties; never have been. I never liked the movement because it was too ideologically based.'" Angela Lambert, "I Haven't Changed One Bit—Interview," *Sunday Telegraph* (London), November 19, 2000. Even if she was not a "movement feminist," she was concerned with the condition of women in Western societies and examined it in several of her books, notably in *The Golden Notebook* (1962) and *The Summer Before the Dark* (1973).

2. Doris Lessing, *Conversations*, edited by Earl G. Ingersoll, Princeton, 1994, p. 105.

3. London, 2002.

4. Lesley Hazelton, "Doris Lessing on Feminism, Communism and Space Fiction," *New York Times Magazine*, July 25, 1982, p. 28.

5. Hitchens, *Letters to a Young Contrarian*, p. 102.

6. Doris Lessing, *Under My Skin*, New York, 1994, p. 284.

7. Lessing, *Walking in the Shade*, New York, 1997, p. 193.

8. Lessing, *Skin*, p. 396.

9. Lessing, *Walking*, p. 265.

10. Lessing, *Skin*, p. 284.

11. Christopher Hitchens, *Why Orwell Matters*, New York, 2002, p. 58.

12. Lessing, *Skin*, p. 179.

13. Lessing, *Conversations*, p. 223.

14. Lessing, *Skin*, p. 281.

15. Ibid., p. 259.

16. Lessing, *Walking*, pp. 57–59.

17. Lessing, *Skin*, pp. 270, 271, 277, 280, 281.

18. Lessing, *Prisons We Choose to Live Inside*, New York, 1987, p. 23.

19. Lessing, *Walking*, pp. 24, 222.

20. Lessing, *Skin*, p. 302.

21. Lessing, *Walking*, pp. 294–295, 166.

22. Ibid., pp. 115–116.

23. Ibid., pp. 194, 218.

24. Lessing, *Conversations*, pp. 210, 211.

25. Lessing, *Skin*, p. 282.

26. Lessing, *Walking*, pp. 76–77, 77, 85, 87.

27. Lessing, *Skin*, p. 397.

28. Louis Menand, "Both Sides Now," review of *The Sweetest Dream*, *New Yorker*, February 18 and 25, 2002, p. 193.

29. Lessing, *Skin*, pp. 15–16.

30. Lessing, *Walking*, p. 380.

31. I met Halperin in Vancouver in 1985, well before the present study was conceived. I was interested in meeting him because he was one of the few academic specialists in Latin American affairs and author of books on Cuba critical of the political system established under Castro.

32. His supposed career as a spy is of no great importance for my examination of the evolution of his political beliefs. It does, however, confirm the depth of his early commitments, which he later abandoned. The biography cited below thoroughly examines the matter of his spying without reaching definitive conclusions. In a later article the biographer regretfully concluded—based on an extensive review of the evidence—that he had spied for the Soviet Union during World War II while working for the Office of Strategic Services. See Don S. Kirschner, *On Oral History: A Cautionary Note*, unpublished manuscript, 2002.

33. Halperin's books are: *The Rise and Decline of Fidel Castro*, Berkeley, Calif., 1972; *The Taming of Fidel Castro*, Berkeley, Calif., 1981; and *Return to Havana: The Decline of Cuban Society Under Castro*, Nashville, Tenn., 1994.

34. Don S. Kirschner, *Cold War Exile: The Unclosed Case of Maurice Halperin*, Columbia, Mo., 1995, pp. 34, 42. The subtitle refers to the possibility that Halperin was in the 1940s a Soviet spy.

35. Kirschner, *Oral History*, p. 19.

36. Halperin, *Return*, p. 7.

37. Kirschner, *Exile*, pp. 34, 42.

38. Kirschner, *Exile*, pp. 53–54. Unless otherwise noted, further quotations from Kirschner are from this book, pp. 34–232, passim.

39. Halperin, *Return*, p. 17. Unless otherwise noted, further quotations from Halperin are from this book, pp. 17–190, passim.

40. Halperin, *Taming*, pp. 86, 136.

41. Boris Yeltsin, *Against the Grain: An Autobiography*, New York, 1990, pp. 70, 162–163.

42. At the beginning of my writing about Sontag's political attitudes, I sent her a letter (in the care of her publisher) informing her of my work and asking if she would respond to some questions about her political attitude change. I received no response.

43. Among her memorable errors, we may recall one that exemplifies projection in its purest form: her belief that the qualities of life she missed in inorganic, dead, dehumanized, inauthentic America were abundant in Castro's Cuba. The latter possessed a "new sensibility" and "a southern spontaneity which . . . our own too white, death-ridden culture denies us. . . . The Cubans know a lot about spontaneity, gaiety, sensuality and freaking out. They are not linear, desiccated creatures of print culture." Quoted in Roger Kimball, *The Long March*, San Francisco, 2000, p. 94. In the same spirit, she reached the conclusion after a short visit to North Vietnam that "the phenomenon of existential agony, of alienation just don't appear among the Vietnamese" who are "'whole' human beings not 'split' as we are." Quoted in Hollander, *Political Pilgrims*, p. 271.

44. There has been much discussion of the decline or disappearance of the public intellectual, supposedly replaced by the rarefied specialist speaking to small audiences about esoteric issues. See, for example, Richard Sennett, *The Fall of Public Man*, New York, Knopf, 1976; Russell Jacoby, *The Last Intellectuals: American Culture in the Age of Academe*, New York, 1987; Richard Posner, *Public Intellectuals, A Study of Decline*, Cambridge, 2002.

45. Carl Rollyson and Lisa Paddock, *Susan Sontag: The Making of an Icon*, New York, 2000, p. 122.

46. Susan Sontag in "Talk of the Town," *New Yorker*, September 24, 2001, p. 32.

47. In her article ostensibly devoted to questioning the propriety of calling the anti-terrorist measures a "war," she wrote: "This antiterror war can never end. That is one sign that it is not a war, but rather a mandate for expanding the use of American power." "Real Battles and Empty Metaphors," *New York Times*, op-ed, September 10, 2002.

48. Peter Berger, "'Sincerity' and 'Authenticity' in Modern Society," *Public Interest*, Spring 1973, p. 83.

49. Quoted in Carol Ianonnone, "Lionel Trilling and the Barbarians at the Gate," *Academic Questions*, Winter 2001–2002, p. 9.

50. Rollyson and Paddock, *Sontag*, p. 17.

51. Leland Poague, ed., *Conversations with Susan Sontag*, Jackson, Miss., 1995, pp. 98, 99, 100, 101, 103–104, 104.

52. "Communism and the Left," *The Nation*, February 27, 1982, pp. 230, 231, 238.

53. Rollyson and Paddock, *Sontag*, p. 222.

54. Charles Ruas, "Susan Sontag: Past, Present and Future," *New York Times Book Review*, October 24, 1982, p. 11.

55. Apparently this essay, or the idea of it, originated in her intention to respond to my *Political Pilgrims*, which was critical of her enthusiastic reports from Cuba and Vietnam. Hilton Kramer reported that at a dinner party she revealed to him her intention to write such an essay: "I asked her what she was working on. Imagine my astonishment upon being told that she was writing an article for the *New York Review of Books* that would constitute a 'reply' to Hollander's book. He shouldn't—she said in a tone of moral indignation—be allowed to get away with it. The article, of course, never appeared. No doubt it was overtaken by events—the crackdown in Poland . . . and the increasing influence here of certain emigré writers from

Communist countries, Joseph Brodsky among them—which would have made a 'reply' to Hollander . . . somewhat problematical. Instead of this lost reply to Hollander, Sontag presently gave us . . . her famous Town Hall speech. . . ." Hilton Kramer: "Anti-Communism and the Sontag Circle," *New Criterion*, September 1986, p. 5.

56. Quoted in Poague, *Conversations*, pp. 209–210. Presumably she was referring to the same essay in which she would rebut *Political Pilgrims*.

57. Ibid., p. 210.

58. Susan Sontag, "A Lament for Bosnia," *The Nation*, December 25, 1995, p. 819.

59. Quoted in Kramer, "Sontag Circle," p. 3.

60. See *Political Pilgrims*, pp. 177–222, 223–277.

61. Rollyson and Paddock, *Sontag*, p. 188.

62. Ibid. The "internal exile" metaphor comes from David Horowitz, "Can There Be a Decent Left? Michael Walzer's Second Thoughts," *FrontPageMagazine.com*, March 26, 2001, p. 2.

63. Rollyson and Paddock, *Sontag*, p. 186.

64. Ibid., p. 303.

65. Christopher Hitchens, *For the Sake of Argument*, New York, 1993, pp. 112, 114.

66. Ibid., p. 114.

67. This was conveyed in a phone conversation on April 17, 2005. The comment paraphrased in the text was a response to my question, "If you were to reprint this article, would you add a postscript or make any changes?"

68. Hitchens, "Minority Report," *The Nation*, April 10, 1989, pp. 474–475.

69. Hitchens, *Prepared for the Worst*, New York, 1988, p. 4.

70. Hitchens, *Love, Poverty and War*, New York, 2004, p. 434.

71. *FrontPageMagazine*, December 29, 2004, p. 3. Page numbers refer to the printed verson of this on-line publication.

72. Much of the preceding and following discussion benefited from the long phone conversation I had with Hitchens on April 14, 2005, and another on the 17th, as well as from earlier email exchanges and a meeting in Washington, D.C., in June 2004.

73. Hitchens, *Letters to a Young Contrarian*, New York, 2001, p. 105.

74. Hitchens, *Love*, p. xiii.

75. Hitchens, *Letters*, pp. 111–112.

76. Hitchens, *Love*, p. xiii.

77. Hitchens, *Letters*, p. 55.

78. He first came to the United States as a visitor in 1970 on a fellowship from Oxford, made further visits during the 1970s already determined to move here, and finally in 1981 came with a one-way ticket. He told me that he felt a strong attraction to the United States from age eighteen that he could not fully explain.

79. Hitchens, "American Notes," *Times Literary Supplement*, September 23, 1983, p. 1020.

80. Hitchens, *Love*, pp. 222, xiv.

81. Ibid., p. 223.

82. Hitchens, "Bukharin Would Have Approved," *New Statesman*, July 25, 1980. In a letter to me dated April 3, 1995, he objected to my characterization of his views on Angola and pointed out that he "had a number of arguments with MPLA [the ruling Communist party] officials and their Western admirers on that trip." He further argued that his interest in and support for Third World revolutions was rooted in the desire "to forestall and to criticize attempted replays of Stalinism."

83. Hitchens, *Prepared*, pp. 281, 174.

84. Ibid., p. 253.

85. Hitchens, *Argument*, p. 110.

86. Hitchens, *Love*, pp. 392–393, 392.

87. Ibid., p. 384.

88. Ibid., pp. 385, 375, 380.

89. Mark Falcoff, "Watching Christopher Hitchens," *Commentary*, January 2003, p. 43.

90. Hitchens, *Love*, p. xi.

91. Personal communication.

92. Interview with Jamie Glazov in *FrontPageMagazine.com*, December 10, 2003.

93. Falcoff, "Watching," p. 42.

94. Hitchens, "Where the Twain Should Have Met," *Atlantic*, September 2003, p. 156.

95. Personal communication.
96. Hitchens, *Letters*, p. 102.
97. Glazov interview.
98. Hitchens, *Letters*, p. 98.
99. Ibid., pp. 137–138.
100. Glazov interview, pp. 1–2.
101. Hitchens, *Letters*, p. 136.
102. Glazov interview, p. 2; Hitchens, *Love*, pp. 43, 46.
103. Hitchens, *Love*, p. 51.
104. Hitchens, "Goodbye to All That," *New York Review of Books*, July 17, 1997, p. 23. In the same article Hitchens in passing refers to I. F. Stone as "a person professionally skeptical" who "forgot himself" when confessing that Che Guevara reminded him of Jesus. This remark was not the only indication of the limits of Stone's alleged "professional skepticism." He rarely evinced skepticism about any sweeping denunciation of American foreign or domestic policies and policymakers. Hitchens's perception of Stone as "professionally skeptical" is probably conditioned by taking for granted (at the time of his writing) that even the most sweeping critiques of the United States were compatible with a skeptical mind-set.
105. Hitchens, *Prepared*, pp. 58–77.
106. *FrontPage* interview 2004, cited p. 8.
107. Ibid.
108. Hitchens, *Love*, p. 426.
109. Ibid., p. 418.
110. Hitchens, "Taking Sides," *The Nation*, October 14, 2002, p. 9. In the same column he announced his resignation as a columnist for *The Nation*.
111. "So Long, Fellow Travelers," *Washington Post*, October 20, 2002.
112. *FrontPage* interview 2004, p. 3.
113. "So Long, Fellow Travelers."
114. Glazov interview 2003.
115. It is of some interest that Hitchens did not support the 1991 war against Iraq occasioned by its occupation of Kuwait, as was made clear in his 1991 article in *Harper's* entitled "Realpolitik in the Gulf: A Game Gone Tilt," reprinted in his *For the Sake of Argument*.
116. Glazov interview 2003, p. 3.
117. *The Nation*, February 27, 1982, p. 231.
118. Hitchens, *Love*, p. 67.

Chapter 7. Disaffection and Resisting It: The Rank and File in the West

1. *Political Will and Personal Belief*, New Haven, Conn., 1999.
2. I was obliged to read this novel as a high school student in Hungary. I also discussed it in my doctoral dissertation, which examined the political functions of socialist realism, the official Soviet doctrine of literary creativity. The novel is a preeminent example of socialist realism at its worst and is most unconvincingly didactic.
3. The interview took place in his home in San Jose, California, on December 28, 1994, and was taped with his agreement. The following discussion is based on this tape.
4. Interview of Herbert Aptheker by Robin D. G. Kelley, *Journal of American History*, June 2000.
5. The long and respectful obituary in the *New York Times* (March 20, 2003), which made barely any reference to his support of the Soviet Union under Stalin and its policies at home and abroad, is another reflection of his excellent reputation in liberal circles.
6. Kelley interview, cited p. 14.
7. Doris Lessing believes that such high expectations are not peculiar to the United States but are widespread in contemporary Western societies.

Chapter 8. Patterns of Disillusionment

1. Geoffrey Wheatcroft, "Old Believers," *Encounter*, March 1990, p. 48.
2. Erica Manfred, "I Was a Red-Diaper Baby," *New York Times Magazine*, November 2, 1997, p. 84.
3. Christopher Hitchens, *Orwell's Victory*, London, 2002, p. 40.

4. The determination of Communist authorities to deceive important visitors is exemplified by the following incident: "Taking a leaf from Potemkin's book . . . the Soviet security services were not at all worried about hosting foreign visitors, and the more intellectual the better. Eduard Herriot, the left-wing French prime minister, visited Ukraine at the time of the famine. He met only smiling children who said they ate meat pies every day. He asked to visit a church and so the Cheka [the name of the political police at the time] turned a warehouse that had been a church back into an appropriate stage set, where they dressed up in disguise as worshipers and their local commander stuck on a false beard and pretended to be a priest. Herriot was . . . entirely assured." Zvetan Todorov, *Hope and Memory: Lessons from the Twentieth Century*, Princeton, N.J., 2003, p. 116. Such deceptions are detailed in my *Political Pilgrims*, Chapter 8, "Techniques of Hospitality."

5. Quoted in D. O. Sears, L. Huddy, and Robert Jervis, eds., *Oxford Handbook of Political Psychology*, New York, 2003, p. 112.

6. This was one of the major findings of *Political Pilgrims*.

7. Horowitz, *Radical Son*, p. 273.

8. Michael Straight is another example of the Western upper-class Communist who "longed for a sense of belonging to some brotherhood." See his *After a Long Silence*, New York, 1983, p. 40.

9. Aczel and Meray, *Cleansing Storm*, pp. 229–230.

10. Alexander Wat, *My Century: The Odyssey of a Polish Intellectual*, Berkeley, Calif., 1990, p. 173.

11. Anna Larina, the widow of Bukharin, the prominent purge victim, was among them (see her *This I Cannot Forget*, New York, 1993). An inmate in the Cuban Gulag exclaimed, upon encountering conditions in the camp, "What's going on here? I am sure Fidel and Raul don't know anything about this." Jose Llovio-Menendez, *Insider*, New York, 1988, p. 151. A Hungarian inmate of the Soviet Gulag, "after the social order that he helped to build had done him almost every evil man can suffer . . . thanked the murderous powers for not having been crueller than they had." Hay, p. 187.

Chapter 9. Resisting Disillusionment

1. The absence of such resistance to disillusionment is not to be confused with a nostalgia for the stability and modest material security that Communist systems provided in the Soviet Union and the East European Communist states. Such nostalgia is most prevalent among the older generations and the less educated; it has little to do with the appeals of ideology or the distant promise of utopia.

2. Kenneth Minogue, "Societies Collapse, Faiths Linger On," *Encounter*, March 1990, p. 3.

3. Enrique Krauze, "The View from La Realidad," *New Republic*, August 13, 2001, p. 31.

4. Quoted in Leon Wieseltier, "The Unreal World of Cornell West," *New Republic*, March 6, 1995, p. 31.

5. Leon Wieseltier, "Under the Spell of Paradise [review of E. Bloch, *Principle of Hope*], *New York Times Book Review*, November 23, 1986.

6. Leszek Kolakowski, *Main Currents of Marxism*, Vol. III, New York, 1978, pp. 525–526.

7. E. P. Thompson, *The Poverty of Theory and Other Essays*, New York and London, 1978, p. 372. Further citations from this book are from pp. 305–393, passim.

8. Stephen Kotkin, "Left Behind," *New Yorker*, September 29, 2003, p. 102.

9. Eric Hobsbawm, *Interesting Times: A Twentieth Century Life*, London, 2002. Further citations from this book are from pp. 41–415, passim.

10. Tony Judt, "The Last Romantic," *New York Review of Books*, November 20, 2003, pp. 43, 45.

11. Quoted in Robert Conquest, *Reflections on a Ravaged Century*, New York, 2000, pp. 10–11. On another occasion Hobsbawm responded this way to the question of why he remained a Communist: "I think the dream we had is a great dream, whether you call it a socialist dream or . . . the dream of general liberation. . . . I think the people who devoted their life to this were enormously good people. . . ." Quoted in Robert Conquest, "Who Was Right, Who Was Wrong and Why," *Encounter*, September 1990, p. 29.

12. Neil McInnes wrote of this attitude: "On the one hand it is admitted that communism failed utterly. . . . On the other hand it is not admitted that it deserved to fail. . . . There

is, on the contrary a hankering to save some hope from the catastrophe. . . ." "The Long Goodbye," *National Interest*, Summer 2001, p. 114.

13. McInnes, "Goodbye," p. 107.

14. Quoted in James Kurth, "'If Men Were Angels . . .': Reflections on the World of Eric Hobsbawm," *National Interest*, Summer 1995, p. 9.

15. Hobsbawm, "Intellectuals and Communism," in *Revolutionaries: Contemporary Essays*, New York, 1973, p. 27.

16. Eugene Genovese wrote: "Hobsbawm's heart remains with the radical left, but his formidable head demolishes its every shibboleth." "Every" is a bit of an overstatement, but there is little doubt about the first part of Genovese's assertion. "The Squandered Century," *New Republic*, April 7, 1995, p. 42.

17. Hobsbawm, *Politics for a Rational Left*, London, 1989, pp. 5, 219–220.

18. Hobsbawm and Chomsky seem to have in common some unarticulated problems and conflicts with their Jewish background, which may have influenced their political attitudes. Both played down their Jewish origins and shared an intense hostility toward Israel.

19. Hobsbawm, *Politics*, p. 220.

20. Tony Judt, "Downhill All the Way," *New York Review of Books*, May 25, 1995, p. 23.

21. Edward Walter, *The Rise and Fall of Leftist Radicalism in America*, Westport, Conn., 1992, p. 90. The remark referred to was witnessed by the author of this book.

22. Alison Edgley, *The Social and Political Thought of Noam Chomsky*, London, 2000, p. 3.

23. "In a Best-seller Chomsky Argues Against Afghan War," *Washington Post*, reprinted in *Daily Hampshire Gazette* (Northampton, Mass.), May 14, 2002.

24. Chomsky, *On Power and Ideology: Managua Lectures*, Boston, 1987, p. 36.

25. These expressions were culled mostly from Noam Chomsky and Edward S. Herman, *After the Cataclysm: Postwar Indochina and the Reconstruction of Imperial Ideology*, Boston, 1987. The quotation regarding the Pol Pot massacres is on p. 290. Also used was his *Managua Lectures*.

26. Sidney Hook, *Out of Step*, New York, 1987, p. 592.

27. Larissa MacFarquhar, "The Devil's Advocate," *New Yorker*, March 31, 2003, p. 75.

28. Ibid., p. 67.

29. "Distortions at Fourth Hand," *The Nation*, June 25, 1977, pp. 789, 791, 792.

30. Chomsky and Herman, *Cataclysm*, Boston, 1979, p. 291.

31. *The Nation*, June 25, 1977, pp. 789, 791, 792.

32. Chomsky and Herman, *Cataclysm*, pp. 147, 162, 207, 208, 209, 136, 137, 141, 225, 292. Paul Berman aptly summed up Chomsky's views of the Pol Pot massacres: "He showed that genocide had never occurred; and, conversely . . . if genocide did occur, it was the fault of American military intervention. . . . In either case, the stories about genocide in Cambodia revealed that America's principal institutions were even more guilty than anyone had previously imagined." *Terror and Liberalism*, New York, 2003, p. 148.

33. Steven Lukes, "Chomsky's Betrayal of Truths," *Times Higher Education Supplement*, November 7, 1980.

34. "Afghan War"; see also Berman, *Terror*, p. 149.

35. Ibid.

36. Jennifer Dempsy, "Chomsky Discusses World Terrorism," *Massachusetts Daily Collegian*, February 26, 1987.

37. Richard Wolin, "Noam on the Range," *Dissent*, Summer 1995, p. 419.

38. Quoted in Bill Moyers, *A World of Ideas*, New York, 1989, p. 47.

39. Cited in Alan Tonelson, "Institutional Structure Blues," *New York Times Book Review*, May 11, 1986. See also Chomsky, *Power*, p. 27.

40. Chomsky, *Power*, p. 36.

41. Ibid., p. 38.

42. Alexander Cockburn, *The Golden Age Is in Us*, London, 1995, pp. 149–151.

43. Wolin, "Noam," p. 421.

44. MacFarquhar, "Devil's," p. 68.

45. Chomsky, "Some Thoughts on Intellectuals and the Schools," *Harvard Educational Review*, Fall 1966, p. 485.

46. See Harvey Klehr, *Far Left of Center: The American Radical Left Today*, New Brunswick, N.J., 1988, pp. 113, 115. Boudin was released in 2003 after serving twenty-two years.
47. For a detailed discussion of what this position entails, see Edgley, *Thought*, pp. 19, 43–47.
48. Quoted in Keith Windschuttle, "The Hypocrisy of Noam Chomsky," *New Criterion*, May 2002, p. 6.
49. P. R. Mitchell and J. Schoeffel, eds., *Understanding Power: The Indispensable Chomsky*, New York, 2002 pp. 148–149.
50. Chomsky, *Managua Lectures*, pp. 6, 7, 9, 10, 115, 116, 125, 133, 127.
51. Quoted in Edgley, *Thought*, p. 3.
52. These were summations of his views on the subject provided by another sympathetic student of his ideas. See James McGilvray, *Chomsky: Language, Mind and Politics*, Cambridge, England, 1999, pp. 203, 220.
53. Stefan Kanfer writing in *City Journal*, Summer 2002, p. 100.
54. MacFarquhar, "Devil's," p. 67.
55. "Questions for Noam Chomsky—The Professional Provocateur," *New York Times Magazine*, November 2, 2002, p. 13.
56. This interpretation follows closely that of Steven Pinker put forward in his *The Blank Slate: The Modern Denial of Human Nature*, New York, 2002, pp. 246–247, 300–301.
57. David J. Langum, *William M. Kunstler: The Most Hated Lawyer in America*, New York, 1999, p. 166. One may take issue with the subtitle: Kunstler was hated by some but admired by vast numbers of people who shared his beliefs and supported his activities on behalf of these convictions. He was a bona fide political celebrity who arguably received more favorable than unfavorable publicity.
58. Ibid., p. 161.
59. William M. Kunstler, *My Life as a Radical Lawyer*, New York, 1994, p. xiii.
60. Langum, *Kunstler*, pp. 6–7.
61. Quoted ibid., p. 156.
62. Ibid., p. 346.
63. Ibid., p. 185.
64. Kunstler, *My Life*, pp. 199–200.
65. Ibid., p. 377.
66. Langum, *Kunstler*, p. 158.
67. The judge thought he was guilty, as he made clear, but not the jury. See Kunstler, *My Life*, p. 323.
68. Ibid., pp. 319, 324.
69. Quoted in Langum, *Kunstler*, p. 322.
70. Ibid., pp. 157–158.
71. Ibid., p. 340.
72. Ibid., pp. 27, 144.
73. Kunstler, *My Life*, p. 166.
74. Ibid., pp. 262, 165.
75. Ibid., pp. xii, 304, xiv, 275.
76. Ibid., p. 285.
77. Ibid., p. 277.
78. Langum, *Kunstler*, p. 316.
79. Kunstler, *My Life*, p. 374.
80. Ibid., pp. 314–315.
81. Ibid., p. 280.
82. Langum, *Kunstler*, pp. 6–7, 164.
83. Kunstler, *My Life*, p. 393.
84. Ibid., p. 49.
85. Langum, *Kunstler*, p. 18.
86. Kunstler, *My Life*, pp. 58, 55, 56, xiv.
87. Langum, *Kunstler*, pp. 21, 23, 28.
88. A. S. Singh and B. G. Johnson, *Interviews with Edward W. Said*, Jackson, Miss., 2004, p. 29.
89. Edward Alexander, "Edward Said (1935–2003)," *Outpost*, November 2003, p. 8.
90. Singh and Johnson, *Interviews*, p. 180.

91. Edward W. Said, *Out of Place: A Memoir*, New York, 2000, p. 261.

92. In the same volume of interviews cited above, on p. 19 he says that he came to the United States at age sixteen, while on p. 84 it is age fifteen.

93. I discussed this phenomenon in some detail in *Political Pilgrims*, New York, 1981, ch. 2 and 9.

94. Said, *Out of Place*, pp. 137, 240, 228, 276, 279.

95. Singh and Johnson, *Interviews*, p. 182.

96. Said, *Out of Place*, p. 81.

97. Stanley Kurtz, "Edward Said, Imperialist," *Weekly Standard*, October 8, 2001, p. 34.

98. Singh and Johnson, *Interviews*, p. 84.

99. Said, *Out of Place*, p. 294.

100. Singh and Johnson, *Interviews*, p. 163.

101. Exactly how much of his life he spent in Palestine (that is, Jerusalem) has been a highly contentious issue, and there is a substantial difference between the autobiographical accounts published before his memoir and the memoir itself. The research of an Israeli scholar indicates that before the publication of his memoir, Said considerably exaggerated, indeed misstated, numerous factual aspects of his Palestinian identity, including his schooling and family ties to Palestine. Apparently he barely attended school in Jerusalem; he was there only on vacations, and his parents did not own the house he had claimed they owned. See Justus Reid Weiner, "'My Beautiful Old House' and Other Fabrications by Edward Said," *Commentary*, September 1999; J. R. Weiner, "The False Prophet of Palestine," *Wall Street Journal*, August 26, 1999; Letters from Readers (on Weiner's article), *Commentary*, January 2000.

102. Singh and Johnson, *Interviews*, p. xxxii.

103. Akeel Bilgrami, Foreword to Edward W. Said, *Humanism and Democratic Criticism*, New York, 2004, p. ix.

104. Singh and Johnson, *Interviews*, p. xviii.

105. Kurtz, "Imperialist," p. 34.

106. Christopher Hitchens, "Where the Twain Should Have Met," *Atlantic*, September 2003, p. 153.

107. This kind of reasoning is similar to the post-1960s assertion that only white people can be racist. It was never clearly explained why this should be the case; the only (irrelevant) basis for this proposition is that nonwhite people are powerless, hence their racism (if any) does not count because it has no consequence.

108. Singh and Johnson, *Interviews*, p. xxi.

109. Said, *Humanism*, p. 124.

110. He wrote this for the benefit of Egyptian readers in the weekly *Al-Ahram*, quoted in Kurtz, "Imperialist," p. 35.

111. Said, *Humanism*, p. 136.

112. Ibid., p. 137.

113. Ibid., pp. 123, 124.

114. *Culture and Resistance: Conversations with Edward W. Said* (David Barsaman, ed.), Cambridge, Mass., 2003, p. 191.

115. Said, *Humanism*, pp. 126–127.

116. Said, *Humanism*, p. 61.

117. Ibid., p. 150.

118. Singh and Johnson, *Interviews*, p. 129.

119. Said, *Culture*, pp. 88–89, 90.

120. Ibid., p. 111.

121. Singh and Johnson, *Interviews*, p. 116.

122. He wrote this in *Blaming the Victim* (London and New York, 1988), which he co-edited with Christopher Hitchens. "Netanyahu" presumably refers to Jonathan Netanyahu (son of Benjamin, former foreign minister of Israel), who was killed in the Entebbe rescue mission in 1976 when Israeli commandos freed one hundred hostages of a hijacking in Uganda.

123. Said, *Culture*, pp. 112–113, 107–108, 115.

124. Pipes, a well-published scholar of the Middle East, has indeed found it difficult to obtain a regular academic position. In all probability this has been the result of his criticism of the views held by Said and his followers who dominate Middle Eastern studies at major American universities.

125. Said, *Culture*, pp. 36, 144–145, 95, 177, 145, 177, 112, 145, 177, 182, 188, 82.

126. Karen Anderson, "Columbia Debates a Professor's 'Gesture,'" *New York Times*, October 19, 2000.

127. Said, *Culture*, p. 145.

128. Ibid., pp. 146, 170.

129. Singh and Johnson, *Interviews*, p. xvi.

130. Norman Podhoretz, *The Bloody Crossroads: Where Literature and Politics Meet*, New York, 1986, pp. 115–116.

131. Alan Wolfe, "Teach Your Children," *New Republic*, November 3, 2003, p. 41.

132. Bill Ayers, *Fugitive Days: A Memoir*, New York, 2001. The quotations that follow are drawn from pp. 7–290, passim.

133. Quoted in Ronald Radosh, "Don't Need a Weatherman: The Clouded Mind of Bill Ayers," *Weekly Standard*, October 8, 2001, p. 38.

134. Brent Staples, "The Oldest Rad," *New York Times Book Review*, September 30, 2001, p. 11; John Patrick Diggins, "The Will to Change," *Los Angeles Times*, September 2, 2001, p. 5; Radosh, "Weatherman," p. 39.

135. Quoted in Horowitz, *Radical Son*, pp. 333–334.

136. Philip Roth, *American Pastoral*, Boston, 1997, p. 134.

137. See "Digesting the Collapse of Communism: Responses of Western Intellectuals," and "Marxism and Western Intellectuals in the Postcommunist Era," in Hollander, *Discontents*.

138. Ayers also differs from those who recognized that "a political line that called for the violent overthrow of American capitalism and the establishment of the dictatorship of the proletariat" was bound to have a limited popular appeal. Harvey M. Teres, *Renewing the Left: Politics, Imagination and the New York Intellectuals*, New York, 1996, p. 4.

139. Dinitia Smith, "No Regrets for a Love of Explosives," *New York Times*, September 11, 2001, p. 1.

140. As to the purpose of this bomb, see Staples, "Rad," and Radosh, "Weatherman."

141. Smith, "No Regrets," p. 2.

142. Todd Gitlin, "White Heat Underground," *The Nation*, December 19, 1981, p. 669.

143. Michael Walzer, "Can There Be a Decent Left?" *Dissent*, Spring 2002, pp. 19, 20.

144. Philip Roth, *The Dying Animal*, New York, 2001, pp. 81–82.

145. Hope Reeves, "Questions for Bill Ayers," *New York Times Magazine*, September 16, 2001.

146. Richard Hyland in a special supplement to the *Harvard Crimson*, October 22, 1969, reprinted in *Encounter*, April 1970, p. 30.

147. Norman Mailer too considered sliced white bread a particularly repugnant and alienating symbol of the inauthenticity of American life. See his *Armies of the Night*, New York, 1986, p. 77.

148. Bommi Baumann, *Terror or Love? Bommi Baumann's Own Story of His Life as a West German Urban Guerilla*, New York, 1977, p. 41.

149. Ibid., pp. 30–31, 38.

150. Ibid., pp. 56, 51, 50.

151. Ibid., pp. 18, 23, 33, 82.

152. Sean Wilentz, "The Advocate," *New York Times Book Review*, July 16, 1995.

153. Daniel J. Wakin, "Lives of 60s Revolutionaries Has Quieted but Intensity of Beliefs Hasn't Dimmed," *New York Times*, August 24, 2003, p. 25.

154. Karen de Wit, "Former Stokely Carmichael Still Ready for the Revolution," *New York Times*, April 14, 1996.

155. Reeves, "Questions."

156. This has also been the case of Kathy Boudin, who in 2001 told her parole board that "being underground gave me a certain moral identity." Laura Miller, "A Change in the Weather," *New York Times Book Review*, November 30, 2002.

157. Quoted in Alexander Stille, "Apocalypse Soon," *New York Review of Books*, November 7, 2002, p. 49.

158. Brian C. Anderson, "The Ineducable Left," *First Things*, February 2002, p. 40; Alan Wolfe, "The Snake," *New Republic*, October 1, 2005, pp. 36, 33.

159. Antonio Negri and Michael Hardt, *Empire*, Cambridge, Mass., 2000, pp. 32, 411.

160. Ibid., pp. 13–14, 138, 385, 389.

161. Ibid., pp. xv, 23–24.

162. Ibid., p. xvi.
163. Wolfe, "Snake," pp. 34–35.
164. Negri and Hardt, *Empire*, p. 413.
165. Ibid., pp. 412–413.
166. Stille, "Apocalypse," p. 51.
167. Quoted in Rachel Zabarkes Friedman, "Lawyer of Jihad," *National Review*, August 23, 2004, p. 29.
168. George Packer, "Left Behind," *New York Times Magazine*, September 22, 2002, pp. 42, 44, 45.
169. Ibid., p. 42.
170. Julia Preston, "Lawyer Accused of Aiding Terrorism Sees Fear as Obstacle," *New York Times*, June 22, 2004.
171. Packer, "Left Behind," p. 44.
172. Quoted in David Horowitz, *Unholy Alliance: Radical Islam and the American Left*, Washington, D.C., 2004, pp 200–201.
173. Packer, "Left Behind," p. 44.
174. Michael Tremoglie, "Terrorist Law School Mentor," *FrontPageMagazine.com*, November 18, 2002.
175. Deborah L. Rhode, "Terrorists and Their Lawyers," *New York Times*, op-ed, April 16, 2002.
176. John B. Judis, "The Strange Case of Ramsey Clark," *New Republic*, April, 22, 1991.
177. A comparably puzzling case (also connected with Iraq) is that of Scott Ritter. Ritter is a former Marine officer and UN inspector in Iraq who became a fierce critic of U.S. policy in Iraq and the Middle East (and throughout the world), a peace activist, and a popular speaker on college campuses (see, for example, "Former UN Inspector Ritter warns U.S. Meddling in Iran," *Daily Hampshire Gazette*, June 25, 2005).
178. Lizzy Ratner, "Ramsey Clark: Why I'm Taking Saddam's Case," *New York Observer*, January 10, 2005, p. 17. See also John F. Burns, "In Defending Hussein an American Contrarian Seeks to Set the Historical Record Straight," *New York Times*, December 6, 2005.
179. Judis, "Clark."
180. Ratner, "Clark."
181. Judis, "Clark."
182. Ratner, "Clark," p. 17.
183. Judis, "Clark."
184. Michael Klare chastised him for his critique of Gorbachev's policies of reducing the Soviet role in the Third World and seeking to improve relations with the West. Quoted in Alexander Cockburn, *The Golden Age Is in Us*, London, 1995, pp. 74–75.
185. Ibid., p. 269.
186. Ibid., p. 290.
187. Marx and Engels, *The Communist Manifesto*, Moscow, 1955, pp. 56, 57, 58.
188. Alexander Cockburn, "A Million Here, a Million There," *The Nation*, March 5, 1989.
189. Cockburn, *Golden Age*, p. 76.
190. Ibid., p. 77.
191. Ibid., p. 164.
192. Ibid., p. 70.
193. Ibid., p. 150.
194. Claud Cockburn, *Crossing the Line*, London, 1958, p. 184. Subsequent quotations from this volume are drawn from pp. 49–178, passim.
195. Warren Hoge, "Great Grandmother Comes in from the Cold," *New York Times*, September 13, 1999.
196. Ibid.
197. Ibid.
198. Obituary, *The Guardian*, June 27, 2005.
199. Sam Tanenhaus, "Gus Hall, Unreconstructed American Communist of 7 Decades, Dies at 90," *New York Times*, October 17, 2000.
200. Quoted in Horowitz, *Unholy Alliance*, p. 80.
201. Eric Hoffer, *The True Believer*, New York, 1950, p. 96.

Chapter 10. Conclusions: "Regions Where No Persuasion Can Penetrate": The Personal and the Political

1. The familiar concept was, of course, introduced by Eric Hoffer in *The True Believer*. Ted Goertzel, *Turncoats and True Believers*, Buffalo, N.Y., 1992, also addresses the dynamics of belief and disbelief in a wide range of cases ranging from Auguste Comte to Linus Pauling, Holocaust revisionists, and Fidel Castro.

2. Pankaj Mishra, *An End to Suffering*, New York, 2004, pp. 221–222, 394.

3. Hoffer, *Believer*, p. xiii.

4. Gerda Lerner, *Firewood: A Political Autobiography*, Philadelphia, 2002, p. 370. To her credit, she also acknowledged that her political beliefs effectively filtered and neutralized available information that contradicted these beliefs. She wrote: "I wanted the Soviet Union to be a successful experiment . . . and so I checked my critical faculties when it came to that subject, and instead accepted what I wanted to hear." She would deny that information undermining her beliefs was "part of a larger picture." She added: ". . . I cannot evade my complicity in studied ignorance. . . . I believed what I wanted and needed to believe, as I clung to the certainty of my fixed paradigm" (pp. 255, 370); Tzvetan Todorov, *Hope and Memory: Lessons from the 20th Century*, Princeton, N.J., 2003, p. 96.

5. My friend Harold Skulsky drew my attention to these propositions. They were quoted from Spinoza's *Opera*, published in German in Heidelberg in 1925 (pp. 277, 278) and translated by Skulsky.

6. David M. Potter, *History and American Society*, New York, 1973, pp. 385, 387.

7. The glorification of individualism, however, coexists with a similarly regnant egalitarianism, creating further conflicts and confusion for those seeking to attain the most satisfactory sense of identity.

8. Potter, *History*, pp. 363–364.

9. Hoffer, *Believer*, p. 37.

10. Robert Nisbet, *The Quest for Community*, New York, 1953.

11. Hoffer, *Believer*, p. 381.

12. It may be objected that in the United States in the early 1950s, loyalty oaths were required in some occupations and some people lost their jobs as a result of McCarthyism. This is true, but it was a short-lived phenomenon impacting on relatively small numbers of people and scarcely represented the kind of institutionalized intolerance that prevailed in Communist and other authoritarian systems.

13. Potter, *History*, p. 381.

14. James R. Abbott, Richard Farnum, and Harold J. Bershady, "On Ressentiment as a Motive Force in Sociological Research," paper presented at the annual meeting of the American Sociological Association, Chicago, 2002, pp. 6, 15.

15. Potter, *History*, pp. 368–369.

16. Ibid., pp. 360–361.

17. Abbott, et al., "Ressentiment," p. 24.

18. Such a conflation of the personal and the political realms may not be peculiar to American society. In a recent novel by V. S. Naipaul (*Magic Seeds*, New York, 2004), individuals who joined revolutionary guerrilla movements in India are portrayed as deeply frustrated and consumed by rage stimulated by a wide range of personal failures and failings; most of them are educated and of middle- or upper-middle-class background.

19. I exclude from this discussion Islamic societies where the subordination of the individual to the collectivity is taken for granted and fiercely affirmed by religious teachings. On the other hand, suicide bombing may be seen as the ultimate submission to religious/political objectives and fantasies *as well as* a peculiar form of individual self-assertion.

20. Edmund White, Introduction to Jean Genet, *Prisoner of Love*, Hanover, N.H., 1989, pp. viii, ix, xvii; Horowitz, *Radical Son*, p. 176.

21. I learned about this in the long conversation I had with him on December 28, 1994, in San Jose, California, referred to earlier.

22. Mary McCarthy, "Portrait of an Intellectual," from *The Company She Keeps*, New York, 1942, p. 170.

23. Quoted from the novel *I Married a Communist*, in Derek Parker Royal, ed., *Philip Roth: New Perspectives on an American Author*, Westport, Conn., 2005, p. 197.

24. See, for example, Nathan Leites, *A Study of Bolshevism*, Glencoe, Ill., 1953, pp. 348, 135.

25. Hoffer, *Believer*, pp. xi, 15, 84, 86.
26. Ibid., pp. 78–79.
27. Quoted in ibid., pp. 78–79, 81.
28. For instance, two Hungarian writers, first idealistic supporters and later idealistic opponents of the Communist regime, wrote: ". . . the decisive push [for breaking with the party] was provided by the moral factor. . . . The moral sensibility of Imre Nagy—and this was his most unusual quality—remained intact even after the experience of the Soviet practices; he could not remain indifferent in face of the dark series of the newly excavated crimes. . . ." Aczel and Meray, *Vihar*, p. 286.

Index

A NOTE ON THE AUTHOR

Paul Hollander is professor emeritus of sociology at the University of Massachusetts at Amherst. Born in Budapest, he studied at the London School of Economics, the University of Illinois, and Princeton University, where he received a Ph.D. in sociology. He has been a Ford Foundation and a Guggenheim fellow, and an associate of the Davis Center for Russian and Eurasian Studies at Harvard University. He lives in Northampton, Massachusetts.